BIBLICA ET ORIENTALIA

(SACRA SCRIPTURA ANTIQUITATIBUS ORIENTALIBUS ILLUSTRATA)

34

ROMAE
E PONTIFICIO INSTITUTO BIBLICO
1978

JOSEPH A. FITZMYER, S.J. and DANIEL J. HARRINGTON, S.J.

A MANUAL OF PALESTINIAN ARAMAIC TEXTS

(Second Century B. C. — Second Century A. D.)

ROME
BIBLICAL INSTITUTE PRESS
1978

PRINTED IN ITALY

TYPIS PONTIFICIAE UNIVERSITATIS GREGORIANAE — ROMAE

The publication of this manual
has been made possible by
generous grants-in-aid
from
WESTON SCHOOL OF THEOLOGY
Cambridge, Massachusetts
and
THE CATHOLIC BIBLICAL ASSOCIATION
OF AMERICA
Washington, D. C.

TABLE OF CONTENTS

PREFACE xi

LIST OF SIGLA FOR " OTHER COLLECTIONS " ENTRIES xv

LIST OF ABBREVIATIONS xvii

PALESTINIAN ARAMAIC TEXTS 1

1. 4Q Jeremiah^{b} (= Jer 10:11) — 4QJer^{b} 2
2. 4Q Prayer of Nabonidus — 4QprNab (*or* 4QṣNab) 2
3. 4Q Pseudo-Daniel — 4QpsDan ar^{a-c} 4
4. 1Q Daniel^{a,b} — 1QDan^{a,b} (1Q*71*, *72*) 8
5. 11Q Targum of Job — 11QtgJob 10
6. 1Q New Jerusalem — 1QJN ar (1Q*32*). 46
7. 2Q New Jerusalem — 2QJN ar (2Q*24*). 50
8. 5Q New Jerusalem — 5QJN ar (5Q*15*). 54
9. 11Q New Jerusalem — 11QJN ar 64
10. 4Q Enoch^{c} — 4QEn^{c} frg. 1, col. i 64
11. 4Q Enoch^{c} — 4QEn^{c} frg. 1, col. ii 66
12. 4Q Enoch^{e} — 4QEn^{e} 66
13. 4Q Enoch Astronomical^{b} — 4QEnAstr^{b} 66
14. 1Q Enoch Giants — 1QEnGiants (1Q*23*) 68
15. 2Q Enoch Giants — 2QEnGiants (2Q*26*) 72
16. 4Q Enoch Giants^{a} — 4QEnGiants^{a}. 72
17. 4Q Enoch Giants^{b} — 4QEnGiants^{b} 74
18. 4Q Enoch Giants^{c} — 4QEnGiants^{c}. 76
19. 6Q Enoch Giants — 6QEnGiants (6Q*8*) 76
20. 1Q Testament of Levi — 1QTLevi ar (1Q*21*) 80
21. 4Q Testament of Levi^{a} — 4QTLevi ar^{a} 88
22. 4Q Visions of ʿAmram^{a} — 4QʿAmram^{a} 90
23. 4Q Visions of ʿAmram^{b} — 4QʿAmram^{b} 92
24. 4Q Visions of ʿAmram^{c} — 4QʿAmram^{c} 94
25. 4Q Visions of ʿAmram^{d} — 4QʿAmram^{d} 94
26. 4Q Visions of ʿAmram$^{e(?)}$ — 4QʿAmram$^{e(?)}$ 96
27. 4Q Testament of Qahat — 4QTQahat 96
28. 4Q " Messianic " Text — 4QMess ar 96
29. 1Q Genesis Apocryphon — 1QapGen (+ 1Q*20*) 100
30. 4Q Testuz (Unidentified Fragment) — 4QTestuz ar 126
31. 1Q Unidentified Fragments — 1Q*24* 126
32. 1Q Unidentified Fragments — 1Q*63-68*. 128
33. 3Q Unidentified Fragments — 3Q*12*, 3Q*14* 132

34. 5Q Unidentified Fragment — 5Q*24* 134
35. 6Q Unidentified Fragments — 6Q*14*, 6Q*19*, 6Q*23*, 6Q*26*, 6Q*31* . . 134
36. Masada Letter on an Ostracon — MasOstr 136
37. Hyrcania Funerary Inscription — Hyrcania 136
38. Murabbaʿat List of Names and Rations — Mur 8 ar 136
39. Murabbaʿat IOU (A.D. 56) — Mur 18 ar 136
40. Murabbaʿat Writ of Divorce — Mur 19 ar 138
41. Murabbaʿat Marriage Contract — Mur 20 ar 140
42. Murabbaʿat Marriage Contract — Mur 21 ar 142
43. Murabbaʿat Deed of Sale — Mur 23 ar 144
44. Murabbaʿat Easement — Mur 25 ar 144
45. Murabbaʿat Deed of Sale — Mur 26 ar 148
46. Murabbaʿat Deed of Sale — Mur 27 ar 148
47. Murabbaʿat Property Record — Mur 28 ar 150
48. Murabbaʿat IOU(?) — Mur 32 ar 150
49. Murabbaʿat Ostracon — Mur 72 ar 152
50. Murabbaʿat Unidentified Fragments — Mur 31, 33-35 ar. 152
51. ? Ḥever Contract B (Deed of Sale A.D. 134) — pap?ḤevB ar . . 154
52. ? Ḥever Contract C (Deed of Sale) — pap?ḤevC ar. 156
53. 5/6 Ḥever Letter of Bar Cochba 1 — 5/6ḤevEp 1 158
54. 5/6 Ḥever Letter of Bar Cochba 2 — 5/6ḤevEp 2 158
55. 5/6 Ḥever Letter of Bar Cochba 4 — 5/6ḤevEp 4 160
56. 5/6 Ḥever Letter of Bar Cochba 8 — 5/6ḤevEp 8 160
57. 5/6 Ḥever Letter of Bar Cochba 10 — 5/6ḤevEp 10 160
58. 5/6 Ḥever Letter of Bar Cochba 11 — 5/6ḤevEp 11 160
59. 5/6 Ḥever Letter of Bar Cochba 14 — 5/6ḤevEp 14 160
60. 5/6 Ḥever Letter of Bar Cochba 15 — 5/6ḤevEp 15 162
61. 5/6 Ḥever Babatha Archive, Greek Document 1 — 5/6ḤevBA 1 . 162
62. 5/6 Ḥever Babatha Archive, Greek Document 2 — 5/6ḤevBA 2 . 162
63. 5/6 Ḥever Babatha Archive, Docket on Marriage Contract — 5/6ḤevBA Docket 162
64. 5/6 Ḥever Nabatean Contract — 5/6ḤevA nab 164
65. Jerusalem Stone Weight 168
66. Storage Jar Inscription 168
67. Kidron Valley Dipinto 168
68. Givʿat Ha-Mivṭar Abba Inscription 168
69. Jebel Ḫallet eṭ-Ṭuri Ossuary 168
70. Uzziah Tomb Slab. 168
71. Kidron Epitaph 168
72. Dominus Flevit Ossuary 11 170
73. Dominus Flevit Ossuary 13 170
74. Dominus Flevit Ossuary 19 170
75. Dominus Flevit Ossuary 20 170
76. Dominus Flevit Ossuary 24 170
77. Dominus Flevit Ossuary 25 170
78. Dominus Flevit Ossuary 26 170
79. Dominus Flevit Ossuary 27 170
80. Dominus Flevit Ossuary 32 170

81. Dominus Flevit Ossuary 33 170
82. Dominus Flevit Ossuary 34 170
83. Dominus Flevit Ossuary 36 170
84. Dominus Flevit Ossuary 38 172
85. Giv'at Ha-Mivṭar Ossuary 1 172
86. Giv'at Ha-Mivṭar Ossuary 2 172
87. Giv'at Ha-Mivṭar Ossuary 3 172
88. Giv'at Ha-Mivṭar Ossuary 14. 172
89. Jason Tomb Inscription 172
90. Kallon Family Ossuary 1 172
91. Kallon Family Ossuary 2 172
92. Kallon Family Ossuary 3 174
93. Kallon Family Ossuary 4 174
94. Kallon Family Ossuary 5 174
95. Jerusalem Hypogeum Ossuary 1 174
96. Jerusalem Hypogeum Ossuary 2 174
97. Jerusalem Hypogeum Ossuary 4 174
98. Jerusalem Hypogeum Ossuary 5 174
99. Jerusalem Tomb Ossuary 1. 174
100. Jerusalem Tomb Ossuary 2. 174
101. Jerusalem Tomb Ossuary 3. 176
102. Jerusalem Tomb Ossuary 4. 176
103. Jerusalem Tomb Ossuary 5. 176
104. Jerusalem Tomb Ossuary 6. 176
105. Jerusalem Tomb Ossuary 7. 176
106. Jerusalem Tomb Ossuary 8. 176
107. Jerusalem Tomb Ossuary 9. 176
108. Nicanor Tomb Inscription 176
109. Nazareth Ossuary 176
110. Siloam Ossuary 1 176
111. Siloam Ossuary 3 176
112. Siloam Ossuary 6 178
113. Siloam Ossuary 7 178
114. Siloam Ossuary 14. 178
115. Silwan Tomb Ossuary 1 178
116. Silwan Tomb Ossuary 2 178
117. Silwan Tomb Ossuary 3 178
118. Talpioth Ossuary 1 178
119. Talpioth Ossuary 2 178
120. Talpioth Ossuary 5 178
121. Mt. Scopus Tomb Inscription 1. 178
122. Mt. Scopus Tomb Inscription 2. 178
123. Mt. Scopus Tomb Inscription 3. 178
124. Mt. Scopus Ossuary 6 178
125. Mt. Scopus Ossuary 12 180
126. Mt. Scopus Ossuary 180
127. Abu Gosh Ossuary 180
128. Wadi Aḥmedieh Inscription 1. 180

129. Wadi Aḥmedieh Inscription 2. 180
130. Gezer Tomb Inscription 1 180
131. Gezer Tomb Inscription 2 180
132. Helen of Adiabene Tomb Inscription 180
133. Ḥizmeh Ossuary 2. 180
134. Isawwiya Ossuary 4 180
135. Jaffa Ossuary 180
136. Masada Ostracon 182
137. Qaṭ'a Ossuary B 182
138. Ramat Raḥel Ossuary 182
139. Šaf'at Ossuary 1 182
140. Šaf'at Ossuary 10. 182
141. Šaf'at Ossuary 11 182
142. Beit Saḥur Ossuary 182
143. Wadi Yasul Ossuary 2. 182
144. Er-Ram Ossuary 182
145. Trilingual Jerusalem Ossuary 182
146. Gezer Ossuary. 184
147. Mt. Zion Ossuary 184
148. French Hill Ossuary 184
149. El-Mal Dedicatory Inscription 184
150. *Mĕgillat Ta'ănît* 184

TEXT DESCRIPTION AND BIBLIOGRAPHY 189

APPENDIX : Palestinian Aramaic Inscriptions of Later Date (Synagogal, Funerary, and Other) 251
List of Inscriptions 252
Aramaic Texts and Translations 254
Text Description and Bibliography 277

GLOSSARY TO THE MAIN TEXTS. 305

GLOSSARY TO THE APPENDIX 347

INDEXES 357
I. Index of Subjects. 359
II. Index of Modern Scholars 362

COMPARATIVE TABLE OF TEXTS IN THIS COLLECTION WITH OTHER COLLECTIONS 368

PREFACE

Aims. This is an attempt to gather together Palestinian Aramaic texts of various sorts and varying lengths from the last two centuries B.C. and the first two centuries A.D. (roughly from 200 B.C. to A.D. 135). The texts are of diverse character: a few of them are biblical (revealing the form of the text in this period); a number belong to the so-called intertestamental literature of Palestinian Jews; some of them are letters, contracts, or business documents of different sorts, reflecting various elements of Palestinian life of that period. The last part of the collection of texts presented here comes from ossuaries or tombstone inscriptions and often contains no more than a few words or names. Indeed, it is not at all easy to decide whether such texts are really written in Aramaic (and not in the Hebrew of the day). They are included here only to the extent that they have something in them that may indicate an Aramaic relationship.

It is hoped that this collection of texts will give some idea of the kind of Aramaic in use in Palestine during this period. It has often been said that between the final redaction of the Book of Daniel and the first of the rabbinic writings, viz., the *Mĕgillat Ta'ănît*, there was a virtual absence of Aramaic material, save for some tombstone inscriptions and ossuary texts. Indeed, it was at times thought that Aramaic was somewhat on the decline in the period in question. But the discoveries of the last half-century have brought to light all sorts of Palestinian Aramaic texts from this period. They are scattered widely in publications of all kinds. It has been thought wise to present them here, even though many of the documents or inscriptions are fragmentary, in order to allow them to give a picture of the Aramaic of this period. Though many of them are not extensive, they do reveal at least Palestinian Aramaic vocabulary, phonological problems, morphological types, and some syntactic usage.

The kind of Aramaic that is found in these texts belongs to the period of Middle Aramaic, as this has been defined by J. A. Fitzmyer in *The Genesis Apocryphon of Qumran Cave 1: A Commentary* (BibOr 18A; 2d ed.; Rome: Biblical Institute, 1971) 22-23, and explained in his forthcoming article, "The Phases of the Aramaic Language" (*A Wandering Aramean: Collected Aramaic Essays*). It is part of the development of Imperial or Official Aramaic, which began about 200 B.C., along with the emergence of the dialects of Palmyra, Nabatea, Hatra, and early Syriac.

The last text presented in this collection is really the first of the rabbinic writings, the *Mĕgillat Ta'ănît.* Though it may date from the period which is being covered by this collection, it also reflects the reworking of a later period. It is incorporated here merely to stand as a contrast to the preceding texts. Similarly, the widely scattered synagogue inscriptions of the 3d to 6th centuries are gathered in an appendix to illustrate the same sort of contrast.

Discussions of the language of Jesus in recent decades have been legion, and much of that discussion has been based on texts that are of questionable relevance. Our purpose in gathering the Palestinian Aramaic texts of the period with which we are dealing is to try to illustrate what should be the background to that discussion.

Principles of Inclusion and Presentation. When it has been possible to date the texts, we have tried to present the material in chronological order. Obviously, this has not always been possible, especially in the case of the tombstone inscriptions and ossuaries. These have been grouped by importance and then by provenience.

The collection made here provides the text of these documents (often with emendations and restorations, to the extent that these are possible), a translation of the text, a brief introduction, and a bibliography of secondary literature on each of the texts. A glossary of the texts completes the collection.

We have included some of the very small unidentified fragments in this collection, when they have preserved at least a whole word, lest the testimony of such bits to the small, but growing, corpus of Aramaic texts of this period be lost. When the letters preserved on some of them have not formed recognizable Aramaic words, the fragments have been omitted. Anyone who wishes to check such omitted fragments may consult 1Q*21* 2, 13-17, 20-21, 33-36, 38-42, 44, 46-49, 59-60 ; 1Q*23* 5-8, 10-12, 16, 18, 23-26, 28, 31 ; 1Q*32* 6, 8-13, 18-21, 23 ; 1Q*68* 2, 7, 9 : 3Q*12* 2 ; 3Q*13* 1-5 ; 3Q*14* 9 ; 6Q*8* 7-25, 27-33 ; 6Q*23* 3, 4 ; 6Q*26* 2 ; Mur 21 ar frgs. 4, 5.

The student who is interested in the state of preservation of single letters should consult the *editiones principes.* Since our purpose has not been to produce a critical edition of these texts or to duplicate the work of the original editors, we have not marked with a dot or a superior small circle possible or probable readings. Our purpose in this regard has rather been to reflect the current state of study of the text and to present a reading of it that will contribute to a knowledge of the Aramaic of this period as a whole. Serious students of these texts will always want to check the readings against the *editiones principes* and the photographs or facsimiles available. This is the purpose of the bibliographical notes.

Similarly, we have introduced into the lines themselves words or letters that in the original have been written as either infrascript or suprascript (e.g., between the lines). This has been done, not only to make easier the printing of these texts, but also to incorporate such material into the words or sentences concerned.

Our translation of these texts has tried to be as accurate as possible, rendering them into good, but not overly literal, English. In some cases alternative translations have been given in parentheses. Because of the fragmentary nature of some of these texts, certainty of interpretation or translation is obviously impossible. The purpose of the translation is to give a simple interpretation of the text.

We have attempted in this manual no analysis of the grammar of the Aramaic language of this period. That will have to wait for a later date, and perhaps a second volume. However, the glossary will enable the student to see how we have analyzed some of the forms.

It should be further realized that in some of the short ossuary inscriptions a mixture of Hebrew and Aramaic sometimes occurs. Then the question arises: Was the inscription intended as Aramaic with Hebraism(s) or Hebrew with Aramaism(s)? Since it is practically impossible to resolve this question, we have incorporated the texts as Aramaic and commented on the obvious Hebraism(s) in the notes.

All of the texts given in this collection have been discovered in or near Palestine. This is more or less the rationale behind the collection. We are fully aware that one or other might possibly have been composed outside of this geographical area. But they are included on the basis that they would not have been found in or near Palestine, if someone there were not making use of them, reading them, and understanding them. T. Muraoka ("The Aramaic of the Old Targum of Job from Qumran Cave XI," *JJS* 25 [1974] 425-43) has argued that the text of the targum reflects eastern Aramaic. Whether it does or not remains to be seen. It is highly problematic whether the distinction between eastern and western Aramaic is valid at this period; and in any case the reason for including the text is given above.

The manuscript of this book had already been accepted for publication by the time that we received a copy of the long-awaited publication of a group of important Aramaic texts : J. T. Milik, *The Books of Enoch : Aramaic Fragments of Qumrân Cave* 4 (Oxford : Clarendon, 1976). Most of Milik's Enoch material should have been included here, but it will have to await another edition of this book. Milik's publication provides an excellent presentation of these texts, which one can easily use alongside of what we have assembled here. We have made what adjustments we could in the Enoch material gathered here in the light of Milik's most recent work on it.

A similar remark has to be made about two fragmentary targums of Qumran Cave 4 recently published by Milik ; see R. de Vaux and J. T. Milik, *Qumrân Grotte* 4, *II : I. Archéologie ; II. Tefillin, mezuzot et targums* (4*Q*128—4*Q*157) (DJD 6 ; Oxford : Clarendon, 1977), 4QtgLev (4*Q*156), pp. 86-89 ; 4QtgJob (4Q157), p. 90.

It is our pleasant duty to thank the many persons and groups that have aided the publication of this manual. An initial grant for research on this topic was made to J. A. Fitzmyer by the Faculty Research Grants of Fordham University, Bronx, N.Y. Once most of the work of compilation and translation was done, we were further favored by two special grants-in-aid. We are indebted to the individuals who helped us to obtain these grants for the publication of this highly technical material. In particular, we wish to thank the Rev. John W. Padberg, S. J., president of Weston School of Theology, Cambridge, Massachusetts, who secured assistance for us from the school ; and the Rev. Joseph Jensen, O.S.B., the executive secretary of the Catholic Biblical Association of America, who supported our request for aid. All users of this manual will be indebted to them, because these funds have helped to keep the price of this book within a reasonable range. Finally, we are grateful to the Rev. Carlo Martini, S.J., rector of the Biblical Institute in Rome, and to Rev. Peter Heitmann, S.J., editor of the series, Biblica et orientalia, for accepting this manual into that series.

For an explanation of the system used to designate the sigla for texts from Qumran, Murabbaʿat, Naḥal Ḥever, etc., see J. A. Fitzmyer, *The Dead Sea Scrolls : Major Publications and Tools for Study* (SBL-SBS 8 ; Missoula, MT ; Scholars Press, 1975) 3-8.

Joseph A. Fitzmyer, S.J.
The Catholic University of America
Washington, DC 20064

Daniel J. Harrington, S.J.
Weston School of Theology
Cambridge, MA 02138

LIST OF SIGLA FOR "OTHER COLLECTIONS" ENTRIES

AC J. J. Koopmans, *Aramäische Chrestomathie : Ausgewählte Texte (Inschriften, Ostraka und Papyri) bis zum 3. Jahrhundert n. Chr. für das Studium der aramäischen Sprache gesammelt* (2 parts ; Leiden : Nederlands Instituut voor het Nabije Oosten, 1962)

AH F. Rosenthal (ed.), *An Aramaic Handbook* (Porta linguarum orientalium ns 10 ; parts I/1-2, II/1-2 ; Wiesbaden : Harrassowitz, 1967)

ASG H. Kohl and C. Watzinger, *Antike Synagogen in Galilaea* (29. Wissenschaftliche Veröffentlichung der deutschen Orient-Gesellschaft ; Leipzig : Hinrichs, 1916 ; reprinted, Wiesbaden : Harrassowitz, 1976)

ASP E. L. Sukenik, *Ancient Synagogues in Palestine and Greece* (Schweich Lectures, 1930 ; London : British Academy, 1934)

ATQ B. Jongeling, C. J. Labuschagne, and A. S. van der Woude, *Aramaic Texts from Qumran with Translations and Annotations* (SSS 4 ; Leiden : Brill, 1976)

CIH D. Chwolson, *Corpus inscriptionum hebraicarum* (St. Petersburg : H. Schmitzdorff, 1882)

CII J.-B. Frey, *Corpus inscriptionum iudaicarum : Recueil des inscriptions juives qui vont du IIIe siècle avant Jésus-Christ au VIIe siècle de Notre-Ere* (2 vols. : I. Europe ; II. Asie-Afrique ; Vatican City : Pontificio istituto di archeologia cristiana, 1936, 1952 ; vol. 1 has been reprinted with a prolegomenon by B. Lifshitz under the title, *Corpus of Jewish Inscriptions from the Third Century B. C. to the Seventh Century A. D.* [Library of Biblical Studies ; New York : Ktav, 1975])

CIS *Corpus inscriptionum semiticarum* (Paris : Imprimerie nationale), 2/1-2 : Inscriptiones aramaicae (1888, 1893)

DadWJ E. Koffmahn, *Die Doppelurkunden aus der Wüste Juda : Recht und Praxis der jüdischen Papyri des 1. und 2. Jahrhunderts n. Chr. samt Übertragung der Texte und deutscher Übersetzung* (STDJ 5 ; Leiden : Brill, 1968)

Ephem. M. Lidzbarski, *Ephemeris für semitische Epigraphik* (3 vols. ; Giessen : Töpelmann, 1902, 1908, 1915)

Epigr. M. Lidzbarski, *Handbuch der nordsemitischen Epigraphik nebst ausgewählten Inschriften* (2 vols. ; Weimar : E. Felber, 1898 ; reprinted, Hildesheim : Olms, 1962)

IR R. Hestrin (ed.), *Inscriptions Reveal : Documents from the Time of the Bible, the Mishna and the Talmud* (2d ed. ; Jerusalem : Israel Museum, 1973)

JPCI S. Klein, *Jüdisch-palästinisches Corpus Inscriptionum (Ossuar-, Grab- und Synagogeninschriften)* (Vienna/Berlin : R. Löwit, 1920 ; reprinted, Hildesheim : H. A. Gerstenberg, 1971)

JS E. R. Goodenough, *Jewish Symbols in the Greco-Roman Period* (13 vols. ; Bollingen Series, 37 ; New York : Pantheon, 1953-68)

PI T. C. Vriezen and J. H. Hospers (eds.), *Palestine Inscriptions* (Textus minores, 17 ; Leiden : Brill, 1951)

PS S. Klein, *Palästina-Studien* (Vienna : " Menorah," 1925)

SEG *Supplementum epigraphicum graecum* (eds. L. Robert, M. N. Tod, and E. Ziebarth ; Leiden : A. W. Sijthoff, 1937), 8/1.

SHY S. Klein, *Spr Hyšwb* (Jerusalem : Mosad Bialik, 1939), vol. 1.

SWDS *Scrolls from the Wilderness of the Dead Sea : A Catalogue of the Exhibition,* The Dead Sea Scrolls of Jordan, *Arranged by the Smithsonian Institution in Cooperation with the Government of the Hashemite Kingdom of Jordan and the Palestine Archaeological Museum* ([Berkeley] : University of California for ASOR, 1965)

Thomsen P. Thomsen, "Die lateinischen und griechischen Inschriften der Stadt Jerusalem und ihrer nächsten Umgebung," *ZDPV* 43 (1920) 138-58 ; 44 (1921) 1-61, 90-168 ; also published separately, Leipzig : Hinrichs, 1922.

LIST OF ABBREVIATIONS

(Full details for those marked with an asterisk can be found in the preceding list of sigla for "Other Collections" entries.)

AASOR	Annual of the American Schools of Oriental Research
AB	Anchor Bible
*AC**	J. J. Koopmans, *Aramäische Chrestomathie*
AGJU	Arbeiten zur Geschichte des antiken Judentums und des Urchristentums
*AH**	F. Rosenthal (ed.), *An Aramaic Handbook*
AJA	*American Journal of Archaeology*
AJBA	*Australian Journal of Biblical Archaeology*
APOT	R. H. Charles, *Apocrypha and Pseudepigrapha of the Old Testament*
ArOr	*Archiv Orientální*
*ASG**	H. Kohl and C. Watzinger, *Antike Syngaogen in Galilaea*
*ASP**	E. L. Sukenik, *Ancient Synagogues in Palestine and Greece*
*ATQ**	B. Jongeling et al., *Aramaic Texts from Qumran*
BA	*Biblical Archaeologist*
BANE	G. E. Wright (ed.), *The Bible and the Ancient Near East*
BASOR	*Bulletin of the American Schools of Oriental Research*
Bib	*Biblica*
BibOr	Biblica et orientalia
BIES	*Bulletin of the Israel Exploration Society*
BJPES	*Bulletin of the Jewish Palestine Exploration Society*
BL	*Booklist*
BO	*Bibliotheca orientalis*
BTB	*Biblical Theology Bulletin*
BTS	*Bible et terre sainte*
BVC	*Bible et vie chrétienne*
BZ	*Biblische Zeitschrift*
BZAW	Beihefte zur *ZAW*
BZNW	Beihefte zur *ZNW*
CBQ	*Catholic Biblical Quarterly*
*CIH**	D. Chwolson, *Corpus inscriptionum hebraicarum*
*CII**	J.-B. Frey, *Corpus inscriptionum iudaicarum*
*CIS**	*Corpus inscriptionum semiticarum*
CRAIBL	*Comptes rendus de l'académie des inscriptions et belles-lettres*
*DadWJ**	E. Koffmahn, *Die Doppelurkunden aus der Wüste Juda*
DBS	L. Pirot and H. Cazelles (eds.), *Dictionnaire de la Bible, Supplément*
DJD	Discoveries in the Judaean Desert

*Ephem.**	M. Lidzbarski, *Ephemeris für semitische Epigraphik*
*Epigr.**	M. Lidzbarski, *Handbuch der nordsemitischen Epigraphik*
ETL	*Ephemerides theologicae lovanienses*
ETR	*Etudes théologiques et religieuses*
GerefTTs	*Gereformeerd theologisch tijdschrift*
GLECS	*Groupe linguistique d'études chamito-sémitiques*, Comptes rendus
HAT	Handbuch zum Alten Testament
HeyJ	*Heythrop Journal*
HTR	*Harvard Theological Review*
HUCA	*Hebrew Union College Annual*
IEJ	*Israel Exploration Journal*
Int	*Interpretation*
*IR**	R. Hestrin (ed.), *Inscriptions Reveal*
ITQ	*Irish Theological Quarterly*
IZBG	*Internationale Zeitschriftenschau für Bibelwissenschaft und Grenzgebiete*
JAC	*Jahrbuch für Antike und Christentum*
JANESCU	*Journal of the Ancient Near Eastern Society of Columbia University*
JAOS	*Journal of the American Oriental Society*
JBL	*Journal of Biblical Literature*
JDS	Judean Desert Studies
JEOL	*Jaarbericht ex Oriente Lux*
JJPES	*Journal of the Jewish Palestine Exploration Society*
JJS	*Journal of Jewish Studies*
JNES	*Journal of Near Eastern Studies*
*JPCI**	S. Klein, *Jüdisch-palästinisches Corpus Inscriptionum*
JPOS	*Journal of the Palestine Oriental Society*
JQR	*Jewish Quarterly Review*
*JS**	E. R. Goodenough, *Jewish Symbols*
JSJ	*Journal for the Study of Judaism in the Persian, Hellenistic and Roman Period*
JSS	*Journal of Semitic Studies*
JTC	*Journal for Theology and the Church*
JTS	*Journal of Theological Studies*
LMRF Bulletin	*Louis M. Rabinowitz Fund for the Exploration of Ancient Synagogues, Bulletin*
MGWJ	*Monatsschrift für Geschichte und Wissenschaft des Judentums*
MTZ	*Münchener theologische Zeitschrift*
MUSJ	*Mélanges de l'université St.-Joseph*
NedTTs	*Nederlands theologisch tijdschrift*
NovT	*Novum Testamentum*
NTA	*New Testament Abstracts*
NTS	*New Testament Studies*
OLZ	*Orientalistische Literaturzeitung*
PEFQS	*Palestine Exploration Fund Quarterly Statement*

PEQ	*Palestine Exploration Quarterly*
*PI**	T. C. Vriezen and J. H. Hospers (eds.), *Palestine Inscriptions*
PJ	*Palästina-Jahrbuch*
*PS**	S. Klein, *Palästina-Studien*
PVTG	Pseudepigrapha Veteris Testamenti graece
QDAP	*Quarterly of the Department of Antiquities of Palestine*
RArch	*Revue archéologique*
RB	*Revue biblique*
RechBib	Recherches bibliques
REG	*Revue des études grecques*
REJ	*Revue des études juives*
RevScRel	*Revue des sciences religieuses*
RHPR	*Revue d'histoire et de philosophie religieuses*
RHR	*Revue de l'histoire des religions*
RivB	*Rivista biblica*
RQ	*Revue de Qumran*
RSR	*Recherches de science religieuse*
RTL	*Revue théologique de Louvain*
SBFLA	*Studii biblici franciscani liber annuus*
SBLSBS	Society of Biblical Literature, Sources for Biblical Study
SBM	Stuttgarter biblische Monographien
SBT	Studies in Biblical Theology
SEA	*Svensk exegetisk Årsbok*
*SEG**	*Supplementum epigraphicum graecum*
Sem	*Semitica*
*SHY**	S. Klein, *Spr Hyšwb*
SPAW	*Sitzungsberichte der preussischen Akademie der Wissenschaften*
SSS	Semitic Study Series
STDJ	Studies on the Texts of the Desert of Judah
SVTP	Studia in Veteris Testamenti pseudepigrapha
*SWDS**	*Scrolls from the Wilderness of the Dead Sea*
TGl	*Theologie und Glaube*
Thomsen*	P. Thomsen, "Die lateinischen und griechischen Inschriften"
TLZ	*Theologische Literaturzeitung*
TRu	*Theologische Rundschau*
TToday	*Theology Today*
VDI	*Vestnik Drevnii Istorii*
VT	*Vetus Testamentum*
VTSup	Vetus Testamentum, Supplements
WZKM	*Wiener Zeitschrift für die Kunde des Morgenlandes*
ZAW	*Zeitschrift für alttestamentliche Wissenschaft*
ZDMG	*Zeitschrift des deutschen morgenländischen Gesellschaft*
ZDPV	*Zeitschrift des deutschen Palästina-Vereins*
ZNW	*Zeitschrift für die neutestamentliche Wissenschaft*
ZTK	*Zeitschrift für Theologie und Kirche*

PALESTINIAN ARAMAIC TEXTS

PALESTINIAN ARAMAIC TEXTS

ARAMAIC TEXT

1. 4Q Jeremiah[b] (= Jer 10:11) — 4QJer[b]

1 [ ]יאבדו מן ארעא

2. 4Q Prayer of Nabonidus — 4QPrNab (*or* 4QṣNab)

frgs. 1-3

1 מלי צלתא די צלי נבני מלך א[רעא די ב]בל מלכא [רבא כדי הוא כתיש]

2 בשחנא באישא בפתגם א[להא עלי]א בתימן [בשחנא באישא]

3 כתיש הוית שנין שבע ומן [אנשא] שוי א[נה וצלית לאלהא עליא]

4 וחטאי שבק לה גזר והוא [גבר] יהודי מ[ן בני גלותא ואמר לי]

5 החוי וכתב למעבד יקר ור[בות הד]ר לשם א[להא עליא וכן כתבת]

6 כתיש הוית בשחנא ב[אישא] בתימן [ומן אנשא שוי אנה]

7 שנין שבע מצלא הוי[ת לכל] אלהי כספא ודהבא [נחשא ופרזלא]

8 אעא אבנא חספא מן די [הוית סב]ר די אלהין ה[מון]

TRANSLATION *

1.

[May the gods who did not make the heavens and the earth] perish from the earth [and from under the heavens.]

2.

frgs. 1-3

1. The words of the prayer which Nabonidus prayed, the king of [the] la[nd of Bab]ylon, the [great] king, [when he was smitten]
2. with the evil disease by the decree of the [Most High] Go[d] in Teima [" With the evil disease]
3. was I smitten (for) seven years' and unlike [man] was I made ; [and I prayed to the Most High God,]
4. and an exorcist remitted my sins for Him ; he (was) a Jew fr[om (among) the deportees. He said to me,]
5. ' Make (it) known and write (it) down, to give glory and gr[eat hono]r to the name of G[od Most High.' And thus I have written,]
6. ' I was smitten with [the] e[vil] disease in Teima, [and unlike man was I made]
7. (for) seven years. [I] prayed [to all] the gods of silver and gold, [of bronze and iron,]
8. of wood (and) stone (and) clay from the time that [I thou]ght that t[hese] were gods [who would be able to cure me ...' "]

* Square brackets [ ] in the translation indicate lacunae in the Aramaic text. Material so enclosed is subject to various degrees of conjecture ; see the *editiones principes* or a commentary for the state of the question. Parentheses ( ) enclose material added for the sake of the sense of the English translation. Angular brackets < > enclose editorial additions. Braces { } enclose superfluous (e.g., dittographical) words. Italics in the translation indicate a literal Aramaic translation of the Hebrew text of the Bible in other than targumic texts.

frg. 4

1]]·· בר המון אחלמת
2]] מנה אח[ל]ף שלם של[ותי [
3]]··נו רחמי לא יכלת[[
4]]כמה דמא אנתה לד[ניאל [
5]]···[[

3. 4Q Pseudo-Daniel — 4QpsDan ar[a-c]

A.

ms. b

1]]··ן[[
2]]מן בתר מבולא[[
3] נ]וח מן לובר [טורא [
4]]· קריה[[
5] [
6]]א מגדלא רו[מה [

ms. a

7]]···[[
8] ע]ל מגדלא ושל[[
9] ל]בקרה בבנינ[א [
10]].ס.[[

B.

ms. a

1] שנין אר]בע מאה ··[[
2 יח . [. הו]ן וי .]]כולהון ויתון מן גוא
3 מצרין ביד .] ולהוא] מעברהון ירדנא יובל[א]
4]]ובניהון . [[
5]]. ית .[[

frg. 4

1. [ ].. apart from them I was made strong again
2. [ ] from it pas[s]ed the calm of [my] repo[se]
3. [ ].. my friends I was not able [ ]
4. [ ] how you resemble Da[niel]
5. [ ]... [ ]

3.

A.

1. [ ]..*n*[ ]
2. [ ]after the flood[ ]
3. [N]oah (came down) from [Mt.] Lubar[ ]
4. [ ]. a city[ ]
5. [ ]
6. [ ]' the tower, [its] heig[ht]

7. [ ]...[ ]
8. [up]on the tower and *šl*[ ]
9. [to] make an inspection in the building[ ]
10. [ ].*s*.[ ]

B.

1. [fo]ur hundred [years]..[ ]
2. he *ḥ*[the]m and he .[ ] all of them, and they will come from the midst of
3. Egypt through .[and he will] make them cross (?) the Jordan River
4. [ ]and their sons .[ ]
5. [ ].*yt*.[ ]

C.

mss. b and a

1 [ ]בחרו בני ישראל אנפיהון מן [אנפי אלהין]

2 [והוו דב]חין לבניהון לשידי טעותא ורגז עליהון אלוהין וא[מר] למנתן

3 אנון ביד נב[כדנצר מלך ב]בל ולאחרבא ארעהון מנהון מאדי ש[ ]

4 [ ] . בני גלותא . [ ]

5 [ ]ובדר אנון[ ]

D.

ms. a

1 [ ]איץ שב[ע]ין שנין . [ ]

2 [מלכותא] דה רבתא ויושע אנו[ן]

3 [ ]חסינין ומלכות עממ[יא]

4 [ ]היא מלכותא קד[מיתא]

E.

ms. a

1 [ ]מלך שנין . [ ]

2 [ ] . . בלכרוס [ ]

3 [ ] . תה[ ]

4 [ש]נין . . [ ]

5 [ ]רהוס בר[ ]

6 [ ]וס שנין ת[ ]

7 [ ]י מללה [ ]

F.

ms. a

1 [רש]ע[א] אטעו . [ ]

2 [בעדנא] דנה יתכנשון קריאי . [ ]

3 [מלכי] עממיא ולהוה מן יום [ ]

C.

1. [ ]the Israelites chose their presence rather than [the presence of God]
2. [and they sacr]ificed their children to the demons of error. God became angry with them and he gave or[ders] to give
3. them (over) into the hand of Nebu[chadnezzar, the king of Ba]bylon, and to destroy their land for them, from the hands (?) of š[ ]
4. [ ]. the deportees .[ ]
5. [ ]and he scattered them[ ]

D.

1. [ ]oppressed (?) se[v]enty years .[ ]
2. [ ]this great [kingdom] and he rescued the[m]
3. [(they became)] mighty and a kingdom of natio[ns]
4. [ ]This (is) the fi[rst] kingdom[ ]

E.

1. [ ]ruled ( ) years .[ ]
2. [ ].. Balakros [ ]
3. [ ].*th*[ ]
4. [y]ears ..[ ]
5. [ ]*rhws* son of[ ]
6. [ruled]*ws* [2/8/9] years[ ]
7. [ ]*y* to speak [ ]

F.

1. [in wicked]nes[s] they caused to stray .[ ]
2. [at] this [time] the ones called .[ ]will gather[ ]
3. [the kings of] the nations, and he/there will be from the day of[ ]

4] קדי]שין ומלכי עממיא [[
5] ע]בדין עד יומא [דנה [

ms. c

6] [. [ ]
7] ל]מסף ר[ש]עא
8]]אלן כעור יטער
9] א]לן אנון יקומון
10] ק]דיש[י]א ויתובון
11] [.] רשעא [

4. 1Q Daniel[a,b] — 1QDan[a,b] (1Q*71*, *72*)

(a) *1QDan*[a] *col. 2* (= Dan 2:2-6)

1 כשדיים להגיד] [
2 המלך 3 ויאמר להם ה[מלך [
3 לדעת את החלום 4 וידברו] [
4 מלכא לעלמין ח]יי [
5 ופשרא נחוה 5 ענא מלכא] [
6 אזדא די הן לא תהוד[עונני [
7 תתעבדון ובתיכון] 6 [
8] מ]תנן ו[נבזבה [

(b) *1QDan*[b] *frgs. a, b* (= Dan 3:22-30)

1] ד]י נור[א [
2 23]]מכפתין] [
3 24] מל]כא תוה וקם באת[בהלה [
4] ל]גו נורא מכפתין ענין ואמרין למ[לכא 25 [
5]]חזה גברין ארבעה שרי[ן [

4. [ho]ly ones and the kings of the nations[[
5. [sl]aves/doing until [this] day[[

6. [ ].[ ]
7. [to] put an end to wi[ck]edness
8. [ ]these will stray like a blind man
9. [ ]these, they will rise
10. [ ]the [h]oly on[e]s and they will return
11. [ ]. wickedness[ ]

4.

(a) (Dan 2:2-6)

1. (Hebrew :) let the Chaldeans [be summoned] to tell [the king his dreams. So they came in and stood before]
2. the king. [3]And the [king] said to them, [" I have had a dream, and my spirit is troubled]
3. to know the dream." [4]Then [the Chaldeans] spoke [to the king,]
4. (*vacat* [Aramaic :]) " O king, li[ve] forever! [Tell your servants the dream,]
5. and we shall make known the interpretation." [5]The king answered, [" The word from me is]
6. certain: If you do not make kno[wn to me the dream and its interpretation, (into) pieces]
7. you shall be made, and your houses [shall be laid to ruin. [6]But if you make known the dream and its interpretation, you shall get]
8. [from me g]ifts and [rewards]

(b) (Dan 3:22-30)

1. [the flame o]f fir[e slew those men who took up Shadrach, Meshach, and Abednego.]
2. [23][ ]bound.
3. [24][Then Ki]ng [Nebuchadnezzar] was astonished and rose in has[te. He said to his counselors, " Did we not throw three men]
4. bound [in]to the fire ? " They spoke up and answered the ki[ng, " True, O king." [25]He answered,]
5. [" But I] see four men loos[e, walking in the midst of the fire, and they are not hurt; and the appearance]

6 די רביע[יא ד]מא לבר אלה[ין [26] [

7 ואמר שד[ר]ך מיש[ך [

8 באדין נפקין שדר[ך [27] [

9 ופחותא והדברי מל[כא [

10 לא התחרך ושרבל[יהון עד]ה בהון [28] [

11]]ומשך ועבד[[

12 ושזב לע[בדוהי]שניו ויהבו גשמ[הון [

13 ולא[ש]ימו טעם די כול עם אומ[ה [29]]

14] נ]גו דמין יתעבד ובית[ה [

15] ל]הצלה כדנה [30] באד[ין [

5. 11Q Targum of Job — 11QtgJob

col. 1

Hebrew Job

17:14, 15 — 1 [ואמי ואחתי לתולע]תה ומא אפו א[ן]

16 — 2]]העמי לשאול ת[נחת]

3 [הכחדא על עפר נ]שכב (*vacat*)

18:1 — 4] ענ]א בלדד שוחא[יא ואמר]

2 — 5]] . תשוא סוף למלי[ן

2, 3 — 6 [ונמלל למא לב]עירא דמינא[

4 — 7]] העל דב[רתך

4 — 8]]מן את[רה

6. of the four[th (is) l]ike a son of (the) god[s." 26Then Nebuchadnezzar came near to the door of the burning fiery furnace]
7. and said, "Shad[r]ach, Mesha[ch, and Abednego, servants of the Most High God, come forth, and come here!"]
8. Then Shadra[ch, Meshach, and Abednego] came out [from the fire. 27And the satraps, the prefects,]
9. the governors, and [the] kin[g]'s counselors [gathered together and saw]
10. was not singed, and [their] mantle[s were not harmed and no smell of fire had co]me upon them. 28[Nebuchadnezzar spoke up and said,]
11. (*vacat*) ["Blessed be the God of Shadrach,] Meshach and Abed[-nego, who has sent his angel]
12. and delivered his se[rvants who trusted in him, and] set at nought [the king's command,] and yielded up [their] bodies;
13. and [they did] not [serve and worship any god except their own God. 29Therefore let] a decree be [m]ade: Any people, natio[n],
14. [or language that says anything against the God of Shadrach, Meshach and Abedn]ego shall be made (into) pieces, and [his] house
15. [shall be laid to ruin; for there is no other god who is able to] deliver like this." 30The[n]

col. 1

Job 17:14–18:4

[If I must call out to the Pit, "You are my father,"]

1. [and "my mother" or "my sister" to] the wo[rm, 15what then? Wh[ere (is)]
2. [my hope? 16Will] it [descend] with me to Sheol? [Shall we together]
3. [in the dust] lie down?" (*vacat*)
4. [1Then] Bildad the Shuhi[te ans]wered, [saying,]
5. [2Whe]n will you put an end to word[s? And we shall speak:]
6. [3Why] are we likened [to ca]ttle? [ ]
7. [4] Is it on accoun[t of you that]
8. [ ] from [its] place? [ ]

col. 2

19:11, 12	[ותק]ף עלי רגזה וח[שבני]	1
12, 13	[א]תון חתפוהי וכבשו[ואחי מני]	2
13, 15	הרחקו וידעי בי[אתהפכו דירי]	3
15	ביתי אמתי לנכר[י]	4
16	לעבדי קרית ולא ע[נא]	5
17	רוח המכת לאנתתי[ ]	6
18	רשיעין יסגפ[ונני]	7
19	כל אנש די[ ]	8

col. 3

19:29	[ב]איש [ ]	1
	[ ] (*vacat*) [ ]	2
20:1, 2	[מלל צופר נעמתיא והתי]ב לכן לבבי י[תיבני]	3
3	[קל]לתי אשמע ורו[ח]	4
4	[הדא יד]עת מן עלמא מן ד[י]	5
5	[ ] . ארו מבע רשיע[ין]	6
5	[ ]לעבע תעדא [ ]	7
6	[וראש]ה לעניא[ימטא]	8

col. 4

21:2, 3	[ ] . לי להות . . . [	1
3, 4	[מ]נדעי תמיק[	2
4, 5	ארו אפו לא ת[תקצר רוחי	3
5, 6	סימו ידיכון על [פמא	4

col. 2

Job 19:11-19

1. [[11]And he in]tensified his wrath against me and con[sidered me his adversary. [12]En masse]
2. have his despoilers come (on), and they have trampled down [their path against me. [13]My brothers from me]
3. have been alienated, and my acquaintances [turned] against me[[15] those dwelling in]
4. my household. My maidservant [regarded me as] a stranger. [ ]
5. [16]I have called my servant, but he does not ans[wer.]
6. [17]I have abased myself before my wife[ ]
7. [18]Evil people afflic[t me]
8. [19]Every one (with) whom [I was intimate]

col. 3

Job 19:29–20:6

1. [[29] e]vil.
2. [ ] (*vacat*)
3. [[1]So Zophar the Naamathite spoke up and answe]red, [2]"Now then my mind makes [answer to me]
4. [[3]] of my [dis]grace I hear and a spir[it answers me...]
5. [[4]Do you k]now [this] from of old, from (the time) tha[t]
6. [on the earth]. [5]For the exulting of wicked m[en (is)]
7. [ ]in haste departs[ ]
8. [[6]]his [head reaches] to the clouds[ ]

col. 4

Job 21:2-10

1. [2]my [wo]rds *lhwt*... (or *lhwwn*...) [[3]]
2. my [k]nowledge you shall mock[[4]]
3. Why then should not [my spirit] be im[patient (shortened)? [5]]
4. Place your hands upon [(your) mouth [6]]

5 ותמהא אחד לי ה] [6, 7
6 והסגיו נכסין זרע[הון [7, 8

7 לעיניהון בתיהון] [8, 9
8 אלהא עליהון] [9, 10
9 הריתהון פל[טו [10

col. 5

1] עי]נוהי במפלתה ומן] חמת מרא [21:20

2] מא] צבו לאלהא בביתה . [[21
3] ומ]נין ירחוהי גזירין הלא[להא [21, 22

4] ו]הוא רמיא מדין אבד] דן [22, 23

5] מו]ח גרמוהי דן ימות בנפ[ש [24, 25

6] ל]א אכל כחדא על [עפר ישכבו [25, 26

7] ע]ליהון ארו ידעת] [26, 27

8] ב]י התעיטתון] [27

col. 6

1] לא]להא 22:3
2]]ארחך 3
3] י]על עמך 4
4] הל]א איתי 4, 5
5] א]חיך מגן 5, 6

6] ל]צהא לא 6, 7

7] ל]חם ואמרת 7, 8
8]]אנפוהי
9] רי]קנה 9

5. and amazement has seized me. [7]How is it that [ ]
6. and have increased (their) possessions. [8][Their] offspring [ ]
7. before their eyes. [9]Their houses [and no rod of]
8. God (is) upon the[m. [10]]
9. their pregnant (cows) have cal[ved]

col. 5

Job 21:20-27

1. [[20]May] his ey[es gaze] upon his fall and from [the wrath of the Lord let him drink]
2. [[21]What] concern (is there) for God in his house .[ ]
3. [when the num]ber of his months (is) cut (short). [22]Is it God [that he will teach]
4. [when] he judges the lofty? [[23]One] has perished [[24]]
5. [and moist (was) the mar]row of his bones. [25]Another will die with (his) sou[l embittered,]
6. [of good he has no]t eaten. [26]Together in/upon [the dust they will lie]
7. [ov]er them. [27]For I have known[ ]
8. [against m]e you plotted. [ ]

col. 6

Job 22:3-9

1. [[3] to G]od
2. [ ]your path ?
3. [[4] Does he] enter with you
4. [into judgment ?][5]Is [n]ot
5. [your wickedness boundless ?[6]]your [br]others for nothing
6. [[7]To] a thirsty person [you gave] no
7. [water ; you withheld br]ead. [8]But you said,
8. [ ]his face
9. [[9] em]pty.

col. 7

Ref.	Text	Line
22:16	די מיתו[ ]	1
17	אמרין ל[מרא מא יעבד]	2
17, 18	לנא אלה[א]	3
18, 19	ועטת רש[יעין]	4
19	ויחאכון ו[ ]	5
20	היך לא[ ]	6
21	הסתכל[ ]	7
22	קבל[ ]	8
	[ ]	9

col. 8

Ref.	Text	Line
24:12	מן קריהון [ונפש הללין]	1
12, 13	תקבל אלהא[ ]	2
13	קדמוהי לנור[א]	3
13, 14	בשבילוהי ל[ ]	4
14, 15	ומסכן ובלי[ליא]	5
15	קבל למא[מר]	6
15, 16	ויחטא ח[תר]	7
16, 17	בבאיש[ ]	8
17	להון[ ]	9

col. 9

Ref.	Text	Line
24:24	והתכ]פפו כיבלא יתקפצון א[ ]	1
25	[מ]ן אפו יתיבנני פתגם וי . [ ]	2
25:1	[ ] [ ] ענא בלד[ד שוחאיא]	3
2	[ואמר ש]לטן ורבו עם אלהא ע[בד שלם]	4
2, 3	[במרו]מה האיתי רחצן להש[היה]	5
3, 4	[ ] או על מן לא תקום [ ]	6

col. 7

Job 22:16-22

1. [16]who died[ ]
2. [17]They have said to [the Lord, What can]
3. God [do] for us ? [[18]]
4. and the advice of impi[ous people [19]]
5. and they will laugh (at them) and [ ]
6. [20]How have [they] not [ ]
7. [21]Consider wisely [ ]
8. [22]Welcome [ ]

col. 8

Job 24:12-17

1. [12]From their cities[the throat of the wounded]
2. complains. God[[13]they have rebelled]
3. before him, against [the] fire[ ]
4. in its paths. [14]At[(the) poor]
5. and (the) needy ; and at nig[ht [15]]
6. dusk, say[ing]
7. and he sins. [16]He brea[ks into houses]
8. on evil[[17]]
9. for them[ ]

col. 9

Job 24:24–26:2

1. [[24] and] they [were] bent over ; like dog-grass they are shrivelled up. ’[ ]
2. [[25] W]ho then can answer me and *y*[ ]
3. [ ] (*vacat*) [25:1]Bilda[d the Shuhite] answered
4. [and said, [2]“ Do]minion and majesty are with God. [He] ma[kes peace]
5. [in] his [heig]hts. [3]Is there security to ke[ep (it there) ?]
6. [ ] Or on whom does [his] not stand ? [[4]And how can a man]

4, 5	[ ]אלהא ומא יצדק[ ]	7
5, 6	[ ] זכי וכוכביא לא[ ]	8
6	[ ]ב]ר אנש תולע[ה ועא [ ]	9
26:1, 2	[ ]איוב ואמ]ר העד[רת]	10

col. 10

26:10	[ ]ע[ד ס]יפי חשוך [	1
11	[ ]עמודי שמיא י]זיע ויתמהון מן *(vacat)*	2
12	[ ]ימא ובמנדעה קטל	3
13	[ ]הד]נח חללת ידה תנין ערק	4
14	[ ]ארחו]הי מא עטר מלא נש[מע]	5
14	[ ]מן]יסתכל	6
	[ ] *(vacat)* [ ]	7
27: 1, 2	[ ]ענא איוב]ואמר חי אלהא[ ]	8
2, 3	[ ]לנפשי הן לכמ[א]	9
3, 4	[ ]ב]אפי הן ימל[ן ספתי]	10

col. 11

27:11	[ ]בי]ד אלהא ועבד	1
11, 12	[מרא לא אכסא הא אתון כ]לכון חזיתון למה	2
12, 13	[ ]אנש רשיעין	3
13, 14	[ ]מן]קדמוהי ינסון הן	4
14	[ ]לחר]ב יפצון ולא ישבעון	5
15	[ ]וארמלתה לא	6

7. [be clean before] God? And how [can one born of a woman] be righteous?
8. [[5] is not] bright, and the stars [are] not [clean in his sight? [6]More so is man, a]
9. [maggot, and a so]n of man, a worm?" [[26:1]Job]
10. [answered and sai]d, [2]" Did [you] hel[p]

col. 10

Job 26:10–27:4

1. [[10]]un[to the en]ds of darkness.
2. [[11]The pillars of the heavens he causes]to tremble, and they are stunned by
3. [[12]]the sea, and with his knowledge he killed
4. [[13] he caused to sh]ine; his hand pierced the fleeing dragon
5. [[14]]*ḥy* What whisp of a word do we he[ar?]
6. [Who] can consider (it) wisely?"
7. [ ] (*vacat*) [
8. [[27:1] Job spoke up] and said, [2]" As God lives, [ ]
9. [ ] my soul; [3]if similar[ly]
10. [in] my nostrils; [4] [my lips] shall not sp[eak]

col. 11

Job 27:11-20

1. [[11] about the h]and of God, and the work of
2. [the Lord I shall not conceal. [12]Look, a]ll of you have seen (it). Why
3. [[13]This is the lot of] evil people
4. [with God, the heritage of oppressors] before him they will carry off. [14]If
5. [for a] sword. They will open (their) mouths, but will not be sated
6. [with food. [15]] and his widow(s) will not

7	[הן כעפרא]זויא כטינא יסגא		16
8	[ומ]מ[ו]ה קשיטה יפלג		17
9	[ ] . . ן כקטותא		18
10	[יש]כב ולא איתחד		18, 19
11	[ ]כמין באיש[ן]		19, 20

col. 12

1	רגל]ן	. [	28:4, 5
2	וחליה[	את]רי	5, 6
3	ספיר . [	. [	6, 7
4	לא . [	לא הד]רכה	7, 8
5	תני]ן	מ]ן	8, 9
6	עק[ר	]ין	9, 10
7	ב[	]לא	10, 11
8	] .	. [	11, 12
9	]	אנ]ש	12, 13

col. 13

1	אתר ערימותא . [	ומן]	28:20, 21
2	צפרי שמיא אסת]תרת	[	21, 22
3	באדנינא שמענא [שמעה	[	22, 23
4	בה ארו הוא יצ[פא אתרה	ארו הוא]	23, 24
5	לקצוי ארעא יב[קא	[	24
6	במעבדה לרוחא[	[	25
7	במכילה במעבד[ה	[	25, 26
8	קלילין באדין]	[	26, 27
9	ואמר לבני[אנש הא	[	28
10	ומסטא[מן באישתה	[	28

col. 14

1	[ב]צפרין בתרעי קריא בשוק[א	[	29:7

7. [mourn. [16]If he heaps up silver coins [like dust,] amasses
[ ] like clay,
8. [[17] and] his [m]on[ey] the true
one will divide
9. [[18]]..*n* like the reed-hut
10. [[19]The rich li]es down and is not seized;
11. [ ][20]Evil[s overwhelm him]
like (flood) waters

col. 12

Job 28:4-13

1. [4]the foot of[[5]].
2. and its mound(s)[[6]The pla]ces of
3. sapphire .[[7]].
4. does not [know [8]has not tr]odden it.
5. A dragon[[9] b]y
6. the roo[ts [10]]*yn*
7. *b*[[11]]*l'*
8. .[[12]].
9. [[13] Ma]n

col. 13

Job 28:20-28

[[20] and where is]
1. the place of subtlety? [21].[even from]
2. the birds of the heavens is it hid[den. [22]]
3. 'With our ears we have heard [a rumor (of it).' [23]]
4. in/by it, for he spi[es out its place, [24]for he]
5. gaz[es upon] the ends of the earth, [ ]
6. [25]In his making for the wind [its]
7. with a measure, [26]in [his] making [ ]
8. [for] light [clouds], [27]then [ ]
9. [28]And he said to the sons of [man, 'Look,]
10. and the turning [from evil is]

col. 14

Job 29:7-16

[[7]As I went out]
1. mornings to the gates of the city (and) in [the] marketplace[ ]

8	[ו]חזוני עלומין טשו וגברין ח[ ]	2
9	[ו]רברבין חשו <מ>מללא וכף ישון[על פמהון]	3
10, 11	קל סגנין הטמרו לחנך דב[ק לשנהון ארו]	4
11	[ת]שמע אדן שבחתני ועין ח[זת .]	5
12	[א]רו אנה שיזבת לענא מן . [ ]	6
12, 13	[ד]י לא עדר להון ברכת [אבד]	7
13, 14	[ב]פם ארמלה הוית לצל[ותא]	8
14, 15	[הלבש]תני וכתתון לבשת[ ]	9
15, 16	[ו]רגלין לחגיר [ ]	10
16	[לא] ידע[ת]	11

col. 15

29:24	[ ]אחאך להון ולא יה[ימנון]	1
24, 25	[ ]ון בחרת ארחי והוית [ראש]	2
25	[כמלך]בראש חילה וכגבר די א[בלין]	3
30:1	[וכען ח]אכו עלי זערין מני ביומין[די]	4
1, 2	[אבה]תהון מלמהוא עם כלבי ע[ני]	5
2	[ ]לא הוא לי צבין ובאכפי[הון]	6
3	[ובכ]פן רעין הוא ירק ד[חשת]	7
3, 4	[ ]באישה די אכל[ו]	8
4	[ועקר רתמ]ין לחמהו[ן]	9

col. 16

30:13	[לסת]רי יתון ופצא לא	1
13, 14	[איתי להון] . בתקף שחנו יתון	2
14, 15	[תחות]באישה אתכפפת התכפפת	3

2. [8]youngsters saw me (and) hid (from me), adult men ḥ[ ];
3. [9]nobles grew silent <from> speaking, putting (their) hand [to their mouth].
4. [10]The voice(s) of chieftains was concealed; to (their) palates clun[g their tongue. [11]For (when]
5. an ear heard, it praised me, and (when) an eye sa[w, it]
6. [12]For I rescued (the) poor from .[ ]
7. those who (had) no helper. [13]The blessing of one about to p[erish ;]
8. in the mouth of the widow I became a pra[yer. [14]]
9. [and it clothed me]. Like a tunic I was clothed [with]
10. [[15] and] feet to the lame [ ]
11. [[16] I did not] know [ ]

col. 15

Job 29:24–30:4

1. [ ] [24]I smile at them, but [they] do not tr[ust (me)]
2. [ ]*wn.* [25]I chose my course and I was [a chief]
3. [, like a king] at the head of his army, like a person who [comforts] mou[rners].
4. [[30:1]But now] they have [la]ughed at me, those younger than I in days, [whose fa]thers [I]
5. [would have kept] from being with the dogs of [my] fl[ock. [2]]
6. [ ]was no delight for me, and with [their] loads[ ]
7. [[3] and in a fa]mine (even) the green of (the) des[ert] was an attraction [for them]
8. [ ]bad; [4]who at[e]
9. [and broom root]s (were) thei[r] food.[ ]

col. 16

Job 30:13-20

1. [[13] to] my [hid]eout they come, but one who opens (for them) [th]ey [do] not
2. [have.] [14]With the severity of purulence they come
3. [beneath] evil am I bowed down. [15]Bent

15	[עלי כ]רוח טבתי ורבותי וכענן	4
15, 16	[ ]ני וכען עלי תתאשד	5
16	[נפשי וי]ומי תשברא יאקפוני	6
17	[ ]גרמי יקדון ועדק[י]	7
17, 18	[ ]חיל יאחדון לבו[שי]	8
18, 19	[יאקפ]ונני אחתוני [לטינא]	9
19, 20	[ע]ליך [ ]	10

col. 17

30:25	[ ]אתה	1
25, 26	[ ]בדי	2
26, 27	[רתח]ו ולא	3
27, 28	[ ]הלכת	4
28	[ ]זעקת	5
29	[לבנ]ת יענה	6
30	[ ]ו מן	7
30, 31	[ ]י	8
31:1	[ ]לא	9

col. 18

31:8, 9	יאכ[ל הן פת]יא	1
9	לבי בא[נתה אטמ]רת	2
10, 11	תטחן ל[אחרן אנתתי ארו ה]וא רגז	3
11, 12	והוא חט[א ארו נורא הו]א עד	4
12, 13	אבדון ת[אכל]הן אתקצרת	5
13, 14	בדין עב[די ו]מא אעבד	6
14, 15	כדי יק[ום אלהא] ארו	7

4. [upon me is like] (the) wind (are) my prosperity and
my honor; and like a cloud
5. [that passes is] my [deliverance]. 16Now for me [my soul]
is poured out,
6. [and d]ays of disgrace will mount about me.
7. [17In the night within me] my bones burn and my sinews
8. [18] force they grasp [my] garment(s)
9. [ ]they [mo]unt about me, 19and they
make me descend [into the mire].
10. [I cry out t]o you[ ]

col. 17

Job 30:25–31:1

1. [25]'*th*
2. [26]*bdy*
3. [27 see]the and are not
4. [28]I walk about
5. [ ] I have cried out
6. [29 to ost]riches
7. [30]. from
8. [31]*y*
9. [31:1]*l'*

col. 18

Job 31:8-16

1. will ea[t 9If] my heart [is
wi]dened
2. for [a] wom[an] I have [hid]den
[myself],
3. 10let [my wife] grind for [another; 11for th]at
(would be a source of) anger,
4. and that (would be) a si[n 12For that
would] be [a fire]
5. (that) con[sumes] unto Abaddon[ ]13If I have
become impatient
6. in the cause of [my] serva[nt]14what [then]
shall I do
7. when [God] rises up ?[ ]15For (he who)

Line	Text	Job
8	עבד[ני ... ח]ד הן	15, 16
9	אמ[נע ... ה]סיפת	16

col. 19

Line	Text	Job
	[... כדי]	
1	דנה ולס[הרא ... ל]בי	31:26, 27
2	ונשקת ידי ל[פמי ... ארו כד]בת	27, 28
3	לאלהא מעל[א ... וה]ללת	28, 29
4	על באישתה[...] . א	29(?)
5	לוטי וישמע[...]ברגזי	29(?)
6	ואחדת א[... למחט]א	29(?), 30
7	חכי למש[אל ... הן לא אמרו א]נש	30, 31
8	ביתי מ[ן ... בברא]	31, 32
9	לא י[בית ...]	32

col. 20

Line	Text	Job
1	תחות חטא[... ותחות שערתא]	31:40
2	באשושה ספ[ו מלי איוב ... גבריא תלתה]	31:40 – 32:1
3	אלין מלהתב[ה פתגם לאיוב ... ארו]	32:1
4	הוא איוב ז[כי בעינוהי ...]	1
5	(*vacat*)] ... [	
6	אדין רגז] אליהוא בר ברכאל בוזיא מן ...]	2
7	זרע רומא[ה ...]	2
8	ואף ע[ל רחמוהי תלתה ...]	3
9	מל[ין ...]	3

col. 21

Line	Text	Job
1	מלי אף אנה ארו סברת[למליכון ... עד]	32:10, 11

8. made[me o]ne. [16]If
9. I wi[thhold] I [p]ut an end to

col. 19

Job 31:26-32

[when]
1. it shone and at [the] mo[on [27] my he]art
2. and my hand kissed [my] m[outh. [28] for] I [should have li]ed
3. to God abov[e. [29] or] I [uttered pr]aise
4. at his misfortune[ ].'
5. my curse, and he hears[ ] in my anger
6. and I caught hold '[[30]I have not allowed] my mouth [to si]n
7. by aski[ng [31]If the m]en of
8. my household [have not said], 'Wh[o .' [32]The sojourner]
9. does not sp[end the night outside ;]

col. 20

Job 31:40–32:3

1. [40]In place of wheat [let thorns come forth, and in place of barley]
2. the stinkweed." (So) have en[ded the words of Job. [32:1]]
3. those [three men ceased] from (trying) to answe[r Job for]
4. he (was) ri[ghteous in his own eyes.]
5. *(vacat)* [ ]
6. [2]Then grew angry [Elihu son of Barachel, the Buzite, from]
7. the descendants of Rum[ah ;]
8. [3]and also a[t his three companions]
9. wor[ds]

col. 21

Job 32:10-17

[let me make known]
1. my words, my very own. [11]For I have awaited [your words until]

2	תסיפון עד תחקרון סוף[ ]	11, 12
3	וארו לא איתי מנכון לא[יוב ומתיב]	12
4	למלוהי די למה תאמרון[ ]	12, 13
5	להן אלהא היבנא ולא א[נש]	13, 14
6	מלין וכמא לא יתיבנה[ ]	14, 15
7	והחשיו ונטרת מנהון[ ]	15, 16
8	קמו ולא ימללון עו[ד]	16, 17
9	[וא]חוה מלי אף א[נה]	17

col. 22

1	[אנה] הן חרגתי לא תס[רדנך]	33:6, 7
2	[לא י]קר הך אמרת באדני וק[ל מליך]	7, 8
3	[זכ]י אנה ולא חטא לי ונקא[אנה]	8, 9
4	[ה]ן עולין השכח אחד לי . [ ]	9, 10
5	[י]שוא בסדא רגלי וסכר כ[ל ארחי]	10, 11
6	[ ]ארו רב אלהא מן אנשא[למה לה]	12, 13
7	[מלין] *רבברן תמלל ארו בכל פ[תגמוהי לא]	13
8	[יתיב א]רו בחדא ימלל אלה[א]	13, 14
9	[ב]חלמין בחדידי לילא[ ]	14, 15
10	[בניו]מה על משכבה[ ]	15, 16
11	[ ]. רה[ ]	16

*read רברבן

col. 23

1	ויאמר פצהי מן חב[ל]ת	33:24, 25
2	אשה ישנקנה ויתמלין [עטמוהי]מן	25

2. you would finish, until you would search out the end of[12]
3. Now look, Jo[b] does not have one from among you [who makes answer]
4. to his words. 13(Beware) lest you sa[y, ' ;]
5. but God has pronounced us guilty, and not a m[an' 14]
6. (his) words, and how (is it that) one does not answer him[15]
7. and they are troubled. I have kept from them [16]
8. they stand (there) and speak no mor[e 17]
9. [but I] shall make known my words, my very [own]

col. 22

Job 33:6-16

1. [, 7I too]. Look, dread of me should not ter[rify you]
2. [will not] bear heavy. 8Surely, you have spoken in my hearing, and (to) the sou[nd of (your) words I listen]
3. [9Innoce]nt am I, and no sin (is) mine ; clean [am I,]
4. [10I]f he has found iniquities, he has caught me. [ ]
5. [11" He] placed my feet in the stocks and has closed up al[l my paths. 12]
6. [ ] For God (is) greater than man. [13Why to him]
7. do you address haughty [words] ? For with none of [his] wo[rds will he]
8. [give answer. 14F]or in one way Go[d] speaks[
9. [15In] dreams, in sharp experiences of the night [ ]
10. [in] his [sle]ep upon his bed. [16]
11. [ ]*.rh*[ ]

col. 23

Job 33:24-32

1. 24and should he say, ' Rescue him from destruc[tion]*t*
2. fire,' he would snuff it out ; and [his bones] will be filled [with marrow 25]than

3 עולים ותב ליומי עלים[ותה … ו]ישמענה 25, 26

4 ויחזא אנפוהי באספ[ליא …]וכעבד 26

5 כפוהי[י]שלם לה ויאמ[ר …]ולא 26, 27

6 כארחי ה[ש]תלמת פר[ק נפשי …]· י 27, 28

7 בנהור תחזא הא [… עם ג]בר 28, 29

8 זמן תרין תלתה לא[תבה נפשה … בנהו]ר 29, 30

9 הי[י]ן הצת דא [איוב … ואנה אמ]לל 30, 31

10 [הן א]יתי מ[לין … [32

col. 24

1 מן חטא מ[ן גבר כאיוב …]א חטיא ומתחבר 34:6, 7, 8

2 לעבדי שקר [… רש]ע ארו אמר לא 8, 9

3 ישנא גבר מ[ן … ב]תר אלהא 9

4 *(vacat)* כען אנש[שמעו לי]חס לאלהא מן שקר 10

5 ומן {ל}חבל א <ל>מ[רא ארו כעבד] אנש ישלם לה 10, 11

6 *(vacat)* […]הכען צדא אלהא 11, 12

7 ישקר ומרא[יעות דינא …]הוא ארעא עבד 12, 13

8 וקשט תב[לא כלא … ונשמ]תה עלוהי יכלא 13, 14

9 וימות [… על עפר]ישכבון 15

10 [… מ]לי הבשק[ר] 16, 17

3. a youth. He returns to the days of [his] you[th ; [26]he prays to God, and] he will listen to him.
4. He will gaze upon his face with as[surance] and according to the product
5. of his hands will [he] requite him. [27]He say[s] and not
6. according to my path was I requited. [28]He has rescu[ed my soul]my[ ].
7. shall gaze upon (the) light. [29]Look, [with a hu]man being
8. once, twice, (or even) three (times) [30]to br[ing back his soul with the ligh]t of
9. li[f]e. [31]Listen to this, [Job, and I shall s]peak
10. [[32]If you h]ave w[ords to say]

col. 24

Job 34:6-17

1. from sin. [7]Wh[o is a man like Job ? He] the sins, [8]and (is) associated
2. with the doers of deceit [and ev]il. [9]For he has said,
3. ' A man is not changed b[y af]ter God.
4. (*vacat*) [10]Now, men of[listen to me !] Far be it from God to do evil,
5. <from> the L[ord] to do harm. [[11]For according to what] a man [produces] will he requite him
6. (*vacat*) [ ] [12]Now will God really
7. do what is deceitful, and [will] the Lord [distort justice ?] [13]He made the earth,
8. and set aright the [whole] wor[ld.] [14]Were he to withhold [and] his [brea]th from it,
9. [[15]all flesh] would die [at once, and]would lie down [in the dust]
10. [[16]] my words. [17]Is it by dece[it]

col. 25

1 [ר]ברבין די לא סוף ויקים א[חרנין] — 34:24
2 [חכ]ם עבדהון וירמא המון באת[ר — 24, 25
3 [מן אר]חה ובכל שבילוהי לא הסתכ[לו] — 27
4 [עלוהי זעקת] מסכנין וקבילת ענין ישמע [ ] — 28, 29
5 [ויסת]ר אנפוהי מן יתיבנה על עם[ועל] — 29
6 [גבר בממ]לך אנש רשיעיא התקלו[ ] — 30, 31
7 [ ]. י לה איחל בלחודוהי[ ] — 31, 32
8 [ ]לא אוסף ארו מ . [ ] — 32, 33
9 [תב]חר ולא אנה [ ] — 33
10 [מ]לין וגבר[ ] — 34

col. 26

1 [ ] . ובסגיא עויתך מא ת[עבד לה הן זכי]ת מא — 35:6, 7
2 תתן לה או מא מידך יקב[ל לגבר כות]ך חטיך — 7, 8
3 ולבר אנש צדקתך מן סגיא[יז]עקון יצוחון — 8, 9
4 מן קדם סגיאין ולא אמר[ין אן]אלהא — 9, 10
5 די עבדנה ודי חלק לנא ל[מנט]ר לנצבתנא — 10
6 בליליא די פרשנא מן בע[ירי ארעא ומן] צפריא — 10, 11
7 חכמנה תמה יזעקון ול[א יענה מן קדם ג]אות — 11, 12
8 [ב]אישין ארו שוא לא יש[מע אלהא ומרא ה]בלא — 12, 13
9 [לא] יצתנה הן תאמר[ ] — 13, 14
10 [ ] . לה א[רו] — 14, 15

col. 25

Job 34:24-34

1. [[24] gr]eat ones endlessly and sets up o[thers].
2. [[25] he kno]ws their deed(s) and will cast them into the pla[ce of]
3. [[27] from] his [pa]th and [they] had no regar[d] for any of his ways.
4. [[28] unto him the cry of] poor people, (that) he may hear the complaint of (the) needy. [[29]]
5. [and hi]des his face, who will bring it back ? (Whether) for a people [or for]
6. [a man, it is the same. [30]When] one of the wicked [ru]les, there are ensnared [[31]]
7. [ ].*y*; of him I shall despair. [32]In him alone [ ]
8. [ ] I shall not again (do it). [33]For *m*. [ ]
9. [you must ch]oose, not I, [ ]
10. [[34] wor]ds, and a man[ ]

col. 26

Job 35:6-15

1. [ ] [6]With the abundance of your transgressions what do you [do to him ? [7]If] you [are innocent], what
2. do you render to him ? Or what does he receive from your hand ? [8][To a man like] yourself (belongs) your sin ;
3. and to a human being your righteousness. [9]Because of an abundance of [misfortunes (people) c]ry out ; they shout (for help)
4. against many. [10]Yet they do not say, '[Where is] the God
5. who made us and who has portioned us out to [guar]d our plantations
6. during the night ? [11]Who has set us apart from the bea[sts of the earth] and
7. made us wiser than the birds.' [12]There they cry out, but he does n[ot answer because of the haught]iness of
8. [e]vil (men). [13]For [God] does not lis[ten] to vanity, [nor] does [the Lord]
9. heed [ai]ry nothings. [14]If you say [that you do not see him]
10. [ ] for him. [15]F[or]

col. 27

1	למלכין יתבי כ[ורסיהון ורח]מוהי לרחצן ירמון	36:7
2	ואף עם אסירין ב[זקין א]חידין בחבלי מסכניא	8
3	ויחוא להון עבדיהו[ן ועוית]הון ארו התרוממו ויגלא	9, 10
4	אדניהון למוסר וא[מר להון]הן יתובון מן באישתהון	10
5	הן ישמעון ויעב[דון ישלמון]בטב ימהון ושניהון	11
6	ביקר ועדנין [והן לא ישמע]ון בחרבא יפלון	11, 12
7	ויאבדון מן כ[סלא ובחנפי ל]בבהון לרנז	12, 13
8	עליהון י[פנא ומ]דינתהון בממתין	13, 14
9	ויפרק מ[סכניא כ]די אדניהון	15
10	[ ]לא[ ]	16

col. 28

1	ע[ולא עבדת ד]כר ארו רברבין עבדוהי ד[י אנש]	36:23, 24
2	חזו ה[מון וכ]ל אנשא עלוהי חזין ובני אנשא	24, 25
3	מרהיק [ב]ה יבקון הא אלהא רב הוא ויומוהי	25, 26
4	סגיא[יא לא נ]דע ומנין שנוהי די לא סוף ארו	26, 27
5	ענ[ין יענן] וזיקי מטר יהכן ועננוהי ינחתון	27, 28
6	ט[על]עם סגיא הן (*vacat*) מן פרס	28, 29
7	ע[ניא]תה מן טלל ופרס נה[ורה]	29, 30
8	[כ]סי ארו בהון ידין ע[ממין]	30, 31

col. 27

Job 36:7-16

[7][they are turned]

1. on kings (who) sit upon [their] th[rones, and] his (i. e., God's) [fr]iends are exalted in security.
2. [8]Moreover, (if they are) with prisoners in [chains, en]meshed in the cords of the poor,
3. [9]he makes the[ir] deeds known to them, and their [transgressions], for they have exalted themselves ; [10]he uncovers
4. their ears for chastisement and s[ays to them], ' If they return from their evil (deeds),
5. [11]if they will listen and ac[t, they will fill out] their days with happiness and their years
6. with honor and delights. [12][But if] they [will not listen], they will fall by the sword
7. and will perish from stu[pidity.' [13]Because of the hypocrisy of] their [hea]rts [he will turn] to anger
8. against them ; [14][and] their [c]ity [will perish] by slayers.
9. [15]But he will rescue the p[oor in their poverty, sin]ce he [uncovers] their ears [ ]
10. [[16]] not [ ]

col. 28

Job 36:23-33

[23][Or who can say,]

1. '[You have done] wr[ong' ? [24]Re]call, for great are his deeds, wh[ich men]
2. have see[n ; [25]al]l mankind gazes upon him, and human beings
3. contemplate [h]im from afar. [26]Look, God is great, and his many days
4. [we do not kn]ow ; the number of his years (is) endless. [27]For
5. [he gathers the] clou[ds] and directs the blasts of rain ; [28]his clouds cause *ṭ*[ ] to come down
6. [upon] a numerous people. [29]Now (?) (*vacat*) who has spread out
7. [the] cl[ouds]*.th*, who has provided shade, [30]and (who) has spread out [the] lig[ht]
8. [or cov]ered [the roots of the sea] ; [31]for through them he will judge pe[oples]

Job	Text	Line
31, 32	[ ]על מאמרה מ[ ]	9
32, 33	[י]שיה על[והי]	10

col. 29

Job	Text	Line
37:10, 11	על אנפי מין אף בהון ימרק ענ[ין] וינפק מן	1
11, 12	ענן נורה והוא אמר ישמעון לה ואזלין לעבדיהון	2
12, 13	על כל די ברא יפקדנון על אנפי תבל הן למכתש	3
13	הן לארעא הן לכפן וחסרנה והן פתגם טב להוא	4
13, 14	עליה הצת דא איוב וקום הסתכל בגבורת באלהא	5
15	[הת]נדע מא שויא אלהא עליהו[ן והו]פע נהור עננה	6
16, 17	[התנ]דע להלבשא עננה גב[ורה ב]דיל די לבושך	7
17, 16, 18	[חמים] ארו הוא ידע מדע[א התנדע למ]נפח ערפלא	8
18, 19	[כמח]זיה עקה ינדע[ ]ל[ ]	9

col. 30

Job	Text	Line
38:3	אסר נא כגבר חל[ציך ואש]אלנך והתיבני (*vacat*) פתגם	1
4	אן הוית במעבדי ארעא החויני הן ידעת חכמה	2
5, 6	מן שם משחתה הן תנדע מן נגד עליה חוטא או	3
6, 7	על מא אשיה אחידין או מן הקים אבן חזיתה במזהר	4
7	כחדא כוכבי צפר ויזעק[ו]ן כחדה כל מלאכי אלהא	5
8	התסוג בדשין ימא ב[ה]גחותה מן רחם תהומא	6
8,9, 10	למפק בשוית עננין [לבו]שה וערפלין חותלוהי ותשוה	7

9. [[32]] at his word *m*[ ]
10. [[33]he wi]ll tell about [it]

col. 29

Job 37:10-19

1. upon the surface of (the) waters. [11]Moreover, with them he brightens (the) clou[ds], and he brings forth from
2. a cloud his fire. [12]And (when) he speaks, they listen to him and proceed to their tasks;
3. he puts them in charge of all that he has created on the face of the earth, [13]either to strike
4. or to smash, either for famine or (for) the lack of it; and if there (is) a good thing, he will be
5. upon it. [14]Listen to this, Job; rise (and) meditate on the power (*or* mighty deeds) of God!
6. [[15]Do you know] what God has laid upon the[m, and (how) he has made] the light of his cloud to shine?
7. [[16]Do you kn]ow (how) to clothe his cloud with po[wer, [17]inas]much as your garment
8. [swelters?] [16]For he has knowledg[e! [18](But) do you know (how) to b]low up the dark cloud?
9. [like a mirr]or worn out. [19]He knows [ ] *l*[ ]

col. 30

Job 38:3-13

1. [3]Now gird [your] loin[s] like a man, [and let me] ask you. Give me an answer.
2. [4]Where were you when I made the earth? Tell me, if you have wisdom!
3. [5]Who set its measurements, if you know? Who stretched the line over it? [6]Or
4. on what (are) its foundations held (fast)? Or who erected its cornerstone, [7]while
5. the morning stars shone (all) at once and all the angels of God cri[ed] out in unison?
6. [8]Is it you who shut in the sea with doors, when it [came gush]ing from the womb of the deep,
7. to surge forth [9]with the donning of clouds (for) its [wra]ps and

8 לה תחומין ובר[יחין ודש]ין ו[עני]ת ואמרת עד תנא 10, 11

9 ולא תוסף [תאתה בגאות ג]לל[יך] הביומיך מנית 11, 12

10 [צפרא הודעת שחרא אתרה למאחד ב]כנפ[י]אר[עא] 12, 13

col. 31

1 ד[י חשכת ל]עדן ע[קת]א ליום קרב ואשתדו[ר רוח קדמא] 38:23, 24

2 היכא יפק ותשוב קדמוהי על ארעא מן שויא 24, 25

3 למטרא זמן וארח לעננין קלילין להנחתה על ארע 25, 26

4 מדבר די לא אנש בה להסבעה שיתא ושביקה 26, 27

5 ולהנפקה צמחי דתאה האיתי למטרא אב או מן 27, 28

6 ילד [ע]נני טלא ומן בטן מן נפק גלידא ושיקו[ע שמיא] 28, 29

7 מ[ן ילד]ה כא[בן] מין התקרמו מנה ואנפי תה[ומא] 29, 30

8 [אחידין]ע . [ ]כימא או סיג נפילא [תפתח] 31

9 [ ]. . . א על בניה תיאש[ ] 32, 33

10 [ ]ענ[נין] 33, 34

col. 32

1 יעלי כפא וחב[ל אילתא תנטר ותמנה י]רחיהין 39:1, 2

2 שלמין ותנדע עדן מולדהין ילדן בניהן ויפלטן 2, 3

dark clouds (for) its swaddling cloths? [10]Is it you who set
8. boundaries, b[olts, and doo]rs for it? [11]And [have you spoken up] and said (to it), "Up to this point!
9. You shall not again [come further with your proud w]aves!" [12]Have you in your days appointed
10. [the morning and shown the dawn its place, [13]to take hold of the] skirt[s of the] ear[th]?

col. 31

Job 38:23-34

1. wh[ich I have reserved for] the time of tr[oub]le, for the day of war and revoluti[on.] [24]How does
2. [the east wind] go forth? Do you blow upon the earth before it? [25]Who has set
3. a time for the rain, a path for light clouds, [26]to make (it/them) descend upon a desert land,
4. where no man is (to be found), [27]to sate the thornbush and the abandoned vine,
5. and to bring forth sprouts of green grass? [28]Does the rain have a father? Or who
6. sired the [cl]ouds of dew? [29]And from whose womb did the ice come forth, and wh[o bor]e the coverin[g of the heavens]?
7. [30]Like a st[one] the waters are frozen over because of it, and the surface of [the de]ep is
8. [held solid. [31]Can you tie up] the Pleiades or [open up] Orion's circuit?
9. [[32]] the [ ] can you set free for her young ones[[33]]
10. [[34]] clou[ds]

col. 32

Job 39:1-11

[Do you know the birth-season of]
1. [1]the mountain-goats? [Do you keep track of] the tra[vail of the hinds? [2]Do you count (when)] their [m]onths (are)
2. complete? Do you know of their birth(s), (when) [3]they bear their young and release (them)?

3, 4	והבליהן תושר יקשן בניהן ויפקן נפקו ולא תבוא	3
4, 5	עליהן מן שלח פראה ברחרין וחנקי ערדא מן	4
5, 6	שרא די שוית דחשת ביתה ומדרה בארע מליחה	5
7	יחאך על מהמא תקף קריא ונגשת שליט לא	6
7, 8	ישמע ויבחר לה טורי[ן] למ. [ו]בתר כל ירוק	7
8, 9	ירדף היבא ראמ[א ל]מפלחך או היבית על	8
9, 10	אוריך התקטר [ראמא ב]ניריה וילג[ן] בבקעה	9
10, 11	[בת]ריך ות. [ה]תתרחץ ב[ה ארו] סגיא	10

col. 33

39:20	[ ] התזיענה בתקף[ ]	1
20, 21	בס[ח]רוהי אימה ודחלה וחפר בבקע וירוט ויחדא	2
21, 22	ובחיל ינפק לאנפי חרב יחאך על דחלה ולא	3
22, 23	יזוע ולא יתוב מן אנפי חרב עלוהי יתלה שלט	4
23, 25	שנן ונזך וחרף סיף ולקל קרנא יאמר האח ומן	5
25	רחיק יריח קרבה ולנקשת זין וזעקת אשתדור	6
25, 26	יחדה [ ] המן חכמתך יסתער נצא ויפרוס	7
26, 27	כנפוה[י] לרוחין או על מאמרך יתגב[ה] נש[רא]	8
27, 28	ועוזא ירים קנ[ה ב]כפא ישכון ויקנן[ ]	9
28, 29	[ ]חפר אכל[א]	10

3. Do you send (forth) their fetuses ? [4]Their young grow up and go
off (on their own) ; they leave and do not return
4. to them. [5]Who has set the wild ass free and loosed the tethers
of the onager ?
5. [6]For it I made (the) desert a home, a dwelling in a salty land.
6. [7]It laughs at the turmoil, the violence of the city ! The driving
of an owner it does not
7. heed. [8]It chooses for itself mountains for past[ure] and goes
in pursuit of all that is green.
8. [9]Is [the] wild ox willing [to] serve you ; or will he pass the
night at
9. your stall ? [10]Can you tie up [the wild ox with] yokes ? Will it
make a fur[row] in a valley
10. [be]hind you ? And will you [ ] ? [11]Can you put your
trust in h[im ? For] much

col. 33

Job 39:20-29

1. [ ] [20]Do you make him tremble with
might [ ] ?
2. Through his snortings (come) terror and fear. [21]He paws at the
plain ; he runs and delights.
3. With might he goes forth to face (the) sword ; [22]he laughs
at fear and does not
4. tremble. He does not turn back from the sight of a sword.
[23]Against him is brandished a sharpened lance —
5. a javelin, and the sharp edge of a sword. [25]To the sound of
the horn he says, " Aha ! " And from
6. afar he sniffs out the battle ; in the clash of arms and the cries
of revolt
7. he delights. [ ] [26]Is it by your wisdom that the falcon
is stirred up and spreads out
8. it[s] wings to (the) winds ? [27]Or is it at your command (that)
the eag[le] lifts itself alo[ft]
9. and (that) the bla[ck eagle] makes [its] nest on high ?
[28][On] the crag it dwells and nests [ ]
10. [[29] from there] it spies out (its) food [
]

col. 34

Job	Text	Line
40:5	[ ]. סוף *(vacat)* [ ]	1
6, 7	ענא אלהא לאיוב מן . [ ] ועננא ואמר לה אסר	2
7, 8	נא כגבר חלציך אשאלנך והתיבני פתגם האף	3
8, 9	תעדא דינה ותחיבנני על דברת די תזכא או	4
9	הא דרע כאלה איתי לך או בקל כותה תרעם	5
10	העדי נא גוה ורם רוח וזוי* והדר ויקר תלבש	6
11, 12	העדי נא חמת רגזך וחזא כל גאה והשפלה וכל	7
12, 13	רמת רוח תתבר והטפי רשיע[ין תח]תיהון וטמר	8
13	[ה]מון בעפר כח[דא בק]טם תכסה	9
14, 15	[ ]. איתי	10

*read וזיו

col. 35

Job	Text	Line
40:23	[ ]	1
23	ירדנא גאפה יתרחץ די יקבלנה א[ ] . .	2
24, 25	במטל עינוהי יכלנה כבחכה יזיב אפה התגד	3
25, 26	תנין בחכא או בחבל תחרז לשנה התשוא	4
26, 27	זמם באפה ובחרתך תקוב לסתה הימלל	5
27, 28	עמך בניה או ימלל עמך בהתחננה לך היקים	6
28, 29	קים עמך ותדברנה לעבד עלם התחאך	7
29, 30	בה כצ[פרא ו]תקטרנה בחוטא לבנתך וי.[ ]ן	8

col. 34

Job 40:5-15

1. [5][ ]. end. (*vacat*) [ ]
2. [6]God answered Job from .[ ] and the cloud and said to him: [7]" Gird
3. now your loins like a man, and let me question you. Give me an answer. [8]Will you again
4. set judgment aside and involve me in guilt so that you may be clean? [9]Or,
5. come now, have you an arm like God? Do you thunder with a voice like his?
6. [10]Now be rid of pride and haughty spirit, and you will be clothed with splendor, honor, and glory.
7. [11]Now be rid of the heat of your anger! Look (rather) at every proud person and bring him low. [12]All
8. haughtiness of spirit you will crush. Snuff out evil [ones in] their [pl]aces, [13]hide
9. them in the dust to[gether, and] cover [their faces with as]hes.
10. [14][ ]. [15]There is

col. 35

Job 40:23-31

1. [[23]Even if]
2. the Jordan [overflows] its bank(s), it is confident that it will take it '[ ]
3. [24]When (it) lifts its eyes, does one restrain it? Does one make its nose ooze as with a hook? [25]Can you draw out
4. (the) dragon with a hook or string its tongue with a rope? [26]Can you put
5. a ring in its nose or pierce its jaw with your gimlet? [27]Will it speak
6. to you with equanimity or speak to you with supplication? [28]Will it make
7. an alliance with you? Will you lead it away as a slave forever? [29]Will you laugh
8. at it like a b[ird?] Will you tie it with a thread for your daughters? [30]Will they [ ]*n*

30 [עלוהי]תין ויפלגון יתה באר . [ ]

31 [ ] ובדגו]גין די נונין[ ]

col. 36

41:7, 8 [ ]והי . . [ ] [

8, 9 להדה ידבקן ורוח ל[א ת]עול בינהן אנתה

9, 10 לחברתה חענן ולא יתפ[ר]שן עטישתה תדלק

10, 11 נורא בין עינוהי כמ<צ>מח פ[ר]א מן פמה לפידין

11, 12 יפקן בלשני אשה ירטון מן נחירוה<י> יפק תנן

12, 13 לכוש יקד ומגמר נפשה ג[מ]רין תגסא וזיקין

13, 14 יפקן מן פמה בצורה יבית תקפה וקדמוהי

14, 15 תרוט עלימו קפלי בשרה דבקין נסיכי[ן עלוהי]

15, 16 כפרזלא ולב[בה נסי]ך כאב[ן] ו[ ]

17 [ ]פח[דו] . . [ ]

col. 37

41:26 [ ] . . . [ ] . . [ן] . [ ]

26 והוא מלך על כל רחש (*vacat*)

42:1, 2 ענא איוב ואמר קדם אלהא ידעת די כלא

2 תכול למעבד ולא יתבצר מנך תקף וחכמה

40:5 חדה מללת ולא אתיב ותרתין ועליהן לא

40:5; 42:4 אוסף שמע נא ואנה אמלל אשאלנך

42:4, 5 והתיבני למשמע אדן שמעתך וכען עיני

5, 6 חזתך על כן אתנסך ואתמהא ואהוא לעפר

6 וקטם (*vacat*) [ ] [ ]

9. [over it]*tyn* and will they divide it up in the la[nd of]
10. [[31] and in bo]ats of fish[ ]

col. 36

Job 41:7-17

1. [[7]] its [[8]one]
2. clings to the other, and a breath does n[ot p]ass between them; [9]each one
3. holds its neighbor tight and they cannot be sepa[r]ated. [10]Its sneeze enkindles
4. a fire between its eyes like the bri<ll>iance of d[aw]n. [11]From its mouth firebrands
5. come forth; with tongues of fire they run. [12]From it<s> nostrils issue smoke,
6. flaming sparks, and live coals. [13]Its breath spews forth c[o]als, and flashes
7. issue from its mouth. [14]Its strength resides in its neck, and before it
8. runs youthful might. [15]The scales of its flesh cling (together), mold[ed on it]
9. like iron. [16][Its] heart is [pour]ed (hard) like stone; and [ ]
10. [[17] become] afrai[d]

col. 37

Job 41:26–42:6

1. [[26]]
2. and it is king over all that creeps.
3. [42:1]Job said in reply before God, [2]“I know that
4. you can do everything; neither power nor wisdom is curtailed in you.
5. [40:5]One thing I have spoken, and I shall not repeat; (even) two things, and to them I shall not
6. add. [42:4](But) listen now and let me speak. Let me ask you,
7. and you answer me. [5]By hearsay I have heard of you, but now my eye
8. has gazed upon you. [6]Therefore, I am poured out and dissolved; I am become dust
9. and ashes.

col. 38

42:9	[ ].[ ].[ ]	1
9	אלהא ושמע א[ל]הא בקלה די איוב ושבק	2
9, 10	להון חטאיהון בדילה ותב אלהא לאיוב ברחמין	3
10, 11	ויהב לה חד תרין בכל די הוא לה ואתון לות	4
11	איוב כל רחמוהי וכל אחוהי וכל ידעוהו ואכלו	5
11	עמה לחם בביתה ונחמוהי על כל באישתה די	6
11	היתי אלהא עלוהי ויהבו לה גבר אמרה חדה	7
	וגבר קדש חד די דהב (*vacat*)	8

(*vacat*)

(The following column is also blank.)

6. 1Q New Jerusalem — 1QJN ar (1Q*32*)

frg. 1

1] · תשוית עמוד[א [

2] ממע]ל לעמוד[א [

frg. 2

1]]...[[

2]]וגוא[[

3]]משח[ת [

frg. 3

1]]ן[ ] [

2]]בחד[[

frg. 4

1]].[ ] [

2]]לתרע[א [

col. 38

Job 42:9-11

1. [9]
2. God. G[o]d hearkened to Job's voice and forgave
3. them their sins on account of him. 10God turned to Job in mercy
4. and gave him twice as much as all that he had before. 11There came to
5. Job all his friends, all his brothers, and all his acquaintances, and they ate
6. bread with him in his house. They consoled him for all the misfortune(s) that
7. God had brought upon him, and each one gave him a ewe
8. and a ring of gold.

6.

frg. 1

1. [ ]. the base of the pillar[ ]
2. [from abov]e to [the] pillar [ ]

frg. 2

1. [ ]...[ ]
2. [ ] and the interior[ ]
3. [the] measurement [ ]

frg. 3

1. [ ]*n* [ ]
2. [ ] in one of [ ]

frg. 4

1. [ ]. .[ ]
2. [ ] to [the] gate[ ]

frg. 5

[ ]ין ת . [ ] 1
[עמו]דין תר[ין] 1a
[ ]ד[ ] 2

frg. 7

[ ] כותל[א] 1
[ ]ין/ץ . [ ] 2

frg. 14

[ ] . כול . [ ] 1
[ ] . גלגל[א] 2
[ ]כיא גלגלא [ ] 3

frg. 15

[ ] . . . . . [ ] 1
[א]מין תלת . . [ ] 2
[ ]די לא . . [ ] 3

frg. 16

[ ]נ . . . . בעת[ ] 1
[ ] . ותשע[ ] 2

frg. 17

[ ]ק . [ ] 1
[ ]דין . [ ] 2
[ ] עד[ ] 3

frg. 22

[ ]חד ע . . [ ] 1
[ ] . קודם[ ] 2
[ ] . . . . . [ ] 3

frg. 5

1. [ ]*yn t*[ ]
1a. [ ]tw[o pil]ars [ ]
2. [ ]. *d*[ ]

frg. 7

1. [the] wall [ ]
2. [ ]*yn/ṣ* .[ ]

frg. 14

1. [ ]. all .[ ]
2. [ ].. [the] wheel/Gilgal[ ]
3. [ ]for the wheel/for Gilgal[ ]

frg. 15

1. [ ].....[ ]
2. [ ] three [cu]bits ..[ ]
3. [ ] which (is) not ..[ ]

frg. 16

1. [ ]*n* .... with the wealth of/he was anxious[ ]
2. [ ]. and nine[ ]

frg. 17

1. [ ]*q* .[ ]
2. [ ]judgment .[ ]
3. [ ] until [ ]

frg. 22

1. [ ] one of ʿ..[ ]
2. [ ]. in front of[ ]
3. [ ].....[ ]

7. 2Q New Jerusalem — 2QJN ar (2Q*24*)

frg. 1

1]   ב]חמשין   וח[ד   [
2]   רו]ח   ושבק סחור   סח[ור   [
3]   ] וכדן אח[זי]נ[י] כול משחת[[

4]   אמין] ארבעין   ותרתין

frg. 2

1]   ]ר אמי[ן   [
2]   ]ה ל[[

frg. 3

1]   ]חד[   ] . . [[
2]   ו]משח עד תרע ספי[רא   [
3 [דנה   פתו]רא די קודמוהי ל[מרא   [

4]   ] . כתול ת[[

frg. 4

1 בשרהון[[
2 לקורבן רעוא[[
3 [וי]עלון להיכלא[[
4 תמנא סאין סול[תא   [
5 ויטלון לחמא . [מן[
6 לקדמין על מד[בחא   וישון לחמא תרין[

7 סדרין על פת[ורא דכיא קודם אל   ועל[
8 תרי סדרי לח[מא יתנון לבונתא דכיתא   [
9 לחמא ויסבון לחמ[א לברא מן היכלא לימין   [

10 מערבה ויתפלג[לחמא לתמנין וארבעה כהנין   [

11 וחזית עד די פל[יגה לחמא מן כול שבעת פלוגת   [

12 רישמתא כ[ ] ע . [ ] . [[
13 שביא די בהון וארבעת עשר כה[נין   [

7.

frg. 1

1. [fifty-one reeds by] fifty-on[e]
2. [for each sp]ace and a peristyle all aroun[d]
3. [ ] And in this (way) he show[ed] m[e] all the measurements of [ ]
4. [ ]forty-two [cubits]

frg. 2

1. [ ]*r* cubi[ts]
2. [ ]*h l*]]

frg. 3

1. [ ] one [ ]..[ ]
2. [and] he measured as far as the Gate of Sapph[ire]
3. [This is] the [ta]ble which (is) before the [Lord (cf. Ezek 41:22)]
4. [ ]. the wall of the *t*[ ]

frg. 4

1. their flesh [ ]
2. for an acceptable offering [ ]
3. [and] they [shall] enter the temple [ ]
4. eight seahs, (wheat) flou[r]
5. and they shall carry the bread .[ ]
6. toward the east upon [the] al[tar and they shall put the bread (in) two]
7. rows upon [the] tab[le before God and upon]
8. the two rows of br[ead they shall put pure incense]
9. the bread, and they shall take [the bread outside the temple to the south]
10. the west, and [the bread] shall be divided [among eighty-four priests]
11. and I watched until [the bread] was div[ided from all seven divisions of]
12. the inscriptions (?) *k*[ ] ʿ.[ ].[ ]
13. the eldest who are among them, and fourteen prie[sts]

14 כהניא תרתי לחמא די הו[ת לבונתא דכיתא עליהון וחזי]

15 הוית עד חדא מן תרתי לחמא יהיבת [ל]כ[הנא רבא]

16 עמה ואחריתא[י]היבת לתנינה די קאם פנב]

17 [ ]א . [ ] חזי הוית עד די יהיב לכ[ול כהניא]

18 [ ]ל די איל ען חד לכול גבר וגבר[ ]

19 [ ]ל[ ]עד עדן די יתבו [ ]
20 [ח]ד בכול [ ]
21 [ ]ל[ ]

frgs. 5-6

1 [ ]מימ[ ]
2 [אורכה ופו]תיה משחא חדא
3 [ ]ה מן כאן
4 [ומן כאן]. א מן דן
5 [ומן דן ק]רן[מדבח]א
6 [ ]מא ופותיה
7 [ ]לכ[ו]ל
8 [רוח] . .

frg. 7

1 [ ]ופותיהון מן כא[ן ומן כאן]
2 [ ]וכול מדבחא[ ]

frg. 8

1 [ ] . [ ]
2 [ע]שרא שורא ארב[עא]
3 [ ] כותליא אבן חו[ר]
4 [ ]ה אחרניא מן בר עשר[י]ן[ ]
5 [ ]בל . [ ] ולהיון מכפרין בה עלו[הי]

6 [ ] . ולא יתכלא עוד כול יום[ויו]ם[ ]

14. the priests. Two (loaves of) the bread [upon] which wa[s the pure incense and I kept]
15. watching until one of the two loaves was given [to the chief] pr[iest]
16. with him. And the other was [g]iven to the second (priest) who was standing apart (?) [ ]
17. [ ]'.[ ] I kept watching until there was given to a[ll the priests]
18. [ ]*l* of a ram of a flock, one for each person[ ]
19. [ ]*l*[ ] until the time when they sat[ ]
20. [o]ne in every [ ]
21. [ ]*l*[ ]

frgs. 5-6

1. [ ]*mym*[ ]
2. [its length and] its [wid]th, the same measurement
3. [ ]*h* from here
4. [and from there].' from this
5. [and from that h]orn [of] the [altar]
6. [ ]*m'* and its width
7. [ ]to eve[r]y
8. [direction]. .

frg. 7

1. [ ]and their width from he[re and from there]
2. [ ]and all the altar[ ]

frg. 8

1. [ ].[ ]
2. [t]en. The wall fo[ur]
3. [ ] the walls, whit[e] stone[ ]
4. [ ]*h* the others from outside, twen[t]y[ ]
5. [ ]*bl.* [ ] and they will be making expiation by it upon [it]
6. [ ].[and it will not yet be terminated. Each [and every] day[ ]

7 [ ]עזרתא [ו]אחזינ[י] . [ ] אוחרי בר מן[ ]

8 [ ]. מאה ועשר[ ]

frg. 9

1 [ ] . עת[ ]
2 [ ]אשי כול [ ]
3 [ ]ק[ ]

frg. 10

1 [ ] אלוה[י]
2 [ ] . [ ]

frg. 11

1 [ ]תר[עא]

8. 5Q New Jerusalem — 5QJN ar (5Q*15*)

frg. 1, col. i

1 [סחור א]מין [תלת מאה ו]חמשין ושבע לכל [רו]ח ושבק סוחר סחור לפרזיתא ברית שוק[קנין תלתה א]מין עשרין

2 [וחדה] (*vacat*) וכדן [אחזיאני מ]שחת פר[זיא כלהן בין פרזה לפרזה שוק] פתה קנין שת[ה] אמין ארבעין ותרתין

3 [ושוק]יא רברביא [די] נפקי[ן] מן מדנחא [למערבא] קנין עשרה פות[י שוקא אמין] שב[עין תרי]ן מנהון ותליתיא

4 [די על] ש[מא]ל מק[דשא מ]שח קנין תמנית עש[ר] פותי אמין מא[ה ועשרי]ן [ו]שת ופו[תי שוקיא] די נפקין מן דרומ[א]

5 [לצפונא תרי]ן מ[נהון] קנין תש[ע]ה ואמין א[ר]בע לשוק חד אמי[ן] שתין ושבע [ו]מצ[יעא די במצ]יעת קריתא

7. [ ]the temple-court. [And] he showed [me] another [ ]
outside of[ ]
8. [ ]one hundred and ten/twenty[ ]

frg. 9

1. [ ].ʿ*t*[ ]
2. [ ]the foundations of every[ ]
3. [ ]*q*[ ]

frg. 10

1. [it]s jambs[ ]
2. [ ].[ ]

frg. 11

1. [the] ga[te]

8.

frg. 1, col. i

1. [around, three hundred and] fifty-seven [cu]bits in every [direc]-tion. And a peristyle (was) all around the block, a portico of a street, [three reeds] (or) twenty-[one cu]bits. (*vacat*)
2. And likewise [he showed me the mea]surements of [all the] blo[cks. Between block and block (there was a street,] si[x] reeds (in) width, (or) forty-two cubits.
3. [And] the great [street]s [that] wen[t] from the east [to the west]: the wid[th of the street] (was) ten reeds (or) seven[ty cubits] (for) [tw]o of them; and (for) the third,
4. [which (is) on] the l[ef]t of the temp[le, the mea]surement (was) of eight[een] reeds (in) width (or) one hund[red and twen]-ty-six cubits. The wid[th of the streets] that go from [the] south
5. [to the north — (there are) tw]o of [them]: ni[n]e reeds and f[o]ur cubits (or) sixty-seven cubi[ts] for each street. As for the cent[ral (street) which (is) in the mid]dle of the city,

6 [משחת פותי]ה קנ[ין תל]תת עשר ואמה חדה לאמין תשע[י]ן ות[רתין] וכל
[שוק]י[א וקריתא ר]ציפין באבן חור

7 [ ] . . [ ]ב . [] . . רג[י]א וא[ ] שש ויהלם (*vacat*)

8 [ואחזיאני משחת שפשיא ת]מנין פות[יהון די] שפשיא קנין תרין [אמין ארבע עשרה
[

9 [ע]ל כל תרע ותרע דשין תרין די אבן פותיה די[דש]א קנה[חד אמין
שבע (*vacat*) [

10 [ואחזיאני משחת בב]יא תרי עשר פותי תרעיהון קנין תלתה אמי[ן עשרין וחדה
על כל]

11 [תרע ותרע דשין תר]ין פותי דשי[א] קנא חד ופלג אמי[ן ע]שר ופלג [
[

12 [וליד כל תרע תרי מגד]לין חד מ[ן י]מינא וחד מן שמ[אל]א פותיהון ואורכהון
משחה חדה קנין חמשה בחמשה]

13 [אמין תלתין וחמש ודרגא די סלק ליד]תרעא בגוא על [ימי]ן מגדליא ברום
מג[דליא פתיה אמין חמש מגדליא]

14 [ודרגיא קנין חמשה בחמשה ואמ]ין חמש ל[אמין א]רבעין בכל רוח תרע[א (*vacat*)]

15 [ואחזיאני משחת תרעי פרזיא פתיהון]קנין תרין אמין ארב[ע] עש[רה ופו]ת[י
. . . יא משחתא אמין]

16 [ומשח]פות[יה די כל א]ספא קנין תרין אמין ארבע עשרה [וית טלולה אמה
חדה]

17 [ומשח על כל] אספא ית ד[שיא ל]ה ומשח בגוא א[ס]פא אורכה אמין [תלת
עשרה ופותיה אמין עשר (*vacat*)]

18 [(*vacat*) ואע]לנ[י ל]גוא אספא [והא] אסף אוחרן ותרעא ליד כותלא גויה [די
ליד ימינא כמשחת תרעא]

6. [the measurement of] its [width] (is) [thir]teen ree[ds] and one cubit (or) in cubits nin[e]ty-t[wo]. All [the str]ee[ts and the city (are) pa]ved with white stone
7. [ ]..[ ]*b*.[ ] .*rg*[*y*]' *w*'[of] marble and jasper. (*vacat*)
8. [And he showed me the measurement of the ei]ghty [postern-gates]; the wid[th of] the posterns (was) two reeds (or) [fourteen cubits].
9. [a]t each and every gate (there were) two doors of stone; the width of the [door] (was) [one] reed (or) seven cubits. (*vacat*)
10. [And he showed me the measurement of] the twelve [portal]s; the width of their gates (was) three reeds (or) [twenty-one] cubit[s. At each]
11. [and every gate (there were) tw]o [doors]; the width of the door[s] (was) one and a half reed[s (or) t]en and a half cubit[s]
12. [And alongside every gate (there were) two to]wers, one o[n] the [ri]ght and one on the l[ef]t; (as to) their width and their length, the measurement (was) the same, five reeds by five (or)
13. [thirty-five cubits. (As for) the stairway that goes up alongside] the gate on the inside to the [rig]ht of the towers, at the top of the to[wers, its width (was) five cubits. The towers]
14. [and the stairways: five reeds by five] and five cubit[s], (or) in [cubits for]ty, on every side of the gat[e (*vacat*)]
15. [And he showed me the measurement of the gates of the blocks: their width] (was) two reeds (or) fou[rte]en cubits; [and the wi]d[th of the measurement, cubits]
16. [And he measured] the wid[th of every thre]shold; two reeds (or) fourteen cubits; [and its lintel: one cubit.]
17. [And he measured at every] threshold the do[ors on] it. He measured inside the thr[esh]old; its length (was) [thirteen] cubits [and its width ten cubits. (*vacat*)]
18. [And he broug[ht me in]side the threshold, [and there (was)] another threshold; and the gate alongside the interior wall [that was on the right side agreed with the measurement of the gate]

19 [בריא פותיה אמ]ין ארבע רומ[ה אמין] שבע ודשין לה תרין וקודם [ת]רעא דן
[אסף עללה פתיה קנה חד אמין]

col. ii

1 שבע וא[ור]כה עלל קנין תרין אמין א[ר]בע עשרה ורומה קנין תרין אמין ארבע
ע[שרה ותרע]

2 ל[קבל תר]ע פתיח לגוא פרזיתא כמשחת תרעא בריא ועל שמאל מעלה דן
אחזיא[ני בית דרג]

3 סחר[וסלק] פותיה ואורכה משחה חדה קנין תרין בתר[י]ן אמין ארבע עשרה
ותר[עין לקבל]

4 תרעין כמשחה ועמוד בגוא גוא די דרגא סח[ר ו]סל[ק] עלוהי פתיה ואו[רכה
אמין שת בשת]

5 מרבע ודרגא די סלק לידה פתיה אמין ארבע וסחר [וס]ל[ק]רום ק[נין תרי]ן
עד[(*vacat*)]

6 ואעלני [לגוא] פרזיתא ואחזיאני בה באתין מן תרע לתר[ע חמשת עשר תמני]ה
בחד[ה רוח עד זויתא]

7 [וש]בעה מן ז[ו]יתא עד תרעא אחרנא פותאהון ארוך בתי[א קנין תלתה אמין
עשרי]ן וחדה ופתיהון]

8 [קני]ן תרין אמין ארבע עשרה וכדן כל תוניא [ורומהון קנין ת]רין א[מי]ן ארבע
ע[שרה ותרעהון]

9 [במציעתא פות]י קנין ת[רי]ן אמין ארבע עש[רה ומשח פותי מצי]עת ביתא וגוהון
די ת[וניא אמין]

10 [ארבע ארוך ורום קנה חד אמין שבע ואחזיאני משחת בתי]מכלא דכא אמין
תשע ע[שרה ארכהון]

11 [פתיהון אמין תר]תי עשרה בית [ע]שרין ות[ר]תין ערש[ין וחדה] עשרה כוין
אטימן עלא מ[ן ערשין]

19. [outside : its width] (was) four [cubi]ts, [its] height seven [cubits]. And the doors on it (were) two. Before this [g]ate (was) [the threshold for entrance ; its width (was) one reed] (or) seven

col. ii

1. [cubits], its [leng]th, as one enters (?), two reeds (or) fou[rt]een cubits ; and its height two reeds (or) four[teen] cubits. [A gate]
2. op[posite (the) gat]e, opening to the interior of the block, agreed with the measurement of the outside gate. On the left of this entrance he showed [me a stairwell]
3. going around [and mounting up]. Its width and its length (had) one measurement : two reeds by t[w]o (or) fourteen cubits. And (the) ga[tes opposite (the)]
4. gates agreed with its measurement. (There was) a column in the midst of the interior of the stairwell that went [a-round] and mount[ed up] on it ; its width and [its] leng[th (were) six cubits by six],
5. square. (As for) the stairway that mounted up at its side, its width (was) four cubits ; and it went around [and w]ent [up (to) a height of [tw]o re[eds] to [(*vacat*)].
6. He brought me [inside] the block and showed me in it houses from gate to ga[te, fifteen (of them) : eig]ht in on[e direction to the corner]
7. [and se]ven from the c[or]ner up to the other gate. Their width (and) the length (?) of the hous[es (were) three reeds] (or) twent[y-one cubits ; and their width (was)]
8. two [re]eds (or) fourteen cubits. And similar to this (were) all the rooms. [Their height (was) t]wo [reeds] (or) four-[teen] cu[bi]ts. Their gates
9. [at the middle] (were) t[wo] reeds (or) fourte[en] cubits (in) width. [And he measured the wid]th of the middle of the house and the inside of the ro[oms ; four]
10. [cubits long and a height of one reed (or) seven cubits. He showed me the measurement of the houses] for dining(?) : The hall (was) nine[teen] cubits (in ?) [their length]
11. [and their width (was) tw]elve [cubits]. (In each) house (there were) [tw]enty-t[w]o couch[es ; and ele]ven windows enclosed abo[ve (the) couches ;]

12 [ולידה אמה בריתא ומשח] . . י כותא רומה [אמ]ין תרתין [פתיה אמין]ועובי פותי כותלא[רום קדמיתא]

13 [אמין ואחרנתא אמין ומשח ת]ח[ו]מי דוכנ[יא אורכהון אמין] תשע עשרה ופות[יהון אמין תרתי עשרה]

14 [ ].[ ]. ורו[מהון] פתיחן ב.[קנין תרין אמין]

15 [ארבע עשרה ופותיהון אמ]ין תל[ת] וארכין [ע]שר[אמה חדה ופלג ורומה בגוא]

frg. 2

1]].א כוין [[
2]] כל בתיא די בגוא .[[
3] תר]עא כולה ואספיא פת[יחין [
4] ע]מודיא אמין תרתי עשרה[[
5]]. עמוד לעמוד [[

frg. 3

1]]. . .[[
2] תר]עיא רבר[ביא [
3] קנין] שתה בשת[ה אמין ארבעין ותרתין]
4]] (*vacat*) [[
5]] ופ. [[

frg. 4

1]].[[
2]]ב וע. .[[
3] מש]חה קנין [[

frg. 5

1]]. .[[
2]]כל תרע[[
3]]עשר[[

12. [and alongside of it the outer gutter. And he measured]. .*y* of the window: Its height (was) two [cub]its, [its width X cubits], and (as for) depth (it was) the width of the wall. [The height of the first (was)]
13. [X cubits; and (of) the other, X cubits. He measured the boun]da[r]ies of (the) platfor[ms: Their length] (was) nineteen [cubits] and [their] width [twelve cubits]
14. [ ].[ ]. and their hei[ght] opened *b*.[two reeds (or) four-]
15. [teen cubits; and their width] (was) thr[ee cub]its; and they (were) [t]en [ ] long [one and a half cubits; and its height on the inside]

frg. 2

1. [ ] ' windows [ ]
2. [ ] all the houses that (were) inside .[ ]
3. [ ]all the [ga]te and the thresholds (were) open[ed]
4. [the col]umns; twelve cubits [ ]
5. [ ]. column to column [ ]

frg. 3

1. [ ]...[ ]
2. [ ]the gre[at ga]tes[ ]
3. [reeds] six by si[x (or) forty-two cubits]
4. [ ] (*vacat*) [ ]
5. [ ]*wp*.[ ]

frg. 4

1. [ ].[ ]
2. [ ]*b w*ʿ..[ ]
3. [measure]ment, reeds[ ]

frg. 5

1. [ ].. *1.* [ ]
2. [ ] every gate[ ]
3. [ ] ten [ ]

frg. 6

[ותרתי] [ ] 1
[שק] . [ ] 2
[ ] . [ ] 3

frg. 7

[ ] . . [ ] 1
[אמ]ין תרתין .]] 2

frg. 8

[ופותי] [ ] 1

frg. 9

[פ]ותי .]] 1
[תר]עיא די]] 2
[ ]ל[ ] 3

frg. 10

[ ] . . . [ ] 1
[ומשח] [ ] 2

frg. 11

[ ]. ותרת[י] 1
[ ] . . . [ ] 2

frg. 12

[ ]אמין]] 1
[ת]רע[ ] 2

frg. 13

[מש]ח[ ] 1

frg. 14

[א]מין .]] 1
[ ] . ת . . [ ] 2

frg. 6

1. [ ] and two of[ ]
2. [ ]. *šq*[ ]
3. [ ].[ ]

frg. 7

1. [ ]..[ ]
2. [ ]two [cu]bits .[ ]

frg. 8

1. [ ] and the width of[ ]

frg. 9

1. [the w]idth of .[ ]
2. [ ] the [ga]tes which[ ]
3. [ ]*l*[ ]

frg. 10

1. [ ]...[ ]
2. [ ] and he measured [ ]

frg. 11

1. [ ]. and two o[f]
2. [ ]...[ ]

frg. 12

1. [ ] cubits [ ]
2. [a g]ate[ ]

frg. 13

1. [ ] he measur[ed]

frg. 14

1. [cu]bits .[ ]
2. [ ]..*t* .[ ]

frg. 15

1 [ת[רין] ק[נ]ין]

frg. 16

1 [ ] . [ ]
2 [ד[י לי]ד]

9. 11Q New Jerusalem — 11QJN ar

frg. 14

1 [כו[ל יום שביעי קודם אל דכר]ן]
2 [[לברא מן היכלא לימין מערב]ה]
3 [[ל]   [ג לתמנין וארבעה כהנין ש]]
3a [[מן כול שבעת פלוגת פתורי]א]

4 [בה[ון וארבעת עשר כה]נין]
5 [תרתי לחמ[א די הות לבונתא]עליהין]
6 [י[היבת לכהנא]רבא]
7 [[ל . . . פנבד .]]

10. 4Q Enoch^c — 4QEn^c

frg. 1, col. i

1 [ולהל[א מנהון ארחקת

2]למדנחא רחיק מנהון ואחזיאת אתר אחרן רב נחל מין ובה[קניא טביא די בשמא די

3]הוא דמא ללבונה ועל צדדי נחליא אלן חזי[ת קונם בשמא ולהלא מן נחל]י[א
4]אלן ארחקת למדנחא ואחזיאת טורי[ן אחרנין ואף בהון חזית אילנין די נפק
5]מנהון דמעא די מתקרא צרי וחלבנ[ה]ול[הלא מן טוריא אלן אחזיאת טור

6]אחרן למדנח סיאפי ארעא ו[כול אילניא א]לן מ[ל]י[ן נטף והוא דמא לקלפי]   [
7 [בש[ם ריח כדי מדקין קלופיא אלן

8 [ולהלא מן טוריא אלן[כלצפון מדנחה]ו[ן אחזיאת טו]ר[ין

frg. 15

1. [t]wo [r]ee[ds]

frg. 16

1. [ ].[ ]
2. [wh]ich (was) along[side]

9.

frg. 14

1. [ev]ery seventh day before God as a memori[al]
2. [ ]outside of the temple, to the right of the west[ ]
3. [ ]*l*[ ]*g* to eighty-four priests *š*[ ]

3a. [ ]from everything the division of the tables filled itself [ ]

4. [in th]em and fourteen prie[sts]
5. [the two (loaves) of brea]d [on which] the incense was [ ]
6. [it] was given to the [chief] priest [ ]
7. [ ]*l*. . . *pnbd* .[ ]

10.

frg. 1, col. i

1. [And further] on from them I was removed
2. [to the east, far from them. And I was shown another great place, a torrentbed of water. And in it] (were) choice reeds of fragrance that
3. [was like incense. And on the sides of these torrentbeds I sa]w sweet cinnamon. And further on from [these] torrentbeds
4. [I was removed to the east. And I was shown] other [mountain]s, and on them too I saw trees [from] which went forth
5. [the sap that is called balsam and galban]um. [And fur]ther on from these mountains I was shown [another] mountain
6. [to the east of the ends of the earth. And] all th[ese] trees [were fu]ll [of resin], and it was like the bark of[ ]
7. [fra]grant odor when they grind these barks.
8. [and further on from these mountains], to the northeast of th[e]m, I was shown (other) mou[nt]ains

11. 4Q Enoch[c] — 4QEn[c]

frg. 1, col. ii

1 תרעין פתי[חין]
2 חשבוניהון בא . [ ]
3 מן תמן אובלת לדרום ס[יאפי ארעא]
4 לרוח דרומא לטל ומט[ר]
5 אחזית תרעין תל[תה]
6 . . . א
7 (*vacat*) [ ]
8 באדין . . . [ ]

12. 4Q Enoch[e] — 4QEn[e]

frg. 1, col. xxvi

31:2 1 [ ] . . . [ ]
2 [ ]. ו באיל[ניא]
32:1 3 [ ]מדקק קלפוהי א[לן ולהלא] מן
4 [טוריא] אלן כלצפון מדנחהון [אחז]ית טורין אחרנין

32:2 5 [מלין נ]רד טב וצפר וקרדמן [ופ]לפלין ומן תמן הובלת

6 [למד]נח כל טוריא אלן רחיק מנהון למדנח ארעא ואחלפ[ת]

7 [על]א מן י[מא] שמוקא וארחקת שגיא מנה ואעברת על[א]

32:3 8 מן חשוכא רה[י]ק מנה ואחלפת ליד פרדס קשט[א]

13. 4Q Enoch Astronomical[b] — 4QEnAstr[b]

frg. 23

6 [וקרין לצפונא צפון] בדי בה צפנין ומתכנסין וסחרין כל ערבי שמיא ואזלין למדנחי שמיא

7 [וקרין למדנחא מד]נח בדי מן תמן דנחין מאני שמיא ואף מזרח בדי מאין זרחין

11.

frg. 1, col. ii

1. gates open[ed]
2. their accounts *b*'.[ ]
3. from there I was brought to the south of the en[ds of the earth]
4. to (?) the wind of the south, for dew and ra[in]
5. I was shown th[ree] gates [ ]
6. ...' [ ]
7. (*vacat*)
8. Then ...[ ]

12.

frg. 1, col. xxvi

1. [ ]...[ ]
2. [ ].*w* in tre[es]
3. [ ]one grinds th[ese] barks of it.[And further on] from
4. these [mountains,] to the northeast of them, I [was shown] other mountains
5. [full of] choice [na]rd, *ṣpr*, cardamom, and pepper. And from there I was brought
6. [to the ea]st of all these mountains, far from them, to the east of the land. And [I] was made to pass
7. ab[ove] the Red S[ea], and I was removed very far from it. I was made to traverse abov[e]
8. the darkness, f[a]r from it, and was made to pass alongside of the Garden of Tru[th]

13.

frg. 23

6. [(They) call the north *ṣippūn*], because in it all the evenings of the heavens hide (*ṣpnyn*), and they are assembled (there), turn around, and go to the east of the heavens.
7. [And (they) call the east *mad*]*naḥ*, because from there the vessels of the heavens shine forth (*dnḥyn*) ; and also *mizraḥ*, because thence rise (*zrḥyn*) (the)

8 שמש [וירח] לאתחזיא [מן] ארעא חד מנהון למדבר בה בני אנשא וחד מנהון [לכ]ל [ימיא]

9 [ולכל נהריא וחד מנהון] למדברין ול[שבע ו]ל[פרד]ס קושטא (*vacat*)

14. 1Q Enoch Giants — 1QEnGiants (1Q*23*)

frg. 1

1 חמרין מאתין ערדי[ן מאתין יעלין מאתין ... מאתין דכרין די]

2 ען מאתין תישין מאת[ין חות]
3 ברא מן כל חוה מן כ[ל עוף ומן כל]
4 על מזג .[ ]

frg. 2

1]]. אנון[[
2]]אין . [[

frg. 3

1]]כל מנה[[
2]] והוית[[
3]]א ושחית[[

frg. 4

1]] . . [[
2]]תקרב[[
3]]ל[[

frgs. 9-14-15 (joined)

1]]ן[[
2]] וידעו ר[זי [
3]]. ה רבה בארעא [[
4]]בה וקטלו לשגי[א [
5]]גברין מ[ן]ה[ ]ל די[[
6]]. . ל ל[[

8. sun [and (the) moon] so as to be seen [from] the earth: One of them to lead mankind by it, and one of them [for all the seas and the]
9. [rivers, and one of them]for deserts, for [the Seven, and for] [the Gar]den of Truth

14.

frg. 1

1. two hundred asses, [two hundred] wild ass[es], [two hundred mountain-goats, two hundred ...], two hundred [rams of (the)]
2. flock, two hund[red he-goats beasts (?) of]
3. the field, from every beast (?), from eve[ry bird, from every]
4. upon *mzg* .[ ]

frg. 2

1. [ ]. they/these[ ]
2. [ ]'*yn* .[ ]

frg. 3

1. [ ]all from it[ ]
2. [ ]and I was[ ]
3. [ ]' defor[med]

frg. 4

1. [ ]. .[ ]
2. [ ]you/it (fem.) will draw near/offer[ ]
3. [ ]*l*[ ]

frg. 9-14-15

1. [ ]*n*[ ]
2. [ ]and they knew the se[crets of]
3. [ ]a great [ ].*h* in the land[ ]
4. [ ]in it, and they killed the abundan[ce]
5. [ ]giants f[rom]*h*[ ]*l* which[ ]
6. [ ]..*l l*[ ]

frg. 13

1]]לארב[ע [
2] ע]תק נהר[א [
3]]. אזל[[

frg. 17

1 ועלו] [
2 בידיהון] [
3 ושרו ל[[

frg. 19

1]בארא[[
2]תב ע[ל [

frg. 20

1]]ן[[
2]]אבוהן באדין[[
3]]. עלמין . [[
4]] כל בני [[
5]]תו . [[

frg. 21

1]]ם[ ] .[[
2]]תמכין בכל דין[[
3]]ל . . . . . [[

frg. 22

1]]ן [[
2] א]לפין מן . [[
3]]באדין . [[

frg. 27

1]]. אלן א[[
2]]מהוי[[
3]]. בין [[
4]] עד[[
5]]כי[[

frg. 13

1. [ ]for fou[r]
2. [ʿ]*tq* [the] river[ ]
3. [ ]. he went[ ]

frg. 17

1. and they entered[ ]
2. in their hands[
3. and they encamped at[

frg. 19

1. [ ]the well[ ]
2. [ ]he returned t[o]

frg. 20

1. [ ]*n*[ ]
2. [ ]their father. Then[ ]
3. [ ]. ages.[ ]
4. [ ]all the sons of[ ]
5. [ ]*tw* .[ ]

frg. 21

1. [ ].[ ]*m*[ ]
2. [ ]taking hold of all that[ ]
3. [ ]*l* .....[ ]

frg. 22

1. [ ]*n*[ ]
2. [th]ousands from .[ ]
3. [ ]Then .[ ]

frg. 27

1. [ ]. these ʾ[ ]
2. [ ]Mahaway[ ]
3. [ ]. between (?)[ ]
4. [ ] until [ ]
5. [ ] for [ ]

frg. 29

1]]אהוא ב[[
2]]לא שיצי[[

15. 2Q Enoch Giants — 2QEnGiants (2Q*26*)

1] י]אדיחו לוחא למ.[[
2]]יסלקו מיא עלא מן [ ] . . א[[
3]] . א ינטלו לוחא מן מיא לוחא די[[
4]] . אחד. לה . . אל . [[

16. 4Q Enoch Giants[a] — 4QEnGiants[a]

frg. 1

1 חברוה[י [
2 חובבש ואדכ.[[
3 ומה תתנונני לק[טלה [

frg. 2

1 ספ[ר [
2 (*vacat*)] [
3 פרשגן לוחא תני[נ]א די אי[גרתא [
4 בכתב יד חנוך ספר פרשא[וקרא עירא]
5 וקדישא לשמיחזה ולכול ח[ברוהי [
6 ידיע להוא לכון ד[י]ל[א [
7 ועובדכון ודי נשיכון] [
8 אנון [ו]בני[הו]ן ונשיא ד[י בניהון [
9 בזנות[כ]ון ב[א]רעא והוה [ע]ליכ[ון וארעא מזעקה]
10 וקבלה עליכון ועל עובד בניכון [וקלה סלק עד תרעי שמיא מזעק וקבל על]
11 חבלא די חבלתון בה (*vacat*)] [
12 עד רפאל מטה ארו אבדנ[א [
13 ודי במדבריא וד[י] בימיא ופשר צבות[כון? [

frg. 29

1. [ ] I shall be in[ ]
2. [ ]he did not finish[ ]

15.

1. [ ] they [will] wash the tablet *lm*.[ ]
2. [ ]the waters will go up higher than [ ] ..'[ ]
3. [ ].' they will lift the tablet from the waters, the tablet which .[ ]
4. [ ].*'ḥd. lh. .'l*.[ ]

16.

frg. 1

1. hi[s] companions[ ]
2. Ḥobabesh and *'Adk*.[ ]
3. and what you will give me to ki[ll (?)]

frg. 2

1. The book of[ ]
2. (*vacat*) [ ]
3. A copy of the seco[n]d tablet of the le[tter]
4. in the handwriting of Enoch the scribe of distinction (?) [The watcher]
5. and the holy one [cried] to Shemiḥazah and to all [his] com[panions]
6. " Let it be known to you th[at] no[t]
7. and your conduct and that of your wives[ ]
8. they [and] th[ei]r sons and the wives o[f their sons]
9. by [yo]ur fornication on the [ea]rth ; and there was [up]on y[ou The earth is crying out]
10. and complaining against you and against the conduct of your sons ; [and its voice mounts up to the gates of the heavens, crying out and complaining against]
11. the harm that you have done to it. (*vacat*) [ ]
12. unto Raphael it reaches. Now we are peris[hing]
13. and (those) which (are) in the deserts and wh[ich] (are) in the seas. The interpretation of [your] desires[ ]

14 עליכון לבאיש וכען שריא אסורכון מח[בל]

15 וצלו *(vacat)* [ ]

17. 4Q Enoch Giants[b] — 4QEnGiants[b]

col. 2

3 באדין חלמו תריהון חלמין
4 ונדת שנת עיניהון מנהון וק[מו]
5 ואתו על [שמיחזה אבוהון]
6 [ ]
7 [שר]שין רברבין נפקו מן עקרהן[ ]
8 [ ]
9 [ ]
10 [ ]ונורא דלק בכל[ ]
11 [ ]
12 [ ]עד כא סוף חלמא[ ]
13 [לא]השכחו גבריא לחויא לה[ון]
14 [חלמא לחנוך] לספר פרשא ויפשור לנא

15 חלמא באדין [הו]ה הודה אחוהי אוהיה ואמר קדם גבריא אף

16 אנה חזית בחלמי בליליא דן גברוא הא שלטן שמיא לארעא נחת

17 [ ]
18 [ ]
19 [ ]
20 [ ] . . . עד כא סוף חלמא[באדין]דחלו כל גבריא

21 [ונפיליא ו]ק[ר]יו מהוי ואתה ל[הון]וב[עו לה]גבריא ושלחוהו על חנוך

22 [ספר פרש]א ואמרו לה אזל[ ]ומותא לכה די

23 [ו]שמעתה קלה ואמר לה די יחו[ינך ו]יפש[ו]ר חלמיא . . .

14. against you for evil. And now loosen your bond (that) ropes you [ ]
15. and pray. (*vacat*)[ ]

17.

col. 2

3. Then two of them dreamed dreams ;
4. and the sleep of their eyes fled from them ; they ro[se]
5. and came to [Shemiḥazah, their father]
6. [ ]
7. great [sh]oots came forth from their trunk [ ]
8. [ ]
9. [ ]
10. [ ]and the fire burned in all [ ]
11. [ ]
12. [ ] thus far the end of the dream. [ ]
13. [ ] the giants were unable to explain to th[em]
14. [the dream. But let us seek out Enoch,] the scribe of distinction(?); he will interpret for us
15. the dream. Then his brother 'Ohyah [de]clared and said before the giants :
16. " I too saw in my dream during this night something wondrous. Look, the ruler of the heavens descended to the earth
17. [ ]
18. [ ]
19. [ ]
20. [ ] . . ." Thus far the end of the dream. [Then] all the giants were afraid,
21. [and the fallen ones (too) ; so] they su[mm]oned Mahaway, and he came to [them] ; and all the giants ques[tioned him] and sent him to Enoch,
22. [the scribe of distinct]ion (?). They said to him, " Go, [ ] and death to you that
23. [and] you heard his voice. Say to him that he should make kn[own to you and] interp[re]t the dreams . . .

col. 3

3 באחת ארכת גבריא [ ]
4 כעלעולין ופרח בידוהי כנש[רין]
5 חלד וחלף לשהוין מדברא רבא[ ]
6 ו[ח]זה חנוך וזעקה ואמר לה מחוי . [ ]
7 לתנא ולכה תנינות למחוי בע[ה אנה]
8 ל[מ]ליך וכל נפילי ארעא [ ]
9-10 . . .
11 [מאתין איל]נין די מן שמין נ[פקו]

18. 4Q Enoch Giants^c — 4QEnGiants^c

frg. 1

3 [הוית מת]גבר ובתקוף חיל דרעי ובחסן גבורתי
4 [מן כ]ול בשר ועבדת עמהון קרב ברם לא
5 [הוית מה]שכח אנה עמ‹הו›ן לאשתררה דבעלי דיני
6 [בשמי]א יתבין ובקדשיא אנון שרין ולא
7 [אנו]ן תקיפין מני (*vacat*)
8 [גע]רה די חיות ברא אתה ואוש ברא קרין
9 [ ]וכדן אמר לה אוהיה חלמי אנסנ[י]
10 [נדת ש]נת עיני למחזא [חז]וה ארו ידע אנה די על

19. 6Q Enoch Giants — 6QEnGiants (6Q8)

frg. 1

1 [ ] . [ ]
2 [ ] . אוהיה ואמר למהוי . [ ]
3 [ ]ולא מרתת מן אחזיך כלא אח[וי לנא]

col. 3

3. in one (hand) the authorization (?) of the giants[ ]
4. like whirlwinds, and he flew with (the aid of) his hands like eag[les (cultivated)]
5. land, and he passed over the wasteland, the great desert [ ]
6. and he [s]aw Enoch, cried out to him, and said to him, " An oracle.[I have come]
7. hither; and of you a second time [I] be[g] for an oracle [ ]
8. to your [w]ords, and all the fallen ones of the earth [ ]

9-10. . . .

11. [two hundred tr]ees which we[nt forth] from the heavens [ ]

18.

frg. 1

3. [I was growing] stronger, by the power of the might of my arm and by the force of my strength,
4. [than a]ll flesh. And I made war with them, but I
5. [was] not able to make my position firm with t<he>m, because those who conducted my suit
6. [ ] were sitting [in the heaven]s and were settled among the holy ones. But
7. [the]y are not more powerful than I. (*vacat*)
8. [the c]ry of the beasts of the field came, and (with) the howl of the field they were calling
9. [ ] Thus did 'Ohyah say to him, " My dream overwhelmed m[e];
10. [and the sl]eep of my eyes [fled] so as to see the [vi]sion of it. Now I know that upon

19.

frg. 1

1. [ ].[ ]
2. [ ]. 'Ohyah, and he said to Mahaway .[ ]
3. [ ]and does not tremble. Who has made you see all (that)? Make kn[own to us]

4]]· ברקאל אבי עמי הוה (*vacat*)] [

5]]ל[עד] לא [ש]יצי מהוי[לא]שתעיה מה די[[

6]אמר אוהיה ל]ה ארו תמהין שמעת הן ילדת סרי[קה [

frg. 2

1 תלתת שרשוהי[ ]וחזי

2 הוית עד די אתת[[

3 פרדסא דן כלה ו .[[

frg. 3

1]] רבה

2]]ע . . . תה

frg. 4

1]] . [[

2 בה וי . [[

3 תמשכון[[

4 . . ולא . [[

frg. 5

1]]ן כל גנני . [[

2]] . ל[[

frg. 6

1]]להון במס . [[

frg. 26

1 לובר ל . [[

2 ל . . ח . . . [[

3 ובחן . [[

4 בני . . [[

4. [ ]. Baraqi'el, my father, was with me. (*vacat*)
5. [ ]*l*[ ]Mahaway had not [yet fi]nished [re]counting what ['Ohyah]
6. [said to] him, " Now I have heard about strange things, whether [a] barr[en woman] has borne (a child) [ ]

frg. 2

1. three of its roots/scions[and]
2. I [wat]ched until there came[ ]
3. all this garden, and .[ ]

frg. 3

1. [ ]great[ ]
2. [ ]'. . .*th*[ ]

frg. 4

1. [ ].[ ]
2. in it and *y*.[ ]
3. you will draw[ ]
4. .. and not .[ ]

frg. 5

1. [ ]*n* all the enclosures of .[ ]
2. [ ].*l*[ ]

frg. 6

1. [ ]to them *bms*.[ ]

frg. 26

1. Lubar *l*.[ ]
2. *l*..*ḥ*...[ ]
3. and he tested .[ ]
4. the sons of/my sons ..[ ]

20. 1Q Testament of Levi — 1QTLevi ar (1Q*21*)

frg. 1

1]]מן די להוון תליתין [[

2]]נוך מלכות כהנותא רבא מן מלכות[ה לא תהוא]

3]]ל[א]ל[ע]ל[יון [

frg. 3

1 [ולמלכות ח]רבא [פגשא לקרבא ונחשירותא ועמלא ונצפתא וקטלא וכפנא זמנין תאכל וזמנין תכפן וזמנין]

2 תעמל וזמין תנ[וח וזמנין תדמוך וזמנין תנוד שנת עיניך כען חזי לך היך רבינך מן כלא והיך יהבנא לך]

3 [רבות ש]לם על[מא [

frg. 4

1] אב יע]קב מעשר[[
2]]ל[[

frg. 5

1]]יצחק[[
2]]...[[

frg. 6

1]]וכדי[[

frg. 7

1]]נתא עד אנתה [[
2]]תמלך עם די [[

3]]ם בעא לא[[

20.

frg. 1

1. [ ]from (the time) that they will become triple [casts]
2. [will cause] you [to inherit (?)] a priestly kingdom, greater than [his] kingdom [there will be none]
3. [ ]to [God most H]i[gh]

frg. 3

1. [and a kingdom of the s]word : [the struggle for the battle, the slaughter, the toil, the shrieking, the killing, and the famine. Sometimes you will eat, sometimes you will be starved, sometimes]
2. you will toil, sometimes you will re[st, sometimes you will sleep, and sometimes the sleep of your eyes will flee. Now see for yourself how we have made you greater than all, and how we have given to you
3. [the greatness] of ever[lasting] pea[ce]

frg. 4

1. [ ]my father Jacob (was) tithing[ ]
2. [ ]*l*[ ]

frg. 5

1. [ ]Isaac[ ]
2. [ ]...[ ]

frg. 6

1. [ ]and when[ ]

frg. 7

1. [ ]*nt'* until you [ ]
2. [ ]you will rule a people which [ ]
3. [ ]*m* sought Not[ ]

frg. 8

1]]ושלם ואנה[[
2]]שלם וכל אנש[[
3]]ן אנה ל[[
4]]ע[[

frg. 9

1] ש]גיאן[[
2] ל]הוין · [[
3]]ד לי עד[[
4]] . . . [[

frg. 10

1]]די להוין[[
2]]ל[[

frg. 11

1]]. ה אדין יהוא[[
2]]. בעא . [[

frg. 12

1]]. . יא ללוט[[
2]]ל[[

frg. 18

1]]שגיא[[

frg. 19

1] י]עקב[[

frg. 22

1]]. רברב[ין [
2]]הוו מ . [[

frg. 8

1. [ ]and peace. And I[ ]
2. [ ]peace and all mankind[ ]
3. [ ]*n* I *l*[ ]
4. [ ]*l*[ ]

frg. 9

1. [m]any[ ]
2. [they wi]ll be[ ]
3. [ ]*d* to me until[ ]
4. [ ]...[ ]

frg. 10

1. [ ]who will be[ ]
2. [ ]*l*[ ]

frg. 11

1. [ ].*h*. Then he shall be[ ]
2. [ ]. he sought .[ ]

frg. 12

1. [ ]..*y*' to Lot[ ]
2. [ ]*l*[ ]

frg. 18

1. [ ]much[ ]

frg. 19

1. [J]acob[ ]

frg. 22

1. [ ]. great[ ]
2. [ ]they were *m*.[ ]

frg. 23

1]]ארי ש[[
2]]חהא[[

frg. 24

1]]נהורא א[[
2]] . . . [[

frg. 25

1]] . . [[
2]] · ד בהון די . [[
3]]ין בחיר[ין [

frg. 26

1] חמדת בכור]י ארעא[[

frg. 27

1]]אדין [[

frg. 28

1]] . מן זרע[[

frg. 29

1] יעק]ב אבי[[
2]]. שיריה[[

frg. 30

1]] . [[
2]]לא לזנו . . [[
3]]בי לה בעא צ[[
4]]ל[[

frg. 31

1] רוח]י טעותא[[

frg. 23

1. [ ]for š[ ]
2. [ ]*ḥh'*[ ]

frg. 24

1. [ ]the light '[ ]
2. [ ]...[ ]

frg. 25

1. [ ]..[ ]
2. [ ].*d* among them who[ ]
3. [ ]*yn* chosen[ ]

frg. 26

1. [the delights of the first-fruits o]f the earth[ ]

frg. 27

1. [ ]Then[ ]

frg. 28

1. [ ]. from the seed of[ ]

frg. 29

1. [Jaco]b my father[ ]
2. [ ]*šyryh*[ ]

frg. 30

1. [ ].[ ]
2. [ ]not for fornication ..[ ]
3. [ ]in me (*or* a house). He sought for himself *ṣ*[ ]
4. [ ]*l*[ ]

frg. 31

1. [spirit]s of error[ ]

frg. 32

1]]ה שמיא ל[[

frg. 37

1]]מין תלה[[
2]]כל משחה ל[[
3]]. לת מה . . שמיא .] [

frg. 43

1]]באש .] [

frg. 45

1]]. . ך ראשא[[

frg. 50

1]]בין ברך[[

frg. 51

1]]. מן קרבא[[
2]]. . [[

frg. 52

1]]מרי ה . .] [
2] ר]עותה[[

frg. 53

1] א]דין .] [
2]]י באר בה[[

frg. 54

1] יה]חזה להון לב[[
2]]שרו . .] [
3]]ל[[

frg. 32

1. [ ]*h* the heavens *l*[ ]

frg. 37

1. [ ]*myn tlh*[ ]
2. [ ]all its measurement *l*[ ]
3. [ ].*lt* what .. the heavens[ ]

frg. 43

1. [ ]evil[ ]

frg. 45

1. [ ]..*yn* the head[ ]

frg. 50

1. [ ]between your son[ ]

frg. 51

1. [ ]. from the war[ ]
2. [ ]..[ ]

frg. 52

1. [ ]my lord *h*..[ ]
2. [ ]his good [pl]easure[ ]

frg. 53

1. [T]hen .[ ]
2. [ ]*y* a well in it[ ]

frg. 54

1. [he] showed to them the *b*[ ]
2. [ ]they encamped ..[ ]
3. [ ]*l*[ ]

frg. 55

1]]הוו . [[
2]]. ת די הוא[[

frg. 56

1]]די כדן מן . [[

frg. 57

1]]· ליומת[[
2]]. הוה רחם[[

frg. 58

1] י]שראל[[

21. 4Q Testament of Levi[a] — 4QTLevi ar[a]

col. 1

1-4] [
5] דן[
6] אנה[
7] אתרחע]ת וכל
8] אדין עיני ואנפי]נטלת לשמיא
9]]ואצבעת כפי וידי
10] וצלית ו]אמרת מרי אנתה
11]ידע א]נתה בלחודיך ידע
12] כל]ארחת קשט ארחק
13]מני ב]אישא וזנותא דחא
14] ח]כמה ומנדע וגבורה
15]הב לי ל]שבחה רחמיך קדמיך

frg. 55

1. [ ]they were .[ ]
2. [ ].*t* which was [ ]

frg. 56

1. [ ]which (is) thus. Whoever .[ ]

frg. 57

1. [ ]. *lywmt*[ ]
2. [ ]. he was loving[ ]

frg. 58

1. [I]srael[ ]

21.

col. 1

1.-4. [ ]
5. [ ]*dn*
6. [ ]I
7. [I washed my]self, and all
8. [Then my eyes and my countenance]
I lifted up to the heavens
9. [ ]and the
fingers of my palms and my hands
10. [I stretched out.... I prayed and] I
said, " My Lord, you
11. [know y]ou yourself
alone know
12. [all] the ways of
truth; remove
13. [from me]the [e]vil and
the fornication. Repel
14. [w]isdom, know-
ledge, and power
15. [grant me to] praise your
mercy before you

16]]דשפיר ודטב קדמיך

17] א]ל תשלט בי כל שטן

18] ע]לי מרי וקרבני למהוא לכה

col. 2

1-4] [

5 לע[יניך [

6 מרי ב[רכת [

7 זרע דק[שטא שמע נא]

8 צלות עב[דך לוי למעבד]

9 דין קשט לכ[ל עלמין אל תעדי]

10 לבר עבדך מן ק[דמיך [

11 באדין נגדת ב[[

12 על אבי יעקוב וכד[י [

13 מן אבל מין אדין[[

14 שכבת ויתבת אנה ע[ל מי דן [

15 אדין חזוין אחזית[[

16 בחזית חזויא וחזית שמ[יא פתיחין וחזית טורא [

17 תחותי רם עד דבק לשמי[א והוית בה ואתפתחו [

18 לי תרעי שמיא ומלאך חד[אמר לי [

22. 4Q Visions of ʿAmram[a] — 4QʿAmram[a]

frg. 1

1]]לי וענו ו[אמרו [

2] כ]ל בני אד[ם [

3]]ל[[

frg. 2

1]]מנ[[

2]]נטלת עיני וחזית וחד מ[נהון [

16. [ ] what is beautiful and what is good before you
17. [do] not let any adversary have power over me
18. [to] me, my Lord, and draw me near to be for you

col. 2

1.-4. [ ]
5. [your] ey[es]
6. my Lord, you have b[lessed]
7. a ri[ghteous] offspring[Hear, now]
8. the prayer of your ser[vant Levi to carry out]
9. a true statute (?) for[ever Turn not away]
10. the son of your servant from be[fore you]
11. Then I set out f[or]
12. to my father Jacob and wh[en]
13. from Abel-main. Then[ ]
14. I lay down and I settled a[t the waters of Dan]
15. Then I was shown visions[ ]
16. As I looked (?) at the visions, I saw the heav[ens opened ; I saw the mountain]
17. beneath me so lofty that it reached the heav[ens, and I was on it ; there were opened]
18. for me the gates of the heavens, and an angel [said to me]

22.

frg. 1

1. [ab]out me." And they answered and [said,]
2. [al]l sons of ma[n]
3. [ ] *l*[ ]

frg. 2

1. [ ]*mn*[ ]
2. [ ]I lifted up my eyes and I looked ; and one o[f them]

3] צב]ענין והשיך חשוך[[
4] (vac[at) ואחרנא חזית וה]א [
5] א]נפוהי חעכין ומכסה ב[[
6]]לחדה[וכ]ל עינוהי[[
7]]ל[[

frg. 3

1]]אנה שליט[[
2] . חנה וש]למה[[

23. 4Q Visions of ʿAmram[b] — 4QʿAmram[b]

frg. 1

10 בחזוי חזוה די חלמא והא תרין דאנין עלי ואמרין [[
11 ואחדין עלי תגר רב ושאלת אנון אנתון מן די כדן מש]לטין עלי ועני ואמרו לי אנחנא]
12 [מהש]לטין ושליטין על כול בני אדם ואמרו לי במן מננא אנת]ה בחר נטלת עיני וחזית]
13 [וחד] מנמון חזוה דח]י[ל [כפ]תן [ומ]ל[ב]ושה צבענין והשיך חשוך [(vacat)]
14 [ואחרנא חזית] והא[ ]ל[ ]בחזוה ואנפוהי העכן ו]מכסה ב [
15 [לחדה וכול עינוהי [

frg. 2

1] מה]שלט עליך[[
2] עירא]דן מן הוא ואמר לי הדן ע]ירא [
3]]ומלכי רשע (vacat) ואמרת מראי מא ש[[
4] וכל ארחה חש]יכה וכל עבדה ח]ש[יך ובחשוכא הוא . [[

3. [d]yed many colors and dark black [ ]
4. [(*va*]*cat*) and I saw the other one; and beho[ld]
5. [his] visage was (like) a snake, and his skin (was) of [ ]
6. [ ]exceedingly, [and al]l his eyes [ ]
7. [ ] *l* [ ]

frg. 3

1. [ ]I have power [ ]
2. [ ]. his favor and [his] pe[ace]

23.

frg. 1

10. in my vision, the vision of the dream: Behold, two were making judgment about me and saying [ ]
11. and they were joined in a great debate about me. I asked them: "Since when do you have power over me in this way?" And they answered and said to me: "We
12. [have been given po]wer, and we have power over all sons of man." They said to me: "Which one of us do you [choose?" I lifted up my eyes and I looked,]
13. [and one] of them, his appearance was fear[so]me, [like a ser]pent; [and] his [g]arm[en]t was dyed many colors, and dark black [(*vacat*)]
14. [and I saw the other one] and behold [ ]*l*[ ]by his appearance, and his visage (was like) a snake, and [his skin was of]
15. [exceedingly, and all his eyes]

frg. 2

1. [ha]ve been given power over you[ ]
2. [this watche]r, who is he?" And he said to me: "Is this [the] wa[tcher]
3. [ ] and Malkî-rešaʿ. (*vacat*) And I said: "My lord, what *š*[ ]
4. and all his way is da]rk, and all his activity is da[r]k, and in the darkness he [ ]

5 [אנת]ה חזה והוא משלט על כול חשוכא ואנה
[משלט על כול נהורא]
6 [מאמר]עליא עד ארעיא אנה שליט על כול נהורא וכו[ל
דאלהא ואנה שליט על אנש]

frg. 3

1 [חנה ושלמה ואנה על כול בני נהו]רא אשלטת ושאלתה[ואמרת לה מה
אנון שמהתך]

2 [וענה וא]מר לי דתלתה שמה[תי]

24. 4Q Visions of ʿAmram^{c} — 4QʿAmram^{c}

frg. 1

1 פרשגן כתב מלי חזות עמרם בר קהת בר לוי כו[ל די]

2 אחוי לבנוהי ודי פקד אנון ביום מו[תה] בשנת

3 מאה ותלתין ושת היא שנתא די מותה [ב]שנת מאה

4 והמשין ותרתין לגל[ו]ת [י]שראל למצרין

25. 4Q Visions of ʿAmram^{d} — 4QʿAmram^{d}

frg. 1

1 [ ]. מאמר ע[ליא]
2 [ ]א ואנה שליט לאנ[ש]
3 [א]ש[לטת ו]שאלתה [ו]אמרת לה מה א[נון]

4 [ ]ל . . . .[ ]

frg. 2

1 [ ]. חזית עירי[ ] . . [ ]
2 [ ]. . . ב . . ומה [ ]
3 [ ]ל[ ]

5. [yo]u see. He has power over all the darkness, and I [have been given power over all the light]
6. [word] of the Most High for the happenings. I have power over all the light and al[l that is God's, and I have power over mankind]

frg. 3

1. [his favor and his peace. And I] have been given power [over all the sons of lig]ht." And I asked him [and I said to him: "What are your names]
2. [And he answered and he sa]id to me, ["My] three nam[es]

24.

frg. 1

1. A copy of a book of words of visions of 'Amram, son of Qahat, son of Levi: Every[thing that]
2. he made known to his sons and that he commanded them on the day of [his] deat[h], in the year
3. one hundred and thirty-six. This (was) the year of his death: [in] the year one hundred
4. fifty-two of the exi[l]e of [I]srael to Egypt.

25.

frg. 1

1. [ ] . word of the Mo[st High]
2. [ ]' and I have power over ma[n]
3. [I] ha[ve power." And] I asked him [and] I said to him: "What a[re]
4. [ ]*l* . . . . [ ]

frg. 2

1. [ ]. I saw watche[rs] . . [ ]
2. [ ]. . . *b* . . and what [ ]
3. [ ]*l*[ ]

26. 4Q Visions of ʿAmram[e(?)] — 4QʿAmram[e(?)]

frg. 1

9 אנה מ[הו]דע [לכון וא]ף יצבתא אנה מודע ל[כון ארי כל בני נהורא]

10 נהירין להוון [וכל בני] חשוכא חשיכין להוון [ארי בני נהורא [

11 ובכל מנדעהון[ל]הוון ובני חשוכא יתקדון [[

12 ארי כל כסל ורש[ע חשיכי]ן וכל [של]ם וקשוט נהיר[ין ארי כל בני נהורא]

13 לנהורא לשמח[ת עלמא ולח]דות[א יהכו]ן וכל בני חש[וכא לחשוכא למותא]

14 ולאבדנא יהכון[ ] . לעמא נהירותא ואחיו[ ]

27. 4Q Testament of Qahat — 4QTQahat

frg. 1

9 וכען לכה עמרם ברי מפק[ד אנה]

10 ו[לבנ]יכה ולבניהון אנא מפקד . [ ]

11 ויהבו ללוי אבי ולוי אבי לי [יהב]

12 כול כתבי בשהדו די תזדהרון בהון[ ]

28. 4Q "Messianic" Text — 4QMess ar

col. 1

1 די ידא תרתין א[ ] כמה [ ]ו שומה שב[ק] מן[ ]

2 שערה[ו]טלופחין על [ ]

3 ושומן זועירן על ירכתה [בתר תרת]ין שנין דן מן דן ידע . .ליה

4 בעלימותה להוה כלהון [כאנ]וש די לא ידע מדע[ם עד] עדן די

5 [י]נדע תלתת ספריא *(vacat)* [ ] *(vacat)*

26.

frg. 1

9. I am in[form]ing [you, and al]so the certainty I am making known to y[ou : for all the sons of light]
10. will be illumined, [and all the sons] of darkness will be darkened ; [for the sons of light]
11. and with all their knowledge [th]ey will be, and the sons of darkness will be cut out[ ] ;
12. for all foolishness and wicked[ness are dar]kened, and all [pea]ce and truth are illumined ; for all the sons of light]
13. wi[ll go] to the light, to [eternal] happine[ss, and to j]o[y ;] and all the sons of dar[kness to darkness, to death,]
14. and to perdition will go ; [ ] for the people (there will be) brightness, and they have revived (?) [ ]

27.

frg. 1

9. Now you, ʿAmram, my son, [I] am comman[ding]
10. and your [sons] and their sons I am commanding. [ ]
11. and they gave to Levi, my father, and Levi my father [gave] to me [ ]
12. all my books in testimony, so that you might be forewarned by them [ ]

28.

col. 1

1. two . . . of the hand. ʾ[ ]*kmh*[ ]*w* it lef[t] a mark from [like (?)]
2. barley [and] lentils on [ ]
3. and tiny marks on his thigh [After tw]o years he will know this from that . .*lyh*.
4. In his youth he will become like *lhwn*[like a ma]n who does not know anyth[ing, until] the time when
5. he shall become skilled in the three books.

6 [בא]דין יערם וידע שו[כלא]שן חזון למאתה לה על ארכובת[ה]

7 ובאבוהי ובא[ב]התוהי . . [ ]היך וזקינה עמה לה[ו]ן מלכה וערמומ[ה]

8 [ו]ידע רזי אנשא וחוכמתה לכול עממיא תהך וידע רזי כול חייא

9 [וכ]ול חשבוניהון עלוהי יסופו ומסרת כול חייא שגיא-תהוא

10 [ה]שבונוהי בדי בחיר אלהא הוא מולדה ורוח נשמוהי

11 [ח]שבונוהי להון לעלמין [ ]

12 [ ]א די ל[ ] . . [ ]לין

13 [ ]ת חשב[ון]

14 [ ]ב
15 [ ]והי
16 [ ].
17 [ ].ש

col. 2

1 .[ ] די מ[ ] נפל לקדמין בני שחוה [ ]

2 [ ]. .תא באיש טלופחא ל. . [ ]

3 [ ]. . . .[ ]
4 [ ]מאתה[ ]
5 [ ]בש[רא]
6 מו[ ]ה[ ]
7 ורוח נש[מוהי חשבונוהי להון]

8 לעלמין [ ]
9 . . . .[ ]
10 [ ]
11 [ ]

6. [Th]en he will become wise and will be endowed with disc[re-
tion]*šn* visions to come to him upon
[his] knees.
7. And with his father and with his forefa[th]ers ..[ ]
life and old age; with him there will be counsel and
prudence,
8. [and] he will know the secrets of mankind. His wisdom will
go forth to all peoples, and he will know the secrets
of all living things.
9. [Al]l their calculations against him will come to naught, although
the opposition of all living beings will be abundant.
10. [But] his [cal]culations [will succeed], because he is the Elect
of God. His birth and the (very) spirit of his breath
11. [ ] his [cal]culations will exist forever.
[ ]
12. [ ]' *dy l*[ ]..
[ ]*lyn*
13. [ ]*t* calcu-
[lation]
14.-17.

col. 2

1. .[ ]which *m*[ ] fell to the east. Children of
perdition (?) [ ]
2. [ ]..*t*' (was) bad. The lentil (?)
l..[ ]
3. [ ]....[ ]
4. [ ]to come[ ]
5. [ ]fle[sh]
6. *mw*[ ]*h*[ ]
7. and the spirit of [his] breath [his calculations will exist]
8. forever [ ]
9. ....[ ]
10. [ ]
11. [ ]

12 ומדינן . . [ ]
13 ויחרבון ת . [ ] . מ[ ]ובמלן יתבין די ל . [ ]

14 מין יסופון ת . [ ]מן [ ]בבן יחרבן כול אלן יהכ[ין]

15 ית . [ ] (*vacat*)
16 [ ] . . [ ] . וכל[ה]ן יתבונן כעירין עובדה

17 חלף קלה [ ] יסודה עלוהי יסדון חטאה וחובתה

18 [ ] . . [ ]חדוה[י] . קדיש ועירי[ן]מאמר

19 [א]מרו עלוהי [ ]

20 [ ] . . . . [ ] . [ ] . ב מי[ ]פון[
21 [ ] . זה

29. 1Q Genesis Apocryphon — 1QapGen (+ 1Q*20*)

(A) 1Q*20* (= *DJD* 1. 86-87)

frg. 1, *col. i*

1 [ ]ם רגזך תת . ך ותתק . . ם ומן הוא

2 [ ]ם חמת רגזך
3 [ ]תיא וכביא וש . ליא דאלין ו . . . ין
4 [ ]וכען הא איתי אסירין
5 [ ]ל . . . . . . א
6 [ ]
7 [ק]דישא רבא
8 [ ] . . ודיא כול
9 [ ] . . . . תוהי
10 [ ] . . . .

col. ii

1 . [ ]
2 . . ל[ ]
3 יום . [ ]
4 כול . . . ין . [ ]
5 . . . ין . . . ין . . [ ]

12. and cities ..[ ]
13. and they will lay waste *t*.[ ].*m*[ ]
and with *mln* dwelling which *l*.[ ]
14. waters will cease *t*.[ ]from[ ]will
devastate (the) gates (?). All these will co[me]
15. *yt*.[ ] (*vacat*)
16. [ ]..[ ]. and all of [th]em will be
(re)built; like Watchers (will be) his activity.
17. Instead of his voice[ ]upon him they will
base its foundation. Its sin and its guilt
18. [ ]..[in] hi[s] breast[ ]. a Holy One and
Watcher[s] a word
19. [ ]they have [sp]oken against him.
[ ]
20. [ ]...[ ].*b* *my*[ ]*pwn*
21. [ ].*zh*

29. (A)

frg. 1, col. i

1. [ ].you will pour out (?) your wrath, and it will *ttq*..*m*;
and whoever
2. [ ]*m* the fury of your wrath.
3. [ ]*ty' wkby' wš.ly' d'lyn w...yn*
4. [ ] and now look, *'nyty* prisoners
5. [ ]*l*.. ....'
6. [ ]
7. [ ] the Great [H]oly One
8. [ ]..*wdy'* all the
9. [ ].... .*twhy*
10. [ ] ....

frg. 1, col. ii

1. [ ]
2. ..*l*[ ]
3. the day of .[ ]
4. all ...*yn* .[ ]
5. ...*yn* ...*yn* ..[ ]

6 ארע . ת . . . ע ל]   [
7 עזבו גדי . . . .]   [
8 ובישתא למק . .]   [
9 ו . . . . ל]   [
10 . . . . . .]   [

frg. 2

1]   [. . . רת]   [. . . .]   [. מ]   [
2]   [. . ומתמחין מן אחרהון . . . . .]   [
3]   [(*vacat*)
4]   [. ין מת.תנין וב . . . . ל .]   [
5]   [. קודם מרה עלמא   [

frg. 3

1]   [. . . .]   [. נא . . .]   [
2]   [. רו וכול . קבלא . ר]   [
3]   [. ד
4]   [. לדיתם]   [
5]   [. . .]   [

frg. 4

1]   [. . ד .]   [
2]   ]א די א. . . רג .]   [
3]   [. . . . .]   [

(B) 1QapGen (proper)

col. 1

1]   [. . . . . . . ועם נצבתא
2]   [. . אף רז רשעא די
3]   [. תין ורזא די
4]   [. . ל . מדעין
5]   [.
6]   [. . . .
7]   [. . . . ן

6. land of *.t.. ..ʿ l*[ ]
7. *ʿzbw gdy* ....[ ]
8. and the evil for *mq..* .[ ]
9. and .... *l*[ ]
10. ....[ ]

frg. 2

1. [ ]....*rt*[ ]. .. .[ ].*m*.[ ]
2. [ ].. and were struck from behind them .....[ ]
3. [ ] (*vacat*)
4. [ ].*yn mt.tnyn wb*.........*l*.[ ]
5. [ ]. before the eternal Lord.

frg. 3

1. [ ]*n'*[ ]
2. [ ].*rw* and all the *qbl' r*[ ]
3. [ ]. *d*
4. [ ]. *ldytm*[ ]
5. [ ]...[ ]

frg. 4

1. [ ]..*k* .[ ]
2. [ ]' which '..*rg* .[ ]
3. [ ]... ... ... [ ]

(B)

col. 1

1. [ ]...... and with the planting (?)
2. [ ].. Moreover, the mystery of evil which
3. [ ]. *tyn* and the mystery which
4. [ ]
5. [ ]
6. [ ]
7. [ ]

col. 2

1 הא באדין חשבת בלבי די מן עירין הריאנתא ומן קדישין ה[י]א ולנפיל[ין]

2 ולבי עלי משתני על עולימא דנא (*vacat*)
3 באדין אנה למך אתבהלת ועלת על בתאנוש אנ[תתי ואמרת]

4 [ ]אנא ועד בעליא במרה רבותא במלך כול ע[למים]

5 [ ] בני שמין עד כולא בקושטא תחוינני הן[ ]

6 [בקושטא] תחוינני ולא בכדבין הדא ב[ ]

7 במלך כול עלמים עד בקושט עמי תמללין ולא בכדבין [ ]

8 אדין בתאנוש אנתתי בחלץ תקיף עמי מללת וב[כת]

9 ואמרת יא אחי ויא מרי דכרלך על עדינתי א[ ]
10 [ ]ם ענתא ונשמתי לגו נדנהא ואנה בקושט כול[א אחוינך]

11 [ ]ול.א ושגי לבי עלי אדין אשתני [ ]

12 וכדי חזת בתאנוש אנתתי די אשתני אנפי עלי[ ]

13 באדין אנסת רוחהא ועמי תמלל ולי תאמר יא מרי ויא [אחי דכרלך]

14 עדינתי יאמיא אנה לך בקדישא רבא במלך ש[מיא]

15 די מנך זרעא דן ומנך הריונא דן ומנך נצבת פריא[דן]

16 ולא מן כול זר ולא מן כול עירין ולא מן כול בני שמ[ין למא צלם]

17 אנפיך כדנא עליך שנא ושחת ורוחך כדן עליבא[ארי אנה]

18 בקושט ממללא עמך (*vacat*) [ ]
19 באדין אנה למך רטת על מתושלח אבי וכולא לה [חוית חנוך]

20 אבוהי וכולא מנה ביצבא ינדע בדי הוא רחים ורגי[ג ועם קדישיא]

col. 2

1. So then I thought in my mind that the conception was due to Watchers or that it w[a]s due to Holy Ones, or to Nephi-[lim... ;]
2. and my mind wavered because of this child. (*vacat*)
3. Then I, Lamech, became frightened and I went to Bitenosh, my wi[fe and said, " ...]
4. [ ]'*n*' *w'd* by the Most High, by the Great Lord, by the King of all A[ges,]
5. [with] the sons of heaven, that you truthfully make everything known to me, whether [ ]
6. you must tell me [truthfully] and without lies whether this *b*[... Swear]
7. by the King of all Ages that you are speaking to me truthfully and without lies [ ]."
8. Then Bitenosh, my wife, spoke to me with great vehemence; she we[pt]
9. and said, "O my brother and my lord, recall my pleasure '[ ]
10. [ ]*m* the time, and my breath in the midst of its sheath. For [I shall tell you] everythi[ng] truthfully [ ]."
11. [ ]*wl*.' and then my mind was much changed within me. [ ]
12. But when Bitenosh, my wife, noticed that my expression had changed [ ],
13. then she suppressed her emotion, speaking to me and saying to me, " O my lord and [my brother, recall]
14. my pleasure. I swear to you by the Great Holy One, by the King of h[eaven]
15. that this seed is from you; from you is this conception, and from you the planting of [this] fruit [ ],
16. and not from any stranger, nor from any of the Watchers, nor from any of the sons of hea[ven. Why is the expression]
17. of your face so changed and deformed? (Why) is your spirit so depressed? [For I]
18. am speaking to you truthfully. (*vacat*) [ ]
19. Then I, Lamech, ran to Methuselah, my father, and [told] him everything [that he might go (and) ask Enoch],
20. his father, and learn everything from him with certainty, since he (Enoch) is a favorite and o[ne cherished ... and with the Holy Ones]

21 עדבה פליג ולה מחוין כולא   וכדי שמע מתושל[ח פתגמיא אלן]

22 [רט] לחנוך אבוהי למנדע מנה כולא בקושטא [ ]

23 רעותה ואזל לארך מת לפרוין ותמן אשכחה ל[חנוך אבוהי]

24 [ו]אמר לחנוך אבוהי יא אבי ויא מרי די אנה לך [אתית]

25 [ ] ל [ ] ואמר לך דאל תרגז עלי די להכא אתית ל[ך]

26 דחיל לעליך [ ]

col. 3

3 ארי ביומי ירד אבי [ ]

col. 5

3 אנה חנוך[ ]
4 [לא מן בני] שמין להן מן למך ב[רך]

9 וכען לכא̇ אנה אמר . . . ולך אנה מחוה [ ]
10 אזל אמר ללמך ברך [ ]
24 וכדי שמע מתושלח [פתגמיא אלן]
25 ועם למך ברה . . . מלל[ ]
26 וכדי אנה למך [ ]
27 די מני אנפק . . . [ ]

col. 6

2 וקושטא כול יומי דברת . . . .] [
6 [ ]אנה נוח גבר . . .] [

col. 7

1 [תשלט ב]ארעה וכול די עליהא בימיא . . . . [ ]

7 [ ]וחדית למלי מרה שמיא [ ]

21. is his lot apportioned; and they make everything known to him. When Methusela[h] heard [those things],
22. [he ran] to Enoch, his father, to learn from him the truth about everything [ ]
23. his good pleasure. And he went through the length of the land of Parvaim, and there he found [Enoch his father]
24. [And] he said to Enoch, his father, " O my father and my lord, to whom I [have come]
25. [ ]*l*[ ] and I say to you, 'Do not be angry with me, because I have come here to [you]
26. reverenced (?) by you ... [ ]

col. 3

3. for in the days of Jared, my father ...

col. 5

3. I, Enoch, [ ]
4. [not from the sons of] heaven, but from Lamech, [your] so[n ...]
9. and now I say to you ... and to you I make known [ ]
10. go, say to Lamech, your son [ ]
24. And when Methuselah heard [these things]
25. and he spoke ... to Lamech, his son [ ]
26. And when I, Lamech, [ ]
27. that he brought forth from me[ ]

col. 6

2. and (during) all my days I have practised the truth ... [ ]
6. [ ]I, Noah, a man ... [ ]

col. 7

1. [you shall rule over] the earth and all that (is) on it, over the seas... [ ]
7. [ ]and I rejoiced at the words of the Lord of heaven [ ]

col. 10

12 [ ]תבותא נחת חד מן טורי הארט . . . [ ]
13 לכול ארעא כולהא כפרת . . . [ ]
15 [ ]על מדבחא אקטרת . . . . [ ]

col. 11

17 כול דם לא תאכלון[ ]

col. 12

10 [ ]ארפכשד תרתין שנין בתר מבולא . . . כול בני שם כולהון [ ]

11 [ ]פוט וכנען [
13 שרית אנה ובני כולהון למפלח בארעא ונצבת כרם . . . בלובר טורא ולשנין ארבע
עבד לי חמר[ ]

15 ושרית למשתיה ביום חד לשתא חמישיתא[ ]
16 קרית לבני ולבני בני ולנ[שי כולוא ולבנתהון ואתכנשנא בחדא ואזלנה[ ]

17 [ ]למרה שמיא לאל עליון לקדישא רבא די פלטנא מן אבדנא[ ]

col. 16

11 [ ]כול ארע צפונא כולהא עד די דבק ל. . .[ ]
12 [עד] תחומא דן מי ימא רבא . . . . . .[ ]
16 [ ]טינה נהרא [ ]

col. 17

8 [ ]למערבא לאשור עד דבק לחדקל[ ]
9 לארם ארעא די. . . . עד די דבק לראיש[ ]
10 [ ]טור תורא דן ועבר חולקא דן למערבא עד דבק[ ]

11 [ ]ועל ראיש תלתת חולקיא . . . לארפכשד[ ]

16 [ ]לגמר יהב לקדמין בצפונא עד די דבק לטינה נהרא וכתרה ל[מג]וג . . .

col. 10

12. [ ]the ark settled (upon) one of the mountains of Ararat ... [ ]
13. I atoned for all the land ... [ ]
15. [ ]I burned incense on the altar ... [ ]

col. 11

17. [ ]you must eat no blood[ ]

col. 12

10. [and became the father of] Arpachshad two years after the flood, ... all the sons of Shem[ ]
11. [ ]Put and Canaan[ ]
13. I and all my sons began to cultivate the earth, and I planted a vineyard ... on Mount Lubar, and in the fourth year it produced wine for me[ ]
15. And I began to drink it on the first day of the fifth year[ ]
16. I invited my sons and the sons of my sons and the wives of all of us and their daughters, and we gathered together and went[ ]
17. [ ]to the Lord of heaven, to the Most High God, to the Great Holy One, who rescued us from destruction[ ]

col. 16

11. [ ]all the land of the north until it reached[ ]
12. [as far as] this boundary the waters of the Great Sea[ ]
16. [ ]the Tina River[ ]

col. 17

8. [ ]to the west, to Asshur, until it reached the Tigris[ ]
9. For Aram, the land which ... until it reached the head of [ ]
10. [ ]this Mount of the Ox and he crossed this portion toward the west, until it reached[ ]
11. [ ]and upon the head of the three portions ... for Arpachshad [ ]
16. [ ]to Gomer he gave the east in the north, until it reached the Tina River and its circuit; to [Mag]og ...

col. 19

7 [ובנית תמן מדבח]א [וקרית] תמ[ן בשם א]ל[הא] ואמרת אנתה הוא

8 ל[י א]ל [ע]ל[מא]לל[ ]ל[ ] למאלם [ ]ם עד כען לא דבקתה לטורא קדישא ונגדת

9 ל[ ] והוית אזל לדרומא [ ]א[ ]עד די דבקת לחברון ול[ה זמנא] אתב[נ]יאת חברון ויתבת

10 [תרתין שנ]ין [תמן] והוא כפנא בארעא דא כולא ושמעת די ע[בו]רא ה[וא] במצרין ונגדת

11 ל[מעל] לארע מצרין [ ]א די .ל[ ]והוא [דבק]ת לכרמונא נהרא חד מן

12 ראשי נהרא אמ[ ] עלא[ ]ל[ ] כען אנחנא [ ] ארענא [וח]לפת שבעת ראשי נהרא דן די

13 [ ]לל[ ]מ[ ]מל[ ]א[ ]א כען חלפנא ארענא ועלנא לארע בני חם לארע מצרין

14 וחלמת אנה אברם חלם בלילה מעלי לארע מצרין וחזית בחלמי [וה]א ארז חד ותמרא

15 חדא [יאי]א [שגיא]וב[ני] אנוש אתו ובעון למקץ ולמעקר ל[א]רזא ולמשבוק תמרתא בלחודיהה

16 ואכליאת תמרתא ואמרת אל תקוצו ל[א]רזא ארי תרינא מן שר[בא חד]א ושביק ארזא בטלל תמרתא

17 ולא [אתקץ] *(vacat)* ואתעירת בליליא מן שנתי ואמרת לשרי אנתתי חלם

18 חלמת [וא]דחל [מן] חלמא דן ואמרת לי אשתעי לי חלמך ואנדע ושרית לאשתעיא לה חלמא דן

19 [וחוית] ל[ה פשר] חלמא [דן] וא[מר]ת . . . . די יבעון למקטלני ולכי למשבק [ ]ום דא כול טבותא

20 [די תעבדין עמי] בכול [אתר] די [נהוה בה אמרי] עלי די אחי הוא ואחי בטליכי ותפלט נפשי בדיליכי

21 [יבעון] לאע[ד]יותכי מני ולמקטלני ובכת שרי על מלי בליליא דן

col. 19

7. [... and I built there an alta]r, [and I called on the name of G]o[d] ther[e ...], and I said, " You are indeed
8. to [me the eterna]l [Go]d[ ]*ll*[ ]*l*[ ]*lm'lm*[ ]*m*." Up till now I had not reached the holy mountain ; so I set out
9. for [ ] and I kept going *southward* [ ] until I reached Hebron. At [that time] Hebron was bu[i]lt, and I dwelt
10. [for two ye]ars [there]. *Now there was a famine in* all this *land* ; but *I heard that* [*there was*] *gr*[*ai*]*n in Egypt.* So I set out
11. to [enter] the land of Egypt [ ]' which .*l* [ ] *whw*' ; I ar[rived] at the Carmon River, one of the
12. heads of the River. '*m*[ ]. Now we [ ]our land (?), and I [cro]ssed the seven heads of this river, which
13. [ ]*ll*[ ]*m*[ ]*ml*[ ]'[ ]' Now we crossed (the border of) our land and entered the land of the sons of Ham, the land of Egypt.
14. And I, Abram, had a dream in the night of my entering the land of Egypt and I saw in my dream [that there wa]s a cedar, and a date-palm (which was)
15. [very beautif]ul ; and some men came, intending to cut down and uproot the cedar, but to leave the date-palm by itself.
16. Now the date-palm remonstrated and said, " Do not cut down the cedar, for we are both from [on]e fam[ily]." So the cedar was spared with the help of the date-palm,
17. and [it was] not [cut down]. (*vacat*) (That) night I awoke from my sleep and said to Sarai my wife, " I have had a dream,
18. [and I] am frightened [by] this dream." She said to me, " Tell me your dream that I may know (it too)." So I began to tell her this dream ;
19. [and I made known] to [her the meaning of this] dream, [and] s[aid], " [ ] who will seek to *kill me* *and to spare you.* [No]w this (is) all the favor
20. [that you must do for me] ; whe[rev]er [we shall be, *say*] about me, ' He is my brother.' Then I shall live with your help, *and my life will be saved because of you.*
21. [they will seek] to [ta]ke you away from me and to kill me." And Sarai wept at my words that night.

22 [ ]ל . ל[ ] . ופרעו צ[ען ו]ל[א עוד . . . .] שרי
למפנה לצען

23 [עמי ארי דחלת י]תירא בנפשה די לא יחזנה כול [בר אנוש]ולבתר
חמש שניא אלן

24 [אתון] תלתת גברין מן רברבי מצרי[ן] די פרע[ו] צע[ן]
על מל[י] ועל אנתתי והווא יהבין

25 [לי מתנן שגיאן ושא]לו ל[י] טבתא וחכמתא וקושטא וקרית קודמיהון
ל[כתב] מלי חנוך

26 [ ] בכפנא די א[ ]תה ולא [ ] ואתון למקם עד די[
]צ להה[ ]מלי

27 [ ]ל [ ] במאכל שגי ובמשתה
[שגי] ל[ ]חמרא

col. 20

1 [ ]א[ ]

2 [ ]ל[ ] כמה נצ[י]ח ושפיר
לה צלם אנפיהא וכמא

3 [ו]כ[מא] רקיק לה שער ראישה כמא יאין להין לה עיניהא ומא
רגג הוא לה אנפהא וכול נץ

4 אנפיהא [ ] כמא יאא לה חדיה וכמא שפיר לה כול לבנהא דרעיהא
מא שפירן וידיהא כמא

5 כלילן ו[חמיד] כול מחזה ידיהא כמא יאין כפיה ומא אריכן וקטינן כול
אצבעת ידיהא רגליהא

6 כמא שפירן וכמא שלמא להן לה שקיהא וכל בתולן וכלאן די יעלן לגנון
לא ישפרן מנהא ועל כול

7 נשין שופר שפרה ועליא שפרהא לעלא מן כולהן ועם כול שפרא דן חכמא
שגיא עמהא ודלידיהא

8 יאא וכדי שמע מלכא מלי חרקנוש ומלי תרין חברוהי די פם חד תלתהון
ממללין שגי רחמה ושלח

9 לעובע דברהא וחזהא ואתמה על כול שפרהא ונסבהא לה לאנתא ובעא
למקטלני ואמרת שרי

22. [ ]*l*.*l*[ ]. and Pharaoh Zo[an ... so that] Sarai [no longer wished] to go toward Zoan
23. [with me, for she feared very m]uch within her, lest any[one] should see her [ ]. And after those five years
24. three men of the *nobles* of Egyp[t came] of *the Phara*[*oh*] Zoa[n] concerning [my] words and my wife. They gave
25. [me many gifts and as]ked of [me] kindness, wisdom, and truth. And I read before them the [book] of the words of [En]och (?)
26. [ ] about the famine which '[ ]*th* and not [ ] and they came to the place (?) in order to [ ]*ṣ* to her [ ] the words of
27. [ ]*l*[ ] with much eating and [much] drinking *l*[ ] the wine

col. 20

1. [ ]'[ ]
2. [ ] how splen[did] and beautiful the form of her face, and how
3. [ ] and how soft the hair of her head; how lovely are her eyes and how pleasant is her nose and all the radiance
4. of her face [ ]; how lovely is her breast and how beautiful is all her whiteness! Her arms, how beautiful! And her hands, how
5. perfect! And (how) [attrac]tive all the appearance of her hands! How lovely (are) her palms, and how long and dainty all the fingers of her hands. Her feet,
6. how beautiful! How perfect are her legs! There are no virgins or brides who enter a bridal chamber more beautiful than she. Indeed, her beauty
7. surpasses that of all women; her beauty is high above all of them. Yet with all this beauty there is much wisdom in her; and whatever she has
8. is lovely." When the king heard the words of Hirqanos and the words of his two companions — for the three of them spoke as one person — he coveted her very much. He sent off
9. in haste (and) had her brought (to him). When he beheld her, he marvelled at all her beauty and took her to himself as a wife. He sought to kill me, but Sarai said

10 למלכא דאחי הוא כדי הוית מתגר על דילהא ושביקת אנה אברם בדילהא ולא קטילת ובכית אנה

11 אברם בכי תקיף אנה ולוט בר אחי עמי בליליא כדי דבירת מני שרי באונס *(vacat)*

12 בליליא דן צלית ובעית ואתחננת ואמרת באתעצבא ודמעי נחתן בריך אנתה אל עליון מרי לכול

13 עלמים די אנתה מרה ושליט על כולא ובכול מלכי ארעא אנתה שליט למעבד בכולהון דין וכען

14 קבלתך מרי על פרעו צען מלך מצרין די דברת אנתתי מני בתוקף עבד לי דין מנה ואחזי ידך רבתא

15 בה ובכול ביתה ואל ישלט בליליא דן לטמיא אנתתי מני וינדעוך מרי די אנתה מרה לכול מלכי

16 ארעא ובכית וחשית בליליא דן שלח לה אל עליון רוח מכדש למכתשה ולכול אנש ביתה רוח

17 באישא והואת כתשא לה ולכול אנש ביתה ולא יכל למקרב בהא ואף לא ידעהא והוא עמה

18 תר֯תין שנין ולסוף תרתין שנין תקפו וגברו עלוהי מכתשיא ונגדיא ועל כול אנש ביתה ושלח

19 קרא לכול [חכימי] מצרין ולכול אשפיא עם כול אסי מצרין הן יכולון לאסיותה מן מכתשא דן ולאנש

20 ביתה ולא יכלו כול אסיא ואשפיא וכול חכימיא למקם לאסיותה ארי הוא רוחא כתש לכולהון

21 וערקו *(vacat)* באדין אתה עלי חרקנוש ובעא מני די אתה ואצלה על

22 מלכא ואסמוך ידי עלוהי ויחה ארי בחלם [חזני] ואמר לה לוט לא יכול אברם דדי לצליא על

23 מלכא ושרי אנתתה עמה וכען אזל אמר למלכא וישלח אנתתה מנה לבעלהא ויצלה עלוהי ויחה

10. to the king, "He is my brother," so that I might be benefited by her. And *I, Abram,* was spared *because of her*; I was not killed. But I wept
11. bitterly — I, Abram, and Lot, my nephew, with me — on the night when Sarai was led away from me by force. (*vacat*)
12. That night I prayed, I entreated, and I asked for mercy; in (my) sorrow I said, as my tears ran down (my cheeks), "Blessed (are) you, O God Most High, my Lord, for all
13. ages! For you are Lord, and Master over all, and have power to mete out justice to all the kings of the earth. Now
14. I lodge my complaint with you, my Lord, against the Pharaoh Zoan, the king of Egypt, because my wife has been led away from me by force. Mete out justice to him for me and show forth your great hand
15. against him and against all his house. May he not be able to defile my wife tonight — that it may be known about you, my Lord, that you are the Lord of all the kings of
16. the earth." And I wept and talked to no one. (But) that night God Most High sent him a pestilential spirit *to afflict him* and all the men of *his household,* an evil spirit
17. that kept afflicting him and all the men of his household. He was not able to approach her, nor did he have intercourse with her, though he was with her
18. for two years. At the end of two years the plagues and afflictions became more severe and more intense for him and all the men of his household. So he sent
19. for all the [wise men] of Egypt, all the magicians, and all the physicians of Egypt, (to see) if they could cure him of this plague, and the men
20. of his household. But none of the physicians, the magicians, nor any of the wise men were able to rise up (and) cure him, for the spirit afflicted all of them (too),
21. and they fled. (*vacat*) Then Hirqanos came to me and begged me to come and pray over
22. the king and lay my hands upon him that he might be cured, for [he had seen me] in a dream. But Lot said to him, "Abram, my uncle, cannot pray for
23. the king, while Sarai his wife is with him. Now go, tell the king that he should send his wife away from him, (back) to her own husband. Then he (Abram) will pray for him that he might be cured."

24 *(vacat)* וכדי שמע חרקנוש מלי לוט אזל אמר למלכא כול מכתשיא ונגדיא

25 אלן די מתכתש ומתנגד מרי מלכא בדיל שרי אנתת אברם יתיבו נה לשרי לאברם בעלה

26 ויתוך מנכה מכתשא דן ורוח שחלניא וקרא לי אלו‹הי› ואמר לי מא עבדתה לי בדיל [שר]י ותאמר

27 לי די אחתי היא והיא הואת אנתתך ונסבתהא לי לאנתה הא אנתתך דברה אזל ועדי לך מן

28 כול מדינת מצרין וכען צלי עלי ועל ביתי ותתגער מננה רוחא דא באישתא וצלית על [מר]דפא

29 הו וסמכת ידי על [ראי]שה ואתפלי מנה מכתשא ואתגערת [מנה רוחא] באישתא וחי וקם [או]דע

30 לי מלכא ב . [ ] . אמנת . עות . וימא לי מלכא במומה די לא [ ]הא ו[ ] והא [דברו] ל[י]

31 לש[ר]י ויהב לה מלכא [כסף וד]הב [ש]גיא ולבוש שגי די בוץ וארגואן [ושם אנון]

32 קודמיהא ואף להגר וא[ש]למה לי ומני עמי אנוש די ינפק[וני מן מצרין]

33 ואזלת אנה אברם בנכסין שגיאין לחדא ואף בכסף ודהב וסלקת מן [מצרי]ן [ולוט]

34 בר אחי עמי ואף לוט קנה לה נכסין שגיאין ונסב לה אנתה מן בנת [מצרין] וה[וי]ת ש[רא עמה]

col. 21

1 [ב]כל אתר משריאתי עד די דבקת לבית אל לאתרא די בנית תמן בה מדבחא ובניתה תניאני

2 [ו]אקרבת עלוהי עלואן ומנחה לאל עליון וקרית תמן בשם מרה עלמיא והללת לשם אלהא וברכת

24. *(vacat)* When Hirqanos heard Lot's words, he went (and) said to the king, " All these plagues and afflictions
25. with which my lord, the king, is beset and afflicted (are) because of Sarai, the wife of Abram. Let Sarai be returned to her husband, Abram,
26. and this plague will depart from you, as well as the spirit of purulence." So he (the Pharaoh) *summoned* me to him and *said* to me, " *What have you done to me* for [Sar]ai's sake, in *telling*
27. *me*, ' *She is my sister*,' when *she was* (*really*) *your wife* ? *And I took her to be my wife. Here is your wife*; lead her away; *go*, depart from
28. all the provinces of Egypt. But now pray for me and for my household that this evil spirit may be commanded (to depart) from us." So I prayed for that [perse]cutor
29. and I laid my hands upon his [he]ad. The plague was removed from him, and the evil [spirit] was commanded (to depart) [from him], and he was cured. And the king rose (and) [made] known
30. to me *b*.[ ]. .*'mnt* .*'wt*. ; and the king swore an oath to me that [he had] not [touched] her (?) *w*[ ]. And then [they brought]
31. Sa[r]ai to [me]. The king gave her [mu]ch [silver and go]ld, many garments of fine linen and purple [and he laid them]
32. before her, and Hagar too. H[e hand]ed her over to me, and appointed men to escort [me out of Egypt].
33. So I, *Abram*, went (forth) *with very many flocks* and *with silver and gold* too, and I *went up from* [*Egy*]*pt*. [Lot],
34. my brother's son, (was) *with* me, and *Lot too* (had) acquired many flocks; he had taken for himself a wife from the daughters [of Egypt]. And I [cam]ped [with him]

col. 21

1. at every place of my (former) encampments, *until* I reached *Bethel, the place where I* (*had*) *built the altar*, and I built it again.
2. I offered upon it holocausts and an offering to God Most High, *and there* I *called upon the name of the Lord* of the ages, and I praised the name of God, and I blessed

3 [א]להא ואודית תמן קודם אלהא על כול נכסיא וטבתא די יהב לי ודי עבד עמי טב ודי אתיבני

4 לארעא דא בשלם *(vacat)*

5 בתר יומא דן פרש לוט מן לואתי מן עובד רעותנא ואזל ויתב לה בבקעת ירדנא וכול נכסוהי

6 עמה ואף אנה אוספת לה על דילה שגי והוא רעה נכסוהי ודבק עד סודום וזבן לה בסודם בי

7 ויתב בה ואנה הוית יתב בטורא די בית אל ובאש עלי די פרש לוט בר אחי מן לואתי

8 ואתחזי לי אלהא בחזוא די ליליא ואמר לי סלק לך לרמת *(vacat)* חצור די על שמאל

9 ביתאל אתר די אנתה יתב ושקול עיניך וחזי למדנחא ולמערבא ולדרומא ולצפונא וחזי כול

10 ארעא דא די אנה יהב לך ולזרעך לכול עלמים וסלקת למחרתי כן לרמת חצור וחזית ארעא מן

11 רמתא דא מן נהר מצרין עד לבנן ושניר ומן ימא רבא עד חורן וכול ארע גבל עד קדש וכול מדברא

12 רבא די מדנח חורן ושניר עד פורת ואמר לי לזרעך אנתן כול ארעא דא וירתונה לכול עלמים

13 ואשגה זרעך כעפר ארעא די לא ישכח כול בר אנוש לממניה ואף זרעך לא יתמנה קום הלך ואזל

14 וחזי כמן ארכהא וכמן פתיהא ארי לך ולזרעך אנתננה אחריך עד כול עלמיא *(vacat)*

15 ואזלת אנה אברם למסחר ולמחזה ארעא ושרית למסחר מן גיחון נהרא ואתית ליד ימא עד די

16 דבקת לטור תורא וסחרת מן ל[יד] ימא רבא דן די מלחא ואזלת ליד טור תורא למדנחא לפותי ארעא

3. [G]od. I gave thanks there before God for all the flocks and the good things which he had given me, because he had done good to me, because he had brought me back
4. to this land in safety. (*vacat*)
5. After this day Lot parted from me because of the conduct of our shepherds, and he went and *settled* in the valley of the Jordan; (he took) all his flocks
6. with him, and I too added greatly to what he had. He pastured his flocks and came (eventually) *to Sodom.* He bought himself a house in Sodom
7. and dwelt in it. But I was dwelling (then) on the mountain of Bethel, and it grieved me that Lot, the son of my brother, had parted from me.
8. (*vacat*) God appeared to me in a vision of the night and *said to me,* " Go up to Ramath-Hazor, which is to the north of
9. Bethel, *the place where you are* dwelling; *lift up your eyes and look to the east, west, south, and north,* and see *all*
10. this *land which I am giving to you and to your descendants forever.*" The next day I climbed up to Ramath-Hazor and I looked at the land from
11. this height, from the River of Egypt to Lebanon and Senir, and from the Great Sea to Hauran, and all the land of Gebal as far as Kadesh, and at all the Great Desert
12. which is (to the) east of Hauran and Senir as far as the Euphrates. And he said to me, " To your descendants I shall give all this land; they will inherit it forever.
13. *I shall make your descendants* as numerous *as the dust of the earth which no man can number; so too your descendants will be without number. Rise, walk about,* and go (around)
14. to see how great is *its length* and how great is *its width. For I shall give it to you* and to your descendants after you for all ages." (*vacat*)
15. So I, Abram, set out to go around and look at the land. I started going about from the Gihon River, moving along the Sea, until
16. I reached the Mount of the Ox. I journeyed from [the coast] of this Great Salt Sea and moved along the Mount of the Ox toward the east through the breadth of the land,

17 עד די דבקת לפורת נהרא וסחרת ליד פורת עד די דבקת לימא שמוקא למדנחא והוית אתה לי ליד

18 ימא שמוקא עד די דבקת ללשן ים סוף די נפק מן ימא שמוקא וסחרת לדרומא עד די דבקת גחון

19 נהרא ותבת ואתית לי לביתי בשלם ואשכחת כול אנשי שלם ואזלת ויתבת באלוני ממרה די בחברון

20 כלמדנח צפון חברון ובנית תמן מדבח ואסקת עלוהי עלא ומנחא לאל עליון ואכלת ואשתית תמן

21 אנה וכול אנש ביתי ושלחת קרית לממרה ולערנם ולאשכול תלתת אחיא אמוראא רחמי ואכלו כחדא

22 עמי ואשתיו עמי *(vacat)*

23 קדמת יומיא אלן אתה כדרלעומר מלך עילם אמרפל מלך בבל אריוך מלך כפתוך תדעל מלך גוים די

24 הוא בין נהרין ועבדו קרב עם ברע מלך סודם ועם ברשע מלך עומרם ועם שנאב מלך אדמא

25 ועם שמיאבד מלך צבוין ועם מלך בלע כול אלן אזדמנו כחדא לקרב לעמקא די סדיא ותקף מלך

26 עילם ומלכיא די עמה למלך סודם ולכול חברוהי ושויו עליהון מדא תרתי עשרה שנין הווא

27 יהבין מדתהון למלך עילם ובשנת תלת עשרה מרדו בה ובשנת ארבע עשרה דבר מלך עילם לכול

28 חברוהי וסלקו ארחא די מדברא והווא מחין ובזין מן פורת נהרא ומחו לרפאיא די בעשתרא

29 דקרנין ולזומזמיא די בעמן ולאימיא [די ב]שוה הקריות ולחוריא די בטורי גבל עד דבקו לאיל

30 פרן די במדברא ותבו ומחו ל[ ] בחצצן תמר *(vacat?)*

17. until I reached the Euphrates River. I travelled along the Euphrates, until I came to the Red Sea in the east. (Then) I moved along
18. the Red Sea, until I reached the tongue of the Reed Sea, which goes forth from the Red Sea. (From there) I journeyed to the south, until I reached the Gihon
19. River. Then I returned, came home safely, and found all my men safe and sound. I *went and dwelt at the Oaks of Mamre, which are in Hebron,*
20. to the northeast of Hebron. *There I built an altar* and offered on it a holocaust and a offering to God Most High. I ate and drank there,
21. I and all the men of my household. And I sent an invitation to *Mamre*, Arnem and *Eshcol*, the three Amorite brothers, (who were) my friends; and they ate together
22. with me and drank with me. *(vacat)*
23. Before those days there came *Chedorlaomer, the king of Elam, Amraphel, the king of* Babylon, *Arioch, the king of* Cappadocia, (and) *Tidal, the king of Goiim* which
24. is between the two rivers; *and they made war on Bera, the king of Sodom, on Birsha, the king of Gomorrah, on Shinab, the king of Admah,*
25. on *Shemiabad, the king of Zeboiim, and* on *the king of Bela. All of these joined* together to (fight) a battle in *the valley of Siddim.* But the king of Elam
26. and the kings who were with him prevailed over the king of Sodom and all his allies. They imposed tribute on them. *For twelve years* they kept paying
27. their tribute to the king of Elam, but in *the thirteenth year they rebelled* against him. *And in the fourteenth year* the king of Elam led (forth) all
28. his allies; they came up (by way of) the desert route, and they set about destroying and plundering from the Euphrates River (onward). *They destroyed the Rephaim who (were) in Ashteroth-*
29. *Karnaim*, the Zumzammim who (were) in Ammon, *the Emim* [who were *in*] *Shaveh*-Hakerioth, *and the Hurrians* who (were) *in the mountains* of Gebal, *until* they reached *El-*
30. *Paran which is in the desert. Then they returned and struck* the [Amorites who dwelt (?)] *in Hazezon-Tamar. (vacat ?)*

31 ונפק מלך סודם לעורעהון ומלך [עומרם ומ]לך אדמא ומלך צבואין
ומלך בלע ו[ע]בד[ו] קרבא

32 בעמקא ד[י סדיא] לקובלי כדרלע[ומר מלך עילם ומלכיא] די עמה ואתבר
מלך סודום וערק ומלך עומרם

33 נפל בעגיאין [די חימרא] ובז מלך עילם
כול נכסיא די סודם ודי

34 [עומרם]ש[ ] ושבו
לוט בר אחוי

col. 22

1 די אברם די הוא יתב בסודם כחדא עמהון וכול נכסוהי ואתה חד מן רעה

2 ענה די יהב אברם ללוט די פלט מן שביא על אברם ואברם באדין הוא

3 יתב בחברון וחויה די שבי לוט בר אחוהי וכול נכסוהי ולא קטיל ודי

4 נגדו מלכיא ארחא ‹די› חלתא רבתא למדיתון ושבין ובזין ומחין וקטלין
ואזלין

5 למדינת דרמשק ובכא אברם על לוט בר אחוהי ואתחלם אברם וקם

6 ובחר מן עבדוהי גברין בחירין לקרב תלת מאא ותמניאת עשר וערנם

7 ואשכול וממרה נגדו עמה והוא רדף בתרהון עד דבק לדן ואשכח אנון

8 שרין בבקעת דן ורמה עליהון בליליא מן ארבע רוחיהון והווא קטל

9 בהון בליליא ותבר אנון והוא רדף להון וכולהון הווא ערקין מן קודמוהי

10 עד דבקו לחלבון די שימא על שמאל דרמשק ואצל מנהון כול די שבוא

11 וכול די בזו וכול טבתהון ואף ללוט בר אחוהי פצא וכול נכסוהי וכול

12 שביתא די שבאו אתיב ושמע מלך סודם די אתיב אברם כול שביתא

31. *The king of Sodom went out* to face them, *and* (likewise) *the king of* [*Gomorrah*], *the king of Admah, the king of Zeboiim, and the king of Bela*; [and they f]ough[t] the *battle*
32. *in the valley of* [*Siddim*] against *Chedorla*[*omer, the king of Elam,* and the kings] who (were) with him. But *the king of Sodom* was routed, and he fled; *the king of Gomorrah*
33. *fell into pits* [of bitumen]; and the king of Elam plundered *all the wealth of Sodom and of*
34. [*Gomorrah.*]*š*[ ] *and they carried off Lot, the son of Abram's brother,*

col. 22

1. *who was dwelling in Sodom,* together with them — *and* all *his flocks.* But one of the herdsmen of the flock
2. which Abram had given to Lot, who *escaped* from the captives, *came to Abram.* At that time Abram *was*
3. *dwelling* in Hebron; and *he informed* him that Lot, his nephew, *had been carried off* with all his flocks, but (that) he was not killed, and that
4. the kings had set out (by way of) the route <of> the Great Valley toward their province, taking captives, plundering, destroying, killing, and making
5. their way toward the province of Damascus. Abram wept for Lot, his nephew; then he summoned up his courage, rose up,
6. and chose from his servants the best men for war, *three hundred and eighteen* (of them); and Arnem,
7. Eshcol, and Mamre set out with him. *He went in pursuit* of them *until* he reached *Dan* and found them
8. encamped in the valley of Dan. He fell *upon them by night* from all four sides. He slaughtered
9. some of them (that) night, routed them, and *pursued them,* as all of them went fleeing before him,
10. *as far as* Helbon *which is* situated *to the north of Damascus.* So he rescued from them all that they had captured
11. and all that they had plundered — and all their own goods. *Lot too,* his nephew, *he saved with all his flocks*; *and* all
12. the captives which they had taken *he brought back. The king of Sodom* heard that Abram had brought back all the captives

13 וכול בזתא וסלק לעורעה ואתה לשלם היא ירושלם ואברם שרא בעמק

14 שוא והוא עמק מלכא בקעת בית כרמא ומלכיצדק מלכא דשלם אנפק

15 מאכל ומשתה לאברם ולכול אנשא די עמה והוא הוא כהן לאל עליון וברך

16 לאברם ואמר בריך אברם לאל עליון מרה שמיא וארעא ובריך אל עליון

17 די סגר שנאיך בידך ויהב לה מעשר מן כול נכסיא די מלך עילם וחברוהי

18 *(vacat)* באדין קרב מלכא די סודם ואמר לאברם מרי אברם

19 הב לי נפשא די איתי לי די שביא עמך די אצלתה מן מלך עילם ונכסיא

20 כולהון שביקין לך *(vacat)* אדין אמר אברם למלך סודם מרים אנה

21 ידי יומא דן לאל עליון מרה שמיא וארעא אן מן חוט עד ערקא דמסאן

22 אן אסב מן כול די איתי לך דלמא תהוה אמר דמן נכסי כול עתרה די

23 אברם ברא מן די אכלו כבר עולימי די עמי וברא מן חולק תלתת גבריא די

24 אזלו עמי אנון שליטין בחולקהון למנתן לך ואתיב אברם כול נכסיא וכול

25 שביתא ויהב למלך סודם וכול שביא די הואת עמה מן ארעא דא שבק

26 ושלח כולהון *(vacat)*

27 בתר פתגמיא אלן אתחזי̇ אלהא לאברם בחזוא ואמר לה הא עשר שנין

28 שלמא מן יום די נפקתה מן חרן תרתין עבדתה תנה ושבע במצרין וחדא

29 מן די תבת מן מצרין וכען בקר ומני כול די איתי לך וחזי כמן כפלין שגיו מן

30 כול די נפקו עמך ביום מפקך מן חרן וכען אל תדחל אנה עמך ואהוה לך

13. and all the booty, and *he went* up *to meet him.* He came to Salem, that is, Jerusalem, while Abram was camped in the *Valley of*
14. *Shaveh — this is the Vale of the King,* the Valley of Beth-haccherem. *Melchizedek, the king of Salem, brought out*
15. *food and drink* for Abram and for all the men who were with him ; *he was a priest of the Most High God and he blessed*
16. Abram *and said,* " *Blessed be Abram by the Most High God, the Lord of heaven and earth. Blessed be the Most High God*
17. *who has delivered your enemies into your hand.*" *And he gave him a tithe of all* the flocks of the king of Elam and his confederates.
18. (*vacat*) Then *the king of Sodom* approached *Abram* and *said,* " My Lord Abram,
19. *give me the men* that are mine who are captives with you and whom you have rescued from the king of Elam ;
20. all *the goods* (are) left *for you.*" (*vacat*) *Abram* then *said to the king of Sodom,* " *I raise*
21. *my hand* (in oath) this day *to the Most High God, the Lord of heaven and earth, that I shall not take so much as a thread or a sandalstrap*
22. *from anything that is yours, lest you say,* ' From my possessions (comes) all of *Abram*'s wealth ' —
23. *except for what* my *young men* who are with me *have* already *eaten, and* except for *the portion of the* three *men who*
24. *went with me* ; they are masters over *their portion,* to give it to you (or not)." Then Abram returned all the goods and all
25. the captives and gave (them) to the king of Sodom. All the captives who were with him from this land he set free
26. and sent them all away. (*vacat*)
27. *After these things God* appeared *to Abram in a vision* and said to him, " Look, ten years
28. have elapsed since the day you departed from Haran ; you passed two (years) here, seven in Egypt, and one
29. since you returned from Egypt. Now examine and count all that you have ; see how they have doubled and multiplied
30. beyond all that went forth with you on the day when you set out from Haran. Now *do not fear* ; *I* am with you ; and I shall be to you

31 סעד ותקף ואנה מגן עליך ואספרך לך לתקיף ברא מנך עתרך ונכסיך

32 ישגון לחדא (*vacat*) ואמר אברם מרי אלהא שגי לי עתר ונכסין ולמא לי

33 כול [א]לן ואנה כדי אמות ערטלי אהך די לא בנין וחד מן בני ביתי ירתנני

34 אליעזר בר [ביתי]לד ירתנ‹נ›י ואמר לה לא ירתנך דן להן די יפוק

30. 4Q Testuz (Unidentified Fragment) — 4QTestuz ar

1 זרעך וישתארון כל צדיקיא וישי[וכל]

2 עול וכל שקר לא עוד ישתכח [ ]

3 וכען סב לוחיא יקריא כי לא [ ]

4 [כ]ל עקתי וכל די יתאעל [ ]

5 [ ] לוחא מן . [ ]

31. 1Q Unidentified Fragments — 1Q*24*

frg. 1

1 [ ]ן ורוח[ ]

2 [ ] . שין ובחשין וה . [ ]

3 [ ]ל . . יא ולנהן [ ]

4 [ ]תיא ולחבריא ו[ל]

5 [ ]א ולכול[ ]

6 [ ] . פיא ולמכן[ ]

7 [ ]א ולברקיא [ ]

8 [ ]ל . [ ] . [ ]

frg. 2

1 [ ] . [ ]

2 [ ]על אר[עא]

3 [ ]ל[ ]

31. both support and strength. I (shall be) *a shield over you* and and a buckler for you against one stronger than you. *Your wealth* and your flocks
32. will *increase very much.*" (*vacat*) *And Abram said,* "*My Lord God,* my wealth and (my) flocks are vast (indeed); but why do I have
33. all [th]ese things, seeing that when I die I shall *depart* (from this life) *barren* (and) without sons? Even one of *my household servants is to inherit me,*
34. *Eliezer, a son* [born in the house]*ld* shall inherit me." But he said *to him,* "*This one shall not inherit you, but* rather *one who shall go forth*

30.

1. your seed, and all the righteous will be left and they will *yšy*[and no]
2. perversion and no deceit will any longer be found [ ]
3. And now, take the precious tablets, for not [ ]
4. [al]l my troubles. And everyone who will be introduced [ ]
5. [ ] the tablet from .[

31.

frg. 1

1. [ ]*n* and wind[ ]
2. [ ]*šyn* and hot ashes and *h*.[ ]
3. [ ]*l* . . *y*' and *lnhn*[ ]
4. [ ]*ty*' and for the dark fogs and [*l*]
5. [ ]' And for all [ ]
6. [ ].*py*' and *lmk*[ ]
7. [ ]' and for the lightnings [ ]
8. [ ]*l* .[ ].[ ]

frg. 2

1. [ ].[ ]
2. [ ]upon [the] ear[th]
3. [ ]*l*[ ]

frg. 3

[ ] תא[ ] 1
[ו]לכול חש[וכא] 2

frg. 4

[ ] לכול] מיא ה . [ ] 1

frg. 5

[ ] . [ ] 1
[ ] רוש ויצ . [ ] 2
[ ] . ריהון ולכול[ ] 3
[ ] . ולמטרא ולטל[א] 4
[ו]ל[כו]ל [ ] 5

frg. 6

[ ] לכול . [ ] 1
[כו]ל . גי פו[ ] 2

frg. 7

[ ] . יום לקץ [ ] 1
[ ]כולא גמירת[ ] 2
[ע]ליהון די[ ] 3

frg. 8

[ ] ׳ ן [ ] 1
[ ]לא שלם לכון [ ] 2

32. 1Q Unidentified Fragments — 1Q*63-68*

(a) 1Q*63*

[ ] . . [ ] 1
[ ] בדגליהון [ ] 2
[ ]ין [ ] 3
[ ] . . ואמר [ ] 4

(b) 1Q*64*

[ ] . . . . [ ] 1

frg. 3

1. [ ]*t'* [ ]
2. [and] for all the dark[ness]

frg. 4

1. [for all] the water *h*.[ ]

frg. 5

1. [ ].[ ]
2. [ ]*rwš wyṣ*.[ ]
3. [ ].*ryhwn* and for all[ ]
4. [ ] and for the rain and the de[w]
5. [and] for a[l]l [ ]

frg. 6

1. [ ]for all[ ]
2. [al]l .*gy pw*[ ]

frg. 7

1. [ ] day for the end-time of [ ]
2. [ ] all (of it) a decision of[ ]
3. [up]on them who[ ]

frg. 8

1. [ ].*n* [ ]
2. [ ] he did not recompense you[ ]

32.

(a)

1. [ ]..[ ]
2. [ ] in their detachments [ ]
3. [ ]*yn* [ ]
4. [ ]. and he said [ ]

(b)

1. [ ]....[ ]

2]]. בתמרירותא [[
3]]מני אל . . [[

(c) 1Q*65*

1]]בדקו ועלו [[
2]]מין זקפין . [[
3] י]שראל [[

(d) 1Q*66* 1

1]] . . [[
2]] זבדתון [[
3]] למפלח [[

(e) 1Q*66* 2

1]]מלף וא[[
2]]ל[[

(f) 1Q*67* 1

1]] מחאך
2]] בריחוהי
3]]ל

(g) 1Q*67* 5

1]]ר . [[
2]] תליתי [[
3]]ו אנון [[

(h) 1Q*68* 1

1]] . ש שיצ[י [
2]] . תן לה נפש[[
3]]ל . [[

(i) 1Q*68* 3

1]] להון ולחם וק . [[
2]] . תע[[

2. [ ]. in the bitterness[ ]
3. [ ] from me *'l*..[ ]

(c)

1. [ ]they broke through and entered[ ]
2. [ ]*myn* erecting[ ]
3. [I]srael [ ]

(d)

1. [ ]. .[ ]
2. [ ]you presented (as a gift)[ ]
3. [ ] to cultivate [ ]

(e)

1. [ ]a teacher and '[ ]
2. [ ]*l*[

(f)

1. [ ]to laugh
2. [ ] by its smell
3. [ ]*l*

(g)

1. [ ]*r* .[ ]
2. [ ] third [ ]
3. [ ]*w* they are[ ]

(h)

1. [ ].*š* complet[ed]
2. [ ].*tn* to him *npš*[ ]
3. [ ]*l* .[ ]

(i)

1. [ ]*lhwn* and bread and *q*.[ ]
2. [ ].*tʿ*[ ]

(j) 1Q*68* 15

1]]למפל[[
2]]. ל[[

33. 3Q Unidentified Fragments — 3Q*12*, 3Q*14*

3Q*12*, *frg. 1*

1 ל .[ ]יום] [
2 בת ולמחרת] [
3 שמיא וארע[א [

3Q*14*, *frg. 4*

1 בש[[
2 רע .] [
3 דר] [
4 לעדני[א [
5 בכול[[
6 בכול י .[[

3Q*14*, *frg. 5*

1]]מחזורית[א [
2]]. רו ·]ל[מעל] [
3]]אתון על .]]ה[[
4]]לת .] [

3Q*14*, *frg. 6*

1]] סתרין] [
2]]תרין א .] [
3]] (*vacat*)] [

3Q*14*, *frg. 7*

1]] וחנוך[[
2]]חמשין[[
3]]. [[

3Q*14*, *frg. 8*

1 ..] [
2 די סדום ו[[

(j)

1. [ ]to fall[ ]
2. [ ].*l*[ ]

33.

frg. 1

1. *l*.[ ] day[ ]
2. he spent the night, and on the morrow[ ]
3. the heavens and [the] earth[ ]

frg. 4

1. *bš*[ ]
2. *r*ʿ.[ ]
3. *dr*[ ]
4. for [the] seasons[ ]
5. in all[ ]
6. in all *y*.[ ]

frg. 5

1. [the] return[ ]
2. [ ].*rw*.[to] enter [ ]
3. [ ]they came to .[ ]*h*[ ]
4. [ ]*lt* .[ ]

frg. 6

1. [ ] tearing down [ ]
2. [ ] two ʾ.[ ]
3. [ ] (*vacat*) [ ]

frg. 7

1. [ ]and Enoch[ ]
2. [ ]fifty[ ]
3. [ ].[ ]

frg. 8

1. ..[ ]
2. of Sodom and [ ]

34. 5Q Unidentified Fragments — 5Q*24*

1]].[ ] [
2]]. בא ת.[[
3]]עליכון [[

35. 6Q Unidentified Fragments — 6Q*14*, 6Q*19*, 6Q*23*, 6Q*26*, 6Q*31*

(a) 6Q*14*, *frg. 1*

1]]בלל.[[
2]]מן די.[[
3]]פה לגב[ה] כפיל[[
4]]יא יפוק מן א.[[
5]]ה יבדה ע[ל [
6]] כול חות ב[רא [
7]]עמין מן.[[
8]]יא[[

(b) 6Q*14*, *frg. 2*

1]]עק יקום [[
2]] עד די כ[[
3] א]בל ובכי [[
4]]... בלא כ[[

(c) 6Q*19*

] ארעא[
1 די בני חם [[
2] ע]ממיא [[
3]]א ח.[[

(d) 6Q*23*, *frg. 1*

1 עלמא [[
2 ואחר [[
3 רוח [[

(e) 6Q*23*, *frg. 2*

1]]ילל[[
2]]רבו מרא[[
3] מ]לפא וסר[[

34.

1. [ ].[ ]
2. [ ].*b' t*.[ ]
3. [ ]upon you[ ]

35.

(a)

1. [ ]he mixed .[ ]
2. [ ]ever since .[ ]
3. [ ]*ph* to a doubled height[ ]
4. [ ]*y'* will go forth from '.[ ]
5. [ ]*h* will devise a[gainst]
6. [ ] all the beasts of [the] fi[eld]
7. [ ] peoples from[ ]
8. [ ]*y'*[ ]

(b)

1. [ ]*'q* will arise[ ]
2. [ ] until *k*[ ]
3. [mou]rning and weeping [ ]
4. [ ]..*bl' k*[ ]

(c)

1. [the land] of the sons of Ham[ ]
2. [ ]the [p]eoples[ ]
3. [ ]' *ḥ*.[ ]

(d)

1. eternity[ ]
2. and after[ ]
3. a wind (*or* a spirit)[ ]

(e)

1. [ ]lamented[ ]
2. [ ]they extolled (the) Lord (of ?) [ ]
3. [ ]the [te]acher and *sr*[ ]

(f) 6Q*26*, *frg. 3*

1] [. . . תע .] [
2] [נפשך .] [
3] [. . . .] [

(g) 6Q*31*, *frg. 1*

1] נטר עמא[[

36. Masada Letter on an Ostracon — MasOstr

1 [מנח]ם בר מעזי שלם די ת . . . [ ]
2 [ת]שלמן לכספא זוין חמשה מנין [ ]

37. Hyrcania Funerary Inscription — Hyrcania

frg. 1

1] מנפא[ ] [
2] [חבל] [
3] א דכל[[
4] [. . .] [

frg. 2

1] אם[[
2] [. . . . למרת אי] [
3] לנפשנא קדם הר] [

38. Murabbaʿat List of Names and Rations — Mur 8 ar

1 למנין סערין ס 20 ס 19 ק 3
2 ישוע אח[י] ס 40
3 טרפ . א . ס 16 ק ½
4 ישוע בר הרקק
5 . צוק [כ]בר ממניה

39. Murabbaʿat IOU (A. D. 56) — Mur 18 ar

recto

1] [.] שנ]ת תרתין לנרון קסר . [ ] .

(f)

1. [ ]...*t*ʿ.[ ]
2. [ ] yourself (*or* your soul) [ ]
3. [ ]....[ ]

(g)

1. [ ]the people guarded[ ]

36.

1. [Menaḥ]em, son of Maʿazi, greetings! That you ...[ ]
2. [you] are to pay the sum, five zuzim (in) number[ ]

37.

frg. 1

1. [ ]*mnp*'[ ]
2. [ ] alas ![ ]
3. [ ]' of all[ ]
4. [ ] . . .[ ]

frg. 2

1. [ ]'*m*[ ]
2. [ ].... to the mistress of '*y*[ ]
3. [ ] for our souls (*or* for ourselves) before *hr*[ ]

38.

1. On account: Barley, 20 s(eahs), 19 s(eahs), 3 q(abs)
2. Jesus, (son of) 'Aḥ[ai], 40 s(eahs)
3. Lentils (?), 16 s(eahs), $^1/_2$q(ab)
4. Jesus, son of Ḥarquq,
5. [from] Ṣuq, [al]ready delivered (?)

39.

recto

1. [the ye]ar two of the Emperor Nero .[ ],

2 בצויה איתודי אבשלום בר חנין מן צויה
3 בנפי מניה עמי אנה זכריה בר יהוחנן בר ה . . [ ]

4 יתב בכסלון כסף זוזין עס[רי]ן [וכספא] מש[לם]

5 אנה . [ ]ן [ ] . [ ] . לא די זבינת עד זמ[נא]
6 דנה אפרועגך בחמש ואפשר בתמ[ימותא]

7 ושנת שמטה דה והן כן לא אעבד תשלומ[תא]

8 לך מנכסי ודי אקנה לקובליך

verso

9 [זכ]ריה בר יהוח[נן ע]ל נפשה
10 [כת]ב יהוסף ב[ר] . שהד
11 יהונתן בר יהוחנא שהד
12 יהוסף ב[ר י]הודן עד

40. Murabbaʿat Writ of Divorce — Mur 19 ar

recto, col. 1

1 באחד למרחשון שנת שת במצדא
2 שבק ומתרך מן רעתי יומא דנה אנה {יהוסף
3 בר נ} יהוסף בר נקסן מן [ ]ה יתב במצדא לכי אנתי

4 מרים ברת יהונתן [מ]ן הנבלטא יתבא
5 במצדא די הוית אנתי מן קדם דה די את
6 רשיא בנפשכי למהך ולמהי אנת<ה> לכול גבר
7 יהודי די תצבין וב[די]ן להוי לכי מני ספר תרכין

8 וגט שבקין בדין [גמי]קא יהבנא וכול חריבין

9 ונזקן ו . . . ן .[אפר]וע לכי כדן יהי קים

10 ומשלם לרבעין ובז[מן]די תמרין לי אחלף לכי

11 שטרה כדי חיא

2. at Ṣiwaya, Absalom, son of Ḥannin, from Ṣiwaya, has declared
3. in my presence that there is on account with me, me Zechariah, son of Yoḥanan, son of *H*..[ ],
4. living at Cheaslon, the sum of twe[nt]y zuzin. The sum I am to rep[ay]
5. b[y But if] I have not paid (?) by this
6. time, I will reimburse you with (interest of) a fifth and will settle in en[tirety],
7. even if this is the Year of Release. And if I do not do so, indem[nity]
8. for you (will be) from my possessions, and whatever I acquire (will be) at your disposal.

verso

9. [Zech]ariah, son of Yoḥan[an, f]or himself.
10. Joseph, so[n of], [wro]te (this), witness.
11. Jonathan, son of John, witness.
12. Joseph, so[n of J]udan, J]udan, witness [Hebrew word].

40.

scriptura interior

1. On the first of Marḥeshwan, the year six, at Masada:
2. I divorce and repudiate of my own free will today, I {Joseph
3. son of N} Joseph, son of Naqsan, from [ ]*h*, living at Masada, you my wife,
4. Miriam, daughter of Jonathan, [fro]m Hanablaṭa, living
5. at Masada, who have been up to this (time) my wife, so that you
6. are free on your part to go and become a wife of any Jewish
7. man that you please. And n[ow] you have from me a bill of repudiation
8. and a writ of divorce. Now I give (back) [the dow]ry, and (for) all ruined
9. and damaged goods and ...*n* .[I reimbur]se you. So let it be determined
10. and paid fourfold. And at (any) ti[me] that you say to me, I shall replace for you
11. the document, as long as I am alive.

recto, col. 2

12 בא[ה]ד למרחש[ון]שנת שת במצדא
13 שבק ומתרך א[נ]ה מן רעתי יומא דנה
14 יהוסף בר נ[קסן]לכי אנתי מרים ‹ברת›
15 יהונתן [מ]ן [ה]נבלטא יתבא
16 במצדא די ה[וי]ת אנתתי
17 מן קדמת דנא די אתי רשיא
18 בנפשכי למ[ה]ך למהי אנתא
19 לכול גבר יהודי די תצבין
20 בדין להי לכי מני ס[פ]ר תרכין
21 וגט שבק[ין ב]דין כו[ל גמי]ק יהבנה
22 וכל חר[יבי]ן [ונזקן] . כדן

23 [יהי קים] ו[מש]לם לרבעין ובזמן

24 [די ת]מרין לין א]חלף לכי שטרה כדי

25 [חי]א

verso

26 יהוסף בר נק[סן] על נפש[ה]
27 אליעזר [בר] מלכה שהד
28 יהוסף בר מלכה שהד
29 אלעזר בר חננה שהד

41. Murabbaʿat Marriage Contract — Mur 20 ar

recto, col. 1

1 [ב]שבעה לאדר שנת חדה ע[שרה [
2 [בר] מנשה מן בני אלישיב] [
3 [את]י תהוא לי לאנתה כדין מ[ושה [
4 [ו]לעלם מן {נכס} נכסי וע[לי [
5 טב טביע כסף זוזין] [
6 [ו]להוא קים אם תש[תבקי [

7 [ה]ן לבית עלמא תהך [מקדמי [
8 [ ]הוראה ואם בנן לה[וין [
9 [ל]בעלין או הן אנה לבת] עלמא אהך [

scriptura exterior

12. On the [fir]rst of Marḥesh[wan], the year six, at Masada:
13. [I] divorce and repudiate of my own free will today,
14. I Joseph, son of Na[qsan], you, my wife Mariam, <daughter>
15. of Jonathan, [fro]m [Ha]nablaṭa, living
16. at Masada, who ha[ve be]en my wife
17. up to this (time), so that you are free
18. on your part to [g]o to become the wife
19. of any Jewish man that you please.
20. Now you have from me a bill of repudiation
21. and a writ of divor[ce. N]ow I give (back) the who[le
22. dow]ry and (for) all ru[in]ed [and damaged goods and]. So
23. [let it be determined] and [pa]id fourfold. And at (any) time
24. [that you] say to me, [I shall] replace for you the document, as long as
25. [I am al]live.

verso

26. Joseph, son of Naq[san], for himsel[f].
27. Eliezer, [son] of Malka, witness.
28. Joseph, son of Malka, witness.
29. Eleazar, son of Ḥanana, witness.

41.

recto, col. 1

1. [On] the seventh of Adar, the year ele[ven , X]
2. [son] of Manasseh, from (among) the sons of Eliashib, [ ]
3. [yo]u shall be my wife according to the law of M[oses]
4. [and] forever. From {property} my property, and upo[n me]
5. good coinage, a sum of zuzin [ ]
6. [and] it shall be determined. And if you are di[vorced from me]
7. [I]f you go to the house of eternity [before me]
8. [ ] the law. And if there sha[ll be] children[ ]
9. [to] marriage. Or if I [go] to the house [of eternity before you, you]

10 ומתזנה ומכסיא]   [
11 ארמלו די לך מן בת[רי   [
12]א[קנא אחראין וער[בין   [
13 וקודם ירתיך מן כול[[
14 לכי שטרא כ[די חיא   [

recto, col. 2

15 בשבעה]   [
16 בחרדונא]   [
17 מן בני אלי[שיב   [

verso

18 יהודה בר יהו[על נפשה]

42. Murabba'at Marriage Contract — Mur 21 ar

frgs. 1-3

recto, col. 1

1] ב 21 ל [. . שנת]   [
2]   לע[ותון ברת]   [
3]   [הב לעות[ון   [
4]   [.ל הב.א .]   [
5]   [ת מן כל ד[י   [

recto, col. 2

6] בעשרי[ן ואח[ד   ] . . [[
7]   [א ע . נ .]   אנת ת[הוה[לי לאנתה   [
8]   [. ון לות .]   ]ן תמ]   [
9]   [. . .   ] ה[ן אפט[רנך   [
10 ואתבנ[ך כסף כ[תבתיך עם כל ע[ליך די ע[מי והן ב[נן יהון לך מני]
11 כנמסא וה[נן י[הון יתבן ביתי ו[יהון]מתזנן מ[ן נכסי] . . . [עד]
12 לבעלין [או מ[ן בתר[י ע[מך . . . מזגהו[ן וה[ן אנת ל[בית עלמא ת[הך מק[דמי]

10. and are to be nourished and clothed [ ]
11. your widowhood aft[er me]
12. [I shall ac]quire are guarantees and sure[ties]
13. and in favor of your heirs against every [ ]
14. for you the document, as lon[g as I am alive.]

recto, col. 2

15. On the seventh [ ]
16. at Ḥarodon [ ]
17. from (among) the sons of Elia[shib]

verso

18. Judah, son of Yo[, for himself]

42.

frgs. 1-3

recto, col. 1

1. [On the 21st of]. ., the year [ ]
2. [Leʿ]uthon, daughter of [ ]
3. [ ]*hb* Leʿuth[on]
4. [ ].*l* *hb*.ʾ .[ ]
5. [ ]*t* from all th[at]

recto, col. 2

6. [On the twen]ty-fir[st]. .[ ]
7. [ ]ʾ ʿ.*n*.[you shall] be [my wife]
8. [ ].*wn* at .[ ]*n* *tm*[ ]
9. [ ]. . . [i]f I div[orce you]
10. I will return [to you the sum of your con]tract along with everything of y[ours that is with] me. And if there be [children to you by me],
11. legitimately, th[ey a]re to live (at) my house and [be] nourished fr[om my possessions]. . .[up]
12. to marriage [or a]fter me (i. e., my death) along with you. . . their matching. [I]f [you] go to [the house of eternity] be[fore me],

13 בניך מנ[י ירתון] כסף כתבתיך ו[כל] די עלי[ך די עמי ודי כתיב] ממעלא

14 בבת וב[ברא ה]ן אנה אהך לבית[א]דך מקד[מיך אנת תהוה יתבה]

15 ומתזנה [מנכסי] כל ימין ביתהון ד[י בנינ]א בת די ארמ[לו די לך עד]

16 למתות[ך וכת]בתיך ת[ ]ה[ ] אית לך [ ]ן [ ]

17 ואנה מנחם [בר]מע[ ] די מן לע[ו]ת[ו]ן . [ ]ת . . [ ]

18 ואנה לעות[ון ברת]ע[ ] די מן לעל[א כתיב]

19 וב[ז]מן די ת[אמרין לי אח]לף ל‹ו›תך ית ש[טרא]

20 [כדי] חיא

verso

21 [מנחם בר על] נפשה
22 [בר י]הוסף ספר[א]
23 [לעותון ברת]מן נפשה כתב
24 [בר]מן . . יה [ ]
25 [בר] חסדי [ ]
26 [בר י]הוחנן ע[ד]
27 [ ] . שהד

43. Murabba'at Deed of Sale — Mur 23 ar

recto

1, 3 ב10 לשבט שנת חדה לחר[ות ירושלם]

5 זבנת לך בכסף סלע[ין]
7 למקנה[ ]

44. Murabba'at Easement — Mur 25 ar

frg. 1

1 [ב למרחשון שנ]ת תלת לחרות ירו{ו}שלם ב[
חנינא בר יהוחנן]

13. your sons [shall inherit] from [me] the sum of your contract and [everything] of you[rs that is with me and that is written] above,
14. inside and out[side.] If I go to that hou[se] be[fore you, you are to dwell]
15. and be nourished [from my possessions] all the days at the house o[f our son]s, the house of your widow[hood, until]
16. your dea[th, and your] contract *t*[ ]*h*[ ] is yours [ ]*n* [ ]
17. and I Menaḥem, [son of] *m*ʿ[ ] which is on the part of Leʿ[u]th[o]n. [ ] *t*..[ ]
18. and I Leʿuth[on, daughter of] ʿ[ ] and whatever [was written a]bove.
19. At (any) t[i]me that you [say to me, I shall re]place for you the doc[ument]
20. [as long as] I am alive.

verso

21. [Menaḥem, son of , for] himself.
22. [, son of J]oseph, the scribe.
23. [Leʿuthon, daughter of] wrote for (?) herself.
24. [, son of] from ..*yh* [ ]
25. [, son of] Ḥasdai [ ]
26. [, son of Yo]ḥanan, witness [*Hebrew word*]
27. [ ], witness.

43.

recto

1, 3. On the tenth of Shebat, the year one of the libera[tion of Jerusalem]
5. I have sold to you for the sum of [ ] sel[as]
7. to acquire [ ]

44.

frg. 1

1. [On the of Marḥeshwan, the ye]ar three of the Liberation of Jerusalem, at [, Ḥannina, son of Yehoḥanan]

2] ..[ל....] [
3] וכל די בה ודי הי]א עלה מעלא ומפקא [ ]

4] תחומי אתרא ד]ך מדנחא בית ברשבא מ[ערבא [

5]]י . [ ]א וכספא אנה מקב[ל [

6 [ו]אנה חנינא מזבנה ו[כל די
איתי לי ודי אקנה]
7 [זבנא דך מן כל חרר ותג]ר וריק ובטלן די יתנך [ע]ל [אתרא
דך]

8] ....[ ]ל[[

frg. 3

1] . למרחש[ון [
2]]ל[ ] . [[

frg. 4

1] חנינ]ה בר יהוח[נ]ן [[

frg. 6

1] ..]א [
2] . בדרתא . [[

frgs. 9-10

1] מד]נח[א] בית [ברשבא [
2]]ל דרומא [[
3]]ל[[

frg. 13

1]]ן [ ] . [[
2] . ככל די מעל[א [

frg. 15

1] . בתא רבא[[

2. [ ].. *l*....[ ]
3. [and everything that is in it and that i]s on it, the entrance and exit [ ]
4. [the boundaries of th]at [site] : (to) the east, the house of Barsabba ; (to) [the] we[st,]
5. [ ]*y* .[ ]' and the sum I am in recei[pt of]
6. [and] I, Ḥannina, (am) the seller, and [all that belongs to me and that I shall acquire]
7. [(is) that purchase from every litigation and clai]m ; and invalid and useless (is) whatever (someone) may give you [concern]ing [that site]
8. [ ]....[ ] *l*[ ]

frg. 3

1. [ ]. of Marḥesh[wan]
2. [ ]*l*[ ].[ ]

frg. 4

1. [Ḥannin]a, son of Yehoḥa[n]an[ ]

frg. 6

1. [ ]. .'[ ]
2. [ ]. in the courtyard.[ ]

frgs. 9-10

1. [(to) the e]ast, the house of [Barsabba]
2. [ ]*l* ; (to) the south [ ]
3. [ ]*l*[ ]

frg. 13

1. [ ]*n* [ ].[ ]
2. [ ]. according to all that is abo[ve]

frg. 15

1. [ ].*bt'* the great[ ]

frg. 17

1] מ]ן יומ[א דנה [

frg. 23

1]]...ן [[
2] קדמך] וקדם ירתי[ך [

45. Murabba'at Deed of Sale — Mur 26 ar

frg. 1

1 .]]טין די יה[ ]..[[
2 מן [יומא דנה ולעל]ם וקים ע[לי]ה מ[[
3 ש[ואנה]ס אנתת[מזב]נתה [וכל די איתי לי]
4 אחריא וערבה [ל]מרקא ולקימא [זבנ]ה [דך קדמכן וקדם]
5 ירתכן מן כל חרר [ו]תגר ובטלן [די י]תנכן [על אתרא דך]
6 ולעלם ותשלמתא מן נכסי[נה ודי נקנה] ל[ק]ב[לכן ובזמן די]
7 תאמר לנה נחלף לכן ש[טרא דנה לעלם]
8 רשין זבניה די מן עלא [באתרא דך [

46. Murabba'at Deed of Sale — Mur 27 ar

1]].[ ]. [
2] א]נחנה מזבנין
3] מן כל חרר ות]גר וכלן מן נכסי אחרין
4]] ויהבין לך מן דלנה
5]] ובזמן די תאמר לי אחלף לך
6 [שטרא דנה]בר חנינה על נפשה

frg. 17

1. [fr]om this d[ay]

frg. 23

1. [ ]...*n* [ ]
2. [before you] and before [your] heirs[ ]

45.

frg. 1

1. [ ]*ṭyn dy yh*[ ]..[ ]
2. from [this day (forward) and forev]er, and it (is) confirmed for [me]*h m*[ ]
3. *š*[and I,]*s*, the wife of [ ] am the [sel]ler; [and all that belongs to me is]
4. the guarantee and the surety [to] clear and confirm tha[t purcha]se [for you and for]
5. your heirs from every litigation [and] claim; and invalid (is) [whatever] (anyone else) may present to you [concerning that site];
6. and (so) forever. The indemnity from [our] possessions [and what we shall acquire] (shall be) at [your dis]po[sal. At (any) time that]
7. you say to us, we shall replace for you [this doc]ument. [For-ever]
8. the above-mentioned buyers shall have a claim [to that site]

46.

1. [ ].[ ]
2. [w]e are selling
3. [from every litigation and cla]im; and all of us from our posses-sions give guarantee
4. [ ]and give to you from what is ours
5. [ ] And at (any) time that you say to me, I shall replace for you
6. [this document.], son of Ḥannina, for himself.

47. Murabba'at Property Record — Mur 28 ar

frgs. 1-2, recto, col. 1

1] . מן הרמנה אמר ל . .]
2] ד]י לי ולאתרא די ל[י]
3] . מה]

frgs. 1-2, recto, col. 2

4] . . . מין וארס]
5]]ן . . .] [
6 ואנה יוסף בר גבניס ואנה .] [
7 . . ל . . ל . . . . א . . . לל .] [
8 . . .]]ען דך לי ל . ן . ן .] [
9 ואנה שמעון בר פנחס ח . . .] [
10 אחרי וערב לך [ו]קים די [ב]שטרא [ד]נה . . ל] [

frgs. 1-2, verso

1] . . ל . . . על נפש[ה]
2]]ן בר . . . על נפשה

frg. 3

1 [יהו]סף

48. Murabba'at IOU (?) — Mur 32 ar

1] . . . ין .] [
2 כספא זך זו[ז]ין מאתין [אנה מ]קב[ל] . . . ויהב [אנ]ה כספא
3 ליהודה זך . . . א כסף זוזין מאה ויהונתן זך זי קבל
4 כסף זוזין תש[ע]ין ותרין פ . . ת ערבא ואחריא לך ולשארא
5] [ ] . ל .] [ ] . . . לי לרש[ו]ת מן קצת . . . ולאו
6] . [ ] . [

47.

frgs. 1-2, recto, col. 1

1. [ ]., from Rimmon, said to[ ]
2. [wh]ich belongs to me and to the site that is mi[ne]
3. [ ].*mh*

frgs. 1-2, recto, col. 2

4. [ ]...*myn* and I engage
5. [ ]*n* ...[ ]
6. And I, Joseph, son of Gabinius, and I .[ ]
7. [ ]*l*[ ]*l*[ ]'[ ]*ll* .[ ]
8. ...[ ]'*n* that for me *l.n.n* .[ ]
9. And I, Simeon, son of Phinehas, *ḥ*[ ]
10. guarantee and surety for you. [And] confirmed (is) what is [in th]is document ..*l*[ ]

frgs. 1-2, verso

11. [ ]..*l*[ ], for himsel[f]
12. [ ]*n*, son of [ ], for himself.

frg. 3

[Jo]seph

48.

1. [ ]...*yn* .[ ]
2. [I am in re]ceipt of that sum: two hundred zu[z]in [ ] and [I] give the sum
3. to that Judah, the [ ], the sum of one hundred zuzin. That Jonathan, who has received
4. a sum of nin[e]ty-two zuzin, *p..t* the surety and the guarantee for you. And as for the rest
5. [ ].*l*.[ ]...to me as autho[riza]tion for a part ... *wl'w*
6. [ ].[ ].

49. Murabbaʿat Ostracon — Mur 72 ar

frg. 1

1 ליהו[חנן [
2 פדוי בר ר . [[
3 הוה יהוחנן זנה מתנא[[
4 זי לא איתיני ידע למן הוה אמר על[[
5 [על יה]וחנן זנה כן אמר זי שמע הוית זי אמר יהוחנן זנה .] [
6]]באנפי יהוחנן זנה כלקבל זי מן עלא כת[יב [
7]]לשבט זי ה[וה] יומא ז[נה [
8]]הוית קאם יומא ז[נה [
9]]תלוש זי אנת עכיר ואמר[[
10]]. וסלקת מן תמן למצדא ויהו[חנן זנה [
11] ק]צת לחם השוהי .] [
12]] . מה . . יא ב[.] [

frg. 2

1 יה[וחנן [
2 הוית ענ[ה [

50. Murabbaʿat Unidentified Fragments — Mur 31, 33-35 ar

(a) *Mur 31, frg. 1*

1] [.] [
2 דמין] [
3 למקנ[ה [
4 שמ[עון [

(b) *Mur 31, frg. 3*

1]]בית [י]וסף [ד]ך . . .] [
2]]ל[[

49.

frg. 1

1. To Yeho[ḥanan]
2. Paddui, son of *R*. .[ ]
3. This Yehoḥanan was recounting [ ]
4. since I did not know to whom he was speaking ab[out]
5. [about] this [Yeh]oḥanan. He spoke thus : I have heard that this Yehoḥanan said .[ ]
6. [ ] in the presence of this Yehoḥanan, according to what is writ[ten] above
7. [ ] of Shebat, which i[s] thi[s (very)] day [ ]
8. [but] I was standing [to]day
9. [ ]you are to knead whatever you *'kyr*. And he said [ ]
10. [ ]. And I went up from there to Masada. And [this] Yeho[ḥanan]
11. [a li]ttle bread, divide it in equal parts .[ ]
12. [ ].*mh* ..*y' b*[ ]

frg. 2

1. Yeh[oḥanan]
2. I was answer[ing]

50.

(a)

1. [ ].[ ]
2. the price [ ]
3. to acqui[re]
4. Sim[eon]

(b)

1. [th]at house of [Jo]seph[ ]
2. [ ]*l*[ ]

(c) *Mur 31, frg. 4*

(recto) 1]]בית יוסף דך זבנא דנה
(verso) 2] ש]מעון[[

(d) *Mur 31, frg. 5*

1]]ן[[
2] ד]י המון 33 ס[לעין [
3]]. ואב . [[

(e) *Mur 33, frg. 1*

1 בעשרין וארבעה לן[[
2 מקבל אנה שמעון בר חנין] [
3 בר . א . ה מן . . . ין דמין . . .] [
4 ח. לח . . א שמעון בר חנין כסף
5]]קלופו בר .] [

(f) *Mur 34*

1] אנ]ה מן רעותי

(g) *Mur 35*

1] יתבא [

51. ? Ḥever Contract B (Deed of Sale, A. D. 134) — pap?ḤevB ar

1 בעסרי[ן] ל . . ר שנת תלת לחרת ישראל בכפרבביו
2 ח . . בר יהודה מן כפרבביו אמר לאלעזר בר אלעזר שטרא
3 מן תמן אנה מן רעותי יומא דנה זבנת לך ימה דנה לבתה דילי
4 די פתיח צפן לגה דרתי די תפתחנה לגה בתך
5 ורשה לא איתי לך {לך} עמי בגו דרתה דך זבנת לך בכסף
6 זוזין די המון תמנ[י]א וסלעין תרתן דמין גמרין לעלם רשי
7 אלעזר בזבן בתה דך אבניא ושרית[א] ודגריא* כול די בה

(c)

1. [ ]that house of Joseph, this sale (*or* purchase)
2. [Si]meon [ ]

(d)

1. [ ]*n* [ ]
2. [whi]ch are 33 se[las]
3. [ ]. and '*b*[ ]

(e)

1. On the twenty-fourth of [ ]
2. I, Simeon, son of Ḥannin, am in receipt of [ ]
3. son of .'.*h* from ...*yn*, the price ... [ ]
4. *ḥ*. *lḥ*..' Simeon, son of Ḥannin, a sum of
5. [ ]Klopas, son of .[ ]

(f)

1. [I] of my own free will

(g)

1. [ ] dwelling at

51.

1. On the twentie[th] of ..*r*, the year three of the Liberation of Israel, at Kephar-Bebayu,
2. *Ḥ*.., son of Judah, from Kephar-Bebayu, said to Eleazar, son of Eleazar, the administrative officer
3. from there: I have this day of my own free will sold to you this day the house which belonged to me,
4. which opens on the north into my courtyard, so that you may make an opening for it into your own house.
5. But there is no authorization for you {for you} from me over the interior of that courtyard. I have sold (the house) to you for the sum of eig[h]t
6. zuzin, which (equal) two selas, total price forever. Eleazar
7. is given authority by the purchase of that house (over) stones, beam[s], and stairs, (and) everything that is in it,

8 בניה וקרקעא תחמא ‹די› בתה דך [די לך ל]אלעזר זבנה מדנחא

9 יחונתן [בר י]שוע לצפנה דרתה מערבא ודרמא בנה ורשה לא

10 איתי לך עמי בגו דרתה דילי ולא מעל ול[א] מפק עלי אנ{ת}ה ח . .

11 [מן] ימה דנה ולעלם ואנה אחרי ‹ו›ערב ל[ך בז]בן בתה דך מן ימה דנה

12 ולעלם ואנה שלם ברת שמעון את[ת] ח . . דנה מלין לאיתי

13 לי {ו}ל[ש]לם בזבן בתה דך ‹מן יומא דנה**› ולעלם ותש[למ]תה ‹מן
נכסינה› ודי נקנה לקובלך

14 כ[ת]בה דנה פשיט וחתמו בגוה
15 ח . . בר יהודה על ‹נ›פשה
16 שלם ב[ר]ת שמעון על נפשה כתב
17 אלעזר בר מתתא ספרה
18 שמעון בר יהוסף עד
19 אלעזר בר . . . שהד
20 יהודה בר יהודה שהד

*read דרגיא **or ימה דנה

52. ? Ḥever Contract C (Deed of Sale) — pap?ḤevC ar

recto

1 [ ] . . ך . . [ ] . . [ ]ן[ ]
2 [ ] . לין בית זרע חנטין סאין תלת וקבין תלתה ומח[ס]ר

3 [ולי]תיר לזבנה תחומי אתרא דך מדנחא אלנה בר מ . חי מערבא

4 חוני ואחרנין די הוא מן קדמת דנה ל[י]ה[ו]נתן בר ר[ו]בא דרומא

5 אפתלמיס ופ . . יון אחה צפונא אורחא אתרא דך בתחומה

6 ובמצרה תאניא וכל די בה ודי חיא עלה מעלא ומפקא בה

8. (the) building and terrain. The boundary <of> that house, [which belongs to you], Eleazar, the buyer: (to) the east,
9. Jonathan, [son of J]esus; to the north, the courtyard; (to) the west and the south, (what) is constructed. No authority
10. is given to you by me over the interior of the courtyard that belongs to me, nor (any) entrance o[r] egress against my (will), me *Ḥ*..
11. [from] this day (forward) and forever. And I (am giving) guarantee <and> surety to [you in the sa]le of that house from this day (forward)
12. and forever. As for me, Salome, daughter of Simeon, wif[e] of said *Ḥ*.., there are no claims
13. for me, {and} for Salome, in the sale of that house <from this day> (forward) and forever. And in[dem]nity <from our possessions> and whatever we shall acquire (is) at your disposal.
14. This document was set out, and they set a seal on it:
15. *Ḥ*.., son of Judah, for <h>imself.
16. Salome, dau[gh]ter of Simeon, wrote for herself.
17. Eleazar, son of Mattathah, the scribe.
18. Simeon, son of Joseph, witness [*Hebrew word*].
19. Eleazar, son of ..., witness.
20. Judah, son of Judah, witness.

52.

recto

1. [ ]..*n*..[ ]..[ ]*n*[ ]
2. [ ].*lyn* a farm-land (yielding) wheat — three seahs and three qabs, more or
3. [l]ess (?), to sell (it). The boundaries of that site: (to) the east, 'Elnah, son of *M.ḥy*; (to) the west,
4. Ḥoni and others, which belonged prior to this to Jonathan, son of Roba'; (to) the south,
5. Ptolemaios and *P..ywn*, his brother (?); (to) the north, the road. That (is the) site with its boundary
6. and with its border, the fig-trees, and everything that is on it. (As for) whatever animal is on it, the animal (has) the entrance and the egress of it.

7 חיא ‹אתרא› דך זבנת לכן בכסף זוזין שבעין ותמניה די המון

8 סלעין תשע עשרה ותקל חד לחין וכספא אנה מקבל דמין

9 לעלם רשאין זבניא די מן עלא באתרא דך וירתהן למקנה ולמזבנה

10 ולמעבד בה כל די יצבון וירתהן מן יומא דנה ולעלם ואנה

11 או . . . ס מזבנה וכל די איתי לי ודי אקנה אחראין ו[ערבין]

12 למרקא ולקימא זבנה דך קדמ[כן] וקדם ירתכן [ ]

verso

13 [ ]Ευ[ ]Ευ

14 [ ] . . [ ] . .

15 [ ] . על [נפשה כ]תב

16 [ ] . . . [ ]ה

17 [ש]הד [מ]ן . קר .

18 [מ]נשה כתב ספר{י}א

19 [ ] מן ירושלם

20 [ ] שהד מן חברן

53. 5/6 Ḥever Letter of Bar Cochba 1 — 5/6ḤevEp 1

1 שמעון בר כוסבה הנסי על ישראל ליהונתן ולמסבלה סלם[ ] ותתנון

2 יתהן באספליא [ ]ואם לא כן תעבדון די מנכן פרענותא תתעבד [ ]

3 כל גבר תקועי[ ] דמנכן אעבד ית פרענותה[ ]ישוע בר תדמריה
[ ]ולא תבסרון למחד

4 ית סיפה די עלוי[ ]שמואל בר עמי

54. 5/6 Ḥever Letter of Bar Cochba 2 — 5/6ḤevEp 2

1 וית כול[ ]די[ ]כתבת לכון ושלחת

2 לכון[ואם] לא תעבד[ון]

7. I have sold to you that <site> for the sum of seventy-eight zuzin, in bad condition, which (equal)
8. nineteen selas and one shekel. And the sum that I am in receipt of (is the) price
9. forever. The buyers who are (mentioned) above and their heirs have the right over this site, to acquire (it) and to sell it,
10. and to do in it everything that they please, and their heirs (as well), from this day (forward) and forever. I
11. '*w*...*s* am the seller; and everything which belongs to me and which I shall acquire are a guarantee and [surety]
12. to clear and confirm that purchase for you and for your heirs [ ]

verso

13. Eu[ ] Eu[ ]
14. [ ]..[ ]..
15. [wr]ote for [himself]
16. [ ]...[ ]*h*
17. [wit]ness [fr]om .*qr*
18. [Man]asseh, the scribe, wrote (this document).
19. [ ] from Jerusalem.
20. [ ] witness, from Hebron.

53.

1. Simeon, son of Kosiba, the ruler over Israel, to Jonathan and Masabbala, peace! [ ] and you are to give
2. them with assurance [ ]; and if you do not do so, whatever punishment is to be exacted from you [ ]
3. every Teqoan man [ ] who is from (among) you, I shall exact his (*or* the) punishment[ ]. (As for) Jesus, son of the Palmyrene [ ] and you are not to despise taking
4. his (*or* the) sword that is upon him [ ] Samuel, son of ʿAmmi.

54.

1. And every [ ] that [ ] I wrote to you and sent (a message)
2. to you [and if] you do not do [so]

55. 5/6 Ḥever Letter of Bar Cochba 4 — 5/6ḤevEp 4

1 אגרת שמעון בר כוסבה שלם
2 ליהונתן בר בעיה דכל דאלישע
3 אמר לך עבד לה והתשדר
4 עמה[ ]בידה
5 הוא שלם

56. 5/6 Ḥever Letter of Bar Cochba 8 — 5/6ḤevEp 8

1 שמעון בר כשבה
2 ליהונתן בר בעין
3 ולמשבלה בר שמעון
4 די תשלחון לי ית אלעזור
5 בר חטה שוה קדם
6 שבה
7 שמעון בר יהודה כתבה

57. 5/6 Ḥever Letter of Bar Cochba 10 — 5/6ḤevEp 10

1 [שמע]ון לינתן ולמסבלה
2 [ש]לם די תנמרן ותשלחן למחניה[ ]

58. 5/6 Ḥever Letter of Bar Cochba 11 — 5/6ḤevEp 11

1 שמעון בר כוסבה ליהונתן בר בעין ולמסבלה
2 [ ] רהומיה [ ]ותדברון ית תירסיס בר תינינוס ויתה עמכון די אנחנה
3 צריכין לה [ ]רבנו בטניה בר מיסה[ ]הוו שלם

59. 5/6 Ḥever Letter of Bar Cochba 14 — 5/6ḤevEp 14

1 שמעון בר כושבה ליהונתן
2 ולמשבלא [ ]כול אנש מתקוע ומתל ארזין[ ]ואם לא תשדרון יתהן
3 ידיע יהוא לכן די מנכן אעבד פרענותא[ ]

55.

1. A letter of Simeon, son of Kosiba, peace!
2. To Jonathan, son of Ba'yah. Everything that Elisha
3. says to you, do for him and make an effort
4. for him [ ] by his hand.
5. Farewell.

56.

1. Simeon, son of Kosiba,
2. to Jonathan, son of Ba'yan,
3. and Masabbala, son of Simeon.
4. You are to send to me Eleazar, (Elazar) not → אליעזר
5. son of *Ḥṭh*, immediately, before
6. (the) Sabbath.
7. Simeon, son of Judah, wrote it.

57.

1. [Sime]on to Jonathan and to Masabbala,
2. [pe]ace! You are to reap and send to the camp[ ]

58.

1. Simeon, son of Kosiba, to Jonathan, son of Ba'yan, and to Masabbala:
2. [ ] the Romans [ ] and you are to take Tirsis, son of Tininos, and let him come with you, because we
3. are in need of him [ ] our leader Beṭenyah, son of Misa, [ ]. Farewell.

59.

1. Simeon, son of Kosiba, to Jonathan
2. and to Masabbala [ ] every man from Teqoa and from Tell Arza [ ] and if you do not send them,
3. let it be known to you that I shall exact the punishment from you[ ]

60. 5/6 Ḥever Letter of Bar Cochba 15 — 5/6ḤevEp 15

1 שמעון ליהודה בר מנשה לקרית ערביה שלחת לך תרי חמרין די תשלח

2 עמהן תר‹י› גברין לות יהונתן בר בעין ולות מסבלה די יעמרן

3 וישלחן למחניה לותך ללבין ואתרגין ואת שלח אחרנין מלותך

4 וימטון לך הדסון וערבין ותקן יתהן ושלח יתהן למחניה[ ]

5 [ ]הוא שלם

61. 5/6 Ḥever Babatha Archive, Greek Document 1 — 5/6ḤevBA 1

24 (Aramaic) יהודה בר כתושיון אדון בבתה בקמיה ש‹ה›דת בבתה ככל
די על כתב יהודה כתבה

25 (Nabatean) עבדעבדת בר אילותא במקמי ובמקם יוחנה חברי בר עגלא
כתבנן שהדתא דא כדי עלא כתיב עבדעבדת כתבה

26 (Aramaic) יהוחנן בר אלכס ביד יהוסף ברה

62. 5/6 Ḥever Babatha Archive, Greek Document 2 — 5/6ḤevBA 2

11 בבתיה ברת שמעון אתקבליה מן שמעון ב[ר יו]חנה בר

12 יהוסף אפ[טרפא] ישוע ברי לכסות [ול]מ[ז]ון ד[י] ישוע [ברי כס]ף
ד[י]נרין שתיה מחדא בתמוז ועדי

13 תלת{ל}ין באלולא שנת עשרין ושבע [די הון י]רחין תלתא שו[י]ן
די בבלי בר מנחם כתביה

63. 5/6 Ḥever Babatha Archive, Docket on Marriage Contract — 5/6ḤevBA Docket

1 כתבת בבתא ברת שמען

60.

1. Simeon to Judah, son of Manasseh, of Qiryat ʿArabaya : I have sent to you two asses, with which you are to send
2. tw<o> men to Jonathan, son of Baʿyan, and to Masabbala, (with instructions) that they should load (them)
3. and send (them) to the camp, to you, (with) palm branches and citrons. And you, send others from your own quarters,
4. and let them bring to you myrtle branches and willow boughs. Prepare them and send them to the camp[ ]
5. [ ]. Farewell.

61.

24. (Aramaic) Judah, son of Chthusion, guardian of Babatha, in her presence (?), the te<st>imony of Babatha, according to all that (is) in the deed. Judah wrote it.
25. (Nabatean) ʿAbdoʿabdat, son of ʾIlutha, in my place (?) and in their place (?), Yoḥanah, my companion, son of ʿEgla : we have written this testimony as it is written above. ʿAbdoʿabdat wrote it.
26. (Aramaic) Yehoḥanan, son of ʾAlex, by the hand of Joseph, his son.

62.

11. I, Babatha, daughter of Simeon, have received from Simeon, so[n of Yo]ḥanah, son of
12. Joseph, the guar[dian] of Jesus, my son, for clothing [and for] fo[o]d fo[r] Jesus, [my son, a su]m of six d[e]narii from the first of Tammuz until
13. the thirtieth of Elul, the year twenty-seven, [which are] three equ[a]l [m]onths. (This is) what Babelis, son of Menaḥem, has written.

63.

The contract of Babatha, daughter of Simeon

64. 5/6 Ḥever Nabatean Contract — pap5/6ḤevA nab

recto, frg. 1

1 [ב לאלו]ל שנת עשרי[ן למנכו מלכא מלך נבטו]

2 על שקיא במחוז עגלתין כדי גנתא הי ותחומיה כתיבין בשטר עדוא הו ומן באתר

3 דמן שטר עדוא הו כריזת גנתא ה[י וכ]תב כרוז בני חת....ן...כא די כתב כרוזא הנפק

4 בשם א[פ]תח בר תימאלהי וכתיב[ ]ככל כתב כרוזא הו..ב...א ימליך בר עבדי כרז גנתא

5 הי ובצע דמי כרוזא הו ודי לותה [ק]רב כדי בה וד‹י› אכתב כרוזא הו לותך אנתא ימליך

6 דנה[כ]תיב מין........ושחד וחד.......ק[מי]ת נ[י]קרכס אבי

7 ומית בני דדי בר נב[ו]מא ודי אנה אלעזר דנה אצדק וירת ניקרכס אבי ולא שבק בני דדי

8 ולא איתי לה ילד ואנה אלעזר דנה [אצד]ק [ויר]ת בני דדי הו ודי ב[י]ום די כתיב שטרא

9 דנה הוה מאת בי אנה אלעזר דנה לותך אנתא ימליך דנה ובעית מנך די תנפק לי שטר

10 עדוא הו ואקרב מה די לך עמי מן פגעון חקק ותחשב בתי בפגעונא ואפרק מנך שטר

11 עדוא הו ואנפקת שטר עדוא ה[ו ואת]קרי וערבת וחשבת בתי ומנית לי בפגעונא הו

12 כל די קבלת ועבדי אבוך א..............אגר וק......לל תרתי חנותא

13 [ ]טע[ ]......כלא נחשב ביני לביניך ושבקת לי

14 [ ]ל[ ]ל

64.

recto, frg. 1

1. [On the ? day of Elu]l, the year twent[y of Maliku the King, king of Nabatea,]
2. on the (public) markets in Maḥoz-ʿEglatain. Whereas that garden and its boundaries are mentioned (lit., written) in that document of seizure, in accordance with
3. that document of seizure th[is] garden has been publicly proclaimed and the writ of proclamation of Bannai *ḥt. . . . n. . . k'*, since the writ of proclamation was issued (?)
4. on the estimate of 'A[ph]taḥ, son of Taim'ilahi, and was recorded[ ] according to that whole writ of proclamation . . *b*. . .' Yamlik, son of ʿAbdai, has publicly proclaimed
5. that garden and has settled the price of that proclamation and (of) what is [rela]ted to it as well as in it, and since he has caused that proclamation to be written for you, you Yamlik,
6. this [was w]ritten *myn* . . . . *wšḥd wḥd*. . . . . . . *q* [ ] N[i]karchos, my father, has [die]d,
7. and Bannai, my uncle, son of Neb[o]ma, has died. Since I, this Eleazar, have the right and am the heir of Nikarchos, my father, and (since) Bannai, my uncle, did not leave
8. and has no offspring, I, the said Eleazar, [have the rig]ht [and am the h]eir of Bannai, that uncle of mine, and since on the day that this document was written
9. he died, I, said Eleazar, came (?) to you, you the said Yamlik, and I requested of you that you produce for me that document
10. of seizure, and I offer whatever is yours from my side on a determined agreement; you are to evaluate my house in this agreement, and I shall redeem from you that document
11. of seizure. You produced th[at] document of seizure [and it was] read; you have taken in guarantee and evaluated my house and you have made an accounting to me in that agreement.
12. Everything that you have received and ʿAbdai, your father, '[ ] has rented *wq*[ ]*ll* the two shops
13. [ ]*tʿ*[ ]. . . . . . We shall evaluate [that as] all between you and me, and you have left for me
14. [ ]*l*[ ]*l*

recto, frg. 2

1 ועמזו שגיא ודי[אלע]זר דנה מן כל די אבעי ודי תב[עי]

2 בשמי עליך ככל די[אל]עזר ושגיא . . . . הוה ביניך

3]ובני דדי הו . . . מן מנסב [

4]בעה ותלי ושטרין וכתבין וכרוזין [

5]ר ובלע ובין ומטי וחשב[ ] [

6]עלין וסכלו ושל . . וקצץ ונעי [

7]קק וק . . י . . . . . ו . . . ובצע וחליפה ובשריה [

8]בשר בעו וקבלת מלך ודין ופתור יאירת [

recto, frg. 3

1 ימלי]ך בר עבדי על ניקרכס אבי אנה אלעזור [

2 דנה ועל בני דד[י ב]ר נבומא[כסף סל]עין ארבע מאה כפס ראש רבין מן דמנה כדי בה

3 ביום ע]שרין לטבת [שנ]ת ארבע למנכו מלכא מלך נבטו די ש[ט]רא הו כתיב [

4]די בנצת משכוני שטר עדוא הו מש . קי ניקרכס ובני [

5 אנו תרתי חנותא ותוניא די גוא מנהם . . . . י בשוק מחוז עגלתין ומנעלהם ומנפקהם

6 כדי אנו נקיבין בשמהן ותחומין [ב]שטר עדוא הו מ . . . . .] [

7] ג]וא גן]מ[ ]א ו[ ] [

recto, frg. 4

1]מא ותני תרתי [חנותא] [

2 ומנפקהם

recto, frg. 2

1. and much *'nzw*, and whatever[ ] the said [Elea]zar. From all that I request and that you re-[quest]
2. in my name for yourself, according to all that [Ele]azar, and much ..... was between you
3. [ ] and Bannai, that uncle of mine, ... *mn mnsb*
4. [ ] he requested *wtly* and documents, writs, and proclamations
5. [ ]*r* and he suffered loss, *wbyn wmṭy* and he counted[ ]
6. [ ] *'lyn wsklw wšl.. wqṣṣ wn'y*
7. [ ]*qq wq..y .....w ... wbṣ' wḥlyph wbšryh*
8. [ ]*bšr b'w* and I complained (before) king and judge and *ptwr y'yrt*

recto, frg. 3

1. [Yamli]k, son of 'Abdai, against Nikarchos, my father, (of) me the said Eleazar,
2. and against Bannai, [my] uncle, [so]n of Neboma, [(to) a sum] of four hundred [sel]ahs, (the) interest as part of the principal — whatever from it as in it —
3. [on the day twe]nty of Tebet, the [yea]r four of Maliku] the King, king of Nabatea, when that deed was written
4. [ ]which in part of the pledges (?) of that document of seizure *mš.qy* Nikarchos and Bannai :
5. *'nw* two shops and the chambers that are within them ....*y* in the market of Maḥoz-'Eglatain, and their entrances and exits
6. as these are marked by their names, and (the) boundaries (are) [in] that document of seizure *m.* .....[ ]
7. [inter]ior of a garden[ ]*m*[ ]' *w*[ ]

recto, frg. 4

1. [ ]*m'* and the chambers of the two [stores]
2. and their exits

verso

3 יסף בר יהודה

65. Jerusalem Stone Weight

1 [ד]בר קתרס

66. Storage Jar Inscription

1 בלזמה / בלזם

67. Kidron Valley Dipinto

1 כוכה דנה עביד
2 לגרמי אבהתנה
3 ארך אמין תרתין
4 ולא למפתח עליהון

68. Giv'at Ha-Mivṭar Abba Inscription

1 אנה אבה בר כהנה א
2 לעז‹ר› בר אהרן רבה אנ
3 ה אבה מעניה מרד
4 פה די יליד בירושלם
5 וגלא לבבל ואסק‹ת› למתת
6 י בר יהוד וקברתה במ
7 ערתה דזבנת בגטה

69. Jebel Ḥallet eṭ-Ṭuri Ossuary

1 כל די אנש מתהנה בחלתה דה
2 קרבן אלה מן דבגוה

70. Uzziah Tomb Slab

1 לכה התית
2 טמי עוזיה
3 מלך יהודה
4 ולא למפתח

71. Kidron Epitaph

1 אבהתנ[ה]
2 ולא למפ
3 תח לעל[ם]

verso

3. Joseph, son of Judah

65.

[Of] Bar Qathros

66.

Balsam (*Aram.*) / balsam (*Hebr.*)

67.

1. This sepulchral chamber was made
2. for the bones of our fathers.
3. (In) length (it is) two cubits.
4. (It is) not (permitted) to open them! (*or* Not to be opened!)

68.

1. I, Abba, son of the priest Ele-
2. az<ar>, son of Aaron the elder, I
3. Abba, the oppressed and the perse-
4. cuted, who (was) born in Jerusalem
5. and went into exile to Babylon, brought (back to Jerusalem) Matta-
6. thi(ah), son of Jud(ah); and I buried him in the
7. cave which I had acquired by the writ.

69.

1. Everything that a man will find to his profit in this ossuary
2. (is) an offering to God from the one within it.

70.

1. Hither were brought
2. the bones of Uzziah,
3. the king of Judah.
4. (It is) not (permitted) to open! (*Or* Not to be opened!)

71.

1. Ou[r] fathers!

2-3. (It is) not (permitted) to open eve[r]! (*Or* Never to be opened!)

72. **Dominus Flevit Ossuary 11**

שמעון בר . . נה

73. **Dominus Flevit Ossuary 13**

שפירא

74. **Dominus Flevit Ossuary 19**

שלם ברת עזי

75. **Dominus Flevit Ossuary 20**

י[ה]וסף בר א . . .

76. **Dominus Flevit Ossuary 24**

יהונתן בר ס

77. **Dominus Flevit Ossuary 25**

. . . בר אלעזר

78. **Dominus Flevit Ossuary 26**

(a, d, e) חנניה בר מנחם
(b, c) חנניה בר מנחמ

79. **Dominus Flevit Ossuary 27**

מתיה בר חקוה

80. **Dominus Flevit Ossuary 32**

יהוסף בר אגרה

81. **Dominus Flevit Ossuary 33**

טוביה בר אגרה

82. **Dominus Flevit Ossuary 34**

(a) חנניה בר שמעון
(b) חנניה בר שמעון

83. **Dominus Flevit Ossuary 36**

עזריה בר זכריה

72.
Simeon, son of . . *nh*

73.
Sapphira

74.
Salome, daughter of ‘Awwai

75.
J[o]seph, son of ’. . .

76.
Jonathan, son of *S*[ ]

77.
..., son of Eleazar (*or* Elazar)

78.
(a, d, e) Ḥananiah, son of Menaḥem
(b, c) Ḥananiah, son of Menaḥem

79.
Matthiah, son of *Ḥqwh*

80.
Joseph, son of ’Agrah

81.
Tobiah, son of ’Agrah

82.
(a) Ḥananiah, son of Simeon
(b) Ḥananiah, son of Simeon

83.
Azariah, son of Zechariah

84. Dominus Flevit Ossuary 38

שלום אתת שפיר

85. Giv'at Ha-Mivṭar Ossuary 1

(a) סמון בנה הכלה
(b) 1 סמון
2 בנא הכלה

86. Giv'at Ha-Mivṭar Ossuary 2

יהונתן קדרה

87. Giv'at Ha-Mivṭar Ossuary 3

מרתא

88. Giv'at Ha-Mivṭar Ossuary 14

1 חלת שלום ברת שאול
2 די שברת שלום ברתה

89. Jason Tomb Inscription

1 קינא עלמא עיבד ליסון בר פ. . . אחי שלם די בנת לך קבור סבא הוה שלם

2 . . . ס
3 כדנין קינא עלמא רחמיא למעבדא לך זי הוית שוא שלם

4 חני . . סגי מח . . . קינא היכילין שלם

90. Kallon Family Ossuary 1

יהוסף בר שמעון

91. Kallon Family Ossuary 2

(a) 1 מרים יועזר שמעון בני יחזק
2 בן קלון מן בני ישבאב

(b) 1 מרים ויהועזר ושמעון
2 בני יחזק בר קלון
3 ברי ישבאב

84.

Salome, wife of Shappir

85.

(a) Simon, builder of the Temple
(b) 1. Simon,
2. builder of the Temple

86. Jonathan, the potter (*or* the pot-seller; *or* the Black)

87.

Martha

88.

1. The ossuary of Salome, the daughter of Saul,
2. who hoped for (?) Salome, her daughter.

89.

1. Make an everlasting lament for Jason, son of P ..., my brother. (It is) Salome who has built for you an elder's tomb. Be (at) peace!
2. ...*s*
3. Friends are joined to make an everlasting lament for you who were worthy (of it). Peace!
4. Ḥoni.. very much *mḥ*... a lament *hykylyn*. Peace!

90.

Joseph, son of Simeon

91.

(a) 1. Miriam (*or* Mariam), Yoʿezer (*or* Yoʿazar), and Simeon, children of Yeḥzaq,
2. son of Kallon, of the sons (?) of Yeshab'ab.
(b) 1. Miriam and Yehoʿezer and Simeon,
2. children of Yeḥzaq, son of Kallon,
3. sons of Yeshab'ab.

92. Kallon Family Ossuary 3

(a) 1 יהועזר בר
2 שמעון בר
3 קלון
(b) 1 יועזר
(c) 1 יהועזר בר
2 שמעון בן קלון

93. Kallon Family Ossuary 4

(a) שמעון בר יהועזר בר קלון
(b) שמעון בר יהועזר בן קלון

94. Kallon Family Ossuary 5

(a) שלמציון ברת גמלא
(b) 1 שלמציון איתת
2 יהועזר בר קלון ברת גמלא

95. Jerusalem Hypogeum Ossuary 1

(a) אבא דוסתס
(b) דוסתס אבונה ולא למפתח

96. Jerusalem Hypogeum Ossuary 2

(a) שלמצין אמנה
(b) אמ<א> שלמציון

97. Jerusalem Hypogeum Ossuary 4

(a) אתת מתיה וברה
(b) שלם ומתיה ברה

98. Jerusalem Hypogeum Ossuary 5

אנתת אלעזר

99. Jerusalem Tomb Ossuary 1

יהודה בר אלעזר הסופר

100. Jerusalem Tomb Ossuary 2

שמעון בר ישוע

92.

(a) 1. Yeho'azar, son of
2. Simeon, son of
3. Kallon

(b) Yo'azar

(c) 1. Yeho'azar, son of
2. Simeon, son of Kallon

93.

(a) Simeon, son of Yeho'azar, son of Kallon

(b) Simeon, son of Yo'azar, son of Kallon

94.

(a) Shelamṣion, the daughter of Gamla'

(b) 1. Shelamṣion, wife of
2. Yeho'azar, son of Kallon, daughter of Gamla'

95.

(a) Father, Dosithos

(b) Dosithos, our father! (It is) not (permitted) to open! (*Or* Not to be opened!)

96.

(a) Shelamṣion, our mother

(b) Moth<er>, Shelamṣion

97.

(a) The wife of Matthiah and her son

(b) Salome and Matthiah, her son

98.

The wife of Eleazar (*or* Elazar)

99.

Judah, son of Eleazar (*or* Elazar), the scribe

100.

Simeon, son of Yeshua' (*or* Jesus)

101. Jerusalem Tomb Ossuary 3

. . . אלעזר בר נתי

102. Jerusalem Tomb Ossuary 4

יהודה בר חנניה

103. Jerusalem Tomb Ossuary 5

מרים אתת יח‹ז›קיה

104. Jerusalem Tomb Ossuary 6

אלישבע אתת טרפון

105. Jerusalem Tomb Ossuary 7

יהוחנן בר . . .

106. Jerusalem Tomb Ossuary 8

ישוע בר יהוסף

107. Jerusalem Tomb Ossuary 9

[   ]תא קרבן

108. Nicanor Tomb Inscription

נקנר אלךסא

109. Nazareth Ossuary

1 סועם
2 בר מנחם
3 נוח נפש

110. Siloam Ossuary 1

1 אבונה
2 שמעון סבא
3 יהוסף ברה

111. Siloam Ossuary 3

1 שלמציון ברת
2 שמעון

101.

... Eleazar (*or* Elazar), son of Nattai

102.

Judah, son of Ḥananiah

103.

Miriam (*or* Mariam), wife of Yeḥe<z>qiah (*or* Hezekiah)

104.

Elisheba' (*or* Elizabeth), wife of Tarphon (*or* Tryphon)

105.

Yehoḥanan, son of ...

106.

Yeshua' (*or* Jesus), son of Joseph

107.

(For) the [ ]*t*' an offering

108.

Nicanor, the Alexandrian

109.

1. So'am,
2. son of Menaḥem,
3. repose of soul!

110.

1. Our father,
2. Simeon the elder (*or* Simeon [son of] Sabba);
3. Joseph, his son

111.

1. Shelamṣion, daughter of
2. Simeon

112. Siloam Ossuary 6

שמעון בר יואמץ (?)

113. Siloam Ossuary 7

יהוסף בר שמעון

114. Siloam Ossuary 14

אמא

115. Silwan Tomb Ossuary 1

אבישלום

116. Silwan Tomb Ossuary 2

אבא יהוחנן

117. Silwan Tomb Ossuary 3

שפרא

118. Talpioth Ossuary 1

שמעון ברסבא

119. Talpioth Ossuary 2

מרים ברת שמעון

120. Talpioth Ossuary 5

מתי

121. Mt. Scopus Tomb Inscription 1

חניה בר יהונתן הנזר

122. Mt. Scopus Tomb Inscription 2

שלום אנתת חניה בר הנזיר

123. Mt. Scopus Tomb Inscription 3

אשוני בר שמעון בר אשוני

124. Mt. Scopus Ossuary 6

יהודה בר יהוחנן

112.
Simeon, son of Yo'amaṣ (?)

113.
Joseph, son of Simeon

114.
Mother (*or* 'Imma)

115.
Abishalom

116.
Father, Yehoḥanan

117.
Sapphira

118.
Simeon Barsabba (*or* son of Sabba)

119.
Miriam (*or* Mariam), daughter of Simeon

120.
Mattai

121.
Ḥananiah, son of Jonathan, the Nazirite

122.
Salome, wife of Ḥananiah, son of the Nazirite

123.
'*šwny*, son of Simeon, son of '*šwny*

124.
Judah, son of Yehoḥanan

125. **Mt. Scopus Ossuary 12**

גרידא

126. **Mt. Scopus Ossuary**

(a) יהוחנן בר צביא
(b) סרי חיסה

127. **Abu Gosh Ossuary**

יהוסף גנבי

128. **Wadi Aḥmedieh Inscription 1**

סבורא

129. **Wadi Aḥmedieh Inscription 2**

שמעון בר טפזאי

130. **Gezer Tomb Inscription 1**

סרו בר אליעזר

131. **Gezer Tomb Inscription 2**

חנון בר יחוני

132. **Helen of Adiabene Tomb Inscription**

(a) צרן מלכתא (*Estrangela*)
(b) צרה מלכתה (*Aramaic*)

133. **Ḥizmeh Ossuary 2**

הושע בר שמעון

134. **Isawwiya Ossuary 4**

(a) שלום ברת יהוחנן
(b) שלום
(c) יונה

135. **Jaffa Ossuary**

יהוסף בר יהוחנן

125.

Gerida'

126.

(a) Yehoḥanan, son of Ṣibyā'
(b) Saray *Ḥys*'

127.

Joseph, the thief (?)

128.

Sibbura

129.

Simeon, son of Ṭiphzai

130.

Saru, son of Eliezer

131.

Ḥannun, son of Yeḥoni

132.

Ṣaran, the Queen (*Estrangela*)
Ṣarah, the Queen (*Aramaic*)

133.

Hosea, son of Simeon

134.

(a) Salome, daughter of Yehoḥanan
(b) Salome
(c) Jonah

135.

Joseph, son of Yehoḥanan (*or* John)

136. **Masada Ostracon**

1 חנני בר שמעון
2 מן שמעה

137. **Qaṭʻa Ossuary B**

קרסא
ΚΑΣΣΑ

138. **Ramat Raḥel Ossuary**

[שמע]ון בר אלעזר

139. **Šafʻat Ossuary 1**

פינחס ויעקיביה כהנה

140. **Šafʻat Ossuary 10**

אלקצדרין בר ת...

141. **Šafʻat Ossuary 11**

1 דה קוקא
2 קימו חבב
3 די טרוסיה
4 חבל וברתה

142. **Beit Saḥur Ossuary**

יהודה בר יהוחנן בר יתרא

143. **Wadi Yasul Ossuary 2**

יהוחנן בר יהוסף

144. **Er-Ram Ossuary**

(a) יהודה בן תודוס
(b) יהודה בר תודוס

145. **Trilingual Jerusalem Ossuary**

(a) חנין הבשני *(Hebrew)*
(b) Ἀνὶν Σκυθοπολείτης *(Greek)*
(c) 1 יהוסף בר אנין עניה *(Aramaic)*
2 אבה קבר בריה

136.

1. Ḥanani, son of Simeon,
2. from Shim'ah

137.

Qarsa (*Aramaic*)
Kassa (*Greek*)

138.

[Sime]on, son of Eleazar

139.

Phinehas and Ya'aqibyah, the priest

140.

Alexandrin(us), son of *T* ...

141.

1. This (is) the sepulchral chamber <of>
2. Qaymu *Ḥbb*
3. of *Ṭrwsyh.*
4. Alas! And his daughter.

142.

Judah, son of Yehoḥanan (*or* John), son of Yithra

143.

Yehoḥanan (*or* John), son of Joseph

144.

(a) Judah, son of Theudos
(b) Judah, son of Theudos

145.

(*Hebrew*) Ḥanin, the Bashanite
(*Greek*) Anin, the Scythopolitan
(*Aramaic*) 1. Joseph, son of 'Anin, the poor man;
2. the father buried his son

146. Gezer Ossuary

אלעזר בר גני

147. Mt. Zion Ossuary

שפירא אינתת שמעון

148. French Hill Ossuary

יהוסף בר חגי

149. El-Mal Dedicatory Inscription

1 [בירה]
2 שנת תלת מה
3 וחמש יקים
4 בר חמלת בר
5 נצרמלך
6 בנה בית אלה

150. *Mĕgillat Taʿănît*

אלין יומיא די לא לאתענאה בהון ומקצתהון די לא למספד בהון:

(1) מן ריש ירחא דניסן עד תמניא ביה אתוקם תמידא די לא למספד: מן תמניא ביה ועד סוף מועדא אתותב חגא די לא למספד ודי לא להתענאה:

(2) בשבעה לאייר חנכת שור ירושלם ודי לא למספד: בארבעת עשר ביה פסחא זעירא די לא למספד ודי לא להתענאה: בעשרין ותלתא ביה נפקן בני חקרא מן ירושלם: בעשרין ושבעה ביה אתנטילו כלילאי מן ירושלם די לא למספד:

(3) בארבעת עשר לסיון אחידת מגדל צור: בחמיסר ביה ובשתת עשר ביה גלו אנשי בית שאן ואנשי בקעתא: בעשרין וחמשה ביה אתנטילו דימוסנאי מיהודה ומירושלם:

(4) בארבעה בתמוז עדא ספר גזרתא:
(5) בחמשת עשר באב זמן אעי כהניא ודי לא למספד: בעשרין וארבעה ביה תבנא לדיננא:

146.

Eleazar, son of Gannai

147.

Sapphira, wife of Simeon

148.

Joseph, son of Haggai

149.

1. [In the month of],
2. (in) the year three hundred
3. and five, Yaqim,
4. son of Ḥamilat, son of
5. Neṣarmilk,
6. built the house of a god.

150.

These are the days on which one is not to fast, and on some of them one is not to mourn.

1. From the beginning of the month of Nisan until the eighth thereof the daily sacrifice was settled; one is not to mourn. From the eighth thereof until the end of the determined time, the Feast (of Weeks) was restored; one is not to mourn and one is not to fast.
2. On the seventh of Iyyar, the dedication of the wall of Jerusalem; one is not to mourn. On the fourteenth thereof, the Little Passover; one is not to mourn and one is not to fast. On the twenty-third thereof the men of Akra departed from Jerusalem. On the twenty-seventh thereof the crowns were removed from Jerusalem; one is not to mourn.
3. On the fourteenth of Siwan the taking of the tower of (Beth-)Zur. On the fifteenth thereof and on the sixteenth thereof, the people of Beth-shean and the people of the Plain were banished. On the twenty-fifth thereof the tax-collectors were removed from Judah and Jerusalem.
4. On the fourth in Tammuz the Book of Decrees was abrogated.
5. On the fifteenth in Ab, the season of the (bringing of the) wood for the priests; one is not to mourn. On the twenty-fourth thereof we returned to our own judicial system.

(6) בארבעה באלול חנכת שור ירושלם ודי לא למספד: בשיבסר ביה נפקו
רומאי מן ירושלם: בעשרין ותרין ביה תבו לקטלא משמדיא:

(7) בתלתא בתשרי בטילת אדכרתא מן שטריא:

(8) בעשרין ותלתא למרחשון אסתתר סוריגה מן עזרתא: בעשרין וחמשא ביה
אחידת שור שמרון: בעשרין ושבעה ביה תבת סלתא למסק על מדבחא:

(9) בתלתא בכסלו אתנטילו סימואתא מן דרתא: בשבעה ביה יום טב: בעשרין
וחד ביה יום הר גרזים די לא למספד: בעשרין וחמשה ביה חנכתא
תמניא יומין די לא למספד בהון:

(10) בעשרין ותמניא לטבת יתיבת כנשתא על דינא:

(11) בתרין בשבט יום טב ודי לא למספד: בעשרין ותרין ביה בטילת עבידתא
די אמר סנאה לאיתאה להיכלא די לא למספד: בעשרין ותמניה ביה אתנטיל
אנטיוכוס מלכא מן ירושלם:

(12) בתמניה ובתשעה לאדר יום תרועת מטרא: בתרין עשר ביה יום טיריון:
(בתרין עשר ביה יום טורינוס): בתלת עשר ביה יום ניקנור: בארביסר
ביה ובחמיסר ביה יומי פוריא אנון די לא למספד: בשתת עשר ביה שריו
למבני שורא דירושלם די לא למספד: בשובעת עשר ביה קמו עממיא על
פלטת ספריא במדינת כלקיס בבית זבדי והוה פרקן: בעשרין ביה צמון
עמא על מטרא ונחת להון: בעשרין ותמניא ביה אתת בשורתא טבתא
ליהודאי דילא יעדון מן אוריתא ולא למספד
להן כל אנש דאיתי עלוהי מן קדמת דנה ייסר בצלו:

6. On the fourth in Elul, the dedication of the wall of Jerusalem; one is not to mourn. On the seventeenth thereof the Romans departed from Jerusalem. On the twenty-second thereof they began again to execute evildoers.
7. On the third in Tishri the mention (of a foreign ruler ?) was removed from the (public) documents.
8. On the twenty-third of Marḥeshwan the partition-wall was torn down from the (temple's) inner court. On the twenty-fifth thereof the wall of Samaria was captured. On the twenty-seventh thereof the finely-sifted flour began to be offered on again the altar.
9. On the third in Kislew the images were removed from the outer court (of the temple). On the seventh thereof, a feast day (possibly the day of the death of Alexander Janneus). On the twenty-first thereof, the day of Mount Gerizim; one is not to mourn. On the twenty-fifth thereof, the Feast of Dedication for eight days; one is not to mourn on them.
10. On the twenty-eighth of Ṭebet the Sanhedrin took its seat for judgment.
11. On the second in Shebat, a feast day (reference obscure); and one is not to mourn. On the twenty-second thereof, the cessation of the (pagan) service which the enemy ordered brought into the temple; one is not to mourn. On the twenty-eighth thereof, Antiochus the king (probably, Antiochus VII Sidetes) was removed from Jerusalem.
12. On the eighth and ninth of Adar, the day of blowing the trumpet for rain. On the twelfth thereof, the day of *Ṭyrywn*. (On the twelfth thereof, Trajan's Day.) On the thirteenth thereof, the day of Nicanor. On the fourteenth and fifteenth thereof are the days of Purim; one is not to mourn. On the sixteenth thereof they began to build the wall of Jerusalem; one is not to mourn. On the seventeenth thereof the Gentiles rose up against the remnant of the scribes in the province of Calchis in Beth-Zabdai, but there was deliverance. On the twentieth thereof the people fasted for rain, and it came down upon them. On the twenty-eighth thereof, good tidings came to the Jews that they need not turn from the Law; one is not to mourn.

Therefore, everyone who has previously made a vow (of abstinence) is to be in prayer.

TEXT DESCRIPTION AND BIBLIOGRAPHY

TEXT DESCRIPTION AND BIBLIOGRAPHY

1. *4Q Jeremiah*[b] (*= Jer 10:11*) — *4QJer*[b]. This text is as yet unpublished. The phrase quoted here is found in F. M. Cross, *The Ancient Library of Qumran and Modern Biblical Studies* (Anchor Books, A272 ; rev. ed. ; Garden City : Doubleday, 1961) 187 n. 38. It is listed here because it gives an interesting Qumran variant reading of Jer 10:11 ; cf. the MT *mēʼarʻāʼ*, which has often been suspected of being a Hebraism (with the prefixed preposition *mē-*, instead of the more usual *min*).

Bibliography

S. Segert, " Bedeutung der Handschriftenfunde am Toten Meer für die Aramaistik," *Bibel und Qumran : Beiträge zur Erforschung der Beziehungen zwischen Bibel- und Qumranwissenschaft : Hans Bardtke zum 22.9.1966* (Berlin : Evangelische Haupt-Bibelgesellschaft, 1968) 183-87, esp. p. 185.

J. G. Janzen, *Studies in the Text of Jeremiah* (Harvard Semitic Monographs, 6 ; Cambridge : Harvard University, 1973) 181-82.

2. *4Q Prayer of Nabonidus* — *4QprNab* (*or 4QṣNab*). First published by J. T. Milik, " ' Prière de Nabonide ' et autres écrits d'un cycle de Daniel : Fragments araméens de Qumrân 4," *RB* 63 (1956) 407-15, esp. pp. 407-11. The fragment recounts the sojourn of Nabonidus, the last neo-Babylonian king, in the oasis of Teima in the Arabian desert and his miraculous healing from sickness there. Milik believes that it is the source (either in a written or oral form) that was used by the author of Daniel when he described the sickness of the persecutor of the Jews, Nebuchadnezzar. " Beneath his pen the name of the great king displaces that of Nabonidus, Teima is replaced by the more illustrious Babylon, and the illness, although still lasting seven years, acquires features unknown to medical science " (*Ten Years of Discovery in the Wilderness of Judaea* [SBT 26 ; Naperville, IL : Allenson, 1959] 36-37 ; Milik offers here a revised translation of the fragment).

Other Collections : *AC* §62 ; *ATQ*, 121-31.

Bibliography

E. Vogt, " Precatio regis Nabonid in pia narratione iudaica (4Q)," *Bib* 37 (1956) 532-34.

D. N. Freedman, " The Prayer of Nabonidus," *BASOR* 145 (1957) 31-32.

H. M. I. Gevaryahu, " Tplt nbn'yd mmglwt mdbr yhwdh [The Qumran Fragment of the Prayer of Nabonidus]," *Studies in the Dead Sea Scrolls : Lectures Delivered at the Third Annual Conference (1957) in Memory of E. L. Sukenik* (Jerusalem : Kiryat Sepher, 1957) 12-23.

A. H. Habermann, *Had-Do'ar* 37/12 (16 Shevat 1957) 215.

H. Bardtke, *Die Handschriften am Toten Meer : Die Sekte von Qumran* (Berlin : Evangelische Haupt-Bibelgesellschaft, 1958) 301.

M. Burrows, *More Light on the Dead Sea Scrolls : New Scrolls and New Interpretations, With Translations of Important Recent Discoveries* (New York : Viking, 1958) 169, 400.

I. D. Amusin, " Le fragment Koumran de la ' Prière ' du roi de Babylon Nabonid," *VDI* 4/66 (1958) 104-17.

I. M. Diakonoff, " Ancient Near East in Soviet Research," *ArOr* 27 (1959) 143-48, esp. p. 148.

A. Dupont-Sommer, " Remarques linguistiques sur un fragment araméen de Qoumrân (" Prière de Nabonide ")," *GLECS* 8 (1957-60) 48-50.

A. Dupont-Sommer, " Exorcismes et guérisons dans les écrits de Qoumrân," *Congress Volume, Oxford, 1959* (VTSup 7 ; Leiden : Brill, 1960) 246-61.

A. Dupont-Sommer, *Les écrits esseniens découverts près de la Mer Morte* (Bibliothèque historique ; Paris : Payot, 1959) 337-39, 446. Engl. *The Essene Writings from Qumran* (tr. G. Vermes ; Oxford : Blackwell, 1961 ; reprinted, Magnolia, MA : Peter Smith, 1973) 320-25.

R. Meyer, " Das Qumranfragment ' Gebet des Nabonid,' " *TLZ* 85 (1960) 831-834 ; see also *Deutsche Literaturzeitung* 82 (1961) 183-84.

L. F. Hartman, " The Great Tree and Nabuchodonosor's Madness," *The Bible in Current Catholic Thought* (ed. J. L. McKenzie ; St. Mary's Theological Studies, 1 ; New York : Herder and Herder, 1962) 75-82.

R. Meyer, " Das Gebet des Nabonid : Eine in den Qumran-Handschriften wiederentdeckte Weisheitserzählung," *Sitzberichte der sächsischen Akademie der Wissenschaften zu Leipzig* (Phil.-hist. Kl., 107/3 ; Berlin : Akademie Verlag, 1962).

Reviews : V. Hamp, *BZ* 7 (1963) 294-95 ; P. Grelot, *RQ* 4 (1963-64) 115-21 ; G. Fohrer, *ZAW* 75 (1963) 142 ; J. A. Emerton, *BL* (1964) 72 ; R. de Vaux, *RB* 71 (1964) 473-74.

G. Vermes, *The Dead Sea Scrolls in English* (Pelican Book A 551 ; Baltimore : Penguin, 1962) 229.

G. Fohrer, " 4 Q Or Nab, 11 Q tg Job und die Hioblegende," *ZAW* 75 (1963) 93-97.

J. Carmignac, " Un équivalent français de l'araméen ' gazir ' (Daniel et Prière de Nabonide)," *RQ* 4 (1963-64) 277-78.

H. M. I. Gevaryahu, " 'ywnym bspr dny'l hmnwy ldny'l wḥbryw whm'wr' bbq't dwr'," *Beth Miqra* 16 (1963) 139-46.

G. Bornkamm, " Lobpreis, Bekenntnis und Opfer," *Apophoreta : Festschrift für Ernst Haenchen* (BZNW 30 ; Berlin : Töpelmann, 1964) 46-63, esp. p. 63 n. 47.

W. Dommershausen, *Nabonid im Buche Daniel* (Mainz : Matthias Grünewald, 1964) 68-76.

Reviews : J. L. Koole, *GerefTTs* 67 (1965) 187 ; J. Haspecker, *Scholastik* 40 (1965) 606-7 ; O. Schilling, *TGl* 55 (1965) 65 ; M. Rehm, *MTZ* 17 (1966) 125-26 ; V. Hamp, *BZ* 11 (1967) 286-87.

S. Segert, " Sprachliche Bemerkungen zu einigen aramäischen Texten von Qumran," *ArOr* 33 (1965) 190-206, esp. pp. 193-95, 198-99, 200.

A. Szörényi, " Das Buch Daniel, ein kanonisierter Pescher ? " *Volume du congrès international pour l'étude de l'Ancien Testament, Genève 1965* (VTSup 15 ; Leiden : Brill, 1966) 278-94.

M. Delcor, " Le Testament de Job, la prière de Nabonide et les traditions targoumiques," *Bibel und Qumran : Beiträge zur Erforschung der Beziehungen zwischen Bibel- und Qumranwissenschaft : Hans Bardtke zum 22.9.1966* (Berlin : Evangelische Haupt-Bibelgesellschaft, 1968) 57-74.

D. S. Attema, " Het gebed van Nabonidus," *Schrift en uitleg : Studies ... aangeboden aan Prof. Dr. W. H. Gispen* (Kampen : J. H. Kok, 1970) 7-20.

M. McNamara, " Nabonidus and the Book of Daniel," *ITQ* 37 (1970) 131-49.

L. Moraldi, *I manoscritti di Qumrān* (Classici della religione : La religione ebraica ; Turin : Unione tipografico, 1971) 671-76.

A. Mertens, *Das Buch Daniel im Lichte der Texte vom Toten Meer* (SBM 12 ; Stuttgart : Katholisches Bibelwerk ; Würzburg : Echter-Verlag, 1971) 34-42.

W. Kirchschläger, " Exorzismus in Qumran ? " *Kairos* 18 (1976) 135-53, esp. pp. 144-48.

3. *4Q Pseudo-Daniel — 4QpsDan ar^{a-c}*. Published in J. T. Milik, " ' Prière de Nabonide ' et autres écrits d'un cycle de Daniel : Fragments araméens de Qumrân," *RB* 63 (1956) 407-15, esp. pp. 411-15. Ps-Dan^{a} and ps-Dan^{b} are apparently fragments from two different exemplars of the same work and so can be read together. Whether ps-Dan^{c} belongs to the same work is not entirely certain. The fragments deal with (A) the flood and the tower of Babel, (B) the exodus from Egypt, (C) Israel's sin and the exile, (D) the first of the four kingdoms, (E) the Hellenistic era, and (F) the eschatological era. Milik describes the script of the fragments as Herodian but suggests that the document was originally composed toward the end of the Seleucid empire (ca. 100 B.C), because there is no allusion to Roman domination and because Balakros (E. 2) may be Alexander Balas, whose reign was between 150 and 145 B.C.

Bibliography

A. Mertens, *Das Buch Daniel im Lichte der Texte vom Toten Meer* (SBM 12 ; Stuttgart : Katholisches Bibelwerk ; Würzburg : Echter-Verlag, 1971) 42-50.

Related Literature

4QpsDan[d] (4Q*246*), which has also been called 4QpsDan A[a]. Not yet published, this text was discussed in a public lecture by J. T. Milik at Harvard University in December 1972. See J. A. Fitzmyer, "The Contribution of Qumran Aramaic to the Study of the New Testament," *NTS* 20 (1973-74) 382-407, esp. pp. 391-94.

4. *1Q Daniel[a,b] — 1QDan[a,b]* (1Q*71*, *72*). Originally published by D. Barthélemy in *Qumran Cave I* (DJD 1; Oxford: Clarendon, 1955) 150-52 (without photographs), these fragments of Dan 1:10-17; 2:2-6 (1QDan[a]) and 3:22-28, 27-30 (1QDan[b]) come from different scrolls but belong to the same (Herodian) period paleographically. See the discussion (with photographs) in J. C. Trever, "Completion of the Publication of Some Fragments from Qumran Cave I," *RQ* 5 (1964-66) 323-44; 1QDan[a] is on pl. V (= p. 342), and 1QDan[b] is on pl. VI (= p. 343). Since Dan 1:10-17 is from the Hebrew part of the book, we have not reproduced it here. As in the MT of Daniel, 2:2-4a is also in Hebrew. The lacunae in the texts can be filled in by referring to the MT.

Bibliography

J. C. Trever, "1QDan[a], the Latest of the Qumran Manuscripts," *RQ* 7 (1969-1971) 277-86.

A. Mertens, *Das Buch Daniel im Lichte der Texte vom Toten Meer* (SBM 12; Stuttgart: Katholisches Bibelwerk; Würzburg: Echter-Verlag, 1971) 27-28.

J. C. H. Lebram, "Perspektiven der gegenwärtigen Danielforschung," *JSJ* 5 (1974) 1-33.

5. *11Q Targum of Job — 11QtgJob.* Published in J. P. M. van der Ploeg and A. S. van der Woude (avec la collaboration de B. Jongeling), *Le targum de Job de la grotte XI de Qumrân* (Koninklijke nederlandse Akademie van Wetenschappen; Leiden: Brill, 1971). Though the fragments range from Job 17:14 to 42:11, it is only from Job 37:10 on that the text is substantially intact. The more fragmentary columns contain the last part of the second cycle of debates in the dialogue (17:14–21:24), parts of the third cycle of debates (22:1–31:40), and considerable parts of the poetic discourses of Elihu (32:1–37:24). In the later section there is Yahweh's speech from the whirlwind (38:1–41:14), Job's answer (42:1-6), and part of the epilogue (42:9-11). By and large the targum is a rather literal translation of the Hebrew, though there are some added phrases and periphrastic renderings. The editors have dated the Qumran copy to the early

1st century A.D. but suggest that the targum was originally composed sometime between the final redaction of Daniel and the composition of the *Genesis Apocryphon.*
Other Collections : *ATQ*, 1-73.

Bibliography

Reviews of the *editio princeps* : P.-M. Bogaert, *RTL* 3 (1972) 86-90 ; J. Coppens, *ETL* 48 (1972) 221-22 ; E. Cortes, *Estudios Franciscanos* 73 (1972) 124f. ; G. Fohrer, *ZAW* 84 (1972) 128 ; D. Lys, *ETR* 47 (1972) 365-66 ; B. Z. Wacholder, *JBL* 91 (1972) 414-15 ; S. Medala and Z. J. Kapera, *Folia orientalia* 14 (1972-73) 320-23 ; M. Dahood, *Bib* 54 (1973) 283-86 ; G. R. Driver, *BL* (1973) 56 ; P. Grelot, *RQ* 8 (1972-74) 105-14 ; C. T. Fritsch, *TToday* 30 (1973-74) 442-43 ; H. Bardtke, *OLZ* 70 (1975) 468-72.

W. Bacher, " Das Targum zu Hiob," *MGWJ* 20 (1871) 208-23, 283-84 [study of later targum of Job].

G. L. Harding, " Recent Discoveries in Jordan," *PEQ* 90 (1958) 7-18, esp. p. 17.

J. P. M. van der Ploeg, " Le targum de Job de la grotte 11 de Qumran (11Qtg-Job), Première Communication," *Medelelingen der koninklijke nederlandse Akademie van Wetenschappen* (Afd. Letterkunde, Nieuwe reeks, deel 25, No. 9 ; Amsterdam : N. V. Noord-Hollandsche Uitgevers Maatschappij, 1962) 543-57.

Reviews : J. Cantera, *Sefarad* 23 (1963) 143-44 ; B. J. Roberts, *BL* (1963) 64 and *BO* 20 (1963) 348-49 ; P. W. Skehan, *CBQ* 25 (1963) 122-23 ; P. Winter, *RQ* 4 (1962-64) 441-42 ; H. J. de Bie, *NedTTs* 18 (1963-64) 222-23 ; P. Benoit, *RB* 71 (1964) 293-94.

J. P. M. van der Ploeg, " Een Targum van het boek Job : Een nieuwe vondst in de Woestijn van Juda," *Het heilig Land* 15/11 (1962) 145-49.

G. Fohrer, " 4 Q Or Nab, 11 Q tg Job und die Hioblegende," *ZAW* 75 (1963) 93-97.

A. S. van der Woude, " Das Hiobtargum aus Qumran Höhle XI," *Congress Volume* : *Bonn 1962* (VTSup 9 ; Leiden : Brill, 1963) 322-31 ; Engl. *AJBA* 1/2 (1968-69) 19-29.

W. H. Brownlee, *The Meaning of the Qumrân Scrolls for the Bible with Special Attention to the Book of Isaiah* (New York : Oxford, 1964) 81.

J. P. M. van der Ploeg, " Un targum du livre de Job : Nouvelle découverte dans le désert de Juda," *BVC* 58 (1964) 79-87.

A. Dupont-Sommer, " Notes qoumrâniennes," *Sem* 15 (1965) 71-78, esp. pp. 71-74.

S. Segert, " Sprachliche Bemerkungen zu einigen aramäischen Texten von Qumran," *ArOr* 33 (1965) 190-206, esp. pp. 193, 198.

M. Delcor, " Le Testament de Job, la prière de Nabonide et les traditions targoumiques," *Bibel und Qumran* : *Beiträge zur Erforschung der Beziehungen zwischen Bibel- und Qumranwissenschaft* : *Hans Bardtke zum 22.9.1966* (Berlin : Evangelische Haupt-Bibelgesellschaft, 1968) 57-74.

R. Le Déaut, " Le substrat araméen des évangiles : Scolies en marge de l'*Aramaic Approach* de Matthew Black," *Bib* 49 (1968) 388-99, esp. p. 391.

J. A. Sanders, " Cave 11 Surprises and the Question of Canon," *New Directions in Biblical Archaeology* (eds. D. N. Freedman and J. C. Greenfield ; Garden City : Doubleday, 1969) 101-16, esp. pp. 101-2.

E. W. Tuinstra, *Hermeneutische aspecten van de Targum van Job uit grot XI van Qumrân* (Groningen : Dissertation, Rijksuniversiteit te Groningen, 1970).
Reviews : E. G. Clarke, *BL* (1973) 57.

B. Jongeling, " Een belangrijke Dode-Zeerol : Job in het Aramees," *Rondom het Woord* 13 (1971) 282-93.

J. P. M. van der Ploeg, " L'édition des manuscrits de la grotte XI de Qumrân par l'Académie Royale des Sciences des Pays-Bas," *Acta orientalia neerlandica : Proceedings of the Congress of the Dutch Oriental Society Held in Leiden on the Occasion of Its 50th Anniversary, 8th-9th May 1970* (ed. P. W. Pestman ; Leiden : Brill, 1971) 43-45.

D. Sperber, " A Note on the Word qśyṭh," *Acta Antiqua* 19 (1971) 37-39.

H. Bardtke, " Literaturbericht über Qumrān. VI. Teil : II. Das Genesis-Apocryphon 1QGen Ap. ; III. Das Hiobtargum aus Höhle XI von Qumrān (11 QtgJob)," *TRu* 37 (1972) 193-219, esp. 205-19.

M. Dahood, " Is the Emendation of *yādîn* to *yāzîn* Necessary in Job 36,31 ? " *Bib* 53 (1972) 539-41.

J. C. Greenfield and S. Shaked, " Three Iranian Words in the Targum of Job from Qumran," *ZDMG* 122 (1972) 37-45.

P. Grelot, " Note de critique textuelle sur Job xxxix 27," *VT* 22 (1972) 487-89.

B. Jongeling, " Contributions of the Qumran Job Targum to the Aramaic Vocabulary," *JSS* 17 (1972) 191-97.

K. R. Veenhof, " De Job-Targum uit Qumran gepubliceerd," *Phoenix* 18 (1972) 179-84.

M. Delcor, " Le targum de Job et l'araméen du temps de Jésus," *RevScRel* 47 (1973) 232-61 ; also in *Exégèse biblique et judaïsme* (ed. J.-E. Ménard ; Strasbourg : Faculté de théologie catholique, 1973) 78-107.

A. Díez Macho, " Le targum palestinien," *RevScRel* 47 (1973) 169-231, esp. 176-88 ; also in *Exégèse biblique et judaïsme* (ed. J.-E. Ménard ; Strasbourg : Faculté de théologie catholique, 1973) 15-77, esp. pp. 22-34.

S. A. Kaufman, " The Job Targum from Qumran," *JAOS* 93 (1973) 317-27.

Y. Komlosh, " Trgwm spr 'ywb [The Character of the Targum to Job]," *Proceedings of the Fifth World Congress of Jewish Studies*, IV (Jerusalem : World Union of Jewish Studies, 1973) 239-46 (Engl. abstract p. 272).

F. J. Morrow, Jr., " 11 Q Targum Job and the Massoretic Text," *RQ* 8 (1972-1975) 253-56.

M. Pope, *Job : Introduction, Translation, and Notes* (AB 15 ; 3d ed. ; Garden City : Doubleday, 1973) passim.

F. Rundgren, " Aramaica II," *Orientalia Suecana* 22 (1973) 66-81, esp. pp. 72-73.

F. I. Andersen, " The Qumran Targum of Job," *Buried History* 10 (1974) 77-84.

D. Boyarin, " Aramaic Notes I : Column 36 of 11QtgJob," *JANESCU* 6 (1974) 29-33.

A. Caquot, " Un écrit sectaire de Qoumrân : le ' Targoum de Job,' " *RHR* 185 (1974) 9-27.

J. A. Fitzmyer, " The Contribution of Qumran Aramaic to the Study of the New Testament," *NTS* 20 (1973-74) 382-407.

J. A. Fitzmyer, " Some Observations on the Targum of Job from Qumran Cave 11," *CBQ* 36 (1974) 503-24 [= *Patrick W. Skehan Festschrift*].

J. Gray, " The Massoretic Text of the Book of Job, the Targum and the Septuagint Version in the Light of the Qumran Targum (11 QtargJob)," *ZAW* 86 (1974) 331-50.

B. Jongeling, *Een aramees Boek Job uit de Bibliotheek van Qumrân* (Exegetica ns 3 ; Amsterdam : Ton Bolland, 1974).

Reviews : M. J. Mulder, *JSJ* 6 (1975) 104-5.

B. Jongeling, " La colonne XVI de 11 Q tg Job," *RQ* 8 (1972-75) 415-16.

B. Jongeling, " The Job Targum from Qumran Cave 11 (11QtgJob)," *Folia orientalia* 15 (1974) 181-96.

R. Le Déaut, " Targumic Literature and New Testament Interpretation," *BTB* 4 (1974) 243-89.

T. Muraoka, " The Aramaic of the Old Targum of Job from Qumran Cave XI," *JJS* 25 (1974) 425-43.

M. Sokoloff, *The Targum to Job from Qumran Cave XI* (Bar-Ilan Studies in Near Eastern Languages and Culture ; Ramat-Gan : Bar-Ilan University, 1974).

Reviews : B. Jongeling, *JSJ* 6 (1975) 117-20 ; L. H. Schiffman, *JBL* 95 (1976) 158-60 ; L. Frizzell, *CBQ* 37 (1974) 427 ; P. S. Alexander, *JTS* 27 (1976) 166-68 ; J. Robert, *Orientalia* 45 (1976) 459 ; D. Pardee, *JNES* 36 (1977) 216-17.

A. D. York, " The Dating of Targumic Literature," *JSJ* 5 (1974) 49-62.

A. D. York, " *Zr' rwm'h* as an Indication of the Date of 11QtgJob ? " *JBL* 93 (1974) 445-46.

R. Weiss, " Further Notes on the Qumran Targum to Job," *JSS* 19 (1974) 13-18.

M. Dahood, " Four Ugaritic Personal Names and Job 39: 5.26-27," *ZAW* 87 (1975) 220.

R. Weiss, " Zr' rwm' in 11Q tg Job xx,7," *IEJ* 25 (1975) 140-41.

R. Weiss, *Htrgwm h'rmy lspr 'ywb : The Aramaic Targum of Job* (Thesis submitted for the degree ' Doctor of Philosophy,' Jerusalem : Senate of the Hebrew University, 1974) [Study of later targum of Job, not of the Qumran targum].

R. Weiss, " Ḥylwpy nwsḥ byn htrgwm l'ywb mqwmr'n 11 wnwsḥt hmswrh [Recensional Variations between the Aramaic Translation to Job from Qumran Cave 11 and the Massoretic Text], " *Shnaton* 1 (1975) 123-27 (+ p. xxiv [Engl. summary]).

R. Meyer, " Der gegenwärtige Stand der Erforschung der in Palästina neu gefundenen Handschriften. 51. Ein Rückblick, " *TLZ* 101 (1976) 815-25, esp. pp. 819-23.

R. Borger, " Hiob xxxix 23 nach dem Qumran-Targum, " *VT* 27 (1977) 102-5.

T. Muraoka, " Notes on the Old Targum of Job from Qumran Cave XI, " *RQ* 9 (1977-78) 117-25.

A. D. York, " 11 Q tg Job xxi, 4-5 (Job 32, 13), " *RQ* 9 (1977-78) 127-29.

G. Howard, " Fragment 12 of 11QtgJb and the Septuagint of Job 29:7-16, " *Bulletin, IOSCS* 9 (1976) 10-11 [abstract].

W. H. Brownlee, " The Cosmic Role of Angels in the 11Q Targum of Job, " *JSJ* 8 (1977) 83-84.

P. W. Coxon, " The Problem of Nasalization in Biblical Aramaic in the Light of 1 Q GA and 11 Q Tg Job, " *RQ* 9 (1977-78) 253-58.

6. *1Q New Jerusalem — 1QJN ar* (1Q32). First published by J. T. Milik in *DJD* 1. 134-35, pl. XXXI, these fragments may belong to an Aramaic apocalypse inspired by the final chapters of Ezekiel. The few stray phrases that are legible describe the New Jerusalem and the New Temple. This text should be studied in conjunction with the following three texts: 2QJN ar, 5QJN ar, 11QJN ar.

7. *2Q New Jerusalem — 2QJN ar* (2Q24). M. Baillet, who first published this text in " Fragments araméens de Qumrân 2 : Description de la Jérusalem nouvelle," *RB* 62 (1955) 222-45 and then in *DJD* 3. 84-89, pl. XVI, dates the script to the beginning of the 1st century A.D. The text forms part of an apocalyptic vision. The fragments deal with the measurements of the streets(?) of the New Jerusalem (frg. 1); the table for the bread of presence (frg. 3), as in Ezek 41: 21-22; the offering of bread (frg. 4); and the altar of holocausts (frgs. 5-8), as in Ezek 43:13-27.
Other Collections: *AC* §61.

Bibliography

B. Jongeling, " Note additionelle," *JSJ* 1 (1970-71) 185-86.

8. *5Q New Jerusalem — 5QJN ar* (5Q15). Published by J. T. Milik in *DJD* 3. 184-91, pls. XL-XLI. Frg. 1 tells of a visionary inspecting the New Jerusalem in the company of a " divine measurer." It speaks of the blocks in the city (1:1-2), the streets paved with precious stones (1:3-7), the postern gates (1:8-9), the portals (1:10-14), the gates (1: 15–2:5), the houses along the wall from gate to gate (2:6-10), and the dining-houses (2:10-15). The remaining fragments come from the same manuscript as frg. 1 does. Milik describes its script as Herodian (comparable to that of 1QIsa[b], 1QH [first hand], 1QM, and 1QapGen) and its language as a western Aramaic dialect later than the Aramaic of Daniel.

Bibliography

J. Starcky, *RB* 63 (1956) 66; *BA* 19 (1956) 94 (preliminary description).
L. Moraldi, *I manoscritti di Qumrān* (Classici della religione: La religione ebraica; Turin: Unione tipografico, 1971) 723-31.

9. *11Q New Jerusalem — 11QJN ar.* Published by B. Jongeling in " Publication provisoire d'un fragment provenant de la grotte 11 de Qumrân (11Q Jér Nouv ar)," *JSJ* 1 (1970-71) 58-64. See also his

" Note additionelle," *JSJ* 1 (1970-71) 185-86. Jongeling calls attention to the close parallels between this text and 2QJN ar frg. 4, lines 9-16. Both describe the offering of bread in the temple of the New Jerusalem. See also 5QJN ar, published by J. T. Milik in *DJD* 3. 184-91, pls. XL-XLI.

10-11. *4Q Enoch*^{c} — *4QEn*^{c}. J. T. Milik in " Hénoch au pays des aromates (ch. XXVII a XXXII) : Fragments araméens de la grotte 4 de Qumran," *RB* 65 (1958), 70-77, pl. 1, calls this 4En^{b}, but more recently in " Problèmes de la littérature hénochique à la lumière des fragments araméens de Qumrân," *HTR* 64 (1971) 333-78, esp. pp. 336-337 he calls it 4QEn^{c}. The MS is dated by Milik to the last third of the first century B.C. Part of the so-called second journey of Enoch (chaps. 21–36), the first column of this text is equivalent to *1 Enoch* 30:1–32:1 and describes Enoch's sojourn among the aromatic trees on his way to the Garden of Truth. The adjoining column corresponds to 1 Enoch 35:1–36:4 — the end of Enoch's journey to the north, and his journey to the south. Cf. now J. T. Milik, *The Books of Enoch* (see bibliography below), 201-4 (= 4QEn^{c} 1 ii 23-30).

Bibliography

M. Black, " The Fragments of the Aramaic Enoch from Qumran," *La littérature juive entre Tenach et Mischna* : *Quelques problèmes* (ed. W. C. van Unnik ; RechBib 9 ; Leiden : Brill, 1974) 15-28.

P. Grelot, " Hénoch et ses écritures, " *RB* 82 (1975) 481-500.

M. Black, " The ' Parables ' of Enoch (1 En 37-71) and the ' Son of Man, ' " *ExpTim* 78 (1976) 5-8.

J. T. Milik, *The Books of Enoch* : *Aramaic Fragments of Qumrân Cave* 4 (Oxford : Clarendon, 1976).

Reviews : P. Grelot, *RB* 83 (1976) 605-18 ; A.-M. Denis, *Muséon* 90 (1977) 462-69.

J. A. Fitzmyer, " Implications of the New Enoch Literature from Qumran, " *TS* 38 (1977) 332-45.

12. *4Q Enoch*^{e} — *4QEn*^{e}. Published by J. T. Milik in *RB* 65 (1958) 70-77, pl. 1, where it is called 4QEn^{d}, though now in *HTR* 64 (1971) 336-37 it is called 4QEn^{e}. Another section of Enoch's second journey, it is the equivalent of *1 Enoch* 31:2–32:3. It narrates the end of Enoch's travel through the land of the aromatic trees and prepares for his arrival at the Garden of Truth. Milik dates the MS to the first half of the first century B.C. Cf. now *The Books of Enoch*, 232-34 (= 4QEn^{e} 1 xxvi 14-21).

13. *4Q Enoch Astronomical*[b] — *4QEnAstr*[b]. Published by J. T. Milik in *RB* 65 (1958) 70-77, esp. pp. 76-77. Formerly called 4QEnAstr[a], it is described in *HTR* 64 (1971) 336-37 as 4QEnAstr[b], frg. 23 (= *1 Enoch* 76:13–77:4). Milik calls its script " une belle écriture hérodienne," similar to that of 1QIsa[b], 1QapGen, and 1QH (first hand). The correspondences with the Ethiopic version are not very close. In the Ethiopic of *1 Enoch* 78:3 the northern region is divided into three parts: the dwelling of men; the seas of water, the abysses, forests, and rivers, darkness and clouds; the Garden of Truth. The Ethiopic of *1 Enoch* 78:1 simply says that the first region is called the east because it is the first (i.e., a play on *qedem* [" east "] and *qadmônî* [" first "]). Cf. now *The Books of Enoch*, 288-91 (= 4En Astr[b] 23:6-9).

Bibliography

J. T. Milik, *RB* 63 (1956) 60; *BA* 19 (1956) 89 (preliminary description).

J. T. Milik, " Turfan et Qumran: Livre des Géants juif et manichéen," *Tradition und Glaube: Festgabe für Karl Georg Kuhn*, (eds. G. Jeremias et al.; Göttingen: Vandenhoeck & Ruprecht, 1971) 117-27, esp. pp. 121-25.

14. *1Q Enoch Giants* — *1QEnGiants* (1Q*23*). First published by J. T. Milik in *DJD* 1. 97-98, pl. XIX, where he suggested that it might belong to the " Wars of the Patriarchs " — a possible source for *Jubilees* 34:1-9 and the *Testament of Judah* 3–7. In " Turfan et Qumran: Livre des Géants juif et manichéen," *Tradition und Glaube: Festgabe für Karl Georg Kuhn* (eds. G. Jeremias et al.; Göttingen: Vandenhoeck & Ruprecht, 1971) 117-27, esp. p. 120, Milik now identifies frg. 1 as part of the " Book of Giants " preserved in Manichean literature and then joins frgs. 9, 14, and 15 to form another part of the " Book of Giants." Cf. now *The Books of Enoch*, 301-3.

Bibliography

J. T. Milik, " Problèmes de la littérature hénochique à la lumière des fragments araméens de Qumrân," *HTR* 64 (1971) 333-78, esp. p. 366.

M. Philonenko, " Une citation manichéenne du livre d'Hénoch," *RHPR* 52 (1972) 337-40.

15. *2Q Enoch Giants* — *2QEnGiants* (2Q*26*). Published by M. Baillet in *DJD* 3. 90-91, pl. XVII. The script is termed " Herodian calligraphy." Because it describes the washing of a tablet in water, Baillet supposed that it might be a fragment from a ritual. In " Problèmes de la littérature hénochique à la lumière des fragments araméens de Qumrân," *HTR* 64 (1971) 366, J. T. Milik says that it belongs to the "Book of Giants." Cf. now *The Books of Enoch*, 334-35.

Bibliography

S. Segert, Review of M. Baillet et al., *DJD* 3, in *RQ* 4 (1963-64) 279-96, esp. p. 286 ; see also *ArOr* 33 (1965) 205.

16. *4Q Enoch Giants[a] — 4QEnGiants[a].* Published by J. T. Milik in "Turfan et Qumran : Livre des Géants juif et manichéen," *Tradition und Glaube : Festgabe für Karl Georg Kuhn* (eds. G. Jeremias et al. ; Göttingen : Vandenhoeck & Ruprecht, 1971) 117-27, esp. pp. 124-26. Milik says that it was copied by the same scribe as 4QEn[c] and so is to be dated to the turn of the Christian era. Frg. 1 contains the names of two giants, while frg. 2 is a letter from Enoch to Shemiḥazah and the other giants complaining about their conduct (see Gen 6:1-4). Cf. now *The Books of Enoch*, 310-16.

Bibliography

J. T. Milik, "Problèmes de la littérature hénochique à la lumière des fragments araméens de Qumrân," *HTR* 64 (1971) 333-78, esp. pp. 366-72.

17. *4Q Enoch Giants[b] — 4QEnGiants[b].* Published by J. T. Milik in "Turfan et Qumran," 121-25. The copy is dated to 100-50 B.C. Col. 2 tells the story of a dream vision that disquiets the giants to the point that they seek out Enoch for an interpretation, while col. 3 speaks of the mission of Mahawai to Enoch and begins a dialogue between the two. F. M. Cross ("The Development of the Jewish Scripts," *BANE*, 170-264, esp. p. 190, fig. 4, line 3) refers to this text as 4QpsEnoch[a] (Starcky's lot), but Milik (*HTR* 64 [1971] 366-72, esp. p. 367) gives it more recently as 4QHenG[b]. Cf. now *The Books of Enoch*, 304-6.

18. *4Q Enoch Giants[c] — 4QEnGiants[c].* Published by J. T. Milik in "Turfan et Qumran," 124. This fragment seems to contain the end of a speech by Shemiḥazah and the beginning of one by his son 'Ohyah. Shemiḥazah speaks of his defeat in battle, while 'Ohyah starts to recount a dream-vision. The text, as yet unnumbered and not dated by Milik, will be published in more definitive form by J. Starcky. Cf. now *The Books of Enoch*, 307-8.

19. *6Q Enoch Giants — 6QEnGiants* (6Q*8*). Originally published by M. Baillet in *DJD* 3. 116-19, pl. XXIV, who dated the MS to the middle of the 1st century A.D. and suggested an affinity of content and form with 1QapGen. J. T. Milik in " Turfan et Qumran," 119-120, has identified frg. 1 as part of the " Book of Giants." It tells of a vision of Mahawai, in which his father Baraqi'el participates somehow, and of 'Ohyah's taunting(?) response to the recounting of the dream. The other fragments cannot be identified with certainty and are presented here merely for philological reasons. Cf. now *The Books of Enoch*, 300-301.

Bibliography

J. A. Fitzmyer, *The Genesis Apocryphon of Qumran Cave I : A Commentary* (BibOr 18A ; 2d ed. ; Rome : Biblical Institute, 1971) 191-92.

20. *1Q Testament of Levi — 1QTLevi ar* (1Q*21*). J. T. Milik, who published these fragments in *DJD* 1. 87-91, pl. XVII, suggests that the context of frgs. 1 and 7 is like that of *T. Levi* 8:11 and that frgs. 3-6 correspond to parts of the Bodleian Aramaic fragment (see A. E. Cowley and R. H. Charles, " An Early Source of the Testaments of the Patriarchs," *JQR* os 19 [1906-7] 566-83). He also suggests that if *šlm* in frg. 8 is taken as " Salem " rather than " peace," there may be a connection with the Cambridge Aramaic fragment (see H. L. Pass and J. Arendzen, " Fragment of an Aramaic Text of the Testament of Levi," *JQR* os 12 [1899-1900] 651-61). English translations of the Bodleian and Cambridge fragments can be found in *APOT*, 2. 364-67. *Other Collections* : AC §60.

Related Literature

W. Wright, *Catalogue of Syriac Manuscripts in the British Museum, Acquired since the Year 1838* (London : British Museum, 1871) 2.997 (T. Levi syr = Br. Mus. Add. 17193, fol. 71a).

I. Lévi, " Notes sur le texte araméen du Testament de Lévi récemment découvert," *REJ* 54 (1907) 166-80.

R. H. Charles, *The Greek Versions of the Testaments of the Twelve Patriarchs* (Oxford : Clarendon, 1908), esp. pp. liii-lvii, 245-56 (App. III).

J. T. Milik, " Le Testament de Lévi en araméen : Fragment de la grotte 4 de Qumrân," *RB* 62 (1955) 398-406.

A. Dupont-Sommer, " Le *Testament de Lévi* (XVII-XVIII) et la secte juive de l'alliance," *Sem* 4 (1951-52) 33-53.

M. de Jonge, *The Testaments of the Twelve Patriarchs : A Study of their Text,*

Composition and Origin (Assen : van Gorcum, 1953 ; 2d ed. [= corrected reprint], 1975).
P. Grelot, " Le Testament araméen de Lévi est-it traduit de l'hébreu ? A propos du fragment de Cambridge, col. c 10 à d 1," *REJ* ns 14 (1955) 91-99.
M. de Jonge, *Testamenta XII Patriarcharum : Edited According to Cambridge University Library MS Ff 1.24 fol. 203a-262b with Short Notes* (PVTG 1 ; Leiden : Brill, 1964) 10-22.
C. Burchard, " Neues zur Überlieferung der Testamente der Zwölf Patriarchen : Eine unbeachtete griechische Handschrift (Athos, Laura I 48) und eine unbekannte neugriechische Fassung (Bukarest, Bibl. Acad. 580 [341])," *NTS* 12 (1965-66) 245-58.
M. E. Stone, *The Testament of Levi : A First Study of the Armenian MSS of the Testaments of the XII Patriarchs in the Convent of St. James, Jerusalem* (Jerusalem : St. James Press, 1969).
M. de Jonge (ed.), *Studies on the Testaments of the Twelve Patriarchs : Text and Interpretation* (SVTP 3 ; Leiden : Brill, 1975), esp. pp. 247-60.

21. *4Q Testament of Levi*[a] — *4QTLevi ar*[a]. In the original publication (" Le Testament de Lévi en araméen : Fragment de la grotte 4 de Qumrân," *RB* 62 [1955] 398-406), J. T. Milik called this MS 4QTLevi ar[b], but more recently (in *HTR* 64 [1971] 344) he has called it 4QT-Levi ar[a]. As a description of the call and purification of Levi, it runs parallel with an addition to *T. Levi* 2:3 found in the Greek MS e (printed in R. H. Charles's *apparatus criticus* on this verse). On paleographic grounds, Milik dates the MS to the end of the 2d or beginning of the 1st century B.C.
Other Collections : *SWDS*, pl. 8 (pp. 16, 25-26) ; *AC* §60.

Bibliography

P. Grelot, " Notes sur la Testament araméen de Lévi : Fragment de la Bodleian Library, Colonne a," *RB* 63 (1956) 391-406.
M. Burrows, *More Light on the Dead Sea Scrolls* (New York : Viking, 1958) 179-80.
M. Philonenko, " Les interpolations chrétiennes des *Testaments des Douze Patriarches* et les manuscrits de Qoumrân," *RHPR* 38 (1958) 309-43 ; 39 (1959) 14-38 (summary by H. Stegemann in *ZDPV* 83 [1967] 203-5).
M. de Jonge, " Christian Influence in the Testaments of the Twelve Patriarchs," *NovT* 4 (1960) 182-235.
E. Larsson, " Qumranlitteraturen och de tolv patriarkernas testamenten," *SEA* 25 (1960) 109-18.
J. Becker, *Untersuchungen zur Entstehungsgeschichte der Testamente der Zwölf Patriarchen* (AGJU 8 ; Leiden : Brill, 1970).
P. Grelot, " Quatre cent trente ans (Ex. xii, 34) : Du Pentateuque au Testament araméen de Lévi," *Hommages à André Dupont-Sommer* (Paris : A. Maisonneuve, 1971) 383-94.

H. Jacobson, " The Position of the Fingers during the Priestly Blessing, " *RQ* 9 (1977) 259-60.

22. *4Q Visions of ʿAmram^a — 4Qʿ Amram^a*. First published along with the other ʿAmram fragments in J. T. Milik, " 4Q Visions de ʿAmram et une citation d'Origène," *RB* 79 (1972) 77-97, esp. pp. 81 (frgs. 1-2) and 84 (frg. 3). It tells of a vision granted to ʿAmram, the father of Moses (according to Exod 6:20). Milik has read this MS together with the better preserved 4QʿAmram^b (see the next item) so that 4QʿAmram^a, frgs. 1 and 2 are taken as parts of the same text as 4QʿAmram^b, frg. 1, and 4QʿAmram^a, frg. 3 is viewed as part of 4QʿAmram^b, frgs. 2 and 3.

23. *4Q Visions of ʿAmram^b — 4QʿAmram^b*. Published by J. T. Milik in *RB* 79 (1972) 78-84, the text has been filled out in a few places by recourse to 4QʿAmram^{a,d}. The first fragment records ʿAmram's vision of a debate between two angelic figures (one good, the other evil) regarding his fate, while the second and third fragments present a conversation in which the two identify themselves to ʿAmram. The one having power over the darkness is called Malkî-rešaʿ ; the angel of light is probably Malkî-ṣedeq. Milik describes the MS as very old — certainly from the 2d century B.C., possibly even from the first half of that century. He sees an allusion to this work in Origen's 35th homily (on Luke 12:58-59/Matt 5:25-26), even though Abraham rather than ʿAmram is named there.

Bibliography

K. Berger, " Der Streit des guten und des bösen Engels um die Seele : Beobachtungen zu 4Q Amr^b und Judas 9," *JSJ* 4 (1973-74) 1-18.

24. *4Q Visions of ʿAmram^c — 4QʿAmram^c*. Published by J. T. Milik in *RB* 79 (1972) 77-78. This appears to be the beginning of an account of ʿAmram's visions or his testament. According to the MT of Exod 6:20 ʿAmram (Moses' father) lived 137 years, but according to the LXX and this text his life span was 136 years.

Bibliography

P. Grelot, " Quatre cent trente ans (Ex 12,40)," *Homenaje a Juan Prado* (Madrid : C. S. I. C., 1975) 559-70.

25. *4Q Visions of ʿAmram[d] — 4QʿAmram[d].* Published by J. T. Milik in *RB* 79 (1972) 83 (frg. 1) and 84 (frg. 2), these fragments are connected by him with frgs. 2 and 3 of 4QʿAmram[b].

26. *4Q Visions of ʿAmram[e(?)] — 4QʿAmram[e(?)].* Published by J. T. Milik in *RB* 79 (1972) 90-91. Milik suggests that this may be a part of the " Testament of ʿAmram " in which ʿAmram instructs his sons about the meaning of his vision of the two angelic figures.

27. *4Q Testament of Qahat — 4QTQahat.* Published by J. T. Milik, " 4Q Visions de ʿAmram et une citation d'Origène," *RB* 79 (1972) 77-97, esp. p. 97. It is part of the " Testament of Qahat " (Qahat is Levi's son and ʿAmram's father). It alludes to the transmission of traditions from Levi's predecessors (see *Jubilees* 45:16). Milik thinks that the three testaments of the priestly patriarchs (Levi, Qahat, ʿAmram) circulated in a Greek version in the Christian era.

28. *4Q " Messianic " Text — 4QMess ar.* First published by J. Starcky in " Un texte messianique araméen de la grotte 4 de Qumrân," *Ecole des langues orientales anciennes de l'Institut Catholique de Paris : Mémorial du cinquantenaire 1914-1964* (Travaux d'Institut Catholique de Paris, 10 ; Paris : Bloud et Gay, 1964) 51-66. Described wrongly by Starcky as " messianic " and " astrological," this text presents a fragmentary portion of a prediction or pronouncement about a new-born child. It may be related to the descriptions of the birth of Noah (see *1 Enoch* 106–8 ; *Jubilees* 4–10 ; 1QapGen 2 ; 1Q*19*, frg. 3 ; and Josephus, *Ant.* 1.3.1-9 §72-108). Starcky relates the script to the round semiformal type of the Herodian period (30 B.C. to A.D. 20) but prefers a date in the 1st century A.D. According to J. Carmignac, it was most likely copied by the same scribe who copied 4QpPs[a], 4QpIsa[a], and 4QpHos[b].
Other Collections : *SWDS*, pl. 11 (pp. 17, 27-28).

Bibliography

J. Carmignac, " Les horoscopes de Qumrân," *RQ* 5 (1964-66) 199-217, esp. pp. 206-17.

A. Dupont-Sommer, " Deux documents horoscopiques esséniens découverts à Qumran, près de la mer Morte," *CRAIBL* (1965) 239-53.

J. A. Fitzmyer, " The Aramaic ' Elect of God ' Text from Qumran Cave IV," *CBQ* 27 (1965) 348-72 ; slightly revised in *Essays on the Semitic Background*

of the New Testament (London: Chapman, 1971; reprinted, Missoula, MT: Scholars Press, 1974) 127-60.
I. D. Amusin, " ' Izvrannik Voga ' b Kumranskich tekstach," *VDI* 92/1 (1966) 73-79.
R. E. Brown, " J. Starcky's Theory of Qumran Messianic Development," *CBQ* 28 (1966) 51-57.
F. Michelini Tocci, *I manoscritti del Mar Morto: Introduzione, traduzione e commento* (Bari: Laterza, 1967) 349.
J. T. Milik, " Problèmes de la littérature hénochique à la lumière des fragments araméens de Qumrân," *HTR* 64 (1971) 333-78, esp. p. 366.
L. Moraldi, *I manoscritti di Qumrān* (Classici delle religione: La religione ebraica; Turin: Unione tipografico, 1971) 682-84.

Related Literature

A. Dupont-Sommer, " ' Elus de Dieu ' et ' Elu de Dieu ' dans le Commentaire d'Habacuc," *Proceedings of the Twenty-Second Congress of Orientalists Held in Istanbul September 15th to 22nd, 1951* (ed. Z. V. Togan; Leiden: Brill, 1957) 2. 568-72.
P. Grelot, " Hénoch et ses écritures, " *RB* 82 (1975) 481-500, esp. pp. 488-98.
J. C. Greenfield, " Prolegomenon, ", in H. Odeberg, 3 *Enoch or the Hebrew Book of Enoch* (reprint; New York: Ktav, 1973) xx-xxi.

29. *1Q Genesis Apocryphon — 1QapGen* (+ 1Q*20*). 1Q*20* was published by J. T. Milik in *DJD* 1. 86-87, but the *Genesis Apocryphon* proper was published by N. Avigad and Y. Yadin in *A Genesis Apocryphon: A Scroll from the Wilderness of Judaea: Description and Contents of the Scroll, Facsimiles, Transcription and Translation of Columns II, XIX-XXII* (Jerusalem: Magnes Press of the Hebrew University and Heikhal Ha-Sefer, 1956). The legible sections of the *Genesis Apocryphon* are free reworkings of Gen 6:8-9; 9:2-3, 4, 20; Gen 10(?); Gen 12:8–15:4. It first tells about Noah (though most of this section is poorly preserved) and then focuses on Abram's sojourns in Canaan (18:?–19:10a), in Egypt (19:10b–20:33a), and in the promised land (20:33b–21:22) as well as his defeat of the four invading kings (21:23–22:26) and his vision concerning his future heir (22:27–?). The Herodian script of the scroll allows us to set the date of this copy at the end of the 1st century B.C. or the first half of the 1st century A.D. On the basis of a philological analysis of the scroll, E. Y. Kutscher concluded that the language of the scroll dates either from the 1st century B.C. or A.D. Thus it is not impossible that we have a very early copy of the text, perhaps even the autograph itself. The title *Genesis Apocryphon* is misleading; it would be better to call it the *Book of the Patriarchs* (*Kĕtāb 'ăbāhātā'*).
Other Collections: *AC* §66; *AH*, I/1. 51-52; *ATQ*, 75-119.

Bibliography

For the bibliography prior to 1970, see J. A. Fitzmyer, *The Genesis Apocryphon of Qumran Cave I: A Commentary* (2d rev. ed.; BibOr 18A; Rome: Biblical Institute, 1971) 42-46.

Reviews: Anon., *NTA* 16 (1971-72) 130; *Int* 26 (1972) 99; R. J. Clifford, *CBQ* 34 (1972) 359-60; D. Lys, *ETR* 47 (1972) 365; V. Hamp, *BZ* 16 (1972) 304; J. A. Emerton, *BL* (1972) 68; S. Segert, *JSS* 17 (1972) 273-74; C. Mielgo, *Estudio agustiniano* 7 (1972) 384-85; R. Meyer, *TLZ* 97 (1972) 268-70; G. B. Sarfatti, *Lĕšonēnu* 37 (1973) 225; M. Smith, *JBL* 92 (1973) 626-27; R. Murray, *HeyJ* 13 (1972) 445-46; Anon., *IZBG* 19 (1972-73) 411 (§3007); H. Bardtke, *TRu* 37 (1972) 193-204; *BO* 30 (1973) 89-91; M. McNamara, *ITQ* 40 (1973) 283-85; P. Grelot, *RB* 80 (1973) 143-44; L. Rost, *ZDMG* 124 (1974) 143-44; G. Novotný, *MUSJ* 47 (1972) 308-9; M. Delcor, *BLE* 75 (1974) 149-50; A. Paul, *RSR* 60 (1972) 438-42; H. Ringgren, *SEA* 36 (1971) 175; Anon., *OLZ* 70 (1975) 148-49; J. O., *ArOr* 43 (1975) 379-380.

G. L. Archer, Jr., " The Aramaic of the ' Genesis Apocryphon ' Compared with the Aramaic of Daniel," *New Perspectives on the Old Testament* (ed. J. B. Payne; Waco, TX: Word Books, 1970) 160-69.

E. Y. Kutscher, " The Genesis Apocryphon of Qumran Cave I," *Or* 39 (1970) 178-83.

P. Grelot, " Un nom égyptien dans l'*Apocryphe de la Genèse*," *RQ* 7 (1969-71) 557-66.

W. Tyloch, " Aramejski apokryf Ksiegi Rodzaju," *Euhemer* 81 (1971) 13-22.

J. A. Emerton, " Some False Clues in the Study of Genesis XIV," *VT* 21 (1971) 24-47.

J. A. Emerton, " The Riddle of Genesis XIV," *VT* 21 (1971) 403-39.

H. Bardtke, " Literaturbericht über Qumrān. VI. Teil: II. Das Genesis-Apocryphon 1 QGen Ap.; III. Das Hiobtargum aus Höhle XI von Qumrān (11 QtgJob)," *TRu* 37 (1972) 193-219, esp. pp. 193-204.

G. Cowling, " Notes, Mainly Orthographical, on the Galilaean Targum and 1Q Genesis Apocryphon," *AJBA* 2 (1972) 35-49.

T. Muraoka, " Notes on the Aramaic of the Genesis Apocryphon," *RQ* 8 (1972-1974) 7-51.

F. Vattioni, " Aspetti del culto del signore dei cieli," *Augustinianum* 12 (1972) 479-515.

F. Vattioni, " Note sul Genesi (Gen. 14,17-24; 21,33)," *Augustinianum* 12 (1972) 557-63.

B. Dehandschutter, " Le rêve dans l'Apocryphe de la Genèse," *La littérature juive entre Tenach et Mischna: Quelques problèmes* (ed. W. C. van Unnik; RechBib 9; Leiden: Brill, 1974) 48-55.

T. L. Thompson, *The Historicity of the Patriarchal Narratives: The Quest for the Historical Abraham* (BZAW 133; Berlin: de Gruyter, 1974) 187-95.

W. Kirchschläger, " Exorzismus in Qumran? " *Kairos* 18 (1976) 135-53, esp. pp. 136-44.

T. Muraoka, " Segolate Nouns in Biblical and Other Aramaic Dialects, " *JAOS* 96 (1976) 226-35, esp. pp. 231-32.

P. Coxon, " The Nunation Variant in the Perfect of the Aramaic Verb, " *JNES* 36 (1977) 297-98.

P. W. Coxon, " The Problem of Nasalization in Biblical Aramaic in the Light of 1 Q GA and 11 Q Tg Job, " *RQ* 9 (1977-78) 253-58.

G. Garbini, " L' ' Apocrifo della Genesi ' nella letteratura giudaica, " *Annali dell'Istituto Orientale di Napoli* 37 (1977) 1-18.

30. *4Q Testuz (Unidentified Fragment)* — *4QTestuz ar.* Published by M. Testuz in " Deux fragments inédits des manuscrits de la Mer Morte," *Sem* 5 (1955) 37-38, esp. p. 38, pl. I (inverted, with labels confused). The word *lwḥ'* in lines 3 and 5 designates a tablet on which one writes, and its appearance suggests to Testuz a possible connection with the books of *Jubilees* and *Enoch.*

31. *1Q Unidentified Fragments* — 1Q*24*. Published by J. T. Milik in *DJD* 1. 99, pl. XX. The fragments probably belong to an apocalypse, perhaps related to the book of *Enoch.*

Bibliography

J. T. Milik, " Problèmes de la littérature hénochique à la lumière des fragments araméens de Qumrân," *HTR* 64 (1971) 366.

32. *1Q Unidentified Fragments* — 1Q*63-68*. Published by J. T. Milik in *DJD* 1. 147-48, pl. XXXV. 1Q*63* (and *64*, *65*?) may come from a description of a battle, and 1Q*66*, *67* may describe some sacrificial ritual.

33. *3Q Unidentified Fragments* — 3Q*12*, 3Q*14*. Published by M. Baillet in *DJD* 3. 102-4, pl. XIX. Most of the items are so fragmentary that in many not even a single Aramaic word can be read with confidence. On frg. 7, see J. T. Milik, *The Books of Enoch*, 61.

34. *5Q Unidentified Fragments* — 5Q*24*. Published by M. Baillet in *DJD* 3. 196, pl. XLII. The script is dated to the 1st century B.C.

35. *6Q Unidentified Fragments* — 6Q*14*, 6Q*19*, 6Q*23*, 6Q*26*, 6Q*31*. Published by M. Baillet in *DJD* 3. 127-28, pl. XXVI (6Q*14*) ; 136, pl. XXVIII (6Q*19*) ; 138, pl. XXVIII (6Q*23*) ; 138-39, pl. XXIX (6Q*26*) ; 141, pl. XXIX (6Q*31*). Described as an apocalyptic text, the MS of 6Q*14* is dated on paleographic grounds to the 1st century A.D. 6Q*19*, written in the Herodian period, probably has some connection with Genesis (" the sons of Ham "). 6Q*23* is most likely from the 1st century A.D., but its content is not at all clear. 6Q*26* is written in a cursive script (difficult to date) and comes from some kind of financial statement or contract. 6Q*31*, frg. 1 is a papyrus fragment written in Herodian script.

36. *Masada Letter on an Ostracon — MasOstr.* Published by Y. Yadin in " The Excavation of Masada 1963/64, Preliminary Report," *IEJ* 15 (1965) 111. The ostracon is broken on its right side and contains six lines of writing in a semicursive script. It deals with the payment of a sum of money.

37. *Hyrcania Funerary Inscription — Hyrcania.* Published by J. Naveh, " Ktwbt 'rmyt mhwrqnyh," *ʿAtiqot : Hebrew Series* 7 (1974) 56-57, pl. XV/8 (Engl. summary, p. 7*). The inscription consists of two fragments of a stone plaque that cannot be joined. They were found at ancient Hyrcania in the Judean Desert (modern Khirbet el-Mird). Naveh notes that the script on them resembles that of Qumran texts from the Hasmonean period and prefers to date them " within the first half of the first century B.C.E.," noting that no Jewish monumental inscriptions of such an early date have been found so far.

38. *Murabbaʿat List of Names and Rations — Mur 8 ar.* The Aramaic material from the Murabbaʿat caves is published by J. T. Milik in *Les grottes de Murabbaʿât* (2 vols. ; DJD 2 ; Oxford : Clarendon, 1961). Mur 8 ar, which is found in DJD 2. 87-89, pl. XXV, is a list of some kind, dealing with amounts of barley and lentils. Milik describes its script as that of the chancellery with many cursive forms. It could be a list of quantities of produce turned over as taxes.
Other Collections : *IR* §193.

General Bibliography : Murabbaʿat

J. Hempel, " Neue aramäische Texte," *ZAW* 65 (1953) 299-300.
D. Yeivin, " Some Notes on the Documents from Wadi Murabbaʿat Dating from the Days of Bar-Kokh'ba," *ʿAtiqot* 1 (1955) 95-108.
J. J. Rabinowitz, " A Legal Formula in Egyptian, Egyptian-Aramaic and Murabbaʿat Documents," *BASOR* 145 (1957) 33-34.
I. D. Amusin, " Les documents de Vadi-Mourabbaʿat," *VDI* 63/1 (1958) 104-124.
R. Yaron, " The Murabbaʿat Documents," *JJS* 11 (1960) 157-71.
H. L. Ginsberg, " New Light on Tannaitic Jewry and on the State of Israel in the Years 132-135 C.E.," *Proceedings of the Rabbinical Assembly of America* 25 (1961) 132-42.
E. Y. Kutscher, " The Language of the Hebrew and Aramaic Letters of Bar Cochba and His Contemporaries," *Lĕšonēnu* 25 (1961) 117-33 ; 26 (1962) 7-23.
J. A. Fitzmyer, " The Bar Cochba Period," *The Bible in Current Catholic Thought* (ed. J. L. McKenzie ; St. Mary's Theological Studies, 1 ; New York : Herder and Herder, 1962) 133-68 ; slightly revised in *Essays on the Semitic*

Background of New Testament (London: Chapman, 1971; reprinted, SBLSBS 5; Missoula, MT: Scholars Press, 1974) 305-54.
M. R. Lehmann, "Studies in the Murabbaʿât and Naḥal Ḥever Documents," *RQ* 4 (1963-64) 53-81.
S. Segert, "Zur Orthographie und Sprache der aramäischen Texte von W. Murabbaʿāt (Auf Grund von 'Discoveries in the Judaean Desert II')," *ArOr* 31 (1963) 122-37.
E. Koffmahn, "Die 'Restitutionsklausel' in den aramäischen Urkunden von Murabbaʿât," *RQ* 4 (1963-64) 421-27.
E. Koffmahn, "Zur Datierung der aramäisch/hebräischen Vertragsurkunden von Murabbaʿat," *WZKM* 59-60 (1963-64) 119-36.
E. M. Laperrousaz, "L'Hérodium, quartier général de Bar Kokhba ?" *Syria* 41 (1964) 347-48.
M. Delcor, "Murabbaʿât," *DBS*, 5. 1390-99.
E. Koffmahn, *Die Doppelurkunden aus der Wüste Juda: Recht und Praxis der jüdischen Papyri des 1. und 2. Jahrhunderts n. Chr. samt Übertragung der Texte und deutscher Übersetzung* (STDJ 5; Leiden: Brill, 1968).
J. A. Fitzmyer, "Some Notes on Aramaic Epistolography," *JBL* 93 (1974) 201-25.

39. *Murabbaʿat IOU* (A.D. *56*) — *Mur 18 ar.* Published by J. T. Milik in *DJD* 2. 100-4, pl. XXIX, this document is the recognition of a debt owed by one Zechariah to a certain Absalom. Mention of the second year of the emperor Nero leads Milik to date it to A.D. 55/56. Many of the formulas are familiar from the talmuds and Greek papyri. The script is cursive, but relatively close to the literary script of the period.
Other Collections: *DadWJ*, 80-89.

Bibliography

D. R. Hillers, "Revelation 13:18 and a Scroll from Murabbaʿat," *BASOR* 170 (1963) 65.
B. Z. Wacholder, "The Calendar of Sabbatical Cycles during the Second Temple and the Early Rabbinic Period," *HUCA* 44 (1973) 153-96, esp. pp. 169-71.

40. *Murabbaʿat Writ of Divorce* — *Mur 19 ar.* Published by J. T. Milik in *DJD* 2. 104-9, pls. XXX-XXXI, this document is a bill of divorce whose parties are Joseph, son of Naqsan, and his wife Miriam. It contains the formulas of repudiation (2-5, 13-17), of permission for the woman to remarry (5-7, 17-19), and of the transmission of the document from hand to hand (7-8, 20-21). The financial arrangements (8-10, 21-23) and the provisions for replacing the document, if lost (10-11, 23-25), conclude the item. The same or similar formulas are found in the traditional Jewish *gēṭ*. Mention of the "year six" (of

the eparchy of the province of Arabia, begun in A.D. 105) led Milik to date it to October/November of A.D. 111, but Y. Yadin thinks that it refers to the first Jewish revolt with A.D. 64/65 as the first year and 71/72 as the sixth.
Other Collections : *IR* §189 (dated " 72 C.E.[?] ") ; *DadWJ*, 148-55.

Bibliography

E. Koffmahn, " Die ' Restitutionsklausel ' in den aramäischen Vertragsurkunden von Murabbaʿat," *RQ* 4 (1963-64) 421-27.
R. Yaron, " Gyrwšyn bmṣdh," *Ha-'Umah* 10 (1964) 331-41.

41. *Murabbaʿat Marriage Contract — Mur 20 ar.* Published by J. T. Milik in *DJD* 2. 109-14, pls. XXX-XXXI. Despite the fragmentary state of the document, its general structure can be determined by comparison with Mur 21 ar and the traditional Jewish marriage contract. Mur 20 ar is a contract between a man from the priestly family of Eliashib and his future wife. After indication of time and place and the names of the participants (1-2, 15-17), there is the essential clause of the contract (" you shall be my wife according to the law of Moses "). The provisions regarding the dowry and the possibility of divorce (4-6) follow. Then come the sections envisaging the death of either partner (7-11) and the provisions for inheritance. The guarantee and provision for replacement of the document conclude the contract (11ff.). It is dated by Milik to A.D. 117. It has a cursive script with some ligatures.
Other Collections : *AC* §63 ; *DadWJ*, 114-19.

Bibliography

G. L. Harding, " Khirbet Qumran and Wady Murabaʿat [*sic*]," *PEQ* 84 (1952) 104-9.
S. A. Birnbaum, " A Fragment in an Unknown Script," *PEQ* 84 (1952) 118-20.
S. A. Birnbaum, " An Unknown Aramaic Cursive," *PEQ* 85 (1953) 23-41.
S. A. Birnbaum, " The Negeb Script," *VT* 6 (1956) 337-71.
S. A. Birnbaum, " The Kephar Bebhayu Marriage Deed," *JAOS* 78 (1958) 12-18.
S. A. Birnbaum, *The Bar-Menasheh Marriage Deed : Its Relation with Other Jewish Marriage Deeds* (Uitgaven van het Nederlands historisch-archaeologisch Instituut te Istanbul, 13 ; Istanbul : Nederland historisch-archaeologisch Instituut in het Nabije Oosten, 1962).
E. Koffmahn, " Die ' Restitutionsklausel ' in den aramäischen Vertragsurkunden von Murabbaʿat," *RQ* 4 (1963-64) 421-27.
P. Colella, " Trenta denari," *RivB* 21 (1973) 325-27.

42. *Murabba'at Marriage Contract* — *Mur 21 ar.* Published by J. T. Milik in *DJD* 2. 114-17, pls. XXXII-XXXIII. This fragmentary marriage contract contains parts of the following traditional clauses: the possible repudiation of the wife (9-10), the situation of the female children born of the union (10-12), the inheritance in case of the wife's death (12-14), the conditions of her widowhood (14-16), the executory clauses (17-18), and provision for replacement (19-20). It is written in a cursive script with few ligatures; its script suggests to Milik a relatively early date, perhaps even before the first revolt.
Other Collections: *DadWJ*, 120-25.

Bibliography

E. Koffmahn, "Die 'Restitutionsklausel' in den aramäischen Vertragsurkunden von Murabba'at," *RQ* 4 (1963-64) 421-27.

43. *Murabba'at Deed of Sale* — *Mur 23 ar.* Published by J. T. Milik in *DJD* 2. 121-22, pl. XXXIV. Written in cursive script, this deed of sale of some real estate was probably composed in A.D. 132-33 ("the year one of the Liberation of Jerusalem," in the Bar Cochba revolt).
Other Collections: *DadWJ*, 163.

44. *Murabba'at Easement* — *Mur 25 ar.* Published by J. T. Milik in *DJD* 2. 134-37, pl. XXXVIII. Marḥeshwan in the third year of Bar Cochba's revolt would have been October/November of A.D. 134. The document is an easement in which Ḥannina, son of Yehoḥanan, gives someone the right of access to and the use of his real estate. It is written in a cursive script with few ligatures.
Other Collections: *DadWJ*, 164-65.

45. *Murabba'at Deed of Sale* — *Mur 26 ar.* Published by J. T. Milik in *DJD* 2. 137-38, pl. XXXIX. The real estate transaction described in this deed of sale concerned several sellers (one of whom was a woman) and several purchasers. Its script is termed "très belle écriture cursive," practically identical with that of the document published by Milik in *Bib* 38 (1957) 255-64, pls. II-III (see §52).
Other Collections: *DadWJ*, 166-68.

Bibliography

E. Koffmahn, " Die ' Restitutionsklausel ' in den aramäischen Vertragsurkunden von Murabbaʿat," *RQ* 4 (1963-64) 421-27.

46. *Murabbaʿat Deed of Sale — Mur 27 ar.* Published by J. T. Milik in *DJD* 2. 138-39, pl. XXXIX. This text presents the last few lines of a simple contract in which there were several sellers but only one purchaser. Its script is described as a very irregular cursive.

47. *Murabbaʿat Property Record — Mur 28 ar.* Published by J. T. Milik in *DJD* 2. 139-40, pl. XL-XLbis. The text appears to be some kind of agreement regarding boundaries, perhaps even a lease. It is written in a cursive script with many ligatures and indistinct letters. *Other Collections* : *DadWJ*, 169.

48. *Murabbaʿat IOU(?) — Mur 32 ar.* Published by J. T. Milik in *DJD* 2. 149-50, pl. XLIII. Its cursive script may be earlier than that of the documents of the second revolt and even that of Mur 18 ar (A.D. 55/56). The document has to do with sums of money and may be either an IOU or a deed of sale.

49. *Murabbaʿat Ostracon — Mur 72 ar.* Published by J. T. Milik in *DJD* 2. 172-74, pl. LII. Written on a potsherd in a calligraphic script with a strong cursive tendency, this text is part of some kind of narrative (letter, legal record, popular tale?). Milik dates its script to the first half of the 1st century B.C.

50. *Murabbaʿat Unidentified Fragments — Mur 31, 33-35 ar.* Published by J. T. Milik in *DJD* 2. 148-49, pl. XLIIbis (Mur 31 ar) ; 150-51, pl. XLIII (Mur 33 ar) ; 151, pl. XLIII (Mur 34-35 ar). Mur 31 ar, frgs. 1-6 may be a deed of sale for a house, while Mur 33, frg. 1 is some kind of a receipt.

51. *? Ḥever Contract B (Deed of Sale, A.D. 134) — pap?ḤevB ar.* First published by J. T. Milik in " Un contrat juif de l'an 134 après J.-C.," *RB* 61 (1954) 182-90, pl. 4. After giving the date of the contract (= A.D. 133/134), this document provides the names of the principal parties and their places of residence (1-2), the statement of the sale and the waiver (3-5), the price (5-6), the terms of the sale

(6-12), the waiver of rights by the seller's wife (12-13), and the list of witnesses (14-20). Kefar-Bebayu was most likely a site in the Judean Desert.
Other Collections : *AC* §64 (where it is incorrectly said to have been found in " Wâdi Murabbaʿat ") ; *IR* §192.

Bibliography

J. J. Rabinowitz, " Some Notes on an Aramaic Contract from the Dead Sea Region," *BASOR* 136 (1954) 15-16.
S. Abramson and H. L. Ginsberg, " On the Aramaic Deed of Sale of the Third Year of the Second Jewish Revolt," *BASOR* 136 (1954) 17-19.
J. T. Milik, " Note additionnelle sur le contrat juif de l'an 134 après J.-C.," *RB* 62 (1955) 253-54.
S. A. Birnbaum, "The Kepher Bebhayu Conveyance," *PEQ* 89 (1957) 108-32.
J. T. Milik, " Deux documents inédits du Désert de Juda," *Bib* 38 (1957) 245-68, esp. pp. 264-68.
S. A. Birnbaum, " The Kephar Bebhayu Marriage Deed," *JAOS* 78 (1958) 12-18.
E. Puech, " L'Acte de vente d'une maison à Kafar-Bébayu en 135 de notre ère, " *RQ* 9 (1977-78) 213-21.

52. *? Ḥever Contract C* (*Deed of Sale*) — *pap ? ḤevC ar.* First published by J. T. Milik in " Deux documents inédits du désert de Juda," *Bib* 38 (1957) 245-68, esp. pp. 255-64, pls. II-III. The date and the names of the parties are not preserved. There is the statement of intent to sell a piece of real estate (2-3), the boundaries of the land (3-5), the terms of the sale (5-7), the price (7-8), the waiver of rights (9-12), and the list of witnessess (13-20). The first two lines of the list of signatures (13-14) are in Greek.
Other Collections : *AC* §65 ; *DadWJ*, 170-75.

Bibliography

J. J. Rabinowitz, " Some Notes on an Aramaic Deed of Sale from the Judean Desert," *Bib* 39 (1958) 486-87.
I. D. Amusin, " Arameyskii kontrakt 134 g. n. e. iz okrestnostei Mertvogo Morya," *Drevnii Mir* : *Sbornik statei — Akademiku V. V. Struve* (Moscow : Publishing House of Oriental Literature, 1962) 202-13.

53. *5/6 Ḥever Letter of Bar Cochba 1* — *5/6ḤevEp 1.* Published in Y. Yadin's " Expedition D," *IEJ* 11 (1961) 36-52, pl. 22, this letter is discussed on pp. 41-42 of that article. Written on wood, the letter deals with the confiscation of a quantity of wheat and its safe transfer to Simeon bar Cochba, the threat to punish " every Teqoan man," and the arrest of a certain Jesus, son of the Palmyrene. Since the signature of Samuel, son of ʿAmmi, does not correspond to the writing of the letter, we may assume that it was dictated by one of Bar Cochba's aides to a scribe. 5/6 Ḥever is the so-called Cave of Letters. See also E. Y. Kutscher, *Lĕšonēnu* 25 (1961) 119-21.

General Bibliography : *Naḥal Ḥever*

Y. Yadin, " Expedition D," *IEJ* 11 (1961) 36-52 (also in Hebr., " Mnḥ' d'," *BIES* 25 [1961] 49-64 ; 26 [1962] 204-36).
Y. Yadin, " Les lettres de Bar Kokhéba," *BTS* 34 (1961) 14-16.
Y. Yadin, " New Discoveries in the Judean Desert," *BA* 24 (1961) 34-50.
Y. Yadin, " More on the Letters of Bar Kochba," *BA* 24 (1961) 86-95.
E. Y. Kutscher, " The Language of the Hebrew and Aramaic Letters of Bar Cochba and His Contemporaries," *Lĕšonēnu* 25 (1961) 117-33 ; 26 (1962) 7-23.
Y. Aharoni, " The Caves of Naḥal Ḥever," *ʿAtiqot* 3 (1961) 148-62.
M. Cassuto Salzmann, " Ricerche in Israele," *BeO* 3 (1961) 23-25.
M. R. Lehmann, " Studies in the Murabbaʿat and Naḥal Ḥever Documents," *RQ* 4 (1963-64) 53-81.
Y. Yadin, *Hmmṣ'ym mymy br kwkb' bmʿrt h'grwt* [*The Finds from the Bar-Kokhba Period in the* " *Cave of Letters* "] (JDS 1 ; Jerusalem : Israel Exploration Society and Bialik Foundation, 1963).
H. Bardtke, " Der gegenwärtige Stand der Erforschung der in Palästina neu gefundenen Handschriften, 49 : Die Funde in der Wüste Juda. Zum ersten Band der ' Judean Desert Studies (JDS) ' von Yigael Yadin," *TLZ* 90 (1965) 411-24.

54. *5/6 Ḥever Letter of Bar Cochba 2 — 5/6ḤevEp 2.* Published by Y. Yadin in *IEJ* 11 (1961) 42, this is a badly preserved papyrus palimpsest, eight lines of which are in fragmentary state. It seems to be a letter addressed by Bar Cochba to Jonathan and Masabbala. See also E. Y. Kutscher, *Lĕšonēnu* 25 (1961) 122.

55. *5/6 Ḥever Letter of Bar Cochba 4 — 5/6ḤevEp 4.* Published by Y. Yadin in *IEJ* 11 (1961) 43, this is a letter from Bar Cochba to Jonathan that the latter should carry out an order to be transmitted orally by a certain Elisha. The papyrus is a palimpsest. See also E. Y. Kutscher, *Lĕšonēnu* 25 (1961) 122.

56. *5/6 Ḥever Letter of Bar Cochba 8 — 5/6ḤevEp 8.* Published by Y. Yadin in *IEJ* 11 (1961) 44-45, this letter orders Jonathan and Masabbala to send Eleazar, son of Ḥṭh, to Bar Cochba. Here (as in 5/6ḤevEp 14) the name " Kosiba " is written with a *śin* rather than

a *samek*. The communication was written for Bar Cochba by an aide. See also E. Y. Kutscher, *Lĕšonénu* 25 (1961) 124-25. Yadin reads *šbh* in line 6; Kutscher reads *šbt*.
Other Collections: *AH*, I/1. 53.

57. *5/6 Ḥever Letter of Bar Cochba 10 — 5/6ḤevEp 10*. Published by Y. Yadin in *IEJ* 11 (1961) 45-46, this letter is an order from Bar Cochba to Jonathan and Masabbala that they should supply his camp with produce. See also E. Y. Kutscher, *Lĕšonénu* 25 (1961) 125-26.

58. *5/6 Ḥever Letter of Bar Cochba 11 — 5/6ḤevEp 11*. Published by Y. Yadin in *IEJ* 11 (1961) 46, this document mentions the Romans (*rhwmyh*) in a form also found in rabbinic literature and a certain Tirsis, son of Tininos, who may have been either a non-Jewish collaborator or a captive. See also E. Y. Kutscher, *Lĕšonénu* 25 (1961) 126-27.

59. *5/6 Ḥever Letter of Bar Cochba 14 — 5/6ḤevEp 14*. Published by Y. Yadin in *IEJ* 11 (1961) 47-48, the letter may deal with the mobilization of men from Teqoa and Tell Arza(?); it threathens punishment if the order is not carried out. In the upper part it is a palimpsest, in which fragments of several Greek characters are visible. Again (as in 5/6 ḤevEp 8), " Kosiba " is spelled with a *śin* rather than a *samek*. See also E. Y. Kutscher, *Lĕšonénu* 25 (1961) 127-29.

60. *5/6 Ḥever Letter of Bar Cochba 15 — 5/6ḤevEp 15*. Published by Y. Yadin in *IEJ* 11 (1961) 48-49, this is the only letter in the batch not addressed to Jonathan and Masabbala. Here Judah, son of Manasseh, is ordered to send two men along with the two donkeys provided by Bar Cochba to Jonathan and Masabbala so as to furnish the palm branches and citrons for celebrating Sukkoth in the autumn of A.D. 134. See also E. Y. Kutscher, *Lĕšonénu* 25 (1961) 129.
Other Collections: *AH*, I/1. 53.

Bibliography

J. A. Fitzmyer, " The Bar Cochba Period," *The Bible in Current Catholic Thought* (ed. J. L. McKenzie; New York: Herder and Herder, 1962) 133-68, esp. p. 155; reprinted in revised form in *Essays on the Semitic Background of the New Testament* (London: Chapman, 1971; reprinted, SBLSBS 5; Missoula, MT: Scholars Press, 1974) 305-54, esp. p. 336.

Related Literature

B. Lifshitz, " Papyrus grecs du désert de Juda," *Aegyptus* 42 (1962) 240-56.
J. A. Fitzmyer, " The Languages of Palestine in the First Century A.D.," *CBQ* 32 (1970) 501-31, esp. pp. 513-15.
Y. Yadin, *Bar-Kokhba : The Rediscovery of the Legendary Hero of the Last Jewish Revolt against Rome* (London : Weidenfeld and Nicolson, 1971) 130-31.
G. Howard and J. C. Shelton, " The Bar-Kokhba Letters and Palestinian Greek," *IEJ* 23 (1973) 101-2.

61. *5/6 Ḥever Babatha Archive, Greek Document 1 — 5/6ḤevBA 1.* Published in H. J. Polotsky's " Šlwš tʿwdwt mʾrkywnh šl bbth bt šmʿwn," *E. L. Sukenik Memorial Volume* (*1899-1953*) (Eretz-Israel, 8 ; Jerusalem : Israel Exploration Society, 1967) 46-51, esp. pp. 46-49. In this double document (*Doppelurkunde*) the Greek text is written twice, but the *scriptura exterior* is endorsed in Aramaic and Nabatean. It is dated to 12 October A.D. 125. Judah was Babatha's second husband. This and the following item were found in the southern part of Palestine, west of the Dead Sea, but had been written in Nabatean country to the southeast of the Dead Sea. Cf. *IR* §191.

62. *5/6 Ḥever Babatha Archive, Greek Document 2 — 5/6ḤevBA 2.* Published by H. J. Polotsky in " Šlwš tʿwdwt mʾrkywnh šl bbth bt šmʿwn," 50. The main part of the text, which is a copy of a receipt given by Babatha to a Jewish guardian of her orphan son, is written in Greek. It is dated 19 August A.D. 132 and acknowledges the payment of six denarii for the boy's food and clothing. The ten lines in Greek are followed by a three-line Aramaic summary, which in turn is followed by a four-line Greek rendering of the Aramaic. It ends in Greek : Γερμαν[ὸς] 'Ιούδ[ο]υ ἔγραψα.

63. *5/6 Ḥever Babatha Archive, Docket on Marriage Contract — 5/6 ḤevBA Docket.* Only the docket (or label) written on the back of the contract has been published so far. It is found in *IR* §190. It seems to be contract for Babatha's second marriage, to a Judah, son of Eleazar.

64. *5/6 Ḥever Nabatean Contract — 5/6ḤevA nab.* Published in J. Starcky, " Un contrat nabatéen sur papyrus," *RB* 61 (1954) 161-81. This text is very difficult, since it is not yet clearly deciphered or interpreted. Starcky's interpretation of it was a pioneer effort. J. J. Rabinowitz (see bibliography below) has supplied some further information about the nature of the contract. On the basis of his suggestions, we have attempted a fresh translation of the text ; but the whole of it is far from clear. It seems to be a document in which an heir, Eleazar, pays off a debt owed by his deceased father and uncle, to the creditor Yamlik in a settlement that restores to him the garden that had been seized in a public judicial act. Rabinowitz reconstructs the situation thus : " Yamlik, son of ʿAbdai, was the creditor of Nikarchos and Bannai, the father and uncle, respectively, of Elʿazar. By writ of seizure (*šṭr ʿdw*), followed by a writ of proclamation (*ktb krwz*), Yamlik obtained, in satisfaction of his debt, a garden belonging to his debtors. Afterwards both of the debtors died and Elʿazar succeeded to their rights. He succeeded to his uncle's rights by virtue of the fact that the uncle ' did not leave, nor has he, a child '.... As heir to his father and uncle, Elʿazar came to Yamlik, paid him the debt of his father and uncle — principal plus interest from the date of the writ of seizure — and redeemed the garden from him. The debt was paid by Elʿazar partly in cash and partly by transferring to Yamlik a house (building) containing two shops. There was apparently still some balance of the debt left after the cash payment and the transfer of the building, which balance was remitted by Yamlik to Elʿazar as ' counting as nothing between me and between you ' ..." (p. 12).

Bibliography

J. J. Rabinowitz, " A Clue to the Nabatean Contract from the Dead Sea Region," *BASOR* 139 (1955) 11-14.

Y. Yadin, " Expedition D — The Cave of the Letters," *IEJ* 12 (1962) 227-57, esp. p. 229 ; *BIES* 12 (1962) 204-36, esp. p. 206 (another part of the contract was found).

E. Koffmahn, *Die Doppelurkunden aus der Wüste Juda* (STDJ 5 ; Leiden : Brill, 1968) 101-3.

65. *Jerusalem Stone Weight.* Published in N. Avigad, " Excavations in the Jewish Quarter of the Old City, Jerusalem, 1969/70 (Preliminary Report)," *IEJ* 20 (1970) 1-8, esp. p. 7. The weight was found in a house destroyed by fire in A.D. 70. The name of Bar Qathros seems to be that of the owner of the house (and of the weight).
Other Collections : *IR* §233.

Bibliography

N. Avigad, " Excavations in the Jewish Quarter of the Old City, 1969-1971," *Jerusalem Revealed : Archaeology in the Holy City 1968-1974* (Jerusalem : Israel Exploration Society and Shikmona, 1975) 41-51, esp. pp. 47, 49.

66. *Storage Jar Inscription.* Published in *IR* §248, this item contains the word for " balsam " written both in Hebrew and in Aramaic — most likely denoting the contents of the vessel. Its provenience is unknown.

General Bibliography : Palestinian Ossuaries

N. Avigad (" The Palaeography of the Dead Sea Scrolls and Related Documents," *Aspects of the Dead Sea Scrolls* [Scripta hierosolymitana, 4 ; Jerusalem : Magnes, 1958] 56-87, esp. p. 77) gives a general date for these ossuaries : 50 B.C. — A.D. 70 (" allowing a few decades of backward expansion "). See further R. H. Smith (" The Cross Marks on Jewish Ossuaries," *PEQ* 106 [1974] 53-66, esp. p. 53) : " from around 50 B.C. to A.D. 135 or occasionally later."

F. de Saulcy, " Inscription bilingue (sémitique et grecque)," *Bulletin archéologique du Musée Parent* 1 (1867) 9-14.

F. de Saulcy, " Caisses funéraires judaïques," *Bulletin archéologique du Musée Parent* 1 (1867) 21-28.

G. I. Ascoli, *Iscrizioni inedite o mal note, greche, latine, ebraiche, di antichi sepolchri giudaici del Napolitano* (Turin/Rome : Loescher, 1880) 53.

V. Schultze, " Sarkophage und Grabinschriften aus Jerusalem," *ZDPV* 4 (1881) 11-17.

D. Chwolson, *Corpus inscriptionum hebraicarum* (St. Petersburg : H. Schmitzdorff, 1882) 55-236.

C. Clermont-Ganneau, " Epigraphes hébraïques et grecques sur des ossuaires juifs inédits," *RArch* 3/1 (1883) 257-76, pl. IX.

C. Clermont-Ganneau, " Rapports sur une mission en Palestine et en Phénicie entreprise en 1881," *Archives des missions scientifiques et littéraires* 3/11 (1885) 157-251, esp. p. 205.

C. Clermont-Ganneau, *Recueil d'archéologie orientale* (8 vols. ; Paris : Leroux, 1888-1924), passim.

C. Clermont-Ganneau, *Archaeological Researches in Palestine during the Years 1873-1874* (2 vols. ; tr. A. Stewart and J. Macfarlane ; London : Palestine Exploration Fund, 1896, 1899).

M. Lidzbarski, *Ephemeris für semitische Epigraphik* (3 vols ; Giessen : Töpelmann, 1900-15), passim.

R. Dussaud, *Les monuments palestiniens et judaïques au Musée du Louvre* (*Moab, Judée, Philistie, Samarie, Galilée*) (Paris : Leroux, 1912) 33-36, 50.

H. Grimme, " Inschriften auf Ossuarien aus Jerusalem," *OLZ* 15 (1912) 529-534.

G. Dalman, " Inschriften aus Palästina," *ZDPV* 37 (1914) 135-45, 374.

S. Klein, *Jüdisch-palästinisches Corpus Inscriptionum* (*Ossuar-, Grab- und Synagogeninschriften*) (Vienna/Berlin : R. Löwit, 1920 ; reprinted, Hildesheim : Gerstenberg, 1971).

M.-R. Savignac, " Nouveaux ossuaires juifs avec inscriptions," *RB* 38 (1929) 229-36.

E. L. Sukenik, " M'rt qbrym yhwdyt bmwrd hr-hzytym [A Jewish Tomb on the Mt. of Olives]," *Tarbiẓ* 1 (1929-30) 137-43, 5 pls.

S. Krauss, " La double inhumation chez les Juifs," *REJ* 97 (1934) 1-34.

L.-H. Vincent, " Sur la date des ossuaires juifs," *RB* 43 (1934) 564-67.

E. L. Sukenik, " M'rt qbrym yhwdyt bnḥl qdrwn [A Jewish Tomb-Cave in the Kedron Valley]," *Tarbiẓ* 6 (1934-35) 190-96.

J.-B. Frey, *Corpus inscriptionum iudaicarum* (2 vols. ; Vatican City : Pontificio istituto di archeologia cristiana, 1936, 1952), 2. 113-339.

E. L. Sukenik, " M'rwt-qbrym yhwdywt bsbybwt nḥl-qdrwn [Jewish Tombs in the Kedron Valley]," *Kedem* 2 (1945) 23-31.

B. Bagatti, " Resti cristiani in Palestina anteriori a Costantino ? " *Rivista di archeologia cristiana* 26 (1950) 117-31.

E. Dinkler, " Zur Geschichte des Kreuzsymbols," *ZTK* 48 (1951) 148-72 (Engl. " Comments on the History of the Symbol of the Cross," *JTC* 1 [1965] 124-146).

E. R. Goodenough, *Jewish Symbols in the Greco-Roman Period* (13 vols. ; New York : Pantheon, 1953-68), 1. 110-33.

P. Kahane, " Pottery Types from the Jewish Ossuary-Tombs round Jerusalem : An Archaeological Contribution to the Problem of the Hellenization of Jewry in the Herodian Period," *IEJ* 2 (1952) 125-39, 176-82 ; 3 (1953) 48-54.

N. Avigad, *Ancient Monuments in the Kidron Valley* (Jerusalem : Bialik, 1954).

N. Avigad, " The Palaeography of the Dead Sea Scrolls and Related Documents," *Aspects of the Dead Sea Scrolls* (Scripta hierosolymitana, 4 ; Jerusalem : Magnes, 1958) 56-87, esp. pp. 77-81.

J. Daniélou, *Les symboles chrétiens primitifs* (Paris : Seuil, 1961) ; Engl. *Primitive Christian Symbols* (tr. D. Attwater ; Baltimore : Helicon, 1964).

E. Dinkler, " Kreuzzeichen und Kreuz," *JAC* 5 (1962) 93-112.

E. Testa, *Il simbolismo dei giudeo-cristiani* (Pubblicazioni dello Studium Biblicum Franciscanum, 14 ; Jerusalem : Franciscan Printing Press, 1962) 426-513.

E. Testa, " L'uso degli ossuari tra i monaci di Siria," *La Terra Santa* 39 (1963) 36-41.

E. Testa, " I proseliti giudeo-Cristiani," *La Terra Santa* 39 (1963) 132-38.

E. Y. Kutscher, " Kwk (wbny mšpḥth) [*Kwk* and Its Cognates]," *E. L. Sukenik Memorial Volume* (*1889-1953*) (Eretz-Israel, 8 ; Jerusalem : Israel Exploration Society, 1967) 273-79.

J. Finegan, *The Archaeology of the New Testament* (Princeton : Princeton University, 1969) 216-60.

E. Testa, *Nazaret* : *Guideo-Cristiana* : *Riti. Iscrizioni. Simboli* (Pubblicazioni dello Studium Biblicum Franciscanum, collectio minor, 8 ; Jerusalem : Franciscan Printing Press, 1969).

I. Mancini, *Archaeological Discoveries Relative to the Judaeo-Christians* : *Historical Survey* (tr. G. Bushell ; Publications of the Studium Biblicum Franciscanum, collectio minor, 10 ; Jerusalem : Franciscan Printing Press, 1970).

E. M. Meyers, " Secondary Burials in Palestine," *BA* 33 (1970) 2-29.
M. Avi-Yonah, " Ossuaries," *Encyclopedia Judaica* 12 (1971) 1503-6 (with bibliography).
B. Bagatti, *The Church from the Circumcision : History and Archaeology of the Judaeo-Christians* (tr. E. Hoade ; Publications of the Studium Biblicum Franciscanum, smaller series, 2 ; Jerusalem : Franciscan Printing Press, 1971).
E. M. Meyers, *Jewish Ossuaries : Reburial and Rebirth : Secondary Burials in Their Ancient Near Eastern Setting* (BibOr 24 ; Rome : Biblical Institute, 1971).

Reviews : F. Christ, *RB* 80 (1973) 140-42 ; H. Christ, *TZ* 29 (1973) 286-87 ; L. Rahmani, *IEJ* 23 (1973) 121-26 ; N. J. Tromp, *Bib* 54 (1973) 566-68 ; A. Negev, *JJS* 25 (1974) 337-42 ; C. H. J. de Geus, *BO* 32 (1975) 83-84.

E. M. Meyers, " The Theological Implications of an Ancient Jewish Burial Custom," *JQR* 62 (1971) 95-119.
R. H. Smith, " The Cross Marks on Jewish Ossuaries," *PEQ* 106 (1974) 53-66.
E. Dinkler, " *Schalom — Eirene — Pax*: Jüdische Sepulkralinschriften und ihr Verhältnis zum frühen Christentum, " *Rivista di archeologia cristiana* 50 (1974) 121-44, esp. pp. 123-31.

67. *Kidron Valley Dipinto.* A painted cursive inscription found in a tomb-cave in the Kidron Valley and published by E. L. Sukenik, " Mʿrt qbrym yhwdyt bnḥl qdrwn [A Jewish Tomb in the Kidron Valey (*sic*)]," *Tarbiẓ* 6 (1934-35) 190-96, esp. pp. 193-95. N. Avigad (" The Palaeography of the Dead Sea Scrolls and Related Documents," 77-78) assigns it to the first half of the 1st century A.D. The prepositional phrase *ʿlyhwn*, which is difficult to put into good English, is not always included in this stereotyped prohibition ; see §71, 95 below.
Other Collections : *AH*, I/1. 52 ; *CII* §1300 ; *PI*, pp. 38-40.

Bibliography

H. L. Ginsberg, " Lnwsḥ ktwbt hkwk šbnḥl qdrwn [On the Reading of the Inscription of the Tomb in the Kidron Valey (*sic*)]," *Tarbiẓ* 7 (1935-36) 223-226.
J. van der Ploeg, " De in 1947 in de Woestijn van Juda gevonden oude handschriften in het kader van gelijktijdige schriftelijke documenten," *JEOL* 4/11-13 (1949-54) 41-71, esp. p. 50 (+ pl. xvi, fig. 20).
E. Testa, *Il simbolismo dei Giudeo-Cristiani* (Pubblicazioni dello Studium Biblicum Franciscanum, 14 ; Jerusalem : Franciscan Printing Press, 1962) 449.

68. *Givʿat Ha-Mivṭar Abba Inscription.* Found in 1971 opposite the entrance of a tomb-cave at Givʿat ha-Mivṭar in Jerusalem, this Aramaic inscription was written in paleo-Hebrew characters (without spaces between the words). It was first published by E. S. Rosenthal in " The Givʿat ha-Mivtar Inscription," *IEJ* 23 (1973) 72-81, pl. 19.

J. Naveh (" An Aramaic Tomb Inscription Written in Paleo-Hebrew Script," *IEJ* 23 [1973] 82-91, pl. 19) dates it on paleographic grounds to the late 1st century B.C. or the 1st century A.D. The paleo-Hebrew script could suggest a Samaritan origin, but Naveh feels that the site and the contents favor a Jewish origin. The inscription tells of a certain Abba, born in Jerusalem and of priestly origin, who was forced to leave his home but who has now returned to inter the bones of a certain Mattathiah.
Other Collections : *IR* §263.

Bibliography

J. Naveh, " Ktwbt-qbr ḥdšh mgbʿt-hmbṭr [A New Tomb-Inscription from Givʿat ha-Mivṭar]," *Qadmoniot* 6 (1973) 115-18.
J. Naveh, " A New Tomb-Inscription from Givʿat Hamivtar," *Jerusalem Revealed* : *Archaeology in the Holy City 1968-1974* (Jerusalem : Israel Exploration Society and Shikmona, 1975) 73-74 [beware of the readings given here].
P.-E. Dion, " Deux notes epigraphiques sur Tobit," *Bib* 56 (1975) 416-19, esp. pp. 418-19.
M. Cassuto Salzmann, " Una interessante iscrizione di Gerusalemme, " *BeO* 19 (1977) 27-29.
V. Tzaferis, " Mʿrt ʾbhʾ byrwšlym [The ʻ Abba ʼ Burial Cave in Jerusalem], " *ʿAtiqot* : *Hebrew Series* 7 (1974) 61-64 (with English summary, p. 9*).
P. Smith, " The Human Skeletal Remains from the Abba Cave, " *IEJ* 27 (1977) 121-24.
Anon., " Jérusalem : Givʿat HaMivtar : Inscription araméenne (Chronique archéologique), " *RB* 78 (1971) 428-29.

69. *Jebel Ḫallet eṭ-Ṭuri Ossuary*. Published by J. T. Milik in " Trois tombeaux juifs récemment découverts au Sud-Est de Jérusalem," *SBFLA* 7 (1956-57) 232-67, esp. pp. 232-39. The tomb was found at Jebel Ḫallet eṭ-Ṭûrî, a place south of Bîr-ʾAyyûb in the extension of the Kidron Valley just before it becomes the Wâdi en-Nâr. The inscription on the ossuary lid consists of two lines scratched with a fairly broad-pointed nail. It comes from the end of the 1st century B.C., and its script is close to that of 1QIsa^{b}, 1QM, 1QH, 1QapGen — all examples of the Herodian type. Milik's (not entirely correct) translation was this : " Quiconque réutilisera à son profit cet ossuaire-ci, malédiction (*litt.* offrande) de Dieu de la part de celui qui est dedans." But the use of *qrbn* in the inscription is identical to that preserved in Mark 7:11 (Matt 15:5) and should definitely be translated as " offering." Thus the inscription is a warning that whatever of value is in the ossuary has been dedicated to God and is not inten-

ded for any profane use. Cf. §107 (*CII* §1407); B. Mazar, "The Excavations in the Old City of Jerusalem," *W. F. Albright Volume* (Eretz-Israel, 9; Jerusalem: Israel Exploration Society, 1969) 168-70, pl. 45/5.
Other Collections: *AH*, I/1. 53.

Bibliography

J. A. Fitzmyer, "The Aramaic Qorbān Inscription from Jebel Ḫallet eṭ-Ṭûrî and Mark 7.11/Matt 15.5," *JBL* 78 (1959) 60-65; slightly revised in *Essays on the Semitic Background of the New Testament* (London: Chapman, 1971; reprinted, SBLSBS 5; Missoula, MT: Scholars Press, 1974) 93-100.
E. Testa, *Il simbolismo dei Giudeo-Cristiani* (Pubblicazioni dello Studium Biblicum Franciscanum, 14; Jerusalem: Franciscan Printing Press, 1962) 450.
S. Zeitlin, "Korban," *JQR* 53 (1962) 160-63.
J. Bligh, "'Qorban!'" *HeyJ* 5 (1964) 192-93.
Z. W. Falk, "Notes and Observations on Talmudic Vows," *HTR* 59 (1966) 309-12.
S. Zeitlin, "Korban: A Gift," *JQR* 59 (1968) 133-35.
B. Mazar, "The Excavations South and West of the Temple Mount in Jerusalem: The Herodian Period," *BA* 33 (1970) 47-60, esp. p. 55.
B. Mazar, "The Excavations in the Old City of Jerusalem Near the Temple Mount — Second Preliminary Report, 1969-1970 Seasons," *Zalman Shazar Volume* (Eretz-Israel, 10; Jerusalem: Israel Exploration Society, 1971) 1-34, pls. '-*ld*, esp. pl. *kh*.
J. C. Greenfield, Review of J. A. Fitzmyer, *Essays on the Semitic Background of the New Testament*, *JNES* 35 (1976) 59-61, esp. p. 60.

70. *Uzziah Tomb Slab.* Published by E. L. Sukenik in "Ṣiyyûn 'Uzziyāhû melek Yĕhûdāh," *Tarbiẓ* 2 (1930-31) 288-92, pls. I-II. The exact provenience of the inscription is unknown; it was discovered in the collection of the Russian Convent on the Mt. of Olives where it seems to have been since the end of the 19th century. The inscription refers to the transfer of the bones of King Uzziah, who was a leper and so not buried in the royal necropolis within the city (see 2 Chr 26:23), to a new tomb. It would have been affixed on or above the opening of the tomb niche. Avigad (Scripta hierosolymitana 4 [1958] 78) says that a "mid-first century A.D. date for the Uzziah inscription seems quite credible." Cf. 2 Kgs 15:7; Josephus, *Ant.* 9.10.4 §227; *t. B. Bat.* 1:11.
Other Collections: *AH*, I/1. 52; *IR* §255; *PI*, pp. 39-40.

Bibliography

J. N. Epstein, " Lṣywn ʿwzyhw [To the Epitaph of Uzziahu]," *Tarbiẓ* 2 (1930-31) 293-94.
W. F. Albright, " The Discovery of an Aramaic Inscription relating to King Uzziah," *BASOR* 44 (1931) 8-10.
E. L. Sukenik, " Funerary Tablet of Uzziah, King of Judah," *PEQ* (1931) 217-21.
K. Galling, " Ossuar," *Biblisches Reallexikon* (HAT 1 ; Tübingen : Mohr [Siebeck], 1934) 405-7.
K. Galling, *Textbuch zur Geschichte Israels* (Tübingen : Mohr [Siebeck], 1950) §55 (p. 81).
J. van der Ploeg, " De in 1947 in de Woestijn van Juda gevonden oude handschriften in het kader van gelijktijdige schriftelijke documenten," *JEOL* 4/11-13 (1949-54) 41-71, esp. pl. XVIII/29.
N. Avigad, " The Paleography of the Dead Sea Scrolls and Related Documents," *Aspects of the Dead Sea Scrolls* (Scripta hierosolymitana, 4 ; Jerusalem : Magnes, 1958) 56-87, esp. p. 78.
B. Mazar, " Yrwšlym btqwpt hmqrʾ [Jerusalem in the Biblical Period]," *Qadmoniot* 1 (1968) 3-12, esp. p. 11 (photo).

71. *Kidron Epitaph.* A photo of this inscription was first published by H. H. Spoer, " Some Hebrew and Phoenician Inscriptions," *JAOS* 28 (1907) 355-59, esp. p. 358 (§11) ; but Spoer made no attempt to transcribe or translate it (cf. M. Lidzbarski, *Ephem.*, 3. 51). The first attempt to read it was made by E. L. Sukenik, " Verschlussstein mit Inschrift aus einer Grabhöhle bei Jerusalem," *ZDPV* 55 (1932) 124-28 ; see also " Mʿrt qbrym yhwdyt bnḥl qdrwn [A Jewish Tomb in the Kidron Valey (*sic*)]," *Tarbiẓ* 6 (1934-35) 190-96, esp. p. 193. The prohibition of opening gets a new ending here ; cf. §67, 95. The first word could also be restored with a final *aleph*.
Other Collections : *AH*, I/1. 52 ; *CII* §1334.

72. *Dominus Flevit Ossuary 11.* Published by J. T. Milik in *Gli scavi del ' Dominus Flevit ' (Monte Oliveto–Gerusalemme) ; I. La necropoli del periodo romano* (eds. B. Bagatti and J. T. Milik ; Pubblicazioni dello Studium Biblicum Franciscanum, 13 ; Jerusalem : Franciscan Printing Press, 1958) 70-109. On the western slope of the Mt. of Olives, workmen in 1953 came upon the remains of a cemetery that had been in use from the 1st to the 4th century A.D. Bagatti discerned two periods : one extending almost to the end of the second Jewish war in A.D. 135 and marked by tombs in the shape of *kôkîm* ; the later period characterized by graves in the form of *arcosolia* (trough-shaped graves dug parallel with the walls). Milik published 43 inscriptions: Greek (11), Hebrew (19), Aramaic (12), and Greek/Aramaic (1). He maintains that most of the graffiti come from the first half of the 1st century A.D. and the latest (the extreme cursives) are from the interval between the Jewish revolts. Dominus Flevit Ossuary 11, which is published by Milik on p. 83, photo 81, is the inscription found on ossuary no. 19 discovered in chamber 79. The reading of the patronymic is not certain; Milik suggests that either *ywnh* or *zynh* is possible. The script is cursive.

Bibliography

B. Bagatti, " Scoperta di un cimitero giudeo-cristiano al ' Dominus Flevit,' " *SBFLA* 3 (1952-53) 149-84.
B. Bagatti and J. T. Milik, " Nuovi scavi al ' Dominus Flevit,' " *SBFLA* 4 (1953-54) 247-76.
M. Avi-Yonah et al., " The Archaeological Survey of Masada, 1955-1956," *IEJ* 7 (1957) 1-60, esp. pp. 59-60.
F. P. Peterson, *Peter's Tomb Recently Discovered in Jerusalem* (McKeesport, PA: Privately published, 1960) [" Copies may be obtained from the publisher, F. Paul Peterson, P. O. Box 568, McKeesport, PA." Interlibrary-loan: Princeton Theological Seminary, Princeton, NJ 08540 (Pamph. D-40, P4425)].
I. Mancini, *Archaeological Discoveries Relative to the Judaeo-Christians* (Publications of the Studium Biblicum Franciscanum, collectio minor, 10; Jerusalem: Franciscan Printing Press, 1970) 47-64, esp. pp. 60-61.
R. H. Smith, " The Cross Mark on Jewish Ossuaries," *PEQ* 106 (1974) 53-66, esp. pp. 60-65.

73. *Dominus Flevit Ossuary 13.* Published by J. T. Milik in *Gli scavi del ' Dominus Flevit '*, 1. 84, photo 82. On ossuary 21, found in chamber 79, there is a Greek inscription, and on the center of the lid the Semitic name *špyr'* is written, a feminine adjective meaning " beautiful " and attested as a feminine proper name in Acts 5:1 and on some other ossuaries. See §117 below; cf. *CII* §1272, 1282c, 1378. See further E. L. Sukenik, " Mʿrt-qbrym yhwdyt bmwrd hr hzytym [A Jewish Tomb on the Slopes of the Mount of Olives]," " *Yerusalayim* ": *Journal of the Jewish Palestine Exploration Society Dedicated to the Memory of Abraham Mosheh Luncz* (eds. I. Press and E. L. Sukenik; Jerusalem: Darom, 1928) 193-98 (§2).

74. *Dominus Flevit Ossuary 19.* Published by J. T. Milik in *Gli scavi del ' Dominus Flevit '*, 1. 88, photo 87. The inscription is incised on ossuary 69 from chamber 280. The vocalization of the patronymic is uncertain; Milik suggests that either ʿIwya or ʿAwiy is possible. The script is cursive.

75. *Dominus Flevit Ossuary 20.* Published by J. T. Milik in *Gli scavi del ' Dominus Flevit '*, 1. 89, this inscription is on ossuary 75 from chamber 297. Milik says that the patronymic could have been 'Agrah, as in Dominus Flevit ossuaries 32 and 33. The patriarchal name *ywsp* (the hypercorrect orthography being *yhwsp*, as in Ps 81:6) is very common in the Roman period.

76. *Dominus Flevit Ossuary 24.* Found on ossuary 41 from chamber 363 and published by J. T. Milik in *Gli scavi del ' Dominus Flevit '*, 1. 92, photo 89. The patronymic was begun but never completed. The script is calligraphic, but produced by one who was not an expert.

77. *Dominus Flevit Ossuary 25.* Found on ossuary 52 from chamber 376 and published by J. T. Milik in *Gli scavi del ' Dominus Flevit '*, 1. 92, photo 90. The state of the first letters does not allow a satisfactory reading. The name Eliezer/Elazar/Eleazar is a very common one. The script is cursive.

78. *Dominus Flevit Ossuary 26.* Published by J. T. Milik in *Gli scavi del ' Dominus Flevit '*, 1. 93, photos 91-95. On ossuary 57 from chamber 384 the same name is inscribed in five different places; in two instances the medial *mem* is found at the end of Menaḥem. The name Ḥananiah is a very common one. The calligraphic script is dated to the 1st century B.C.

79. *Dominus Flevit Ossuary 27.* Found on ossuary 59 from chamber 384 and published by J. T. Milik in *Gli scavi del ' Dominus Flevit '*, 1. 93-94, photo 96. The name " Matthiah " is a shortened form of " Mattathiah " and has the same meaning as the Greek " Dositheos " (" gift of God ") ; see §97. Milik translates *Ḥqwh* as *tessitore* (" weaver ") and says that Matthiah's father is being described by his profession. The script is calligraphic.

80. *Dominus Flevit Ossuary 32.* Found on ossuary 99 in chamber 437 and published by J. T. Milik in *Gli scavi del ' Dominus Flevit '*, 1. 96, photo 98. Milik dates its script to the period after the First Revolt and suggests that 'Agrah is a nickname meaning " day-laborer," " hired-hand." It is not elsewhere attested as a proper name.

81. *Dominus Flevit Ossuary 33.* Found on ossuary 106 from chamber 437 and published by J. T. Milik in *Gli scavi del ' Dominus Flevit '*, 1. 96. The script is almost calligraphic, of the classical type, and is dated to the 1st century A.D. The name *ṭwbyh* is a shortened form of *ṭwbyhw* (2 Chr 17:18). See ʿAraq el-Emir inscription in L.-H. Vincent, " La date des épigraphes d'ʿarâq el-Emîr," *JPOS* 3 (1923) 55-68, esp. p. 63 ; E. Littmann, *Greek and Latin Inscriptions : Section A. Southern Syria, Part I : Ammonites* (Princeton Archaeological Expedition to Syria in 1904-1905, part 3 ; Leiden : Brill, 1907) 1-4 ; *CII* §868.

82. *Dominus Flevit Ossuary 34.* Found on ossuary 107 from chamber 437 and published by J. T. Milik in *Gli scavi del ' Dominus Flevit '*, 1. 96-97, photos 99-100. Milik suggests that the ossuary belonged to a couple (Ḥananiah and Maria) and that Ḥananiah may have stayed during his last days with his father-in-law's family. He terms the script a timid and not very successful attempt at the calligraphy current at the turn of the Christian era. The first name is written twice.

83. *Dominus Flevit Ossuary 36.* Found on ossuary 112 from chamber 437 and published by J. T. Milik in *Gli scavi del ' Dominus Flevit '*, 1. 97, photo 104. Except for the ligature in *br*, the script is calligraphic and is termed an advanced 1st-century A.D. or an early 2nd-century A.D. form.

84. *Dominus Flevit Ossuary 38.* Found on ossuary 118 from chamber 437 and published by J. T. Milik in *Gli scavi del ' Dominus Flevit '*, 1. 98, photo 106. The name of the husband is the masculine form of *špyr'* (see §73 above). The script is calligraphic.

85. *Givʿat Ha-Mivṭar Ossuary 1.* Published by J. Naveh in " The Ossuary Inscriptions from Givʿat ha-Mivtar," *IEJ* 20 (1970) 33-37, pls. 11-17, esp. pp. 32-33, pl. 11. Inscribed ossuaries were found in two of the four burial caves excavated by V. Tzaferis at Givʿat ha-Mivṭar, in northeastern Jerusalem. On the first ossuary there are two related inscriptions (a, b). There are neither final letters nor spaces between words in inscription a. Naveh takes *smwn* as a defective spelling of the Greek Σίμων, *bnh* and *bn'* as forms of the Aramaic active participle of the verb *bny* (" build "), and *hklh* as a defective form of *hêklā'* (" palace, temple "), known from Biblical Aramaic. Simon was probably one of the builders, master masons, or engineers who took part in Herod's building activities in the Jerusalem Temple.

Other Collections : *IR* §170.

Bibliography

V. Tzaferis, " Jewish Tombs at and near Giv'at ha-Mivtar, Jerusalem," *IEJ* 20 (1970) 18-32.

J. Naveh, " New Inscriptions on Ossuaries from Northern Jerusalem," *Zalman Shazar Volume* (Eretz-Israel, 10 ; Jerusalem : Israel Exploration Society, 1971) 188-90, pls. 65-66 (Hebrew version of the article in *IEJ* 20 [1970] 33-37).

A. Kloner, " M'rt-qbwrh mymy byt šny bgb't-hmbṭr šbyrwšlym [A Burial-cave of the Second Temple Period at Giv'at ha-Mivtar]," *Qadmoniot* 5 (1972) 108-9.

Y. Yadin, " Epigraphy and Crucifixion," *IEJ* 23 (1973) 18-22.

V. Tzaferis, " The Burial of Simon the Temple Builder," *Jerusalem Revealed : Archaeology in the Holy City 1968-1974* (Jerusalem : Israel Exploration Society and Shikmona, 1975) 71-72.

86. *Giv'at Ha-Mivṭar Ossuary 2.* Published by J. Naveh in *IEJ* 20 (1970) 34-35, pl. 12. Naveh suggests that *qdrh* is a *qattāl* form with final *he* (as the ending of the emphatic state) for " the potter " or " the pot-seller," but admits that *paḥār* (< *paḥḥār*) is the otherwise common word for " potter " in all Aramaic dialects.

87. *Giv'at Ha-Mivṭar Ossuary 3.* Published by J. Naveh in *IEJ* 20 (1970) 35, pl. 13. Naveh notes that *mrt'* is a feminine proper name meaning " the mistress, the lady." In contrast to the previous two ossuaries from Giv'at ha-Mivṭar, the ending of the emphatic state on this feminine form is a final *aleph*. Cf. *CII* §1246, 1261, 1263.

88. *Giv'at Ha-Mivṭar Ossuary 14.* Published by J. Naveh in *IEJ* 20 (1970) 36-37, pl. 17. Naveh takes the first part of the second line as the relative pronoun *dy* plus the third person feminine perfect of the root *šbr* (not *tbr*, " break ") and translates " who died giving birth." He says that the last two words could be rendered " Shelam, her daughter," " Salome, his daughter," " Salome the daughter," or " peace, daughter." S. Yeivin has suggested a different word division : *d/ryš brt šlwm brth* (" Dush [*or* Rush], the daughter of Salom[e], his [viz., Saul's] daughter "). This would mean that the bones of both mother and daughter were placed in the same ossuary. But is the name " Duš " or " Ruš " attested for a woman? Could it be read as *rēš bĕrat šĕlām birteh/birtah*, " the head of daughter Salome, his/her daughter "? Better still, could not *śbrt* be taken as an alternate (older) orthography for *sbrt*, " who hoped for Salome, her daughter "? *Other Collections* : *IR* §261.

Bibliography

S. Yeivin, " Prolegomenon," in G. A. Smith, *Jerusalem : The Topography, Economics and History from the Earliest Times to A.D. 70* (reprint, 2 vols. in one ; Library of Biblical Studies ; New York : Ktav, 1972) xi-lxxxiii, esp. p. lxxviii.

89. *Jason Tomb Inscription.* Published by N. Avigad in " Aramaic Inscriptions in the Tomb of Jason," *IEJ* 17 (1967) 101-11, pls. 26-27, esp. pp. 101-9. Found on the northern plastered wall of the porch of Jason's tomb in Reḥov Alfasi in Jerusalem in 1965, this inscription was written in charcoal to the left of the door-opening. Avigad concludes his analysis of the handwriting by calling it the oldest inscription written in a Jewish cursive script found so far and by dating it to the 1st century B.C. The inscription begins with an appeal for the visitor to lament over Jason's death and states that the tomb was built by his sister Salome. The second line consisted of only two or three words, completely missing except for a *samek* at the end. The third line expresses the sorrow of Jason's friends, while the last line may be a lament by a scribe Honi. Avigad translates the end of the first line as " . . . Peace ! . . . Who hast built thyself a tomb, Elder, rest in Peace ! "

Bibliography

N. Avigad, " Ktwbwt 'rmywt bqbr yswn [Aramaic Inscriptions in the Tomb of Jason]," *'Atiqot : Hebrew Series* 4 (1964) 32-37.
B. Lifshitz, " Notes d'épigraphie palestinienne," *RB* 73 (1966) 248-57, esp. 248-255.
P. Benoit, " L'inscription grecque du tombeau de Jason," *IEJ* 17 (1967) 112-113, pl. 28 (in Hebrew in *'Atiqot : Hebrew Series* 4 [1964] 39-40, pl. 20).
L. Y. Rahmani, " Jason's Tomb," *IEJ* 17 (1967) 61-100 (in Hebrew in *'Atiqot : Hebrew Series* 4 [1964] 1-31).

90. *Kallon Family Ossuary 1.* H. Grimme (" Inschriften auf Ossuarien aus Jerusalem," *OLZ* 15 [1912] 529-34) published this and several other inscriptions that came from the vault of the Kallon family.

These were republished (along with more items) by H. Hänsler, " Die Ossuarien des Sionsmuseum," *Das Heilige Land* 57 (1913) 85-95, 129-144. This first inscription has been inscribed on the ossuary lid; a Greek inscription appears on one of the narrow sides. " Kallon " was probably considered the family name by then. Grimme (p. 533) drew attention to the transcription of the letter *pe* in *yhwsp* by the Greek *pi* (not *phi*): Ἰώσηπος Κάλλων. See Mur 103 a 1 (DJD 2. 232); Josephus, *Life* 1 §5; *CII* §1355, 1368.
Other Collections: *CII* §1350; *JPCI*, 8 (§1); Thomsen §206.

91. *Kallon Family Ossuary 2.* Published by H. Grimme in *OLZ* 15 (1912) 531. The (a) part is on the long side of the ossuary, and the (b) part is on the ossuary cover. The inscription, which may be Hebrew and not Aramaic at all, mentions the three children of Yeḥzaq, son of Kallon. The occurrence of Yeshab'ab (cf. 1 Chr 24:13) suggests that this was a priestly family. The two forms of the same name " Yoʿezer " and " Yehoʿezer " and the appearance of the construct plural *bry*, if correct (instead of *bny*), are noteworthy.
Other Collections: *CII* §1352; *JPCI*, 8-9 (§2).

92. *Kallon Family Ossuary 3.* Partially published by H. Grimme in *OLZ* 15 (1912) 532 and republished by H. Hänsler in *Das Heilige Land* 57 (1913) 132-33. The three inscriptions appear on the same ossuary. Again there are variant spellings of the name *yhwʿzr* and *ywʿzr*. In *CII* §1355 *šmʿwn* appears in Greek as Σίμωνος (Κάλλωνος).
Other Collections: *CII* §1351; *JPCI*, 9 (§3).

93. *Kallon Family Ossuary 4.* Partially published by H. Grimme in *OLZ* 15 (1912) 532 and republished by H. Hänsler in *Das Heilige Land* 57 (1913) 133-34. The (a) part appears on the ossuary lid.
Other Collections: *CII* §1354; *JPCI*, 9 (§4).

94. *Kallon Family Ossuary 5.* Published by H. Hänsler in *Das Heilige Land* 57 (1913) 134-35. For the name " Shelamṣion " in Greek, see Josephus, *Ant.* 18.5.4 §130: Σαλαμψιώ. For the name " Gamla'," see *m. Yebam.* 6:4, *b. B. Bat.* 21a, *b. Yoma* 18a.
Other Collections: *CII* §1353; *JPCI*, 9 (§5).

95. *Jerusalem Hypogeum Ossuary 1.* Discovered in 1926 in a tomb-cave near Jerusalem and published by E. L. Sukenik in " A Jewish

Hypogeum near Jerusalem," *JPOS* 8 (1928) 113-21, pls. 1-5. This inscription, which is published on pp. 116-17, pl. 2/3-4, has two parts: (a) occurs on one of the sides, with the word *'b'* added at a later date; (b) is on the lid. The name Dositheos is frequent among Jews of the Hellenistic period (see *IR* §260). Sukenik misread the second part of (b) as *wl'lmnth* (" and for his widow "). See §67, 71 above. *Other Collections*: *CII* §1359.

Bibliography

E. L. Sukenik, " Additional Note on ' A Jewish Hypogeum near Jerusalem,' " *JPOS* 9 (1929) 45-49.

A. Yellin, " On the Newly Discovered Jewish Ossuary Inscriptions," *JPOS* 9 (1929) 41-44.

S. Klein, " Die neuentdeckten jüdischen Ossuarinschriften," *JPOS* 9 (1929) 100-1.

D. Schütz, " Die Ossuarien in Palästina," *MGWJ* 75 (1931) 286-92 (fig. 4).

E. L. Sukenik, " Nochmals ' Die Ossuarien in Palästina,' " *MGWJ* 75 (1931) 462-63.

D. Schütz, " Nachwort," *MGWJ* 75 (1931) 463-64.

N. Avigad, " The Palaeography of the Dead Sea Scrolls and Related Documents," *Aspects of the Dead Sea Scrolls* (Scripta hierosolymitana, 4; Jerusalem: Magnes, 1958) 78-79.

96. *Jerusalem Hypogeum Ossuary 2.* Published by E. L. Sukenik in *JPOS* 8 (1928) 117-18, pl. 3/1-2. The name " Shelamṣion " was often given to women in the last two centuries of the Second Temple period. It was the Hebrew name of Queen Alexandra, wife of Alexander Jannaeus. Inscription (a) is scratched on the lid, while (b) is cut on one of the sides. On (a) the spelling of the name is defective, and on (b) the final letter of *'m'* was not completed. See §114 below. *Other Collections*: *CII* §1363.

97. *Jerusalem Hypogeum Ossuary 4.* Published by E. L. Sukenik in *JPOS* 8 (1928) 118-19, pls. 3/4 and 4/1. Inscription (a) is lightly scratched on the lid, and (b) is lightly scratched on one side. For the name Matthiah, see §79. Since the son has the same name as the father, he may have been born only after the father's death. *Other Collections*: *CII* §1362.

98. *Jerusalem Hypogeum Ossuary 5.* Published by E. L. Sukenik in *JPOS* 8 (1928) 119, pl. 4/2. The inscription is repeated on the lid and on one of the ends.
Other Collections: *CII* §1356.

99. *Jerusalem Tomb Ossuary 1.* Found in 1873 in a cave on the shoulder of the Mt. of Olives, which is called Bât'n el-Hawa (the traditional Mt. of Offense), not far from the road to Bethany, and published by C. Clermont-Ganneau in *Archaeological Researches in Palestine during the Years 1873-1874* (tr. A. Stewart ; London : Palestine Exploration Fund, 1899), 1. 381-412. This inscription, which is published on pp. 393-94 (§4), is written on the right-hand small end of an ossuary and may be related to one inscribed on the front side of a triangular lid (Clermont-Ganneau's §3 on pp. 392-93), which reads *yhwdh hspr* (" Judah, the scribe "). Clermont-Ganneau suggests that both Judah and his father may have been scribes and that this Eleazar the scribe may have some connection with the scribe put to death under Antiochus IV Epiphanes (2 Macc 6:18). On *hswpr*, see Mur 103 a 1 (DJD 2. 232), where ἀσωφήρ follows a proper name (Ἰώσηπος) in a Greek fragment.
Other Collections : *CII* §1308 ; *JPCI*, 19 (§10), 23 (§35).

Bibliography

C. Clermont-Ganneau, " Letters from M. Clermont-Ganneau," *PEFQS* (1874) 3-10, esp. pp. 7-10 ; 261-80.
C. Clermont-Ganneau, " Epigraphes hébräiques et grecques sur des ossuaires juifs inédits," *RArch* 3/1 (1883) 258-76, esp. pp. 259-68.
J. Germer-Durand, " Un musée palestinien," *Jérusalem* 2 (1906-7) 165-71, esp. pp. 167-70.
R. H. Smith, " The Cross Marks on Jewish Ossuaries," *PEQ* 106 (1974) 53-66, esp. pp. 54-57.

100. *Jerusalem Tomb Ossuary 2.* Published by C. Clermont-Ganneau in *Archaeological Researches*, 1. 394. This inscription was cut in very small, almost microscopic letters, at the top right-hand side of the front of the ossuary. Clermont-Ganneau called attention to the appearance of " the Hebrew name of Jesus."
Other Collections : *CII* §1318 ; *JPCI*, 27 (§67).

101. *Jerusalem Tomb Ossuary 3.* Published by C. Clermont-Ganneau in *Archaeological Researches*, 1. 394-95. The inscription is preceded by three marks that do not look like letters and whose meaning is hard to guess. This Eleazar may be the same as the father of Judah, the scribe, in §99. The patronymic " Nattai " is a well-known contracted form of Natanyahu.
Other Collections : *CII* §1304 ; *JPCI*, 21 (§19).

102. *Jerusalem Tomb Ossuary 4.* Painted, or rather written, with a reed pen in cursive characters (badly preserved and difficult to read) on the left of the long front side of an ossuary. C. Clermont-Ganneau (*Archaeological Researches*, 1. 407-8) does not regard the reading as certain, especially that of the patronymic.

103. *Jerusalem Tomb Ossuary 5.* Published in H. H. Spoer, " Some Hebrew and Phoenician Inscriptions," *JAOS* 28 (1907) 355-59. These ossuaries were found to the southeast of Jerusalem, not far from the site of " Schick's amphitheatre." The inscriptions are in Aramaic, Hebrew, and Greek. This inscription, which is published on p. 356, is inscribed on the upper edge of ossuary no. 3 ; the form *'tt* (" wife ") identifies it as Aramaic. The *zayin* in the husband's name is lacking, and Spoer merely transliterates it as Yaḥqiah. The Aramaic inscription is preceded by the Greek name Μαριάμη.
Other Collections : *CII* §1341 ; *Ephem.*, 3. 50-51 ; *JPCI*, 10 (§7) ; *SEG*, 8. §202.

104. *Jerusalem Tomb Ossuary 6.* This item, which is published by H. H. Spoer in *JAOS* 28 (1907) 356, is identified as Aramaic by the occurrence of *'tt* rather than *'št*. The inscription is placed on the upper edge of ossuary 4. The wife's name is also given in Greek as Ἐλισάβη.
Other Collections : *CII* §1338 ; *Ephem.*, 3. 51 ; *JPCI*, 21 (§18).

105. *Jerusalem Tomb Ossuary 7.* Published by H. H. Spoer in *JAOS* 28 (1907) 357, this inscription is found on a broken lid of ossuary 8. The father's name is not preserved.
Other Collections : *CII* §1335 ; *Ephem.*, 3. 51.

106. *Jerusalem Tomb Ossuary 8.* Found ca. 1926 by E. L. Sukenik in the basement of the Department of Antiquities of Palestine (in Jerusalem) and announced by him in *Jüdische Gräber Jerusalems um Christi Geburt* (*Vortrag gehalten am 6. Januar 1931 in der archäologischen Gesellschaft, Berlin*) (Jerusalem : Azriel Printing Press, 1931). An article of the same title appears in *Archäologischer Anzeiger* (1931) 309-16. Sukenik's comment : " Ich möchte hier ausdrücklich betonen, dass ich keine Konsequenzen aus der Auffindung dieser Namen ziehen möchte und sie nicht mit irgendwelchen Persönlichkeiten aus jener Zeit, die im Neuen Testament erwähnt sind, zu identizieren gedenke.

Die Namen waren zu jener Zeit ziemlich häufig und für irgendeine Identifikation fehlen uns jegliche Beweise" (pp. 19-20). The second name also appears merely as *yšw* between the two rosettas on the ossuary. See also C. Clermont-Ganneau, *Archaeological Researches*, 1. 438.

Bibliography

L.-H. Vincent, "Épitaphe prétendue de N.-S. Jésus-Christ," *Atti della Pontificia Accademia Romana di Archeologia*, ser. III: *Rendiconti* 7 (1932) 215-39.
A. Reifenberg, *Ancient Hebrew Arts* (New York: Schocken, 1950) 65 no. 2.
R. H. Smith, "The Cross Mark on Jewish Ossuaries," *PEQ* 106 (1974) 53-66, esp. p. 58.

107. *Jerusalem Tomb Ossuary 9.* Published in J. Germer-Durand's letter of 10 December 1905 to C. Clermont-Ganneau, which was printed in *CRAIBL* (1905) 789-90. In excavations on the eastern slope of Mt. Zion two inscriptions were found on a lintel of a large doorway that was used to cover the confluence of two drains in the Arab period. The beginning of this inscription has been hammered away; the *taw* is only a probable reading. Germer Durand read *l'št qrbn*; Lagrange, *l'št' qrbn*, "an offering for the fire."
Other Collections: *CII* §1407. *Ephem.*, 3. 51-52; *JPCI*, 32 (§101).

Bibliography

M.-J. Lagrange, "Epigraphie sémitique," *RB* os 2 (1893) 220-22.
J. Germer-Durand, "La maison de Caïphe et l'église Saint-Pierre à Jérusalem," *RB* 11 (1914) 71-94, 222-46, esp. pp. 238-40.
L.-M. Vincent and F.-M. Abel, *Jérusalem*: *Recherches de topographie, d'archéologie et d'histoire*: 2. *Jérusalem nouvelle*, fasc. 3 (Paris: Gabalda, 1922) 510.
E. Power, "The House of Caiphas and the Church of St. Peter," *Bib* 10 (1929) 394-416, esp. pp. 404-6.
L.-H. Vincent, "Saint Pierre en Gallicante," *RB* 39 (1930) 226-56, esp. p. 250.

108. *Nicanor Tomb Inscription.* A bilingual ossuary inscription found in a tomb at the north end of the Mt. of Olives and published in C. Clermont-Ganneau, "Archaeological and Epigraphic Notes on Palestine (22. The 'Gate of Nicanor' in the Temple of Jerusalem)," *PEFQS* (1903) 125-40, esp. pp. 125-31 (see also p. 93). The Aramaic is the last line of a four-line inscription; it is preceded by three lines in Greek: ὀστᾶ τῶν τοῦ Νεικά/νορος 'Αλεξανδρέως/ποιήσαντος τὰς θύρας ("The bones of the [sons *or* descendants ?] of Nicanor the Alexandrian who made the doors"). It probably refers to the one

who donated the famous door of Herod's Temple that was known as the " Gate of Nicanor ". While the Greek gives the impression that the sons of Nicanor were buried here, the Aramaic part gives only the name of the tomb's owner. Cf. *b. Yoma* 38a ; *y. Yoma* 41a.
Other Collections : *CII* §1256 ; *Ephem.*, 2. 197-98 ; *JPCI* 17-18 (§9) ; Thomsen, §200 ; *SEG*, 8. §200.

Bibliography

C. Clermont-Ganneau, " La ' Porte de Nicanor ' du Temple de Jérusalem," *Recueil d'archéologie orientale* (8 vols. ; Paris : Leroux) 5 (1903) 334-40 (§53).
G. Dickson, " The Tomb of Nicanor of Alexandria," *PEFQS* (1903) 326-32.
G. Dickson, " Palestinian Ossuaries," *Reliquary and Illustrated Archaeologist* 10 (1904) 145-51.
R. A. S. Macalister, " Further Observations on the Ossuary of Nicanor of Alexandria," *PEFQS* (1905) 253-57.
P. Roussel, " Nikanor d'Alexandrie et la porte du temple de Jérusalem," *REG* 37 (1924) 79-82 (see the comments of R. Dussaud, *Syria* 6 [1925] 99-100).
E. L. Sukenik, *Jüdische Gräber Jerusalems um Christi Geburt* (*Vortrag gehalten am 6. Januar 1931 in der archäologischen Gesellschaft, Berlin*) (Jerusalem : Azriel Printing Press, 1931) 15-17.
L.-H. Vincent, " Épitaphe prétendue de N.-S. Jésus Christ," *Atti della Pontificia Accademia Romana di Archeologia*, ser. III : *Rendiconti* 7 (1932) 215-39.
N. Avigad, " Mʿrwt-qbrym yhwdywt byrwšlym wbhry yhwdh [Jewish Rock-cut Tombs in Jerusalem and in the Judean Hill-Country]," *E. L. Sukenik Memorial Volume (1889-1953)* (Eretz-Israel, 8 ; Jerusalem : Israel Exploration Society, 1967) 119-42, esp. pp. 119-25 and pls. 20, 21.1-2.
R. H. Smith, " The Cross Marks on Jewish Ossuaries," *PEQ* 106 (1974) 53-66, esp. pp. 57-58.

109. *Nazareth Ossuary*. This inscription was on the cover of an ossuary in the Franciscan Museum in Nazareth and was published by G. Dalman in " Inschriften aus Palästina," *ZDPV* 37 (1914) 135-45, esp. p. 136, pl. XL/3. Dalman connects the name *Sōʿām* with the biblical *Šôaʿ* (Ezek 23:23) and the Palmyrene *siʿūnā* and *sauʿān*. He originally read the last line as *kwhn* ʿ*(lwhy)* *š(lm)* [" a priest. Up(on him be) p(eace) ! "]. But in *ZDPV* 37 (1914) 374, he retracted this reading and proposed that the third line be read *nwḥ npš* (" repose of soul ").
Other Collections : *CII* §988 ; *JPCI*, 56-57 (§166).

Bibliography

S. Poznański and D. Yellin, " Zu den von Dalman besprochenen Inschriften aus Palästina," *ZDPV* 41 (1918) 57-59.
D. Schütz, " Die Ossuarien aus Palästina," *MGWJ* 75 (1931) 286-92.

110. *Siloam Ossuary 1.* This and the next four items were published by L. A. Mayer in " A Tomb in the Kedron Valley Containing Ossuaries with Hebrew Graffiti Names," *Bulletin of the British School of Archaeology in Jerusalem* 5 (1924) 56-60. The tomb is situated in the lower Kidron Valley, on the right slope of the mountain, about fifteen minutes' walk from 'En Rogel. It consists of a central vestibule and two small chambers, one of which contained ossuaries, the other one only scattered bones. Thirteen of the nineteen ossuaries were inscribed. Of the inscriptions not studied here, seven are in Hebrew and one is in Hebrew with a Greek transcription. W. F. Albright (*JBL* 56 [1937] 160 n. 43a) stated : " My date for these . . . ossuaries would be the late first century B.C. and the very beginning of the first century A.D." The fact that the bones in ossuary no. 1 belong to one person and that the whole inscription was incised by one person at one time militates against taking it as a funerary inscription for both father and son. Rather, the ossuary was provided for the bones of Simeon by his son Joseph.
Other Collections : *CII* §1299.

Bibliography

M. Lidzbarski, " Epigraphisches aus Syrien II," *Nachrichten von der königlichen Gesellschaft der Wissenschaften zu Göttingen, Phil.-hist. Kl.* (1924) 43-48, esp. pp. 47-48.
E. L. Sukenik, " 'rwnwt wktbwt [Ossuaries and Inscriptions]," *Ha-Shiloaḥ* 42 (1924) 335-44, esp. p. 340.
M. R. Savignac, " Nouveaux ossuaries juifs avec graffites," *RB* 34 (1925) 253-66.
E. L. Sukenik, *Jüdische Gräber Jerusalems um Christi Geburt* (*Vortrag gehalten am 6. Januar 1931 in der archäologischen Gesellschaft, Berlin*) (Jerusalem : Azriel Printing Press, 1931) 17.

111. *Siloam Ossuary 3.* Published by L. A. Mayer in *Bulletin of the British School of Archaeology in Jerusalem* 5 (1924) 56-60. Shelamṣion may be the daughter of the Simeon mentioned in the preceding item.
Other Collections : *CII* §1297 ; *IR* §256.

112. *Siloam Ossuary 6.* Published by L. A. Mayer in *Bulletin of the British School of Archaeology in Jerusalem* 5 (1924) 56-60. On paleographic grounds, Mayer identifies this Simeon as the father of the Joseph in the next item.

113. *Siloam Ossuary 7.* Published by L. A. Mayer in *Bulletin of the British School of Archaeology in Jerusalem* 5 (1924) 56-60. Mayer considers it more likely that Joseph was the son of the Simeon of the preceding item than the Simeon of Siloam Ossuary 1.

114. *Siloam Ossuary 14.* Published by L. A. Mayer in the *Bulletin of the British School of Archaeology in Jerusalem* 5 (1924) 56-60. The word *'m'* may simply mean " mother " (see §96b above ; and Mt. Scopus Ossuary 6, which has the Greek μῆτερ, in C. A. Hornstein, " Newly-discovered Tomb on Mount Scopus," *PEFQS* [1900] 75-76). Or it could be a proper name, either *'Immā'* (R. Eliezer's wife was called 'Imma Shalom) or *'Ammā'* (as in the Judeo-Greek name 'Αμμή).
Other Collections : *CII* §1289 ; *IR* §257.

115. *Silwan Tomb Ossuary 1.* First published in R. A. S. Macalister, " A Tomb with Aramaic Inscriptions near Silwân," *PEFQS* (1908) 341-42. Found in a tomb on the slope of a hill below Deir es-Senneh (near Jerusalem), this inscription (and the next two) were cut in the soft rock and blacked in. Macalister read this and the next item together : " Abishalom, father of Yehoḥanan." But M. Lidzbarski (" The Jewish-Aramaic Inscriptions at the Tomb near Silwân," *PEFQS* [1909] 73) argued that they were written at different times and suggested that *'byšlm* could be divided into two names (*'Abbay* and *Šālôm*), the latter being either masculine or feminine.
Other Collections : *JPCI*, 21 (§14) ; *Ephem.*, 3. 52.

Bibliography

C. Clermont-Ganneau, " Notes on Hebrew and Jewish Inscriptions," *PEFQS* (1891) 240-43, esp. p. 241.
E. L. Sukenik, " 'rwnwt wktbwt [Ossuaries and Inscriptions]," *Ha-Shiloaḥ* 42 (1924) 335-44, esp. p. 340.

116. *Silwan Tomb Ossuary 2.* Published by R. A. S. Macalister in *PEFQS* (1908) 341-42, who took it as part of the preceding inscription and assumed that Abishalom was the father of Yehoḥanan. M. Lidzbarski (*PEFQS* [1909] 73) considered it a separate inscription consisting of two names : *'Abba'* and *Yĕhoḥānān.* See §96b above.
Other Collections : *JPCI*, 21 (§14).

117. *Silwan Tomb Ossuary 3.* Published by R. A. S. Macalister in *PEFQS* (1908) 341-42. The *aleph* had been added in paint but has not been cut in. Macalister read the name as *šmr* (cf. 1 Kgs 16:24), but M. Lidzbarski's reading (*PEFQS* [1909] 73) as *špr'* is clearly correct. See §73 above.

118. *Talpioth Ossuary 1.* First published by E. L. Sukenik in " The Earliest Records of Christianity," *AJA* 51 (1947) 351-65, pls. LXXVIII-LXXXVIII (also printed separately). In 1945 a Jewish chamber-tomb containing a number of ossuaries was discovered in the Talpioth suburb of Jerusalem. The tomb, which was cut in soft limestone, was furnished with five *kôkîm* or burial recesses together with a number of ossuaries. Sukenik stated : " My general impression is that the tomb contains nothing later than the first half of the first century A.D. The tomb was apparently in use from the first century B.C. until the middle of the first century A.D." (p. 365). The first inscription, which is published on p. 357, pl. LXXXIV, is scratched on one of the long sides of ossuary no. 1, close to its top. The first part clearly reads *šmʿwn* ; the *mem* is the final form used in this period, sometimes in beginning or middle of words as well. Sukenik read the second part as a single name (" Barsabba ") and called attention to the appearance of this name in Acts 1:23 and 15:22.

Bibliography

E. L. Sukenik, *The Earliest Records of Christianity* (Philadelphia : *AJA*, 1947).
Reviews : H. R. Willoughby, *JBL* 68 (1949) 61-65 ; S. L. Agnello, *Nuovo Didaskaleion* 4 (1950-51) 86-87.

C. H. Kraeling, " Christian Burial Urns ? " *BA* 9 (1946) 16-20.

O. Moe, " De äldste mindesmerker om kristendommen," *Erevna* 6/1 (1949) 20-26.

B. Reicke, " De judekristna benskrinen fran Jerusalems södra förort Talpijjót," *Svenska Jerusalemsföreningens Tidskrift* 48 (1949) 2-14.

B. Bagatti, " Resti cristiani in Palestina anteriori a Costantino ? " *Rivista di archeologia cristiana* 26 (1950) 117-31, esp. pp. 117-20.

H. Ludin Jansen, " Notes on the Ossuary Inscriptions of Talpioth," *Symbolae Osloenses* 28 (1950) 109-10.

E. Stauffer, " Zu den Kreuzeszeichen von Talpioth," *ZNW* 43 (1950-51) 262.

E. Dinkler, " Zur Geschichte des Kreuzsymbols," *ZTK* 48 (1951) 148-72 (Engl. " Comments on the History of the Symbol of the Cross," *JTC* 1 [1965] 124-146).

J. Munck, " Hat das Judentum den Namen IOY (Jehu) gebraucht ? " *ST* 5 (1951) 167-72.

E. R. Goodenough, *Jewish Symbols in the Greco-Roman Period* (New York : Pantheon, 1953), 1. 130-31.

B. Gustafsson, " The Oldest Graffiti in the History of the Church ? " *NTS* 3 (1956-57) 65-69.
D. Fishwick, " The Talpioth Ossuaries Again," *NTS* 10 (1963-64) 49-61.
I. Mancini, *Archaeological Discoveries Relative to the Judaeo-Christians* (Publications of the Studium Biblicum Franciscanum, collectio minor, 10 ; Franciscan Printing Press, 1970) 19-26.
J. P. Kane, " By No Means ' The Earliest Records of Christianity ' — with an Emended Reading of the Talpioth Inscription IĒSOUS IOU," *PEQ* 103 (1971) 103-8 (+1 chart).
R. H. Smith, " The Cross Marks on Jewish Ossuaries, " *PEQ* 106 (1974) 53-66, esp. pp. 58-60.

119. *Talpioth Ossuary 2.* Published by E. L. Sukenik in *AJA* 51 (1947) 357-58, pl. LXXXIV. A one-line inscription scratched in approximately the middle of the rear of ossuary no. 4. The letters are neatly drawn, and their interpretation presents no difficulty. In contrast to the preceding item, initial/medial *mem* is found throughout.

120. *Talpioth Ossuary 5.* Published by E. L. Sukenik in *AJA* 51 (1947) 358, pl. LXXXIV. One of the short sides of ossuary no. 10 bears three letters, roughly incised. They seem to read *mty*, an abbreviated form of *mttyh* or *mtyh.*

121. *Mt. Scopus Tomb Inscription 1.* This and the next two items were published by N. Avigad in " The Burial-Vault of a Nazirite Family on Mount Scopus," *IEJ* 21 (1971) 185-200, pls. 33-43 ; also in Hebrew in *Zalman Shazar Volume* (Eretz-Israel, 10 ; Jerusalem : Israel Exploration Society, 1971) 41-49. The first inscription, which is published on p. 196, is incised on the front of ossuary no. 7. Its script is described as " somewhat typical of the Jewish cursive of the end of the Second Temple period, often met with in ossuary inscriptions and other written documents " (p. 196). The spelling *hnzr* is an unusual defective form of *hnzyr*, the Hebrew term instead of the Aramaic *nzyr'* (cf. §99 above).

Bibliography

N. Avigad, " M'rt-qbrym mymy Hwrdws 'l hr-hṣwpym [A Jewish Tomb-Cave on Mt. Scopus]," *Qadmoniot* 1 (1968) 37-38.
N. Avigad, " The Tomb of a Nazirite on Mount Scopus," *Jerusalem Revealed : Archaeology in the Holy City 1968-1974* (Jerusalem : Israel Exploration Society and Shikmona, 1975) 66-67 [a modified translation of the preceding article].

122. *Mt. Scopus Tomb Inscription 2.* Incised on the narrow side of ossuary no. 8 and published by N. Avigad in *IEJ* 21 (1971) 197-98, who places its cursive script in the mid-1st century A.D. Salome is a common feminine name, and the form *'ntt* indicates that the language is Aramaic and that *br* rather than *bn* is to be read. The final *t* on *'ntt*, if correctly read, is quite different from the looped *taw* that precedes.

Bibliography

N. Avigad, " The Tomb of a Nazirite on Mount Scopus," *Jerusalem Revealed: Archaeology in the Holy City 1968-1974* (Jerusalem : Israel Exploration Society and Shikmona, 1975) 66-67.

123. *Mt. Scopus Tomb Inscription 3.* Incised on the lid of ossuary no. 16, this inscription was published by N. Avigad in *IEJ* 21 (1971) 198-99. The script is the formal ossuary script, except for the second instance of *br* (which employs a cursive ligature). The person whose bones were deposited was named after his paternal grandfather (papponymy). The name *'šwny* is unknown, but it may stem from *'yšwn* (" pupil " of the eye) or *'šn* (" steadfast ").

124. *Mt. Scopus Ossuary 6.* This inscription is on one of the eight ossuaries found in a Jewish burial cave on Mt. Scopus that was excavated in 1964 and published by D. Barag in " Mʿrt-qbrym yhwdyt bhr-hṣwpym [A Jewish Burial-Cave on Mount Scopus]," *I. Dunayevsky Memorial Volume* (Eretz-Israel, 11 ; Jerusalem : Israel Exploration Society, 1973) 101-3, pl. *yḥ* (Engl. 25*-26*). A Herodian lamp and pottery fragments date the burial cave to the very end of the 1st century B.C. or the 1st century A.D. (no later than 70).

125. *Mt. Scopus Tomb Ossuary 12.* In 1932 twenty-three ossuaries were found in a tomb cave on the slope of Mt. Scopus. The cave and the ossuaries were described by E. L. Sukenik in " Mʿrt-qbrym yhwdyt bmwrdwt hr hṣwpym," *Qôbeṣ* [JJPES] 3 (1934-35) 62-73. This inscription was found on ossuary no. 12 and published on pp. 68-69, 71. The name " Gerida' " is otherwise unknown, and it may be only a nickname. The Aramaic *gĕrîdā'* means " rind " or " crust "; the term *gĕrêdā'* means " alone " or " unqualified."

126. *Mt. Scopus Ossuary.* Found in a tomb-cave on Mt. Scopus and published by L.-H. Vincent in " Chronique : Hypogée judéo-grec dé-

couvert au Scopus," *RB* os 9 (1900) 106-12, esp. 107-8, pl. II. Vincent indicates that the second last letter of the patronymic in inscription (a) can be read as *waw*. But since *Ṣibyā'* is an attested name for a man (see 1 Chr 8:9), it is preferred. *Ṣibyāh* is also a woman's name (2 Kgs 12:2 ; 2 Chr 24:1), and M. Lidzbarski (*Ephem*, 1. 187) considers the possibility of a matronymic — which would be interesting, if true, in the light of the oft-discussed problem of Mark 6:3, ὁ υἱὸς τῆς Μαρίας.
Other Collections : *CII* §1248-49 ; *Ephem.*, 1. 186-87 ; *JPCI* 28 (§69-73).

Bibliography

C. Clermont-Ganneau, " Travaux français : Notes et observations," *RB* os 9 (1900) 307-9, esp. 307-8.
C. A. Hornstein, " Newly-discovered Tomb on Mount Scopus," *PEFQS* (1900) 75-76 (+ 2 folding charts).
B. Lugscheider and E. Kautzsch, " Über ein neuentdecktes jüdisches Grab mit hebräischen und griechischen Inschriften," *Mittheilungen und Nachrichten des deutschen Palästina-Vereins* (1900) 33-41.
E. L. Sukenik, " M'rt qbrym yhwdyt bmwrd hr hzytym," *Qwbṣ yrwšlym* (1928) 193-98.
E. L. Sukenik, " M'rt-qbrym yhwdyt bmwrdwt hr hṣwpym [A Jewish Tomb-Cave on the Slope of Mt. Scopus]," *Qôbeṣ* [JJPES] 3 (1934-35) 62-73.
E. L. Sukenik, " M'rt qbrym yhwdyt bmwrd hṣpwny šl nḥl qdrwn smwk lkpr hšlwḥ," *Spr-hywbl lprwpyswr šmw'l qrwys lml't lw šb'ym šnh* (Jerusalem : R. Mass, 1936) 87-93.

127. *Abu Gosh Ossuary.* The inscription is found on an ossuary discovered at Abu Gosh (not far from Jerusalem) and published by L.-H. Vincent in " Un nouvel ossuaire juif," *RB* os 11 (1902) 276-77. It is written in small but clear cursive script. Though *pe* and *samekh* of the first name are ligated, the reading *yhwsp* is certain. The second word could be read *gnky*, but Vincent prefers either *gnbw* (he calls it a genitive of the absolute form *gnby* or *gnb'*, giving the translation " Joseph, son of *Gnby* ") or *gnby* (understanding the inscription as two names of the same person). Could it be read as *gnb'* and mean " Joseph, the thief " ? Vincent dates the inscription to the 1st century B.C. or early in the 1st century A.D.
Other Collections : *CII* §1190 ; *Ephem.*, 2. 72 ; *JPCI*, 55 (§164).

128. *Wadi Aḥmedieh Inscription 1.* An inscription is found on ossuary no. 2 discovered in the Wadi Aḥmedieh, which flows into the Kidron Valley. It was published by N. Avigad in " M'rwt-qbrym yhwdywt byrwšlym wbhry yhwdh [Jewish Rock-Cut Tombs in Jerusalem and in the Judean Hill-Country]," *E. L. Sukenik Memorial Volume (1899-1953)* (Eretz-Israel, 8 ; Jerusalem : Israel Exploration Society, 1967) 119-42, pls. *k-kd* (Engl. 72*), esp. p. 131. The word " Sibbura " is inscribed twice on the ossuary. It may refer to a " logical " or " reasonable " man. The term would then be an adjective used to describe distinguished kinds of students, teachers, and sages. Or it may merely be a proper name (otherwise unknown).

129. *Wadi Aḥmedieh Inscription 2.* This inscription is found on ossuary 8, discovered in a tomb of the Wadi Aḥmedieh, which flows into the Kidron Valley. It was published by N. Avigad in " M'rwt-qbrym yhwdywt byrwšlym wbhry yhwdh [Jewish Rock-Cut Tombs in Jerusalem and in the Judean Hill Country]," *E. L. Sukenik Memorial Volume (1889-1953)* (Eretz-Israel, 8 ; Jerusalem : Israel Exploration Society, 1967) 131-32. The name is inscribed twice on the ossuary. Avigad suggests a possible connection between *ṭpz'y* and the Aramaic *ṭapzā'* (" coney " or " rock-badger ").

130. *Gezer Tomb Inscription 1.* Published by R. A. S. Macalister in " Ninth Quarterly Report on the Excavation of Gezer," *PEFQS* (1904) 320-54, esp. p. 342. Macalister found what he termed an " exclusively Maccabean cemetery " at Gezer, on a little knoll of rock south of the hill, on the summit of which was the village threshing-floor. This inscription (and the following one) came from tomb 127 where there was large hoard of ossuaries (about 20), all badly broken. An editorial note (by S. A. Cook ?) suggests a connection between *srw* and the Palmyrene *sry* (śry).
Other Collections : *CII* §1181 ; *JPCI*, 53 (§160).

Bibliography

H. Vincent, " Les fouilles anglaises de Gézer," *RB* ns 2 (1905) 100-3, esp. pp. 102-3.

R. A. S. Macalister, *The Excavation of Gezer : 1902-1905 and 1907-1909* (London : John Murray, 1911), 1. 347.

S. Klein, " Ktbwt 'rṣyśr'lywt mtqwpt hbyzntym wh'rbym [Land-of-Israel Inscriptions from the Ages of the Byzantines and the Arabs]," *Qôbeṣ* [JJPES] 1/2-4 (1925) 91-95, esp. p. 93.

131. *Gezer Tomb Inscription 2.* Published by R. A. S. Macalister in *PEFQS* (1904) 342. This inscription was on an ossuary found in the

same place as the previous item. Yeḥoni is probably a short form of *yḥwnyh* (" may Yahweh be gracious "). Its combination with Ḥannun may give evidence of a custom of giving children names related in form to those of kinsmen. On Ḥannun, see 2 Sam 10:1-4 ; 1 Chr 19:2-6.
Other Collections : *CII* §1177 ; *JPCI*, 53 (§161).

132. *Helen of Adiabene Tomb Inscription.* Discovered by F. de Saulcy in 1863 on one of the vaults of the " Tombs of the Kings," which is short distance to the north of the Damascus Gate of Jerusalem, and described by him in *Souvenirs d'un voyage en Terre Sainte* (Paris : Librairie du Petit Journal, 1867), 1. 249. The inscription appears on the front side of the sarcophagus. The first line (" Ṣaran, the Queen ") is drawn in a script close to Estrangela, while the second line (" Ṣarah, the Queen ") repeats the first in Palestinian Aramaic. The reading *ṣrh* rather than *ṣdh* is that of W. F. Albright in *JBL* 56 (1937) 159 n. 41. H. Vincent, in *RB* 16 (1919) 546 n. 2, writes : " . . . sarcophage d'Helène d'Adiabène, qui doit avoir été gravée entre 66 et 70 de notre ère." N. Avigad (Scripta hierosolymitana, 4, p. 78) assigns it on historical grounds to ca. A.D. 50. Josephus provides information about Queen Helen in *J.W.* 5–6 and *Ant.* 20. The identification of this sarcophagus as Queen Helen's seems to rest on the combination of Josephus' report (*Ant.* 20.4.3 §95) about the location of her tomb in the environs of Jerusalem and the description of the person interred in the sarcophagus as a queen. On Ṣaran and Ṣarah, see the remarks about this phenomenon in E. Y. Kutscher, " The Language of the ' Genesis Apocryphon ' : A Preliminary Study," *Aspects of the Dead Sea Scrolls* (Scripta hierosolymitana, 4 ; Jerusalem : Magnes, 1958) 1-35, esp. pp. 23-24.
Other Collections : *CII* §1388 ; *CIH* §72 ; *CIS*, 2. 156 ; M. Lidzbarski, *Epigr.* 117 ; *JPCI*, 26 (§57).

Bibliography

C. Clermont-Ganneau, " Epigraphes hébraïques et grecques sur des ossuaires juifs inédits, " *RArch* 3/1 (1883) 257-76, pl. IX.
C. Clermont-Ganneau, *Archaeological Researches in Palestine during the Years* 1873-1874 (tr. A. Stewart ; London : Palestine Exploration Fund, 1889), l. 381-454.
R. Dussaud, *Les monuments palestiniens et judaïques* (*Moab, Judée, Philistie, Samarie, Galilée*) (Paris : Leroux, 1912) 43-44, §28.
D. Schütz, " Die Ossuarien in Palästina," *MGWJ* 75 (1931) 286-92, esp. p. 290.
I. T. P. Themele, " Taphoi entos kai ektos tēs Ierousalēm," *Nea Sion* 27 (1932) 109-10.

W. F. Albright, " A Biblical Fragment from the Maccabaean Age : The Nash Papyrus," *JBL* 56 (1937) 145-76, esp. p. 159 n. 41.
N. Avigad, " The Palaeography of the Dead Sea Scrolls and Related Documents," *Aspects of the Dead Sea Scrolls* (Scripta hierosolymitana, 4 ; Jerusalem : Magnes, 1958) 56-87, esp. p. 78.
J. Naveh, " An Aramaic Inscription from El-Mal — A Survival of ' Seleucid Aramaic ' Script," *IEJ* 25 (1975) 117-23.

133. *Ḥizmeh Tomb Ossuary 2.* Found in 1931 at the village of Ḥizmeh (northeast of Jerusalem) and published by N. Avigad in " Mʿrwt-qbrym yhwdywt byrwšlym wbhry yhwdh [Jewish Rock-Cut Tombs in Jerusalem and in the Judean Hill-Country]," *E. L. Sukenik Memorial Volume (1889-1953)* (Eretz-Israel, 8 ; Jerusalem : Israel Exploration Society, 1967) 119-42, pls. *k-kd* (Engl. 72*), esp. p. 138. The inscription appears on ossuary no. 2. Avigad notes that this is the first time that the name " Hosea " occurs on an ossuary.

134. *Isawwiya Ossuary 4.* Published by E. L. Sukenik in " Two Jewish Hypogea," *JPOS* 12 (1932) 22-31, esp. p. 30, pl. IV. The ossuary was discovered in a tomb-cave southeast of Isawwiya, a village near Jerusalem. Inscription (a) appears on one of the narrow sides. Sukenik suggests that Salome was the daughter of the Yehoḥanan mentioned on another ossuary (*CII* §1244). In (b) the name Salome is repeated on the edge of the lid, but without any mention of the father's name. The four letters in (c) appear to the right of the inscription on the narrow side. Sukenik reads them as *ywnh* and suggests that the final letter may also be read as *ḥeth*.
Other Collections : *CII* §1245.

135. *Jaffa Ossuary.* Published by C. Clermont-Ganneau in " Ossuaire juif de Joseph, fils de Jean," *RArch* 36 (1878) 305-11. Clermont-Ganneau said that the ossuary was purchased from an inhabitant of Jaffa, but that he had reason to believe that it had been sold previously by one of his own workmen at Wadi Yasul. It is now in the Louvre. The inscription is on the narrow right side, and Clermont-Ganneau drew attention to the appearance of the same two names on other ossuaries from Wadi Yasul (cf. §143).
Other Collections : *CII* §1379 ; *CIH* §11 (col. 77) ; *JPCI* 23 (§42).

Bibliography

V. Schultze, " Sarkophage und Grabinschriften aus Jerusalem," *ZDPV* 3 (1881) 9-17, esp. p. 11.

136. *Masada Ostracon.* Found in the debris near the south wall of the peristyle building at Masada, the ostracon is a fragment of a jar, decorated with a wavy line in red paint. The writing is in two lines of black ink and resembles the script of the ossuaries. It was published in M. Avi-Yonah et al., " The Archaeological Survey of Masada, 1955-1956," *IEJ* 7 (1957) 1-60, esp. pp. 59-60, pl. 16c. The reading of the third letter in the place name is not certain. The name of a family called *Šimʿātîm*, " Shimeathites " (*RSV*), occurs in 1 Chr 2:55.

137. *Qaṭʿa Ossuary B.* Found in 1935 near the small settlement of Qaṭʿa, near the southern channel of the Kidron Valley, and published by N. Avigad in " Mʿrwt-qbrym yhwdywt byrwšlym wbhry yhwdh [Jewish Rock-Cut Tombs in Jerusalem and in the Judean Desert]," *E. L. Sukenik Memorial Volume (1889-1953)* (Eretz-Israel, 8 ; Jerusalem : Israel Exploration Society, 1967) 119-42, pls. *k-kd* (Engl. 72*), esp. pp. 125-26. The Greek ΚΑΣΣΑ may be an error, since it does not reflect the Aramaic *qrs*' exactly. But, on the other hand, the Aramaic *qrs*' may represent the resolution of a doubling by a liquid (cp. Hebrew *kissē*', Akkad. *kussū*, Aram. *korsē*' ; Hebrew *Dammeśeq*, Aram. *Darmeśeq*). Both names appear on ossuary no. 1.

138. *Ramat Raḥel Ossuary.* Published by Y. Aharoni in " Communication (Ramat Raḥel)," *RB* 70 (1963) 572-74, esp. p. 573. Found in a burial cave near Jerusalem that seems to have been in use at the end of the Second Temple period, this ossuary inscription is described as written in " Hébreu aramaïsé " and accompanied by Greek inscriptions that state : " Simonides, Marilla et leurs enfants."

139. *Šafʿat Ossuary 1.* This and the next two items were found in a tomb-cave at Šafʿat, a village 4 km. north of Jerusalem. They were published in F.-M. Abel, " Tombeau et ossuaires juifs récemment découverts," *RB* 10 (1913) 262-77. Inscription (1), which is published on p. 268, is written in Palmyrene script. Abel considered the ending of *khnh* with *he* as noteworthy.
Other Collections : *CII* §1221 ; *JPCI*, 29 (§73).

140. *Šafʿat Ossuary 10.* Published by F.-M. Abel in *RB* 10 (1913) 269-70. This is also written in Palmyrene script. *'lqṣdryn* may be either an Aramaized Greek ethnic designation (" the Alexandrian ") or more probably a proper name.
Other Collections : *CII* §1217 ; *JPCI*, 30 (§81).

141. *Šaf'at Ossuary 11*. Published by F.-M. Abel in *RB* 10 (1913) 271. This is a badly preserved Palmyrene inscription whose interpretation remains uncertain. The beginning of the third line could be read *zwṭr wsrh* ("the little one, and Sarah . . .").
Other Collections: *CII* §1222 ; *JPCI*, 30 (§82).

142. *Beit Saḥur Ossuary*. Published by E. L. Sukenik, "M'rt qbrym yhwdyt bnḥl qdrwn [A Jewish Tomb-Cave in the Kedron Valley]," *Tarbiẓ* 6 (1934-35) 190-96, esp. pp. 195-96. The inscription appears on the top of the front side of an ossuary decorated with two rosettas and what seems to be the drawing of a flower.
Other Collections: *CII* §1301.

143. *Wadi Yasul Ossuary 2*. Found on an ossuary at Wadi Yasul (near Jerusalem), this inscription is written in long and narrow characters. It was published by C. Clermont-Ganneau, "Epigraphes hébraïques et grecques sur des ossuaires juifs inédits," *RArch* 3/1 (1883) 258-76, esp. pp. 269-70. It has the same names (though in reverse order) as the so-called Jaffa Ossuary (§135 above), which Clermont-Ganneau suspected came from Wadi Yasul.
Other Collections: *CII* §1348 ("Wady Beit Sahour"?) ; *JPCI*, 23 (§39).

Bibliography

J. Euting, "Epigraphische Miscellen," *SPAW* 35/36 (1885) 669-88, pls. VI-XII, esp. p. 682 (§58).

144. *Er-Ram Ossuary*. Published in L.-H. Vincent, "Ossuaires juifs," *RB* 4 ns (1907) 410-14, esp. 412-14. The ossuary was found at the southern edge of the Mt. of Olives. The name of the deceased appears twice, once in Hebrew (*bn*) and once in Aramaic (*br*). For "Theudas," see Acts 5:36 and Josephus, *Ant.* 20.5.1. §97-99.
Other Collections: *CII* §1255 ; *JPCI*, 23 (§36).

145. *Trilingual Jerusalem Ossuary*. Discovered in 1905 near the Syrian orphanage in Jerusalem and published in 1906 in M. Lidzbarski, *Ephemeris für semitische Epigraphik* (3 vols. ; Giessen : Töpelmann, 1900-15), 2. 196-97. The Aramaic part seems to have been added later to the Hebrew and Greek inscriptions on the ossuary.
Other Collections: *CII* §1373 ; *JPCI*, 20 (§12) ; Thomsen, §204.

146. *Gezer Ossuary*. Published in R. A. S. Macalister, *The Excavation of Gezer : 1902-1905 and 1907-1909* (London : John Murray, 1911), 1. 349. The inscription appears on the lid of the ossuary from tomb 131. Macalister describes the patronymic as being " rather obscurely scratched."
Other Collections : *CII* §1176.

147. *Mt. Zion Ossuary*. An inscription on an ossuary from the Benedictine collection at Mt. Zion. It was published in E. L. Sukenik, *Jüdische Gräber Jerusalems um Christi Geburt* (*Vortrag gehalten am 6. Januar 1931 in der archäologischen Gesellschaft, Berlin*) (Jerusalem : Azriel Printing Press, 1931) 19. For the female name " Sapphira," see §73 above and Acts 5:1.
Other Collections : *CII* §1384.

148. *French Hill Ossuary*. Found on an ossuary in tomb 1 in the cemetery at French Hill (Karm el-Wiz) north of Jerusalem and published in L. T. Geraty, " A Thrice Repeated Ossuary Inscription from French Hill, Jerusalem," *BASOR* 219 (1975) 73-78. The same Aramaic inscription was incised in clear, easily identified characters by at least two different hands on three different surfaces of the ossuary. A date in the mid-1st century A.D. seems likely on the basis of the script. The name " Haggai " is new in the onomasticon of ossuaries.

Bibliography

J. F. Strange, " Late Hellenistic and Herodian Ossuary Tombs at French Hill, Jerusalem," *BASOR* 219 (1975) 39-67.
B. Arensburg and Y. Rak, " Skeletal Remains of an Ancient Jewish Population from French Hill, Jerusalem," *BASOR* 219 (1975) 69-71.

149. *El-Mal Dedicatory Inscription*. Discovered in the village of el-Mal in southern Syria, this inscription was published by J. Naveh, " An Aramaic Inscription from El-Mal — A Survival of ' Seleucid Aramaic ' Script," *IEJ* 25 (1975) 117-23. It is written in a script that is similar to, but not identical with, Palmyrene ; as the subtitle of his article indicates, Naveh considers it to be a form of " Seleucid Aramaic " script, which he relates to that of the Helen Adiabene Tomb Inscription (see §132 above), and others. The inscription is dated to 305 of the Seleucid era, which is 7/6 B.C. El-Mal is situated due east of Quneitra, 4 kms. east of Masḥara.

Bibliography

D. Urman et al., " Šrydym 'rky'wlwgyym bṣpwn hbšn [Archaeological Remains in Northern Bashan]," *Qadmoniot* 6 (1973) 85-90.
G. Barkay et al., " Archaeological Survey in the Northern Bashan (Preliminary Report)," *IEJ* 24 (1974) 173-84, esp. p. 183.

150. *Mĕgillat Taʿănît.* The " Scroll of Fasting " is a list of days in the calendar celebrating Jewish victories or recognizing Jewish prerogatives. They were celebrated as days of deliverance, and it was not right to mourn or to fast on them. It was called a " scroll of fasting " on the principle of *lucus a non lucendo.* According to one Jewish tradition it was composed ca. A.D. 7, when Judea became part of a Roman province ; according to another it was composed ca. A.D. 66, during the first revolt. It is more than likely a composition that dates from the end of the first century A.D., and there are even later additions mentioning " Trajan's Day " and Hadrian. Though some scholars (e. g., H. L. Strack, *Introduction to the Talmud and Midrash* [Philadelphia : Jewish Publication Society, 1931] 15) would claim that it was composed in part " before the destruction of Jerusalem " and that " in its present form " it " dates from the reign of Hadrian," it must be remembered that it has been handed down in various MSS. and with all sorts of redactions. It is almost impossible to recover the form of the text as it would have been used at the end of the first century A.D. or the beginning of the second. We present a form of the text that is based on the study of H. Lichtenstein, " Die Fastenrolle, eine Untersuchung zur jüdisch-hellenistischen Geschichte," *HUCA* 8-9 (1931-32) 257-351. There follows a select bibliography of the more important and more recent studies of the text ; one should consult the extensive bibliography of older materials supplied by Lichtenstein (pp. 308-16) — but realize that even that is not complete.

Bibliography

L. Zunz, *Die gottesdienstlichen Vorträge der Juden historisch entwickelt* (Berlin : A. Asher, 1832) 127-28 (2d rev. ed., Frankfurt am M. : J. Kauffmann, 1892, pp. 134-35).
J. Derenbourg, *Essai sur l'histoire et la géographie de la Palestine d'après les Thalmuds et les autres sources rabbiniques* (Paris : Imprimerie impériale, 1867), 1. 439-46.
J. Wellhausen, *Die Pharisäer und die Sadducäer : Eine Untersuchung zur inneren jüdischen Geschichte* (Greifswald : Bamberg, 1874) 56-63 ; reprinted, Göttingen : Vandenhoeck & Ruprecht, 1967.

J. Mueller, " Der Text der Fastenrolle," *MGWJ* 24 (1875) 43-48, 139-44.
M. Brann, " Entstehung und Werth der Megillat Ta'anit," *MGWJ* 25 (1876) 375-84, 410-18, 445-60.
H. Graetz, *Geschichte der Judäer* (3d ed. ; Leipzig : O. Leiner, 1878), 3. 597-615 ; 5th ed. (1906) 559-77.
A. Neubauer, *Medieval Jewish Chronicles and Chronological Notes* (Anecdota oxoniensia ; 2 vols. ; Oxford : Clarendon, 1887-1895), 2. 1-25 ; reprinted, Jerusalem : N.P., 1967.
M. Schwab, " La Megillath Taanith ou ' anniversaires historiques,' " *Actes du onzième congrès international des orientalistes, Paris 1897* (Paris : Imprimerie Nationale [E. Leroux], 1898-99), 4. 199-259.
M. Schwab, " Quelques notes sur la *Meghillath Taanith,*" *REJ* 41 (1900) 266-268.
J. Z. Lauterbach, " Megillat Ta'anit," *Jewish Encyclopedia* (New York/London : Funk and Wagnalls, 1904), 8. 427-28.
A. Edersheim, *The Life and Times of Jesus the Messiah* (8th ed. ; New York : Longmans, Green, 1912), 2. 698-700.
S. Zeitlin, " Megillat Taanit as a Source for Jewish Chronology and History in the Hellenistic and Roman Periods, Ch. VII : Megillat Taanit : Text and Translation," *JQR* 10 (1919-20) 237-43. [also printed separately as a Dropsie College dissertation (Philadelphia/Oxford : Dropsie College and Oxford University, 1922)].
A. Schwarz, " Taanith Esther," *Festskrift i Anledning af Professor David Simonsens 70-aarige Fødselsdag* (Copenhagen : Hertz, 1923) 188-205.
J. Morgenstern, " The Three Calendars of Ancient Israel," *HUCA* 1 (1924) 13-78.
G. Dalman, *Aramäische Dialektproben* (2d ed. ; Leipzig : Hinrichs, 1927) 1-3, 41-45 ; reprinted in *Grammatik des jüdisch-palästinischen Aramäisch* (Darmstadt : Wissenschaftliche Buchgesellschaft, 1960).
G. F. Moore, *Judaism in the First Centuries of the Christian Era : The Age of the Tannaim* (3 vols. ; Cambridge : Harvard University, 1927, 1930 [reprinted, 1950, 1954]), 1. 160 ; 2. 54 ; 3. 27, 45-46.
P. Günczler, *Megillath-Thaanith : Bölcseszet-doktori Ertekezes* (Budapest : N. P., 1929).
H. Lichtenstein, " Der Gedenktag des 25. Marcheschwan in der Fastenrolle," *MGWJ* 75 (1931) 202-4.
E. Bickerman, " H'rwt 'ḥdwt lmglt t'nyt [Some Notes on the Megillat Ta'-anît]," *Zion* ns 1 (1935-36) 351-55.
I. H. Weiss, *Dwr dwr wdwršyw : Hw' spr hymym ltwrh šb'l ph* [Zur Geschichte der jüdischen Tradition] (5 vols. ; 6th ed. ; Wilna : Rosenkranz, 1911), 1. 61, 87, 122, 125, 128, 133, 176 ; reprinted, Jerusalem : Ziw, 1963-64.
B. Lurie, *Mgylt T'nyt : Pršywt btwldwt byt ḥšmwny l'wr mšnh qdwmh* (Jerusalem : Bialik, 1964).
M. D. Herr, " 'l ṭybh šl Mgylt T'nyt [On the Character of the Megillat Ta'-ănît]," *Ha-'Aretz*, 5 Iyyar, 1965, p. 10.
S. Zeitlin, *The Rise and Fall of the Judaean State* (2 vols. ; Philadelphia : Jewish Publication Society of America, 1962, 1967), 2. 363-65, 450 (Appendix I : Translation of the text).
H. D. Mantel, " The Megillat Ta'anith and the Sects," *Studies in the History*

of the Jewish People and the Land of Israel (*Zvi Avneri Memorial Volume*) (Haifa : University of Haifa, 1970) 51-70.
N. N. G. [N. N. Glatzer], " Megillat Ta'anit [*sic*]," *Encyclopaedia judaica* (New York: Macmillan, 1971), 11. 1230-1231.
E. Schürer, *The History of the Jewish People in the Age of Jesus Christ* (*175 B.C. — A.D. 135*) (rev. ed. G. Vermes and F. Millar ; Edinburgh : Clark), 1 (1973) 114-15.
A. Pelletier, " La nomenclature du calendrier juif à l'époque hellénistique," *RB* 82 (1975) 218-33 (+ pl. XVII).

APPENDIX

Palestinian Aramaic Inscriptions of Later Date
(Synagogal, Funerary, and Other)

LIST OF INSCRIPTIONS

A1.	'Abellin Synagogue Inscription	254
A2.	'Ain Duk Synagogue Inscription I	254
A3.	'Ain Duk Synagogue Inscription II.	254
A4.	'Ain Duk Synagogue Inscription III	254
A5.	'Ain Duk Synagogue Inscription IV	254
A6.	'Ain Duk Synagogue Inscription V	256
A7.	'Ain Duk Synagogue Inscription VI	256
A8.	'Ain Duk Synagogue Inscription VII	256
A9.	'Alma Synagogue Inscription I	256
A10.	'Alma Synagogue Inscription II	256
A11.	Beth Alpha Mosaic Inscription	256
A12.	Beth Gubrin Synagogue Inscription.	258
A13.	Beth She'an Synagogue Inscription I	258
A14.	Beth She'an Synagogue Inscription II	258
A15.	Capernaum Synagogue Inscription	258
A16.	Chorazin Synagogue Inscription	258
A17.	Dabbura Synagogue Inscription I.	258
A18.	Dabbura Synagogue Inscription II	260
A19.	Dabbura Synagogue Inscription III.	260
A20.	Dabbura Synagogue Inscription IV	260
A21.	Dabbura Synagogue Inscription V	260
A22.	En-Gedi Synagogue Inscription	260
A23.	Fiq Synagogue Inscription	260
A24.	Gaza Synagogue Inscription	262
A25.	Gischala Synagogue Inscription.	262
A26.	Hammath-Gadara Synagogue Inscription I	262
A27.	Hammath-Gadara Synagogue Inscription II	262
A28.	Hammath-Gadara Synagogue Inscription III.	262
A29.	Hammath-Gadara Synagogue Inscription IV	264
A30.	Hammath-Tiberias Synagogue Inscription	264
A31.	Hebron Synagogue Inscription	264
A32.	'Isfiya Synagogue Inscription.	264
A33.	Jerash Synagogue Inscription	264
A34.	Jericho Synagogue Inscription	266
A35.	Kafr Ḥananiah Synagogue Inscription.	266
A36.	Kafr Kenna Synagogue Inscription I	266
A37.	Kafr Kenna Synagogue Inscription II	266
A38.	Khirbet Kanef Synagogue Inscription	266
A39.	Kokhav Ha-Yarden Synagogue Inscription	268

A40. Ma'on Synagogue Inscription 268
A41. Sepphoris Synagogue Inscription 268
A42. Umm El-'Amed Synagogue Inscription 268
A43. Yesud Ha-Ma'ala Synagogue Inscription 268
A44. Bersabee Votive Inscription 268
A45. Beth She'arim Tomb Inscription I 270
A46. Beth She'arim Tomb Inscription II. 270
A47. Beth She'arim Tomb Inscription III 270
A48. Er-Rama Inscription 270
A49. Kafr Bir'im School Inscription 270
A50. Ghôr eṣ-Ṣâfieh Tombstone Inscription I. 270
A51. Ghôr eṣ-Ṣâfieh Tombstone Inscription II 272
A52. Ghôr eṣ-Ṣâfieh Tombstone Inscription III 272
A53. Khirbet Zif Ossuary. 272
A54. Khirbet Susiya Synagogue Inscription I 272
A55. Khirbet Susiya Synagogue Inscription II 272
A56. Eshtemoa' Synagogue Insription 274

ARAMAIC TEXT

A1. ʿAbellin Synagogue Inscription

1 דכיר לטב ראש
2 סדרה (?) ברכה
3 דאתחזק [ועבד]
4 [ה]דין תרעה
5 [אמן] שלום

A2. ʿAin Duk Synagogue Inscription I

1 דכיר לטב פינחס כהנה בר יוסטה דיהב

2 טימי פסיפסה
3 מן דידה ומרושת
4 דכירה
5 לטב רבקה
6 אתתה
7 פינחס

A3. ʿAin Duk Synagogue Inscription II

1 דכירה לטב חליפו ברת רבי ספרה
2 דאתחזק[ת] בהדין אתרה ק[די]שה אמן

A4. ʿAin Duk Synagogue Inscription III

1 [ד]כיר לטב
2 בינימין פרנס[ה]
3 בר יוסה

A5. ʿAin Duk Synagogue Inscription IV

1 [ד]כירין לטב כל מן
2 [ד]מתחזק ויהב או
3 [די]הב בהדן אתרה

TRANSLATION

A1.

1. Remembered for good be the leader
2. of the *sdrh*, Berakah,
3. who gathered his resources [and made]
4. [t]his gate.
5. [Amen !] Peace !

A2.

1. Remembered for good be Phinehas, the priest, son of Justus, who gave
2. the cost of the mosaic
3. from his own resources and the basin.
4. Remembered
5. for good be Rebecca,
6. the wife of
7. Phinehas.

A3.

1. Remembered for good be Ḥalipu, daughter of Rabbi Saprah,
2. who gathered [her] resources for this h[o]ly place. Amen !

A4.

1. [Re]membered for good be
2. Benjamin, [the] administrator,
3. son of Jose.

A5.

1. [Re]membered for good be everyone
2. [who] gathers his resources and contributes or
3. [who has] contributed for this [h]oly

4 [ק]דישה בן דהב בן
5 [כ]סף בן כל מקמה
6 [ד]היא [ואיתו]ן חו‹ל›קהון
7 בהדן אתרה קדישה
8 אמן

A6. ʿAin Duk Synagogue Inscription V

1 דכיר לט[ב]
2 שמואל

A7. ʿAin Duk Synagogue Inscription VI

1 דכי[ר]
2 ד‹כ›יר לטב מרות[ה ק]טינה ויע[י]יר
3 ברה דהנון מתחזקין בה[דן] אתרה
4 [ ]יין בהדן אתר[ה קדיש]ה א[מן]

A8. ʿAin Duk Synagogue Inscription VII

1 דכיר לטב מרו[תה]
2 בר כריס[פה]
3 חולקהון בה[דן אתרה קדישה אמן]

A9. ʿAlma Synagogue Inscription I

1 [א]מן סלה אנה יוסה בר לוי הלוי אומנה דעבד ה[דין]

A10. ʿAlma Synagogue Inscription II

1 [ ]נה טבריה ר[ ]
2 [ ]שקופה מלך ע[למה]

A11. Beth Alpha Mosaic Inscription

1 [הדין פסיפ]סה אתקבע בשתה
2 [למ]לכותה דיוסטינוס מלכ[ה]
3 [ ]חטייה מאת
4 [ ]אתנדבון כל בני
5 ק[רתה]רבי
6 א[דכירין ל]טב כל
7 ב[ני][

4. place, either gold or
5. [si]lver, or any object
6. [what]soever, [and have broug]ht their sh<a>re
7. into this holy place.
8. Amen !

A6.

1. Remembered for go[od] be
2. Samuel.

A7.

1. Remem[bered]
2. Re<mem>bered for good be Marut[ah Qe]tinah and *Y'[y]yr*,
3. his son, who were gathering their resources for th[is] place
4. [ ]*yyn* in this [hol]y plac[e]. Amen !

A8.

1. Remembered for good be Maru[tah]
2. son of Cris[pos and]
3. their share in th[is holy place. Amen !]

A9.

1. A]men ! Selah ! I (am) Jose, son of Levi, the levite, the craftsman who made th[is]

A10.

1. [ ]*nh* of Tiberias *r*[ ]
2. [ ]the lintel. (May) the King of the un[iverse]

A11.

1. [This mosa]ic was composed in the year
2. [in the re]ign of Justin [the] emperor
3. [ ]lentils (?) one hundred
4. [ ]all the people of [the] to[wn] volunteered
5. [ ]Rabbi
6. '[Remembered for] good [be] all
7. the me[mbers]*n*.

A12. Beth Gubrin Synagogue Inscription

1 דכיר
2 לטב קוריס
3 [בר ש]עיי ניח נפ[ש]
4 בר אוכסנטיס
5 דזבן (?) הדין עמודא
6 ליקרה דכנישתא
7 שלום

A13. Beth She'an Synagogue Inscription I

1 דכירין לטב כל בני חבורתה קדישתה
2 דהנון מתחזקין בתקונה דאתרה
3 [קדי]שה ובשלמה תהוי להון ברכתה אמן
4 [ ]רוב שלום חסד בשלום

A14. Beth She'an Synagogue Inscription II

1 דכיר לטב אומנה דעבד חדה** אבידתה*

*Read עבידתה **Read הדה

A15. Capernaum Synagogue Inscription

1 חלפו בר זבידה בר יוחנן
2 עבד הדן עמודה
3 ת[ה]י לא* ברכתה

*Read לה

A16. Chorazin Synagogue Inscription

1 דכיר לטב יודן בר ישמע‹א›ל
2 דעבד הדן סטוה
3 ודרגוה מפעלה יהי
4 לה חולק עם צדיקיה

A17. Dabbura Synagogue Inscription I

1 אלעזר בר [אליעזר ר]בה עבד עמודיה דעל מן
2 כפתה ופצ[ימיה תהי לה ברכתה]

A12.

1. Remembered
2. for good be Kyrios
3. [son of She]ʿay — Repose (for his) soul ! —
4. son of Auxentios
5. who purchased this column
6. in honor of the congregation.
7. Peace !

A13.

1. Remembered for good be all the members of the holy community
2. who gathered their resources for the repair of the [hol]y
3. place and for its completion. May there be a blessing upon them ! Amen !
4. [ ]much peace, piety in peace.

A14.

1. Remembered for good be the craftsman who did this work.

A15.

1. Ḥalphay, son of Zebida, son of John,
2. made this column.
3. May a blessing be upon him !

A16.

1. Remembered for good be Judan, son of Ishmael,
2. who made this colonnade
3. and its staircase with his own skill. May his lot be
4. with (the) righteous !

A17.

1. Eleʿazar, son of [Eliʿezer the gr]eat, made the columns that (are) above
2. the arches and the be[ams. May a blessing be upon him !]

A18. Dabbura Synagogue Inscription II

1 [ב]ר יודה

A19. Dabbura Synagogue Inscription III

1 [ח]יננה[ ]
2 ברכת[ה]

A20. Dabbura Synagogue Inscription IV

1 עבדו בית[ ]
2 תהי לה
3 ברכתה

A21. Dabbura Synagogue Inscription V

1 [ ] עבד תרעה

A22. En-Gedi Synagogue Inscription

1 דכירין לטב יוסה ועירון וחזיקיו בנוה דחלפי

2 כל מן דיהיב פלגו בן גבר לחבריה הי אמר

3 לשן ביש על חבריה לעממיה הי גניב

4 צבותיה דחבריה הי מן דגלי רזה דקרתה

5 לעממיה דין דעינוה משוטטן בכל ארעה

6 וחמי סתירתה הוא יתן אפוה בגברה
7 ההו ובזרעיה ויעקור יתיה מן תחות שומיה

8 וימרון כל עמה אמן ואמן סלה
9 רבי יוסה בן חלפי חזקיו בן חלפי דכירין לטב

10 דרגי סגי אנון עבדו לשמה דרחמנה שלום

A23. Fiq Synagogue Inscription

1 אנה יהודה ח[ז]אנה

A18.

1. [s]on of Judah

A19.

1. [Ḥ]aynanah[ ]
2. [a] blessing[ ]

A20.

1. They made the house [of]
2. May a blessing be
3. upon him !

A21.

1. [ ]made the gate.

A22.

1. Remembered for good be Jose, ʿIron, and Ḥezeqyo, sons of Ḥalphay.
2. Everyone who will set discord between a man and his fellow, either by speaking (with)
3. an evil tongue against (i.e., calumniate) his fellow to the Gentiles, or by stealing
4. the goods of his fellow, or (if) anyone would reveal the secret of the town
5. to the Gentiles, may (the) judge whose eyes range over all the earth
6. and (who) sees hidden things, set his face against that
7. man and against his seed, and may he uproot him from beneath the heavens.
8. Let all the people say : " Amen, amen ! Selah ! "
9. May Rabbi Jose, son of Ḥalphay, (and) Ḥizqio, son of Ḥalphay, be remembered for good.
10. They made the great(?) stairs in the name of the Merciful One. Peace !

A23.

1. I, Judah, (am) the se[x]ton.

A24. Gaza Synagogue Inscription

1 חנניה בר יעקב

A25. Gischala Synagogue Inscription

1 יוסה בר נחום
2 עבד האדן
3 תאה לה
4 ברכתה

A26. Hammath-Gadara Synagogue Inscription I

1 ודכיר לטב
2 קירס הופליס וקירה
3 פרוטון וקירס סלוסטיס
4 חתנה וקומס פרורוס ברה
5 וקיריס פוטיס חתנה וקירס
6 חנינה ברה הננון ובניהון
7 דמיצותון תדירן בכל אתר
8 דהבון הכה חמישה דינרין
9 דהב מלך עלמה יתן ברכתה
10 בעמלהון אמן אמן סלה

A27. Hammath-Gadara Synagogue Inscription II

1 וד[כיר לט]ב רב תנחום הלוי ב[ר חל]יפה דהב חד טרימיסין ודכיר לטב מוניקה דסוסי‹פ›ה צפוריה

2 וק[ירס פ]טריק ד‹כ›פר עקביה ויוסה בר דוסתי דמן כפר נחום דיהבון תלתיהון תלת גרמין מלך

3 ע[למה ית]ן ברכתה בעמל[הון] אמן אמן סלה שלום ודכיר לטב יודן ארדה מן הימאים(?) דיהב תלת

4 ו[דכירין לט]ב ארבילייי דיהבון מהי‹ת›הון מלך עלמ‹ה› יתן ברכתה בעמלהון אמן אמן סלה

A28. Hammath-Gadara Synagogue Inscription III

1 ודכ‹י›ר לטב קיריס ליאנטיס וקירה קלניק דה[בון ······· לי]קרה דכנישתה

A24.

1. Ḥananiah, son of Jacob.

A25.

1. Jose, son of Nahum,
2. made this (column).
3. May a blessing be
4. upon him !

A26.

1. Remembered for good be
2. Lord Hoples and Lady
3. Proton, Lord Sallustius,
4. his son-in-law, *Comes* Phroros, his son,
5. Lord Photios, his son-in-law, and Lord
6. Ḥaninah, his son — these and their children —
7. whose acts of charity are constant in every place,
8. who have given here five denars
9. (of) gold. May the King of the Universe set his (*or* a) blessing
10. on their undertakings. Amen, amen ! Selah !

A27.

1. And remem[bered for go]od be Rab Tanḥum, the levite, so[n of Ḥal]ipah, who gave one *trimēsion.* And remembered for good be Monika, (the wife ?) of Sysipha, the Sepphorite,
2. Lo[rd Pa]trikos of <Ke>far ʿAqabyah, and Jose, son of Dositheos, who (is) from Capernaum, who gave — the three of them — three grams(?). May the King of
3. the Un[iverse se]t his (*or* a) blessing on [their] undertakings. Amen, amen ! Selah ! Peace ! And remembered for good be Judan, the builder(?) from *Hym'ym*, who gave three.
4. And [remembered for go]od be the Arbelites who gave their wo[v]en goods. May the King of the Univer[se] set his (*or* a) blessing on their undertakings. Amen, amen ! Selah !

A28.

1. And rememb[er]ed for good be Lord Leontius and Lady Kalonike, who ga[ve for the ho]nor of the congregation.

2 מלך עלמה יתן ברכתה בעמלה אמן אמן סלה שלום ודכירה לטב חדה אתה

3 אנטוליה ד[יהב]ה חד דינר ליקרה דכנישתה מלך עלמה יתן ברכתה בעמלה

4 אמן אמן [סלה] שלום ודכירין לטב עיריא דהבון חד טר‹ימ›יסין

A29. Hammath-Gadara Synagogue Inscription IV

1 [ודכיר ל]טב אדה בר תנחום
2 [בר מוני]קה דיהב חד טרימיסין ויוסה
3 [בר] קרוצה ומוניקה דיהב‹ו› חד פלגות
4 [די]נר לגו הדן [פסיפ]סה תהוי להון
5 ברכתה אמ[ן סל]ה שלום

A30. Hammath-Tiberias Synagogue Inscription

1 יהי שלמה על כל מן דעבד מצותה בהדן
2 אתרה קדישה ודעתיד מעבד מצותה
3 תהי לה ברכתה אמן אמן סלה ולי אמן

A31. Hebron Synagogue Inscription

1 דכיר לטב
2 סברס(?) בר יו[נ]תן
3 בר[ ]

A32. ʿIsfiya Synagogue Inscription

1 [ ]וברוכה[ ]פו ורתה דברבי
2 [דכיר לטב כל מן דפ]סק ויהב פסקתה תהי [להון ברכתה]

3 [ ]י דכיר לטב דכיר לטב יושיה ד[י]הב[ ]

A33. Jerash Synagogue Inscription

1 שלום על כל
2 ישראל אמן אמן

2. May the King of the Universe set his (*or* a) blessing on his (*or* her) undertakings. Amen, amen! Selah! Peace! And remembered for good be a certain Lady,
3. Anatolia, who g[av]e one denar for the honor of the congregation. May the King of the Universe set his blessing on her undertakings.
4. Amen, amen! [Selah!] Peace! And remembered for good be the guardians(?), who gave one *tr*[*im*]*ēsion*.

A29.

1. [And remembered for] good be 'Adah, son of Tanḥum,
2. [son of Moni]ka, who gave one *trimēsion*; and Jose,
3. [son of] Qaroṣah and Monika, who gav[e] one half
4. [de]nar for this [mosa]ic. May a blessing be upon them!
5. Ame[n! Sel]ah! Peace!

A30.

1. May His peace (*or simply* peace) be upon everyone who has made a donation in this
2. holy place and who will in the future make a donation!
3. May a blessing be upon him (*or* her)! Amen, amen! Selah! And for me. Amen!

A31.

1. Remembered for good be
2. Severus(?), son of Jo[na]than,
3. son of [ ]

A32.

1. [ ]and blessed[ ]*pw wrth* of *BĕRabbi*
2. [Remembered for good be everyone who ple]dged and gave the donation. May [a blessing] be [upon them]
3. [ ]*y* remembered be for good. Remembered for good be Josiah, who [g]ave[

A33.

1. Peace upon all
2. Israel. Amen, amen!

3 סלה פינחס בר
4 ברוך יוסה בר
5 שמואל וי[ו]דן בר חזקיה

A34. Jericho Synagogue Inscription

1 דכירן לטב יהוי דכרונהון לטב כל

2 קהלה קד[י]שה רביה וזעוריה דסייע
3 יתהון מלכיה דעלמה ואתחזקון ועבדון

4 פסיפסה דידע שמהתון ודבניהון ודאנשי

5 בתיהון יכתוב יתהון בספר חייה [עם]
6 צדיקיה חברין לכל ישראל של[ום אמן סלה]

A35. Kafr Ḥananiah Synagogue Inscription

1 דן כלילה[ ]לאתרה קדישה דכפר חנניה דכירין לטב אמן . . . סלה
שלום

A36. Kafr Kenna Synagogue Inscription I

1 דיכר* לטב יוסה בר
2 תנחום בר בוטה ובנוי
3 דעבדין הדה טבלה
4 תהי להון ברכתה
5 אמן

*Read דכיר

A37. Kafr Kenna Synagogue Inscription II

1 ישׁ[ ]
2 הדה טב[לה תהי להון]
3 ברכתה[ ]

A38. Khirbet Kanef Synagogue Inscription

1 [ ]תה דכיר לטב יוסה בר חל[פ]ו בר חנ[ן]

3. Selah ! Phinehas, son of
4. Baruch ; Jose, son of
5. Samuel ; and J[u]dan, son of Hezekiah.

A34.

1. (May they) be remembered for good ! May their memory be for good, all
2. the ho[l]y assembly, the elders and the youth, whom
3. the King of the Universe has helped and (who) have gathered their resources and made
4. the mosaic. (He) who knows their names and (those) of their children and of the people
5. of their households will write them in the book of life [with]
6. the righteous (as) companions for all Israel. Pea[ce ! Amen ! Selah !]

A35.

1. This circle [ ]for the sacred place of Kefar Ḥananiah. (May they be) remembered for good. Amen ! Selah ! Peace !

A36.

1. Remembered for good be Jose, son of
2. Tanḥum, son of Buṭah, and his sons
3. who made this panel(?).
4. May a blessing be upon them !
5. Amen !

A37.

1. *yš*[ ]
2. this pa[nel ?). May] a blessing [be]
3. [upon them !]

A38.

1. [ ]*th*. Remembered for good be Jose, son of Ḥal[p]hu, son of Ḥan[an.]

A39. Kokhav Ha-Yarden Synagogue Inscription

1 דשרן הדה
2 סכופתה מן
3 דרחמנה ומן עמלי
4 אמן אמן סלה

A40. Ma'on Synagogue Inscription

1 [ד]כירין לטב כל קהלה
2 [די] עבדו הדן פספ‹ס›ה
3 וכן דאישן ותמה ויהודה
4 דיהבו תג תרי דינרין....

A41. Sepphoris Synagogue Inscription

1 [ד]כיר
2 [לטב ר]בי יודן
3 [בר תנ]חום בר
4 [בוטה דעבד] הדה [ט]
5 [בלה]
6 [תהי לה ברכתה]

A42. Umm El-'Amed Synagogue Inscription

1 יועזר חזנה
2 ושמעון
3 אחוי עבדו
4 הדן תרא דמרי
5 שומיא

A43. Yesud Ha-Ma'ala Synagogue Inscription

1 דכיר לטב ר׳ מתיה ב[ר]
2 דעביד [הדן] עמו[דה]

A44. Bersabee Votive Inscription

1 ל יהב(?)[ ]ה(?) יהושע
2 מל על נפשיה
3 תנחום בריה

A39.

1. who have established (*1st pl.*) this
2. lintel out of
3. what (is) our own generosity and out of my own toil.
4. Amen, amen ! Selah !

A40.

1. [Re]membered for good be the whole assembly
2. [who] made this mos<a>ic
3. and furthermore Daisan, Thomas, and Judah
4. who gave a sum of two denarii. . . . .

A41.

1. [Rem]embered [for good]
2. [be Ra]bbi Judan,
3. [son of Tan]ḥum, son of
4. [Buṭah, who made] this
5. [panel(?)].
6. [May a blessing be upon him !]

A42.

1. Yoʿezer, the sexton,
2. and Simeon,
3. his brother, made
4. this gate of the Lord
5. of heaven.

A43.

1. Remembered for good be R(abbi) Mattiah, s[on of]
2. who made [this] colu[mn].

A44.

1. *l* gave(?)[ ]*h*(?) Joshua
2. *ml* for himself.
3. Tanḥum, his son.

A45. Beth Sheʿarim Tomb Inscription I

1 כל מן דיפתח
2 הדה קבורתה
3 על{על} מן דבגוה
4 ימות בסוף ביש

A46. Beth Sheʿarim Tomb Inscription II

1 דקביר בהדין
2 שמעון בר יוחנן
3 ובשבועה דכל
4 דיפתח עלוי יהי
5 מאית בסוף
6 ביש

A47. Beth Sheʿarim Tomb Inscription III

1 כל מן דיפתח[ ]

A48. Er-Rama Inscription

1 דכירין לטב רבי אליעזר בר טדאור ובנוי דבנין בית דה דאורחתוה

2 דמיך קדם דתרעה חולקהון [עם צדיקיה]

A49. Kafr Birʿim School Inscription

1 בנ[ה]ו אלעזור בר יהו[נ]תן

A50. Ghôr eṣ-Ṣâfieh Tombstone Inscription I

1 תתניח נפשה
2 דשאול בר [ ]לת
3 דמית בריש ירח
4 מרחשון משתה
5 קדמיתה דשמטתה
6 שנת תלת מא ושתין
7 ורבע שנין לחרבן
8 בית מקדשה שלם

A45.

1. May anyone who will open
2. this grave
3. on the one who is within it
4. die of an evil end !

A46.

1. (He) who is buried in this (grave)
2. (is) Simeon, son of John.
3. With an oath that anyone
4. who will open (it) on him may
5. die of an evil
6. end !

A47.

1. (May) anyone who will open [

A48.

1. Remembered for good be Rabbi Eli'ezer, son of Tede'or, and his sons, who built this hostel(?)
2. situated(?) before the gate. (May) their lot (be) [with the righteous] !

A49.

1. Eleazar, son of Jona[th]an, bui[lt] it.

A50.

1. At rest be the soul
2. of Saul, son of [ ]*lt*,
3. who died at the beginning of the month
4. of Marḥeshwan, in the first
5. year of the release,
6. the year three-hundred and sixty-
7. four (of the) years after the destruction
8. of the house of the Temple. Peace !

A51. Ghôr eṣ-Ṣâfieh Tombstone Inscription II

1 הדה נפשה
2 דאסתר ברתה
3 דעדיו דמיתת
4 בירח שבט
5 שנת ג בשמטת[ה]
6 שנת תלת מא [ותלת]
7 מן שנין לחרבן
8 בית מקדשה
9 שלום שלום
10 עלת

A52. Ghôr eṣ-Ṣâfieh Tombstone Inscription III

1 תתניח נפשה דחלפו
2 ברתה [ ] דמיתת
3 ביום תלתת בהדעשר*
4 יומין בירח אלול בשנת [ב]
5 דשמטתה דהיא שנת
6 ארבע מאה ותלתין
7 וחמש שנין לחרבן
8 בית מקדשה שלום
9 על ישראל שלום

*Read בחדעשר

A53. Khirbet Zif Ossuary

1 קנרוס בר דיטוס רש ‹ע›מרים

A54. Khirbet Susiya Synagogue Inscription I

1 דכיר
2 ישוע יודן
3 [ ] דיהב
4 [ ]
5 [ ]

A55. Khirbet Susiya Synagogue Inscription II

1 [ד]כירן לטב מנחמה ישוע שהדה ומנחמה ש. [ ]

A51.

1. This is the mausoleum
2. of Esther, the daughter
3. of ʿIdyo, who died
4. in the month of Shebat,
5. the year 3 of the relea[se],
6. the year three hundred [and three]
7. of (the) years after the destruction
8. of the house of the Temple.
9. Peace, peace
10. she has entered.

A52.

1. At rest be the soul of Ḥalifu,
2. daughter of [ ], who died
3. on the third day (of the week) on the eleventh
4. day of the month of Elul, in the year [2]
5. of the release, that is the year
6. four-hundred and thirty-
7. five (of the) years after the destruction
8. of the house of the Temple. Peace
9. upon Israel! Peace!

A53.

1. Kynoros, son of Dioṭos, chief of <ci>tizens.

A54.

1. Remembered be
2. Joshua (son of?) Judan
3. [ ] who gave
4. [ ]
5. [ ]

A55.

1. [Re]membered for good be the counselor Yeshuaʿ, the witness, and the counselor Š.[ ]

A56. Eshtemoaʿ Synagogue Inscription

1 דכיר לטב לעזר כהנ[א]

2 ובוני* דיהב חד טר[ימיסין]

3 [ ]יפיו מן פעל[ה**]

*Read ובנוי **or פעל[הון

A56.

1. Remembered for good be La'zar [the] priest
2. and his sons, who gave (sg.) one *tr*[*imēsion*]
3. [ ]*ypyw* with [his (*or* their)] own skill

TEXT DESCRIPTION AND BIBLIOGRAPHY

TEXT DESCRIPTION AND BIBLIOGRAPHY

General Bibliography: Palestinian Synagogues

C. Clermont-Ganneau, *Archaeological Researches in Palestine during the Years 1873-1874* (2 vols.; tr. A. Stewart and J. Macfarlane; London: Palestine Exploration Fund, 1896, 1899), passim.

R. Dussaud, *Les Monuments palestiniens et judaïques* (*Moab, Judée, Philistie, Samarie, Galilée*) (Paris: Leroux, 1912), passim.

J. Juster, *Les juifs dans l'empire romain: Leur condition juridique, économique et sociale* (Paris: P. Geuthner, 1914; reprinted, New York: Burt Franklin, 1969), 1. 456-72.

H. Kohl and C. Watzinger, *Antike Synagogen in Galilaea* (29. Wissenschaftliche Veröffentlichung der deutschen Orient-Gesellschaft; Leipzig: Hinrichs, 1916; reprinted, Wiesbaden: Harrassowitz, 1976).

A. Mader, *Altchristliche Basiliken und Lokaltraditionen in Südjudäa: Archäologische und topographische Untersuchungen* (Paderborn: F. Schöningh, 1918).

S. Krauss, *Synagogale Altertümer* (Berlin/Vienna: Harz, 1922) 384-89.

S. Klein, "Ktbwt mbty-knsywt 'tyqym b'rṣ-yśr'l [Inscriptions from Ancient Synagogues in the Land of Israel]," *Yediot* [Bulletin of the Institute for Jewish Studies at Hebrew University in Jerusalem] 2 (1925) 23-48.

S. Klein, *Palästina-Studien* (Vienna: "Menorah," 1923-28).

K. Galling, "Die Synagogen," *ZDPV* 50 (1927) 310-15, pl. 33.

M. Avi-Yonah, "Mosaic Pavements in Palestine," *QDAP* 2 (1933) 136-81; 3 (1934) 26-73; 4 (1935) 187-93.

S. Krauss, "Bty knsywt 'tyqym b'rṣ yśr'l wb'rṣwt hqdm [Old Synagogues in Palestine and the Orient]," "*Yerushalayim*": *Journal of the Jewish Palestine Exploration Society Dedicated to the Memory of Abraham Mosheh Luncz* (eds. I. Press and E. L. Sukenik; Jerusalem: Darom, 1928) 121-49.

E. L. Sukenik, *Ancient Synagogues in Palestine and Greece* (Schweich Lectures, 1930; London: British Academy, 1934).

J.-B. Frey, *Corpus inscriptionum iudaicarum: Recueil des inscriptions juives qui vont du IIIe siècle avant Jesus-Christ au VIIe siècle de Notre-Ere* (2 vols.; I. Europe; II. Asie-Afrique; Vatican City: Pontificio istituto di archeologia cristiana, 1936, 1952).

S. Klein (ed.), *Spr Hšwyb* [The Book of Settling] (Jerusalem: Mosad Bialik, 1939), vol. 1.

E. R. Goodenough, *Jewish Symbols in the Greco-Roman Period* (13 vols.; Bollingen series, 37; New York: Pantheon, 1953-68).

J. Braslavsky, *Lḥqr 'rṣnw — 'br wšrydym* [Studies in Our Country — Its Past and Remains] (TelAviv: Hakibbutz Hameuḥad, 1954) 271-83.

A. Hiram, " Die Entwicklung der antiken Synagogen und altchristlichen Kirchenbauten im Heiligen Lande," *Wiener Jahrbuch für Kunstgeschichte* 19 [23] (1961) 7-62.

F. Rosenthal (ed.), *An Aramaic Handbook* (Wiesbaden : Harrassowitz, 1967), I/1. 69-70.

B. Baggati, *Gli scavi di Nazaret : Volume I : Dalle origini al secolo XII* (Pubblicazioni dello Studium Biblicum Franciscanum, 17 ; Jerusalem : Franciscan Printing Press, 1967) ; English version, 1969.

S. J. Saller, *A Revised Catalogue of the Ancient Synagogues of the Holy Land* (Publications of the Studium Biblicum Franciscanum, Collectio minor, 6 ; Jerusalem : Franciscan Printing Press 1969). For 1st edition, see *SBFLA* 4 (1953-54) 219-46.

G. Foerster, " Ancient Synagogues in Eretz-Israel, " *Qadmoniot* 5 (1972) 38-42.

K. Hruby, *Die Synagoge : Geschichtliche Entwicklung einer Institution* (Schriften zur Judentumskunde, 3 ; Zürich : Theologischer Verlag, 1971).

J. Naveh, " H'rwt lktwbwt 'rmywt 'ḥdwt mbty-hknst h'tyqym [Notes on Some Aramaic Inscriptions from Ancient Synagogues]," *Lĕšonēnu* 38 (1973-74) 295-99.

S. Safrai, " The Synagogues South of Mt. Judah," *Immanuel* 3 (1973-74) 44-50.

J. Gutmann (ed.), *The Synagogue : Studies in Origins, Archaeology and Architecture : Selected with a Prolegomenon* (Library of Biblical Studies ; New York : Ktav, 1975).

G. Foerster, " Bty knst 'tyqym bmdbr yhwdh wbbq't yryḥw [Ancient Synagogues in the Judean Desert and in the Jericho Valley], " *Teva VaAretz* 15 (1973) ; *Immanuel* 6 (1976) 50-54.

E. Y. Kutscher, *Studies in Galilean Aramaic* (tr. M. Sokoloff ; Bar-Ilan Studies in Near Eastern Languages and Culture ; Ramat-Gan : Bar-Ilan, 1976).

F. Hüttenmeister and G. Reeg, *Die antiken Synagogen in Israel* (2 vols. ; Beihefte zum Tübinger Atlas des vorderen Orients, 19 ; Reihe B (Geisteswissenschaften, Nr. 12) ; Wiesbaden : Dr. Ludwig Reichert Verlag, 1977).

A1. *'Abellin Synagogue Inscription.* This inscribed lintel was found at 'Abellîn (east of Haifa) and described by J. Braslawski in " Lktbt hḥdšh b'blyn [The New Inscription of 'Abellîn]," *Yediot* [BJPES] 2/1 (1934) 31. It was deciphered and interpreted by H. L. Ginsberg and S. Klein (in separate notes) in " Lktwbt 'blyn [The 'Abellîn Inscription]," *Yediot* [BJPES] 2/3-4 (1935) 47-48. We have followed Klein's interpretation. On the formula *dkyr lṭb*, so frequent in these inscriptions, see Neh 13:31 and the Greek translation ([Κύριε μ]νῖσθι εἰς ἀ[γ]αθὸν κὲ ἡ [*sic*] εὐλογίαν. *šālôm*) on an Ashdod chancel screen, published by M. Avi-Yonah, " A New Fragment of the Ashdod Chancel Screen," *LRMF Bulletin* 3 (1960) 69. Klein took *sdrh* as a synonym for *byt knst* (" synagogue ") and *brkh* as a proper name. Could *sdrh* be a misspelling for *snhdryn*? Ginsberg read the last

word in the first line as *brwk* ("Baruch"), the second line as *ksdryy* ("the Alexandrian"), and the bracketed word in the third line as either *wyhb* ("and he gave") or *wʿbd* ("and he made"). No photographs accompany the publications. ʿAbellîn is known as the dwelling place of Rabbi Eleazar ben Judah and his student Rabbi Jose ben Perida' in the late second century A.D.
Other Collections: *SHY*, 1.

A2. *ʿAin Duk Synagogue Inscription I.* Aramaic inscriptions were discovered in a mosaic on the pavement of the synagogue of Naʿaran (near Jericho) and were first published in L.-H. Vincent and B. Carrière, "La synagogue de Noarah," *RB* 30 (1921) 579-601, pls. XV-XVI. Vincent dated the material to the first half of the 1st century A.D. (*RB* 16 [1919] 546), but a 4th or 5th-century date seems more likely. We have worked from the (fuller) texts in J.-B. Frey's *CII* (§1197-1207). The first inscription, which was published by Vincent and Carrière in *RB* 30 (1921) 581-85, pl. XV/1-2, is in two parts. The first three lines form a unit in which the last two are placed on either side of the top of a menorah in the mosaic. The second part is situated on either side of the body of the menorah. The reading *mrwšt* ("basin") is not certain; *metryšt* ("beam") is possible. This is counted as two inscriptions in the original publication; see *CII* §1197-98.
Other Collections: *Yediot* 2 (1925) 39-43 (§17-25); *PS*, 1/2. 34-35; *ASP*, 28-31, 72-76; *SHY*, 109-10; *JS*, 1. 253-57; *AH*, I/1. 70.

Bibliography

H. Vincent, "Le sanctuaire juif d'ʿAïn Douq," *RB* 28 (1919) 532-63; 30 (1921) 442-43.
C. Clermont-Ganneau, "La mosaïque juive de ʿAin Doûq," *CRAIBL* (1919) 87-120.
S. A. Cook, "The 'Holy Place' of ʿAin Dük," *PEFQS* (1920) 82-87.
A. Marmorstein, "The Jewish Inscription from ʿAin Dûk," *PEFQS* (1920) 139-41.
N. Slousch, "Quelques observations relatives à l'inscription juive découverte à Ain Douk," *JPOS* 1 (1920) 33-35.
C. C. Torrey, "The Mosaic Inscription at ʿAin Duk," *JAOS* 40 (1920) 141-42.
H. Lietzmann, "Die Synagoge von Noarah," *ZNW* 20 (1921) 252-54.
S. Krauss, "Nouvelles découvertes archéologues de synagogues en Palestine," *REJ* 89 (1930) 385-413, esp. pp. 395-405.
M. Avi-Yonah, "Mosaic Pavements in Palestine," *QDAP* 2 (1933) 136-81, esp. pp. 155-57 (§69); 3 (1934) 26-73, esp. pp. 51-52 (§69).

E. L. Sukenik, " The Present State of Ancient Synagogue Studies," *LMRF Bulletin* 1 (1949) 7-23, esp. pp. 9-11.
P. Benoit, " Note additionnelle," *RB* 68 (1961) 174-77.

A3. *'Ain Duk Synagogue Inscription II.* Published by L.-H. Vincent and B. Carrière in *RB* 30 (1921) 585-87, pl. XV/3. Done in a square section of the mosaic, this inscription celebrates the memory of a woman who contributed to the construction of the mosaic. Expressions like *'tḥzq[t]* to describe those who have helped in the repair or construction of parts of the synagogue are common in these inscriptions.
Other Collections : CII §1199.

A4. *'Ain Duk Synagogue Inscription III.* Published by L.-H. Vincent and B. Carrière in *RB* 30 (1921) 587-88, pl. XV/4. The inscription was placed on the mosaic between depictions of Daniel and the lions. The *reš* in *prns[h]* is very small and could conceivably be read as *yodh.* See also *JPCI*, 69 (§3).
Other Collections : CII §1202.

A5. *'Ain Duk Synagogue Inscription IV.* Published by L.-H. Vincent and B. Carrière in *RB* 30 (1921) 588-91, pl. XV/5. This inscription is directly beneath the previous item. For the expression *[d]hy' [w'ytw]n ḥw<l>qhwn*, we have followed the interpretation of E. L. Sukenik, *ASP*, 75-76. See also *JPCI*, 69-70 (§3).
Other Collections : CII §1203.

A6. *'Ain Duk Synagogue Inscription V.* Published by L.-H. Vincent and B. Carrière in *RB* 30 (1921) 594-95, pl. XVI/6. At the right of an image (now destroyed) of Daniel in the lions' den, there is a Hebrew inscription (" Danie[l]. Peace "), and beneath that is this Aramaic dedicatory inscription.

A7. *'Ain Duk Synagogue Inscription VI.* Published by L.-H. Vincent and B. Carrière in *RB* 30 (1921) 595-600, pl. XVI/7. Sukenik (*ASP*, 76) observes that it is evident from the different sizes of the *tesserae* that everything between line 1 and the extant part of line 4 is secondary. The repairing mosaicist, instead of continuing line 1 from the undamaged part, began anew with *dkyr* but carelessly omitted the *kaph*, and instead of so laying out the letters as to finish with line 4 he introduced *bhdn 'tr'* unnecessarily in line 3.
Other Collections : CII §1204.

A8. *'Ain Duk Synagogue Inscription VII.* Published by L.-H. Vincent and B. Carrière in *RB* 30 (1921) 600-601, pl. XVI/8. The left side is badly damaged, and the reconstruction is not certain.
Other Collections : *CII* §1205.

A9. *'Alma Synagogue Inscription I.* 'Alma is near Safed. A Hebrew part of the inscribed lintel was published by G. Dalman in "Jahresbericht des Instituts für das Arbeitsjahr 1913/14," *PJ* 10 (1914) 47, pl. VI/2. The Hebrew part said: "May there be peace upon this place and upon all the places of His people Israel." The Aramaic part was discovered in 1957 near the spot where the Hebrew section had been found, and it was published by R. Hestrin in "A New Aramaic Inscription from 'Alma," *LMRF Bulletin* 3 (1960) 65-67, pl. XIV/1. She summarizes her treatment by saying: "We have here a Jewish artisan by the name of Jose the Levite, the son of Levi, who lived in or about the third century A.D. and built or decorated synagogues in the style of the period. He perpetuated his name once in Hebrew [at Kfar Bir'im] and once in Aramaic."

Bibliography

I. Ben-Zvi, "Ktwbt byt-knst ḥdšh bkpr 'lm' [A New Synagogue Inscription at 'Alma]," *Yediot* [BJPES] 15 (1950) 75-77.

Related Literature

Hebrew Part: *Yediot* 2 (1925) 29-30 (§6); *JPCI*, 77-78 (§6); *CII* §973; *SHY*, 122; *JS*, 1. 201, 224; *ASG*, 170.
M. Guérin, *Description geographique, historique et archéologique de la Palestine*: Part 3: *Galilée*, tome 2 (Paris: Leroux, 1880) 445-46.

A10. *'Alma Synagogue Inscription II.* An inscribed fragment found in 1949 and published by R. Amiran in "Another Inscription from 'Alma," *LMRF Bulletin* 3 (1960) 68, pl. XIV/3 (an English version of her article in Hebrew in *'Alon* 2 [1950] 25-26, pl. IVd). The first line refers to the donor, whose name ended in *nh* and who was a native of Tiberias. The second line refers to the making or donating of the lintel and begins the blessing.

Bibliography

I. Ben-Zvi, "Ktwbt byt-knst ḥdšh bkpr 'lm' [A New Synagogue Inscription at 'Alma]," *Yediot* [BJPES] 15 (1950) 75-77.

A11. *Beth Alpha Mosaic Inscription.* On the border of the mosaic in the central nave of the synagogue at Beth Alpha, on the north, between the two animals on either side of the main doorway, and in the very entrance, are two inscriptions, one in Aramaic and a second in Greek. The right side of the Aramaic inscription was badly damaged by heavy stones that fell on it. It was published in E. L. Sukenik, *The Ancient Synagogue of Beth Alpha: An Account of the Excavations Conducted on Behalf of the Hebrew University, Jerusalem* (Jerusalem: University Press, 1932; reprinted, Wiesbaden: Harrassowitz, 1975) 43-46, pl. XXV. Justin I reigned from A.D. 517 to 528 and Justin II from 565 to 578; the former is probably meant here. The interpretation of *ḥṭyyh* in line 3 is not certain.
Other Collections: *ASP*, 31-35; *CII* §1165; *SHY*, 12; *JS*, 1. 241-53.

Bibliography

E. L. Sukenik, "Byt-hknst hʿtyq š-bbyt 'lp' [The Ancient Synagogue of Beth Alpa]," *Tarbiẓ* 1 (1929-30) 111-17, pls. 1-5.
M. Schwabe, "Lktwbt hywnyt šl byt 'lp' [On the Greek Inscription of Beth-Alpha]," *Tarbiẓ* 1/3 (1929-30) 137-40.
E. L. Sukenik, "Ausgrabungen in Bet Alpha," *Encyclopaedia Judaica* (Berlin: Lambert Schneider, 1929) 389-93.
A. Barrois, "Découverte d'une synagogue à Beit Alpha," *RB* 39 (1930) 265-72, pls. 12-14.
S. Krauss, "Nouvelles découvertes archéologiques de synagogues en Palestine," *REJ* 89 (1930) 385-413, esp. pp. 405-8.
C. Watzinger, "Die antiken Synagogen Galiläas: Neue Ausgrabungen und Forschungen," *Der Morgen* 6 (1930) 356-67, esp. 365-66.
M. Avi-Yonah, "Mosaic Pavements in Palestine," *QDAP* 2 (1933) 136-81, esp. 144-45 (§22); 3 (1934) 26-73, esp. p. 50 (§335b).
E. L. Sukenik, "A New Discovery at Beth Alpha," *LMRF Bulletin* 2 (1951) 26, pl. 11.

A12. *Beth Gubrin Synagogue Inscription.* Found in 1925 at Beth Gubrin (Beit Jibrin, Eleutheropolis), this inscription had been engraved on a limestone column 35 cm. in diameter. It was first published by E. L. Sukenik in "Lqṭ 'pygrpy," *Qôbeṣ* [JJPES] 2 (1925) 143-47, esp. pp. 143-45, and republished by him in "A Synagogue Inscription from Beit Jibrin," *JPOS* 10 (1930) 76-78, pl. VI. In line 2 *kwrys* (or *kwrws*) must be a proper name, and lines 3 and 4 seem to have the names of the donor, his recently deceased father (Sheʿay), and his grandfather (Auxentios). In line 5 *dybn* was read at first and interpreted as historical spelling for *dî* and defective writing for *bĕnāh*;

but J. Naveh has corrected the reading to *dzbn*, which we follow. The inscription is dated to the 4th-6th centuries.
Other Collections: *ASP*, 72 ; *CII* §1195 ; *SHY*, 13 ; *JS*, 1. 212, 215.

Bibliography

S. Klein, " Zum Abschnitt IV des archäologischen Jahresberichtes," *ZDPV* 51 (1928) 135-37, esp. p. 135.
S. Krauss, " Nouvelles découvertes archéologiques de synagogues en Palestine," *REJ* 89 (1930) 385-413, esp. pp. 411-13.
S. Klein, " The Synagogue Inscription from Beit Jibrin," *JPOS* 12 (1932) 271, pl. 14. See E. L. Sukenik's response on pp. 271-72.
D. Barag, " An Aramaic Synagogue Inscription from the Hebron Area," *IEJ* 22 (1972) 147-49, pl. 24.
J. Naveh, " H'rwt lktwbwt 'rmywt 'ḥdwt mbty-hknst h'tyqym [Notes on Some Aramaic Inscriptions from Ancient Synagogues] " *Lĕšonēnu* 38 (1973-74) 295-99, esp. pp. 298-99.

A13. *Beth She'an Synagogue Inscription I.* The mosaic pavement in the central nave of the 6th-century synagogue has three inscriptions — two in Aramaic and one in Greek. The Aramaic inscriptions are published in R. Hestrin et al., *IR*, §184 (pp. 186-87 [Hebr.], 84 [Engl.]). The expression " the holy community " refers to the Jewish community in the mixed population of Beth She'an/Scythopolis.

Bibliography

A. Biran, " Archaeological Activities 1962/3," *Christian News from Israel* 14/1 (1963) 14-26, esp. p. 18, pl. 1.
N. Tsori, " Beth Shean," *IEJ* 13 (1963) 148-49.
D. Bahaṭ, " Byt-hknst bbyt-š'n — sqyrh r'šwnh [The Synagogue at Beth-Shean — Preliminary Report], " *Qadmoniot* 5 (1972) 55-58.

A14. *Beth She'an Synagogue Inscription II.* Published in R. Hestrin et al., *IR*, §184 (pp. 186-87 [Hebr.], 84 [Engl.]). The corrupt spellings reflect the regional pronunciation of *aleph* and *'ayin* (see *b. Meg.* 24b and *y. Ber.* 2.4d).

A15. *Capernaum Synagogue Inscription.* In Capernaum in 1924 there were found two inscriptions telling of the donations of columns ; one is in Greek, the other in Aramaic. They were published by G. Orfali, " Deux inscriptions de Capharnaüm," *Antonianum* 1 (1926) 401-12, pls. I-II, the Aramaic on pp. 401-7, pl. I. We follow the reading of E. L. Sukenik (*ASP*, 72). Sukenik suggests that the first two names are the Semitic original of the NT 'Αλφαῖος and Ζεβεδαῖος. The word *l'* is a mistake for *lh*, which is part of a stock phrase in these inscriptions. The date of the synagogue has been the subject of a recent controversy between S. Loffreda (late 4th or early 5th century) and G. Foerster (2d or 3d century).

Other Collections: *ASG*, 4-40; *Yediot* 2 (1925) 37-39 (§16); *PS*, 1/4. 49-50; *ASP*, 7-21, 71-72 (pl. 17b); *CII* §982; *SHY*, 94; *JS*, 1. 181-192; 3. fig. 451; *AH*, I/1. 70.

Bibliography

G. Orfali, *Capharnaüm et ses ruines* (Paris: Picard, 1922).

G. Dalman, *Aramäische Dialektproben* (2d ed.; Leipzig: J. C. Hinrichs, 1927; reprinted, Darmstadt: Wissenschaftliche Buchgesellschaft, 1960) 38 (follows Klein).

E. L. Sukenik, "Die jüdisch-aramäische Inschrift der Synagoge von Kapernaum," *ZDPV* 55 (1932) 75-76, pls. 12a, 13.

E. L. Sukenik, "The Present State of Ancient Synagogue Studies," *LMRF Bulletin* 1 (1949) 7-23, esp. pp. 18-21.

B. Sapir and D. Neeman, *Capernaum (Kfar-Nachum) History and Legacy, Art and Architecture* (Historical Sites Library, N1/9; Tel Aviv: Interfaith Survey of the Holy Land, 1967) 49-54.

G. Foerster, "Notes on Recent Excavations at Capharnaum (Review Article)," *IEJ* 21 (1971) 207-11.

S. Loffreda, "The Synagogue of Capharnaum: Archaeological Evidence for Its Late Chronology," *SBFLA* 22 (1972) 5-29.

S. Loffreda, "The Late Chronology of the Synagogue of Capernaum," *IEJ* 23 (1973) 37-42. See M. Avi-Yonah's note, pp. 43-45.

S. Loffreda, *Guide de Capharnaum* (tr. A. Storme; Lieux saints de Palestine; Jerusalem: Franciscan Printing Press, 1975) 62.

A16. *Chorazin Synagogue Inscription.* Engraved on the lower front of a basalt seat from the synagogue at Chorazin, this inscription was first published by J. Ory, "An Inscription Newly Found in the Synagogue of Kerazeh," *PEFQS* (1927) 51-52. We follow the reading of E. L. Sukenik (*ASP* 60, pl. 15). The term *sṭwh* seems to describe a "colonnade" and by extension the whole synagogue; that it refers to the seat alone is unlikely. The reading and interpretation of *mp'lh* remains uncertain; we have followed the reading of J. Naveh. The last word *ṣdyqym*, as a Hebrew form, was the reading of Ory, but here too we have preferred to read *ṣdyqyh* with Naveh. The synagogue is from the 3d-4th century A.D.

Other Collections: *ASG*, 41-58; *PS*, 1/4. 57-59; *ASP*, 60 (pl. 15); *CII* §981; *SHY*, 98; *JS*, 1. 193-99; *AC*, 71; *AH*, I/1. 70.

Bibliography

A. Marmorstein, " About the Inscription of Judan ben Ishmael," *PEFQS* (1927) 101-2, 687-88 ; (1930) 155.
S. Klein, " Zum Abschnitt IV des archäologischen Jahresberichtes," *ZDPV* 51 (1928) 135-37, esp. p. 136.
E. L. Sukenik, " 'Qtdr' šl mwšh šbbty hknst h'tyqym [' The Chair of Moses ' in Ancient Synagogues]," *Tarbiẓ* 1 (1929-30) A, 145-51, pls. 1-8.
J. N. Epstein, " Lktbt kwrzyn šw. 2-3 [Concerning the Inscription of Chorazin Lines 2-3]," *Tarbiẓ* 1 (1929-30) A, 152.
E. L. Sukenik, " Lktbt kwrzym," [Concerning the Inscription of Chorazin]," *Tarbiẓ* 1 (1929-30) B, 135-36.
S. Krauss, " Nouvelles découvertes archéologiques de synagogues en Palestine," *REJ* 89 (1930) 385-413, esp. 390-95.
C. Watzinger, " Die antiken Synagogen Galiläas : Neue Ausgrabungen und Forschungen," *Der Morgen* 6 (1930) 356-67, esp. 359.
E. L. Sukenik, " The Present State of Ancient Synagogue Studies," *LMRF Bulletin* 1 (1949) 7-23, esp. pp. 18-21.
K. Galling, *Textbuch zur Geschichte Israels* (with E. Edel and E. L. Rapp ; Tübingen : Mohr, 1950) 82 (§57).
Z. Yeivin, " Chorazin," *IEJ* 12 (1962) 152-53.
A. Biran, " Archaeological Activities 1962/63," *Christian News from Israel* 14/1 (1963) 14-26, esp. p. 15.
J. Naveh, " H'rwt lktwbwt 'rmywt 'ḥdwt mbty-hknst h'tyqym [Notes on Some Aramaic Inscriptions from Ancient Synagogues]," *Lĕšonênu* 38 (1973-74) 295-99, esp. 296-97.

A17. *Dabbura Synagogue Inscription I.* In an archaeological survey of the Golan there were discovered at Dabbura five inscriptions in Aramaic and one in Hebrew. They were published by D. Urman, " Jewish Inscriptions from Dabbura in the Golan," *IEJ* 22 (1972) 16-23, pls. 4-7. Urman concludes : " The inscriptions published here indicate the existence of a large Jewish settlement at Dabbura in the Roman period, including a school and a synagogue ; the school was called after the Tanna Rabbi Eli'ezer ha-Qappar or his son." The first item appears on three fragments of a basalt architrave on which are visible traces of an Aramaic inscription carved in two lines and part of a one-line Greek inscription. See D. Urman, *IEJ* 22 (1972) 17-19, pl. 4. The phrase " columns that (are) above the arches and the be[ams] " seems to refer to the upper gallery in the synagogue, i.e., the women's gallery. The Greek part says : " [Ru]sticus bu[ilt] (it)," [Ρο]ύστικος ἔκτ[ισεν].

Bibliography

D. Urman, " Ktwbwt yhwdywt mn hkpr dbwrh šbgwln [Jewish Inscriptions from Dabbura in the Golan]," *Tarbiẓ* 40 (1970-71) 399-402, plates.
D. Urman, " Ktwbwt yhwdywt mn hkpr dbwrh šbgwln [Jewish Inscriptions from Dabbura, Golan]," *Qadmoniot* 4 (1971) 131-33.

A18. *Dabbura Synagogue Inscription II.* Fragment of an Aramaic inscription engraved on a basalt lintel. See D. Urman, *IEJ* 22 (1972) 19, pl. 5a. The form *ywdh* for *yhwdh* appears in Talmudic literature.

A19. *Dabbura Synagogue Inscription III.* Fragment of an Aramaic inscription in two lines, engraved on a basalt lintel. See D. Urman, *IEJ* 22 (1972) 19, pl. 5b. The name appears in talmudic literature in various forms : *ḥnyn'*, *ḥnynh*, *ḥnnyh*, *ḥynn'*, and *ḥynnh*. The second line is part of the conventional blessing.

A20. *Dabbura Synagogue Inscription IV.* Fragment of an Aramaic inscription engraved on the basalt lintel of a synagogue or school of about the 3d century A.D. See D. Urman, *IEJ* 22 (1972) 19-20, pl. 6b. The word *byt* was probably followed by either *knyšt'* (" synagogue ") or *mdršh* (" school ").

A21. *Dabbura Synagogue Inscription V.* Fragment of an Aramaic inscription engraved in relief on a narrow strip of basalt. It was cut at the top of a lintel that probably belonged to the synagogue. See D. Urman, *IEJ* 22 (1972) 20-21, pl. 6a. The missing part may well have been a proper name (" X, son of Y, made the gate ").

A22. *En-Gedi Synagogue Inscription.* First published by B. Mazar in " Ktwbt 'l rṣpt byt-knst b'yn-gdy, sqyrh mwqdmt [The Inscription on the Floor of the Synagogue in En-Gedi : Preliminary Survey]," *Tarbiẓ* 40 (1970-71) 18-23. The first two parts are in Hebrew and give the names of (1) the forefathers from Adam to Japhet according to 1 Chr 1:1-4, (2) the names of the signs of the zodiac, the names of the months, the names of three patriarchs (Abraham, Isaac, Jacob) followed by *šālôm*, and the names of the three companions of Daniel (Hananiah, Mishael, Azariah), followed by *šālôm 'al yiśrā'ēl.* The Aramaic sections present a blessing upon the benefactors of the synagogue and a curse on whoever would betray the " secret " of the

Jewish community. Mazar connects it with the situation brought about by the Persian campaign against Palestine in A.D. 614.
Other Collections: *IR* §185.

Bibliography

D. Barag and Y. Porat, " Byt-hknst bʿyn-gdy [The Synagogue at En-Gedi]," *Qadmoniot* 3 (1970) 97-100.
S. Liebermann, " Hʿrh mwqdmt lktwbt bʿyn-gdy [A Preliminary Remark to the Inscription of En-Gedi]," *Tarbiẓ* 40 (1970-71) 24-26.
E. E. Urbach, " Hswd šbktwbt ʿyn-gdy wnwsḥh [The Secret of the En-Gedi Inscription and Its Formula]," *Tarbiẓ* 40 (1970-71) 27-30.
E. S. Rosenthal, " Ṣbw [Zevu]," *Tarbiẓ* 40 (1970-71) 31-32. See also B. M. Lerner, *Tarbiẓ* 40 (1970-71) 257.
G. B. Sarfatti, " Htrgwm hʿbry šl hktwbt šl byt-hknst šbʿyn-gdy [The Hebrew Translation of the En-Gedi Synagogue Inscription]," *Tarbiẓ* 40 (1970-71) 255.
J. Feliks, " Lʿnyyn ʾhy gnyb ṣbwtyh dḥbryh' bpsyps ʿyn-gdy [Concerning the Expression Hei Ganeiv Zevutei de-Havrei in the En-Gedi Mosaic Pavement]," *Tarbiẓ* 40 (1970-71) 256-57.
A. Dotan, " Hrz bktwbt byt hknst ʿyn-gdy [The ' Secret ' in the Synagogue Inscription of En-Gedi]," *Lĕšonênu* 35 (1971) 211-17.
Y. Yadin, " Pesher Nahum (4Q pNahum) Reconsidered," *IEJ* 21 (1971) 1-12, esp. p. 9 n. 31.
D. Barag, Y. Porat, and E. Netzer, " En-Gedi," *RB* 79 (1972) 581-83.
D. Barag, Y. Porat, and E. Netzer, " ʿwnt hḥpyrwt hšnyyh bbyt-hknst šl ʿyn-gdy [The Second Season of Excavations in the Synagogue of En-Gedil], " *Qadmoniot* 5 (1972) 52-54.

A23. *Fiq Synagogue Inscription.* First published by G. Schumacher in a letter in *ZDPV* 8 (1885) 333-34, this inscription appears on a basalt column beneath an engraved menorah. The first two words are certain. The reading of the second letter of the third word is disputed, but *hz'nh* (" the sexton ") is accepted by most. The inscripion is dated to the 3d or 4th century A.D. Fiq is on the eastern side of the Lake of Galilee, north of the River Yarmuk.
Other Collections: *Yediot* 2 (1925) 33-34 (§11); *JPCI*, 82-83 (§13); *CII* §855; *SHY*, 7; *JS*, 1. 221; *AH*, I/1. 70.

Bibliography

G. Schumacher, " Beschreibung des Dscholan," *ZDPV* 9 (1886) 196-363, esp. pp. 319-22.
G. Schumacher, *The Jaulan* (London: Bentley, 1888) 141.
C. Clermont-Ganneau, " Archaeological and Epigraphic Notes on Palestine," *PEFQS* (1902) 10-29, esp. p. 26.
A. Büchler, " Hebrew Inscription at Fîk," *PEFQS* (1903) 274.

S. A. Cook, " Notes and Queries: Hebrew Inscription at Fik," *PEFQS* (1903) 185-86.
C. Clermont-Ganneau, " Hebrew Inscription from Fik," *PEFQS* (1904) 181.
G. Dalman, " Jahresbericht des Instituts für das Arbeitsjahr 1911/12," *PJ* 8 (1912) 1-63, esp. p. 51.
A. Biran, " Archaeological Activities 1967," *Christian News from Israel* 19/3-4 (1968) 29-48, esp. pl. before p. 37.

A24. *Gaza Synagogue Inscription.* A bilingual (Aramaic and Greek) inscription found beneath a bas-relief of a menorah on one of the columns of the church dedicated to John the Baptist and now a mosque. The column was undoubtedly taken from a synagogue that was built in the 2d or 3d century. The inscription was first published by I. Loeb, " Chandeliers à sept branches," *REJ* 19 (1889) 100-5, esp. pp. 100-1. The Greek part reads: " To Ananiah, son of Jaco<b>," 'Ανανίᾳ υἱῷ 'Ιακώ<β>.
Other Collections: *Ephem.*, 2. 72; *Yediot* 2 (1925) 26-27 (§4); *JPCI* 68-69 (§2); *SEG* 8. §276; *CII* §967; *SHY*, 113-14; *JS*, 1. 223.

Bibliography

C. Clermont-Ganneau, " Séance du 28 Avril," *CRAIBL* (1893) 72-73. See also *Archaeological Researches in Palestine*, 2. 393-96.
D. J. Saul, " Von el-'Akabe über Gaza nach Jerusalem," *Mittheilungen und Nachrichten des deutschen Palästina-Vereins* (1901) 9-14, esp. p. 12.
E. Michon, " Antiquités gréco-romains provenant de Syrie conservées au musée du Louvre," *RB* ns 2 (1905) 564-78, esp. pp. 576-77.
C. Clermont-Ganneau, " Inscription samaritaine de Gaza et inscriptions grecques de Bersabée," *RB* ns 3 (1906) 84-91, esp. pp. 84-86.
M. A. Meyer, *The History of the City of Gaza* (Columbia University Oriental Studies, 5; New York: Columbia University, 1907) 139-41 (§10).
S. Krauss, *Synagogale Altertümer* (Berlin/Vienna: Harz, 1922) 312.
W. R. Taylor, " Recent Epigraphic Discoveries in Palestine," *JPOS* 10 (1930) 16-22, pls. 1-2, esp. pp. 18-19.
W. R. Taylor, " Samaritan Inscription From Gaza," *JPOS* 16 (1936) 131-37, pls. 6-7.
A. Ovadiah, " Byt-hknst b'zh [The Synagogue at Gaza]," *Qadmoniot* 1 (1968) 124-127.
A. Biran, " Archaeological Activities 1967," *Christian News From Israel* 19/3-4 (1968) 29-48, esp. pp. 43-44.
A. Ovadiah, " Excavations in the Area of the Ancient Synagogue at Gaza (Preliminary Report)," *IEJ* 19 (1969) 193-98.

A25. *Gischala Synagogue Inscription.* Found in the 3d/4th-century synagogue at Gischala (= Guš-Ḥalab, near Safed) and first published

by E. Renan in *Mission de Phénicie* (Paris : Imprimerie Impériale, 1864) 778-79, pl. 70/3. The form *h'dn* (" this ") is unusual. In fact, E. Y. Kutscher in *AH*, I/1. 70 (and glossary in I/2. 53, 68) suggests that *'bd h'dn* is the Hebrew phrase " servant of the Lord."
Other Collections : *CIH*, 94-96 (§45) ; *ASG*, 107-11 ; *Yediot* 2 (1925) 34-35 (§12) ; *PS*, 1/2. 35 ; *JPCI*, 78 (§7) ; *CII* §976 ; *SHY*, 29 ; *JS*, 1. 205 ; *AH*, I/1. 70.

Bibliography

C. R. Conder and H. H. Kitchener, *The Survey of Western Palestine* : *Memoirs*, vol. 1 : *Galilee* (London : Palestine Exploration Fund, 1881) 225.
G. Dalman, " Jahresbericht des Instituts für das Arbeitsjahr 1913/14," *PJ* 10 (1914) 1-50, esp. 48.
C. Watzinger, " Die antiken Synagogen Galiläas : Neue Ausgrabungen und Forschungen," *Der Morgen* 6 (1930) 356-67, esp. p. 362.

A26. *Hammath-Gadara Synagogue Inscription I.* The site is on the eastern side of the Lake of Galilee, at the hot springs by the River Yarmuk, near Gadara. The mosaic floor of the synagogue is divided into three panels. The inscriptions on these panels invoke blessings upon donors, but are somewhat unique in specifying the amounts of money contributed and in giving names of Jews from other towns. E. L. Sukenik, who excavated the site and published the inscriptions, assigns the erection of the synagogue to the first half of the 5th century A.D. The first item, which was published by E. L. Sukenik in *ASP*, 81-82 (= *ASH*, 39-47), appears within a wreath with a lemniscus, flanked by a lion and a cypress on either side. The names and titles show how hellenized the Jews in this area had become. The occurrence of *qwms* (= Lat. *comes*) indicates a date before A.D. 438, because after that the Code of Theodosius forbade the conferring of the title on Jews.
Other Collections : *CII* §856-860 ; *SHY*, 46 ; *JS*, 1. 239-41.

Bibliography

E. L. Sukenik, " The Synagogue Inscription from Beit Jibrin," *JPOS* 12 (1932) 271-72 n. 4.
M. Avi-Yonah, " Mosaic Pavements in Palestine," *QDAP* 2 (1933) 136-81, esp. p. 159 (§85).
E. L. Sukenik, " The Ancient Synagogue of Hammath-by-Gadara," *Qobeṣ* [JJPES] 3 (1934-35) 41-61.
M. Avi-Yonah, " Mosaic Pavements in Palestine," *QDAP* 4 (1935) 187-193, esp. pp. 188-89.

E. L. Sukenik, " The Ancient Synagogue of El-Ḥammeh," *JPOS* 15 (1935) 101-80, pls. I-XXIII.
E. L. Sukenik, *The Ancient Synagogue of El-Ḥammeh* (*Ḥammath-by-Gadara*) : *An Account of the Excavations Conducted on Behalf of the Hebrew University, Jerusalem* (Jerusalem : R. Mass, 1935). The same as *JPOS* 15 (1935) 101-80.
L. H. Vincent, " Bulletin : Palestine," *RB* 45 (1936) 465-69, esp. 467-69.
B. Sapir and D. Neeman, *Capernaum* (*Kfar-Nachum*) *History and Legacy, Art and Architecture* (Historical Sites Library, N1/9 ; Tel Aviv : Interfaith Survey of the Holy Land, 1967) 13, 23.

A27. *Hammath-Gadara Synagogue Inscription II.* Published by E. L. Sukenik in " The Ancient Synagogue of El-Ḥammeh," *JPOS* 15 (1935) 101-80, pls. I-XXIII, esp. pp. 137-43 (= *ASH*, 47-53). There are some uncertain words : *swsyph* (perhaps an error for *swsyth*, Susitha [= Hippos]), *'rdh* (perhaps a shortened form of *'rdykl'*), and *ḥym'ym.* The names are both Jewish and Hellenistic.

A28. *Hammath-Gadara Synagogue Inscription III.* Published by E. L. Sukenik, *JPOS* 15 (1935) 143-45 (= *ASH*, 53-55). The names and titles of the donors are Hellenistic. The precise meaning of *'yry'* (" the guardians " < " the watchers " ?) is not certain ; they could be the overseers of the synagogues or perhaps even the secular authorities.

A29. *Hammath-Gadara Synagogue Inscription IV.* Published by E. L. Sukenik, *JPOS* 15 (1935) 145-47, pl. XIIa (= *ASH*, 55-57). The names Tanḥum and Monika also appear in §A27.

A30. *Hammath-Tiberias Synagogue Inscription.* Published by M. Dothan, " Hktwbt h'rmyt mbyt-hknst šl swwyrws bḥmt-ṭbryh [The Aramaic Inscription from the Synagogue of Severus at Hamat Tiberias]," *E. L. Sukenik Memorial Volume* (*1889-1953*) (Eretz-Israel, 8 ; Jerusalem : Israel Exploration Society, 1967) 183-85, pl. *m* and 73*-74* [Engl.]. The synagogue — founded by Severus, who is mentioned in two Greek inscriptions in the same floor (which also contains the signs of the zodaic) — dates from the 4th century A.D. This is the first known instance of an Aramaic inscription appearing alongside a Greek one within a single *tabula ansata.* No individual donors are named. The cryptic " and for me " at the end probably refers to the inscriber.

Bibliography

M. Dothan, " Hammath—Tiberias," *IEJ* 12 (1962) 153-54. See also *RB* 70 (1963) 588-90.
B. Lifshitz, " Die Entdeckung einer alten Synagoge bei Tiberias," *ZDPV* 78 (1962) 180-84. See also *ZDPV* 79 (1963) 97.
A. Biran, " Archaeological Activities 1962/3," *Christian News from Israel* 14/1 (1963) 14-26, esp. 16-17.
M. Dothan, " Bty-hknst bḥmt ṭbryh [The Synagogues at Hammat-Tiberias]," *Qadmoniot* 1 (1968) 116-23.
B. Lifshitz, " L'ancienne synagogue de Tibériade, sa mosaïque et ses inscriptions," *JSJ* 4 (1973) 43-55. Also in Hebrew in *Mḥqryt btwldwt ʿm-yśr'l w'rṣ-yśr'l* [*Studies in the History of the Jewish People and the Land of Israel*] (eds. B. Obed et al., vol. 3 ; Haifa : University of Haifa, 1974) 99-109.

Related Literature

G. M. Fitzgerald, " Notes on Recent Discoveries," *PEFQS* (1921) 175-86, esp. 183-85. See also *ASP*, 57-61 ; *ASH*, 60-61 ; *SEG*, 8. §9-10 ; *CII* §985-86 ; *JS*, 1. 214-16.
N. Slousch, " Ḥpyrwt hḥbrh bḥmt-šl-ṭbrh [Excavations of the Community of Hammath-Tiberias]," *Qôbeṣ* [JJPES] 1 (1921) 5-39 ; 2 (1922-24) 49-52.
L. H. Vincent, " Les fouilles juives d'el-Hamman, à Tibériade," *RB* 30 (1921) 115-22, 438-42.
C. C. McCown, " Epigraphic Gleanings," *AASOR* 2-3 (1923) 109-15, esp. 109-11.
M. Schwabe, " Ṣrwr ktwbwt yhwdywt m'rṣ yśr'l [A Group of Jewish Inscriptions from the Land of Israel]," *BIES* 18 (1954) 157-63.
I. Renov, " The Seat of Moses," *IEJ* 5 (1955) 262-67.

A31. *Hebron Synagogue Inscription.* Although the exact provenience is unknown, there is no doubt that the inscription was found in either Hebron or its vicinity. It is engraved on a marble colonette that probably formed part of the ark of the Law — a feature not appearing in Palestinian synagogues before the 4th century A.D. D. Barag (" An Aramaic Synagogue Inscription from the Hebron Area," *IEJ* 22 [1972] 147-49, pl. 24a) compares it with the Aramaic synagogue inscription from Beth Gubrin and dates both between the 4th and 6th centuries. The donor's name is not entirely certain ; it could also be *Sbns* (Sabinus) or *Smks* (Symmachus).

A32. *ʿIsfiya Synagogue Inscription.* ʿIsfiya is near Haifa. In the ruins of a 6th-century synagogue there were found the fragments of a mosaic pavement representing the zodiac with the four seasons, Jewish symbols, and two inscriptions — one in Hebrew (" Peace upon Israel ") and the other in Aramaic. The Aramaic dedicatory inscription was published in M. Avi-Yonah, " A Sixth - Century Synagogue at

'Isfiyā," *QDAP* 3 (1934) 118-31, esp. pp. 129-30, pl. 43/3. Avi-Yonah thinks that *brwkh* refers to a female donor. The form *brby* (*bĕrabbî*) occurs in rabbinic literature and is usually explained as the contraction of *bêt rabbî* (" house of the rabbi ") and as a title meaning " belonging to the school of an eminent teacher " (M. Jastrow, *Dictionary*, 158, 189). Possibly involved is a confusion of *bê* as a shortened form of the construct *bêt* and *bê* as a full writing of *bĕ*, " son of."
Other Collections : *ASP*, 85-86 ; *CII* §885.

A33. *Jerash Synagogue Inscription.* First published by J. W. Crowfoot and R. W. Hamilton, " The Discovery of a Synagogue at Jerash," *PEFQS* (1929) 211-19, esp. p. 218, pl. V. Jerash was an important Transjordanian site from the 2d-3d centuries A.D. on, and the synagogue is dated by E. L. Sukenik (*ASP*, 35) to the first half of the 5th century. On a mosaic in one of the aisles, this inscription probably commemorates the men who executed the mosaic. E. L. Sukenik (*ASP*, 77) calls it evidence for " Aramaic-speaking mosaicists in the synagogue of a hellenized community," even though the only distinctive Aramaic element in it is *br*. The text begins with the stereotyped Hebrew blessing on Israel.
Other collections : *ASP*, 77 ; *CII* §866 ; *SHY*, 34 ; *JS*, 1. 180 ; 2. 259-260.

Bibliography

A. Barrois, " Découverte d'une synagogue à Djérash," *RB* 39 (1930) 257-65, pls. 9-11.
S. Krauss, " Nouvelles découvertes archéologiques de synagogues en Palestine," *REJ* 89 (1930) 385-413, esp. pp. 408-11.
E. L. Sukenik, " Note on the Aramaic Inscription at the Synagogue of Gerasa," *PEFQS* (1930) 48-49.
J. W. Crowfoot, *Churches at Jerash* : *A Preliminary Report of the Joint Yale-British School Expeditions to Jerash, 1928-1930* (British School of Archaeology in Jerusalem, Supplementary Papers, 3 ; London : W. Clowes, 1931).
C. H. Kraeling, *Gerasa* : *City of the Decapolis* (New Haven : American Schools of Oriental Research, 1938) 236-39, 318-24, 473.
A. H. Detweiler, " Some Early Jewish Architectural Vestiges from Jerash," *BASOR* 87 (1942) 10-17.

A34. *Jericho Synagogue Inscription.* This item appears on the mosaic floor of a synagogue, the remains of which were uncovered in Tell es-Sulṭān (Jericho) and published by D. C. Baramki and M. Avi-Yonah, " An Early Byzantine Synagogue near Tell es-Sulṭān, Jericho," *QDAP* 6 (1938) 73-77, esp. pp. 76-77, pl. XXIII. The inscription is in a panel in front of the door. The *dkyrn* in line 1 is written defectively. The title " King of the Universe " in line 3 appears frequently in the Hammath-Gadara inscriptions. The expression " book of life " in line 5 was originally read as *spr ḥyym*, but we have preferred to follow Naveh's reading of *ḥyyh*, for, though there is no other final *mem* in the text with which to compare it, there are several instances of *he*, the top of which resembles the top of the final letter here. The fact that no individual donors are named makes this inscription somewhat unusual. Baramki dates the building to the early 8th century A.D.

Other Collections : *SHY*, 88 ; *JS*, 1. 260-62 ; *AH*, I/1. 69.

Bibliography

J. Naveh, " H'rwt lktwbwt 'rmywt 'ḥdwt mbty-hknst h'tyqym [Notes on Some Aramaic Inscriptions from Ancient Synagogues]," *Lĕšonēnu* 38 (1973-74) 295-99, esp. pp. 295-96.

A35. *Kafr Ḥananiah Synagogue Inscription.* First published by J.-B. Frey in *CII*, 2. 164-65 (§980). The inscription was engraved on the lower face of a circular bronze chandelier in the synagogue at Kafr Ḥananiah, which is most likely to be identified with el-Mekr (5 km. east of Acre). Between *klylh* and *l'tr'* there are twelve letters that Frey leaves undeciphered ; they probably gave the name(s) of the donor(s). Frey suggested a 6th-century date.

A36. *Kafr Kenna Synagogue Inscription I.* Two inscriptions in a mosaic that was probably part of a synagogue in Kafr Kenna (the traditional " Cana in Galilee "). They were first published in C. Clermont-Ganneau, " Séance du 2 novembre," *CRAIBL* (1900) 555-57. The first item gives the names of Jose's father and grandfather. The precise meaning of *ṭblh* (= Lat. *tabula*) is not entirely clear ; perhaps *tabula ansata* (?). The inscriptions come from the 3d or 4th century A.D.

Other Collections : *Ephem.*, 1. 313-15 ; *Yediot* 2 (1925) 35-37 (§13-14) ; *PS*, 1/2. 34 ; *JPCI*, 74-76 (§4) ; *CII* §987 ; *SHY*, 93 ; *JS*, 1. 264 ; *AH*, I/1. 70.

Bibliography

C. Clermont-Ganneau, " Séance du 6 décembre," *CRAIBL* (1901) 852 + pl.
C. Clermont-Ganneau, " Hebrew Inscription in Mosaic at Kefr Kenna," *PEFQS* (1901) 251.

C. Clermont-Ganneau, " Archaeological and Epigraphic Notes on Palestine,' *PEFQS* (1901) 369-89, esp. pp. 374-89.
C. Clermont-Ganneau, " La mosaïque hebraïque de Kefr Kenna," *Recueil d'archéologie orientale* (Paris : E. Leroux), 4 (1901) 345-60.
D. H. Müller and E. Sellin, " Die hebräische Mosaikinschrift von Kafr Kenna, mit einer Tafel," *Anzeiger der kaiserlichen Akademie der Wissenschaften Wien* : Phil.-Hist. Classe 38 (1901) 107-11, plate. See the comment of J. Halévy in *Revue sémitique* 9 (1901) 374-76 and 10 (1902) 82.
H. Vincent, " Bulletin : Palestine," *RB* 10 (1901) 489-93, esp. 491.
C. Clermont-Ganneau, " Archaeological and Epigraphic Notes on Palestine," *PEFQS* (1902) 132-38, esp. 132-34.
M. Avi-Yonah, " Mosaic Pavements in Palestine," *QDAP* 2 (1933) 136-81, esp. 178-79 (§167).
B. Bagatti, " Le antichità di Kh. Qana e di Kefr Kenna in Galilea," *SBFLA* 15 (1965) 251-92.

A37. *Kafr Kenna Synagogue Inscription II.* Published by C. Clermont-Ganneau in *CRAIBL* (1900) 555-57. This item probably began in the usual way (" remembered for good be ") and gave the name(s) of the donor(s). See A36 above.

A38. *Khirbet Kanef Synagogue Inscription.* Engraved on the lintel of a synagogue in Khirbet Kanef. A facsimile was published by L. Oliphant in " New Discoveries," *PEFQS* (1886) 73-81, esp. p. 76, and republished (with modifications) by G. Dalman, " Inschriften aus Palästina," *ZDPV* 37 (1914) 135-45, esp. p. 138 (§7), pl. XL/7. The name *Ḥlpw*, which is probably the equivalent of the NT 'Αλφαῖος, also occurs in the Capernaum synagogue inscription. Khirbet Kanef is on the eastern side of the Lake of Galilee, north of the Wadi Samak.
Other Collections : *Yediot* 2 (1925) 33 (§10) ; *PS*, 1/2. 36 ; 1/3. 48 ; *JPCI*, 82 (§12) ; *CII* §854 ; *SHY*, 90 ; *JS*, 1. 212-13.

Bibliography

E. L. Sukenik, " Byt hknst h'tyq bḥrbt knp bgwln [The Ancient Synagogue at Khirbet Kanef in the Golan]," *Qôbeṣ* [JJPES] 3 (1934-35) 74-80.
E. L. Sukenik, " The Ancient Synagogue of el-Ḥammeh," *JPOS* 15 (1935) 101-80, esp. pp. 176-77, pl. XXIa. See also *ASH*, 87-91.

A39. *Kokhav Ha-Yarden Synagogue Inscription.* Published by M. Ben-Dov, " Šrydy byt knst bkwkb-hyrdn wb'yyt mqwmh šl grwpynh mwl hšwmrwn bgl'd [Remains of a Synagogue at Kokhav-Hayarden and the Site of Grofina in Gilead]," *Eretz Shomron : The Thirtieth*

Archeological Convention, September 1972 (ed. J. Aviram; Jerusalem: Israel Exploration Society, 1973) 86-98, pl. 16, esp. pp. 92-93 (Engl. 92-93). During the excavation of the Crusader Castle at Belvoir, in the plain of Issachar, many stones that had been put to secondary use were found to have been originally part of a 3d/4th-century A.D. synagogue. The stones include a basalt lintel on which there are menorahs, a holy ark, and this Aramaic inscription, the beginning of which is missing. The inscription probably opened with a blessing on the donors. Note that *skwpth* ("lintel") is spelled here with a *samek* and *kaph* rather than the usual *šin* and *qoph*. There is probably some contamination here from *'iskuppĕtā'* ("threshold"). As for the phrase *drḥmnh wmn ʿmly* Ben-Dov translates, "of their own and of public funds." The fragmentary state of the inscription hinders any certain interpretation.

A40. *Maʿon Synagogue Inscription.* The remains of a synagogue were discovered in 1957 during the construction of a side-road from Nir-Yiṣḥaq to the Magen-Nirim highway. The inscription was inlaid on the top of a mosaic carpet in the central nave. It was published by S. Yeivin, "The Ancient Synagogue of Maʿon (Nirim): F. The Inscription," *LMRF Bulletin* 3 (1960) 36-40, pl. VIIIb. It is the usual type of commemorative inscription in honor of the donor(s) who contributed to the making of the mosaic. The upper right-hand corner has been damaged. Yeivin suggests that the mosaicist did not know any Aramaic and was not familiar with the Hebrew-Aramaic alphabet. The script indicates a date in the late 6th or early 7th century A.D. For *tg* in line 4 we have followed the suggestion of E. Y. Kutscher that it equals Greek ταγή, "stipulated amount to be delivered" (see S. Yeivin, *LMRF Bulletin*, 39), rather than accept the suggestion of J. Naveh. Certain scrawls at the end of line 4 are unintelligible.

Bibliography

M. Avi-Yonah, "The Ancient Synagogue of Maʿon (Nirim): E. The Mosaic Pavement," *LMRF Bulletin* 3 (1960) 25-35. See also (in Hebrew) *Eretz-Israel* 6 (1960) 86-93, pls. XVII-XXII.

J. Naveh, "Hʿrwt lktwbwt 'rmywt 'ḥdwt mbty-hknst hʿtyqym [Notes on Some Aramaic Inscriptions from Ancient Synagogues]," *Lĕšonēnu* 38 (1973-74) 295-99, esp. 298-99.

A41. *Sepphoris Synagogue Inscription.* Sepphoris was the largest and most important city in Galilee in the first four centuries A.D. The Romans called it Diocaesarea. The inscription is on a 3d or 4th-century A.D. Jewish mosaic — at least from before A.D. 352 when Sepphoris was destroyed by Gallus. It was first published by C. Clermont-Ganneau, "Mosaïque juive à inscription, de Sepphoris," *CRAIBL* (1909) 677-83. We have followed the reconstruction printed in J.-B. Frey, *CII*, 2. 173-74 (§989), but this leans heavily on the Kafr Kenna Synagogue Inscription I and is not at all certain.
Other Collections: *JPCI*, 76-77 (§5); *CII* §989; *SHY*, 141.

Bibliography

C. Clermont-Ganneau, *Nazareth et ses deux églises de l'Annonciation et de Saint-Joseph d'après les fouilles récentes* (ed. P. Viaud; Paris: Picard, 1910) 185-91.
M. Avi-Yonah, "Mosaic Pavements in Palestine," *QDAP* 3 (1934) 26-73, esp. 39-40 (§296).

A42. *Umm El-ʿAmed Synagogue Inscription.* The Umm el-ʿAmed synagogue is situated some 30 km. south of ʿEilabūn, near the road passing the east end of the Netopha Valley. The inscription was published by N. Avigad, "An Aramaic Inscription from the Ancient Synagogue of Umm el-ʿAmed," *LMRF Bulletin* 3 (1960) 62-64, pl. XIV/2 (the revision of an earlier Hebrew article in *BIES* 19 [1956-1957] 183-87, pl. 12a). It appears on a stone that was probably built into the wall, not on a lintel. The "gate of the Lord of heaven" refers to the synagogue as a whole, not just to the synagogue gate. The synagogue belongs to the earlier group of Galilean synagogues — from the 3d-4th centuries A.D. The spelling *tr'* is defective for *trʿ*; *šwmy'* is found in Christian Palestinian and Samaritan Aramaic.
Other Collections: *ASG*, 71-79; *JS*, 1. 199-200; *AH*, I/1. 70.

A43. *Yesud Ha-Maʿala Synagogue Inscription.* The site is southwest of Lake Hula. This inscription, engraved on a column from a synagogue, was first published by I. Goldhor in *'dmt qdš, hy' 'rṣ yśr'l* (Jerusalem: L. Woshotpiev (?), 1913) 258 n. 1, and then again by S. Klein, "Zum Abschnitt IV des archäologischen Jahresberichtes," *ZDPV* 51 (1928) 135-37, esp. p. 137. We follow Klein's text. The reading *dʿbyd* is strange, if it is intended to be the perfect; possibly it is intended to be the peal participle.
Other Collections: *PS*, 1/4. 59-60; *CII* §971.

A44. *Bersabee Votive Inscription.* This inscription on a column was transcribed by L.-H. Vincent in 1904 and then published by E. L. Sukenik, " The Ancient Synagogue of el-Ḥammeh," *JPOS* 15 (1935) 101-80, esp. p. 158 (= *ASH*, 68). Because it was encased in the wall of a window, it could be copied only in part. It is dated to the first half of the 5th century.
Other Collections : *CII* §1196 ; *SHY*, 11.

A45. *Beth Sheʿarim Tomb Inscription I.* Beth Sheʿarim was the seat of the Sanhedrin in the days of Rabbi Judah I and a major Jewish center in the talmudic period. The great necropolis there was the central burial place for Diaspora Jews. Four Aramaic inscriptions were discovered in Catacomb no. 12, burial hall A. The first two were published in N. Avigad, " Excavations at Beth Sheʿarim, 1953. Preliminary Report," *IEJ* 4 (1954) 88-107, pls. 8-12 (also in Hebrew in *BIES* 18 [1954] 7-31). All four were published by Avigad in *Byt-šʿrym, krk šlyšy* : *hḥpyrwt h'rky'wlwgywt bšnym tšy''g-tšy''ḥ* [*Beth-Sheʿarim* : *Volume Three, The Archaeological Excavations During 1953-1958*] (Jerusalem : Israel Exploration Society and Mosad Bialik, 1971) 171-73. They are from the 4th century A.D. The first inscription, which was published by N. Avigad (*IEJ* 4 [1954] 95 and *Beth Sheʿarim III*, 171, pl. III/3), was found in room III, written above arcosolium 3. No name is given but the curse (designed to prevent tomb robberies) is similar to that in the next item. *ʿl* is written twice.
Other Collections : *JS*, 1. 208-11 ; 3. fig. 535 ; *AH*, I/1. 70.

Related Literature

B. Maisler [Mazar], " Esh Sheikh Ibreiq," *QDAP* 9 (1942) 212-15 ; 10 (1944) 196-98.
E. L. Sukenik, " The Present State of Ancient Synagogue Studies," *LMRF Bulletin* 1 (1949) 7-23, esp. 16-17.

A46. *Beth Sheʿarim Tomb Inscription II.* Published by N. Avigad (*IEJ* 4 [1954] 95, pl. 10A and *Beth Sheʿarim III*, 171-72, pl. IV/4), this inscription was painted in red in very clear letters above the right-hand loculus in room VIII. The expression " will die of an evil end " is unusual in Jewish-Aramaic epigraphy ; see the preceding item.

A47. *Beth Sheʿarim Tomb Inscription III.* Published by N. Avigad (*Beth Sheʿarim* III, 173), this inscription was painted in red on a fragment of what must have served to close one of the burial places (*kwkym*) or to cover one of the ossuaries in room VIII. It is identical with the first line of Beth She'arim Tomb Inscription I.

A48. *Er-Rama Inscription.* Er-Rama is in Galilee, on the road leading from Safed to Acre. The inscription was published by J. Ben Zevi, " A Third Century Aramaic Inscription in er-Rāma," *JPOS* 13 (1933) 94-96. It is inscribed on a stone that probably was part of a hostel or caravanserai dedicated by Rabbi Eliezer bar Tedeor, who lived in the 3d century A.D. Possibly, however, the stone was part of a tomb, since the noun *'wrḥ'* (lit., " road, path ") was used at times in the sense of " journey " = death, a nuance that may be suggested here by *dmyk* in line 2.
Other Collections: *ASH*, 77-78 n. 2; *CII* §979; *SHY*, 153; *JS*, 1. 213.

Bibliography

S. Klein, " Zur jüdischen Altertumskunde," *MGWJ* 76 (1932) 545-57, esp. 554-556.
A. Marmorstein, " The Inscription of Er-Rame," *PEFQS* (1933) 100-101.

A49. *Kafr Bir'im School Inscription.* In addition to a longer 2d- or 3d-century A.D. Hebrew dedicatory inscription found at Kafr Bir'im (near Safed), a brief Aramaic inscription was also discovered and first published by E. Renan, *Mission de Phénicie* (Paris: Imprimerie Impériale, 1864) 765-70, pl. 70/2. The *nun* and *waw* of the first word and the *he* and *waw* of the last word are written above the line.
Other Collections: *CIH*, 87-94 (§16-17); *ASG*, 89-100; *Yediot* 2 (1925) 27-29 (§5), 31-32, (§9); *JPCI*, 79-80 (§9); *ASP*, 24-26, 70-71; *CII* §974-75; *SHY*, 91; *JS*, 1. 201-3.

Bibliography

R. Dussaud, *Les monuments palestiniens et judaïques* (*Moab, Judée, Philistie, Samarie, Galilée*) (Paris: Leroux, 1912) 85-86 (fig. 116).
R. B. K. Amiran, " A Fragment of an Ornamental Relief from Kfar Bar'am," *IEJ* 6 (1956) 239-45, pls. 31-32. See also (in Hebrew) in *Eretz-Israel* 3 (1954) 178-81, pl. *h*.

A50. *Ghôr eṣ-Ṣâfieh Tombstone Inscription I.* In 1925 H. St. J. B. Philby made a rubbing of this inscription shown to him by the people of Ghôr eṣ-Ṣâfieh, a small agricultural community living in tents in the area south and southeast of the Dead Sea, in the Wadi

Hasa. He was told that it came from the ruins of Qasr el-Tuba (at the base of the hills and close to the left bank of the Wadi Hasa). It was published by A. E. Cowley, " A Jewish Tomb-Stone," *PEFQS* (1925) 207-10, pls. I-II. On the basis of the chronological information presented in the text, Cowley dated it to A.D. 433. He also called attention to the similarity of its script to that of the ʿAin Duk synagogue inscriptions. S. Daiches (" A Jewish Tomb-Stone," *PEFQS* [1926] 31-32) suggested that the first two words be read as *thnyt npšh* and interpreted it as " the resting-place of the (dead) body " (?). *Other Collections* : *CII* §1208 ; *SHY*, 126.

Bibliography

L.-H. Vincent, " Une colonie juive oubliée," *RB* 36 (1927) 401-7.
T. Reinach, " Inscriptions de Touba," *REJ* 85 (1928) 1-10, esp. pp. 1-6.
A. Marmorstein, " Lqwrwt hyhwdym b' " Y bm'h hḥmyšyt lmsprm [The History of the Jews in Palestine in the Fifth Century C.E.]," " *Yerushalyim* " : *Journal of the Jewish Palestine Exploration Society Dedicated to the Memory of Abraham Mosheh Luncz* (eds. I. Press and E. L. Sukenik ; Jerusalem : Darom, 1928) 41-50.
E. L. Sukenik, " Mṣbwt yhwdywt mṣʿr [Jewish Tomb-Stones from Zoar (Ghor es-Safi)]," *Kedem* 2 (1945) 83-88, esp. pp. 83-85.
M. D. Cassuto, " Ht'rybym šbktwbwt ṣwʿr [The Dates in the Inscriptions from Zoar]," *Kedem* 2 (1945) 90-91.
A. A. Akavya, " ʿrbn šl ktwbwt ṣwʿr lkrwnwlwgyh [Contribution of the Zoar Inscriptions to Chronology]," *Kedem* 2 (1945) 92-98.
B. Z. Wacholder, " The Calendar of Sabbatical Cycles during the Second Temple and the Early Rabbinic Period," *HUCA* 44 (1973) 153-96, esp. 180.

A51. *Ghôr eṣ-Ṣâfieh Tombstone Inscription II.* Published in E. L. Sukenik, " Mṣbwt yhwdywt mṣwʿr [Jewish Tomb-Stones from Zoar (Ghor es-Safi)]," *Kedem* 2 (1945) 83-88, esp. pp. 85-86, pl. *w*/1. The inscription marking the tomb of a certain Esther comes from A.D. 372/373. Here *npšh* seems to have the local sense suggested by S. Daiches in *PEFQS* (1926) 31-32.

Bibliography

G. R. Driver, " Seals and Tombstones," *Annual of the Department of Antiquities of Jordan* 2 (1953) 62-65, esp. pp. 64-65.
P. A. H. de Boer, " Naar aanleiding van een inscriptie uit Ṣoʿar," *JEOL* 14 (1955-56) 117-21 (+ pl. II).
B. Z. Wacholder, " The Calendar of Sabbatical Cycles during the Second Temple and the Early Rabbinic Period," *HUCA* 44 (1973) 153-96, esp. p. 181.

A52. *Ghôr eṣ-Ṣâfieh Tombstone Inscription III.* Published by E. L. Sukenik in *Kedem* 2 (1945) 83-88, esp. 86-87, pl. *w*/2. The inscription that marks the tomb of Ḥalifu (a feminine name) comes from A.D. 504/5.

Bibliography

A. H. Fraenkel, " H'rh lktwbt g' mṣw'r [Note on Tomb-Stone 3 from Zoar]," *Kedem* 2 (1945) 89.
B. Z. Wacholder, " The Calendar of Sabbatical Cycles during the Second Temple and the Early Rabbinic Period," *HUCA* 44 (1973) 153-96, esp. p. 181.

A53. *Khirbet Zif Ossuary.* The inscription occurs on an ossuary lid found in a tomb located west of Khirbet Zif and north of Tell Zif, in the Hebron district. The Greek and Aramaic inscriptions appear on the long sides of the lid. They were first published by L. Y. Rahmani in " A Bilingual Ossuary-Inscription from Khirbet Zif," *IEJ* 22 (1972) 113-16, pls. 18-19, esp. p. 114, pl. 19. The general style of the lid as well as the form of the Greek and Aramaic characters indicate a 2d- or early 3d-century date. The Greek inscription runs : Κύνωρος Διο/δό[τ]ου Πρω/τοπολείτης, " Cynoros, (son) of Diodotos, Protopolites." Rahmani explains *Kynōros* as perhaps related to the Greek word for " dog-keeper " and *dwṭws* (" Doṭos ") as a hypocoristic Aramaic form of Diodotos. He originally followed E. Y. Kutscher's suggestion that the last two words be read *rēš mārwān* (" head of the masters "), but later he seems to have accepted Y. Yadin's reading *rēš* <ʿ>*ămārîm*, " head of the citizens " pronounced as one word : *rē-šămārîm.* Yadin also suggested reading the patronymic as *dyṭws* (" Dioṭos ").

Bibliography

E. Y. Kutscher, " Note on the Title *reš mārwān*," *IEJ* 22 (1972) 117.
Y. Yadin, " A Note on the Bilingual Ossuary-Inscription from Khirbet Zif," *IEJ* 22 (1972) 235-36.
L. Y. Rahmani, " Additional Note," *IEJ* 22 (1972) 236.

A54. *Khirbet Susiya Synagogue Inscription I.* This inscription was published by S. Gutman, Z. Yeivin, and E. Netzer, " Ḥpyrt byt-hknst bḥwrbt swsyh [Excavations in the Synagogue at Khirbet Susiya]," *Qadmoniot* 5 (1972) 47-52, esp. p. 50. Four inscriptions were found in all, two in Aramaic (this and the following one), and two in Hebrew. The first two inscriptions were found in the narthex of the synagogue. They date probably from the 4th or 5th century A.D. No photograph is given of this first inscription.

A55. *Khirbet Susiya Synagogue Inscription II.* This inscription was likewise published by S. Gutman, Z. Yeivin, and E. Netzer in *Qadmoniot* 5 (1972) 47-52, esp. pp. 50-51. See the plate 1 (opposite p. 44). The editors consider *mnḥmh* to be a proper name, but admit that it is rare. If it is, the syntax is puzzling, unless we are to take both forms of it as feminine names and understand [*d*]*kyrn* as feminine too, with " daughter/wife of " understood before *Yšw*‘.

A56. *Eshtemoa*‘ *Synagogue Inscription.* This inscription was published by Z. Yeivin, " Byt-hknst b’štmw‘ [The Synagogue at Eshtemoa]," *Qadmoniot* 5 (1972) 43-45. To be noted here is the spelling of the name *l*‘*zr* ; compare the form of the name in the Giv‘at Ha-Mivṭar Abba Inscription (**68**:1-2 above) : *’/l‘z<r>*. Contrast the remarks of G. Vermes, *Jesus the Jew* : *A Historian's Reading of the Gospels* (London: Collins, 1973) 188-91. On the restoration of *ṭr*[*ymysyn*], proposed by Yeivin, see the Hammath-Gadara Synagogue Inscription II (**A27**:1 ; cf. **A28**:4).

GLOSSARY TO THE MAIN TEXTS

GLOSSARY TO THE MAIN TEXTS

The references in brackets indicate that some part of the word has been emended. But the degree of certainty or probability for the restoration varies considerably, and one should always consult the passage itself before discounting the bracketed references.

'b (father) : *'b* (abs.), 5:31.5 ; *'b'* (emph.), **116:**1 ; **95A:**1 ; *'bh,* **145C:**2 ; *'by,* **19:**1.4 ; **20:**4.[1] ; 29.1 ; **21:**2.12 ; **27:**11bis ; **29B:**2.19, 24 ; 3.3 ; **64:**1. 6bis ; 3.1 ; *'bwk,* **64:**1.12 ; *'bwhy,* **28:** 1.7 ; **29B:**2.20, 22, [23], 24 ; *'bwnh,* **95B:**1 ; **110:**1 ; *'bwhn,* **14:**20.2 ; *'bwhwn,* **17:**2.[5] ; *'bhtnh,* **67:**2 ; **71:**[1] ; *'bhthwn,* **5:**15.[5] ; *'bhtwhy,* **28:**1.[7]

'bd (perish, be lost) : *'bd,* **5:**5.[4] ; *'bdn',* **16:**2.[12] ; *y'bdwn,* **5:**27.7 ; *y'bdw,* **1:**1 ; *'bd* (ptc.), **5:**14.[7]

'bdn (perdition) : *'bdn',* **26:**14 ; **29B:** 12.17 ; *'bdwn,* **5:**18.5

'bl (mourn) : *'blyn,* **5:**15.[3]

'bl (mourning) : *'bl* (abs.), **35B:**[3]

'bn (stone) : *'bn* (abs.), **5:**36.[9] ; **5:**31. [7] ; **7:**8.3 ; **8:**1 i 6, 9 ; *'bn* (cst.), **5:**30.4 ; *'bn',* **2:**1.8 ; *'bny',* **51:**7

'gr (rent) : *'gr,* **64:**1.12 ; *mtgr,* **29B:**20.10

'grh (letter) : *'grt,* **55:**1 ; *'ygrt',* **16:**2.3

'd (hand) : see *yd*

'dwn (guardian) : *'dwn* (cst.), **61:**24

'dyn (then) : *'dyn,* **5:**20.6 ; **20:**11.1 ; 27.1 ; 53.[1] ; **21:**1.[8] ; 2.13, 15 ; **29B:**2.8, 11 ; 22.20 ; see also *b'dyn, bdyn*

'dkrh (mention) : *'dkrt',* **150:**7

'dm (man), **22:**1.[2] ; **23:**1.12

'dn (ear) : *'dn* (abs.), **5:**14.5 ; 37.7 ; *'dny,* **5:**22.2 ; *'dnyn',* **5:**13.3 ; *'dnyhwn,* **5:**27.4, 9

'w (or) : *'w,* **5:**9.6 ; 26.2 ; 30.3, 4 ; 31.5, 8 ; 32.8 ; 33.8 ; 34.4, 5 ; 35.4, 6 ; **41:**9 ; **42:**[12]

'wṣ (oppress) : *'yṣ,* **3D:**1

'wrḥ (road, way) : *'wrḥ',* **52:**5

'wryh (law) : *'wryt',* **150:**12

'wš (howl) : *'wš* (cst.), **18:**8

'zd' (certain[ty]) : *'zd',* **4A:**2.6

'zl (go) : *'zl,* **14:**13.3 ; **29B:**2.23 ; 20:24 ; 21.5 ; *'zlt* (I went), **29B:**20.33 ; 21. 15, 16, 19 ; *'zlw,* **29B:**22.24 ; *'zlnh,* **29B:**12.16 ; *'zl* (impv.), **17:**2.22 ; **29B:**5.10 ; 20.23, 27 ; 21.13 ; *'zl* (ptc.), **29B:**19.9 ; *'zlyn,* **5:**29.2 ; **13:**6 ; **29B:** 22.4

'ḥ (brother) : *'ḥy,* **29B:**2.9, [13] ; 19.20 ; 20.10, 11, 34 ; 21.7 ; **89:**1 ; *'ḥwhy,* **5:**38.5 ; **17:**2.15 ; **29B:**22.3, 5, 11 ; *'ḥwy,* **29B:**21.34 ; *'ḥh* (his brother ?), **52:**5 ; *'ḥy',* **29B:**21.21 ; *'ḥy* (my brothers), **5:**2.[2] ; *'ḥyk,* **5:**6.[5]

'ḥd (one [Hebr.]) : *'ḥd,* **40:**1, [12] ; **42:**6 ; *'ḥt,* **17:**3.3

'ḥd (seize) : *'ḥd,* **5:**4.5 ; 22.4 ; *'ḥdt* (I caught), **5:**19.6 ; *y'ḥdwn,* **5:**16.8 ; *m'ḥd,* **5:**30.[10] ; *mḥd,* **53:**3 ; *'ḥdyn* **23:**1.11 ; *'ḥydyn,* **5:**27.[2] ; 30.4 ; 31. [8] ; *'ytḥd,* **5:**11.10

'ḥydh (seizing, taking) : *'ḥydt,* **150:**3, 8

'ḥr (after) : *'ḥr,* **35D:**1.2 ; *'ḥrn',* **22:**2.4 ; *'ḥrhwn,* **29A:**2.2 ; *'ḥryk,* **29B:**21.14

'ḥry (guarantee) : *'ḥry* (abs.), **47:**1-2 r 2.10 ; **51:**11 ; *'ḥry',* **45:**1.4 ; **48:**4 ; *'ḥryn,* **46:**3 ; *'ḥr'yn,* **41:**12 ; **52:**11

'ḥry (other) : *'wḥry,* **7:**8.7 ; *'ḥryt',* **7:** 4.16

'ḥrn (another) : *'ḥrn,* **5:**18.[3] ; **8:**1 i 18 ; **10:**[2], [6] ; *'ḥrn',* **8:**1 ii 7 ; **23:**1.

[14] ; *'ḥrnyn*, **5**:25.[1] ; **10**:4 ; **12**:4 ; **52**:4 ; **60**:3 ; *'ḥrny'*, 7:8.4 ; *'ḥrnt'*, **8**:1 ii [13]

'ḥt (sister) : *'ḥty*, **5**:1.1 ; **29B**:20.27

'ṭm (enclose) : *'ṭymn*, **8**:1 ii 11

'yl (ram) : *'yl* (abs.), **7**:4.18

'ylh (hind) : *'ylt'*, **5**:32.[1]

'yln (tree) : *'ylnyn*, **10**:4 ; **17**:3.[11] ; *'ylny'*, **10**:6 ; **12**:[2]

'ymh (terror) : *'ymh*, **5**:33.2

'ymy (gentilic : Emim) : *'ymy'*, **29B**: 21.29

'yty (there is) : *'yty*, **5**:6.4 ; 9.5 ; 16.2 ; 21.3 ; 23.[10] ; 31.5 ; 34.5, 10 ; **29B**: 22.19, 22, 29 ; **45**:1.[3] ; **44**:1.[6] ; **51**:5, 10, 12 ; **52**:11 ; **64**:1.8 ; **150**:12 ; *'ytyny*, **49**:4 ; *'yt*, **42**:16

'kl (eat) : *'kl*, **5**:5.6 ; *'klt* (I ate), **29B**: 21.20 ; *'klw*, **5**:15.[8] ; 38.5 ; **29B**: 21.21 ; 22.23 ; *y'kl*, **5**:18.[1] ; *t'kl* (3d sg. fem.), **5**:18.[5] ; *t'kl* (2d sg. masc.), **20**:3.[1] ; *t'klwn*, **29B**:11.17

'kl (food) : *'kl'*, **5**:33.[10]

'kp (load) : *'kpyhwn*, **5**:15.[6]

'l (not) : *'l*, **21**:1.[17] ; 2.[9] ; **29B**:2.25 ; 19.16 ; 20.15 ; 22.30

'l (to) : *'lwhy*, **29B**:20.<26>

'l (God) : *'l*, **7**:4.[7] ; **9**:1 ; **20**:1.[3] ; **29B**:12.17 ; 19.[8] ; 20.12, 16 ; 21.2, 20 ; 22.15, 16bis, 21

'l (jamb) : *'lwhy*, **7**:10.1

'lh (god) : *'lh*, **5**:34.5 ; **69**:2 ; **149**:6 ; *'lh'*, **2**:1.[2], [3], [5] ; **5**:4.8 ; 5.2, [3] ; 6.[1] ; 7.[3] ; 8.2 ; 9.4, 7 ; 10.8 ; 11. 1 ; 18.[7] ; 19.3 ; 21.5 ; 22.6, [8] ; 24.3, 4, 6 ; 26.4, [8] ; 28.3 ; 29.5, 6 ; 30.5 ; 34.2 ; 37.3 ; 38.[2]bis, 3, 7 ; **23**:2.[6] ; **28**:1.10 ; **29B**:19.[7] ; 21.2, [3], 3, 8 ; 22.27, 32 ; *'lhyn*, **2**:1.8 ; **4B**:1.6 ; *'lhy*, **2**:1.7

'lwh (god) : *'lwhyn*, **3C**:1, 2

'lwn (oak) : *'lwny*, **29B**:21.19

'lksy (Alexandrian ?) : *'lks'*, **108**:1

'ln (these) : *'ln*, **3F**:8, [9] ; **10**:[3], [4], 5, [6], 7, [8] ; **12**:[3], 4, 6 ; **14**:27.1 ; **28**:2.14 ; **29B**:2.[21] ; 5.[24] ; 19.23 ; 20.25 ; 21.23, 25 ; 22.27, [33] ; *'lyn*, **5**:20.3 ; **150**:1

'lp (thousand) : *'lpyn*, **14**:22.[2]

'm (if [Hebr.]) : *'m*, **41**:6, 8 ; **53**:2 ; **54**:[2] ; **59**:2

'm (mother) : *'m'*, **96B**:<2> ; *'mh*, **114**:1 (possibly a proper name) ; *'my*, **5**:1. [1] ; *'mnh*, **96A**:1

'mh (maidservant) : *'mty*, **5**:2.4

'mh (cubit) : *'mh*, **8**:1 i 6, [16] ; 1 ii [12], [15] ; *'myn*, **6**:15.[2] ; **7**:1.[4] ; 2.1 ; **8**:1 i [1]bis, 2, [3], 4, 5, [5], 6, [8], [9], [10], [11], [13]bis, [14]bis, 15, [15], 16, 17, [17], [19]ter ; 1 ii 1bis, 3, [4], 5, [7], 8, [8], 9, [9], 10, [10], [11], [12]bis, [13]quater, [14], [15] ; 2.4 ; 3.[3] ; 7.[2] ; 12.1 ; 14.[1] ; **67**:3

'mh (people) : *'wmh*, **4B**:[13]

'mwry (Amorite) : *'mwr''*, **29B**:21:21

'mn (be firm ; trust) : *yhymnwn*, **5**: 15.[1]

'mr (say) : *'mr*, **2**:1.[4] ; **3C**:[2] ; **4B**: 1.7 ; **5**:1.[4] ; 9.[4], [10] ; 10.8 ; 13.9 ; 24.2 ; 34.2 ; 37.3 ; **17**:2.15 ; 3.6 ; **18**: 9 ; **19**:1.2, [6] ; **21**:2.[18] ; **23**:2.2 ; 3. [2] ; **29**:2.24 ; 20.22, 24, 26 ; 21.8, 12 ; 22.16, 18, 20, 27, 32, 34 ; **32A**: 4 ; **47**:1.1 ; **49**:1.5bis, 9 ; **51**:2 ; **150**: 11 ; *'mrt* (she said), **29B**:2.9, 16, 18 ; 20.9, 12 ; *'mrt* (you said), **5**:6.7 ; 22.2 ; 30.8 ; *'mrt* (I said), **21**:1.10 ; **23**:2.3 ; 3.[1] ; **25**:1.3 ; **29B**:2.[3] ; 19. 7, 17, [19] ; *'mrw*, **5**:19.[7] ; **17**:2.22 ; **22**:1.[1] ; **23**:1.[11], 12 ; **28**:2.[19] ; *y'mr*, **5**:23.1, [5] ; 33.5 ; *t'mr* (you say), **5**:26.9 ; 20.26 ; **45**:1.7 ; **46**:5 ; *t'mr* (she says), **29B**:2.13 ; *tmryn*, **40**:10, [24] ; *t'mryn*, **5**:21.4 ; **42**:[19] ; *'mr* (I say), **29B**:2.25 ; *'mr* (impv.), **17**:2.23 ; **29B**:5.10 ; 20.23 ; *'mry*, **29B**: 19.[20] ; *m'mr*, **5**:8.[6] ; *'mr*, **5**:27. [4] ; 29.2 ; **29B**:5.9 ; 22.22 ; **49**:1.4 ; **55**:3 ; *'mryn*, **4B**:1.4 ; **5**:7.2 ; 26.[4] ; **23**:1.10

'mrh (ewe) : *'mrh*, **5**:38.7

'n (where) : *'n*, **5**:1.[1] ; 26.[4] ; 30.2

'n (if, whether) : *'n*, **29B**:22.21, 22

'nh (I) : *'nh*, **2**:1.[3], [6] ; **5**:14.6 ; 21.1, [9] ; 22.[1], 3, [3] ; 23.[9] ; 25:9 ;

37:6 ; **17**:2.16 ; 3.[7] ; **18**:5, 10 ; **20**: 8.1, 3 ; **21**:1.6 ; 2.14 ; **22**:3.1 ; **23**:2.5, 6, [6] ; 3.[1] ; **25**:1.2 ; **26**:9bis ; **27**:[9], 10 ; **29B**:2.3, [4], 10, 14, [17], 19, 24 ; 5.3, 9bis, 26 ; 6.6 ; 12.13 ; 19.14 ; 20.10bis, 11, 33 ; 21.6, 7, 10, 15, 21 ; 22.20, 30, 31, 33 ; **39**:3, 5 ; **40**:2, [13] ; **41**:9 ; **42**:14, 17, 18 ; **44**:1.5, 6 ; **45**:1.[3] ; **47**:2.6bis, 9 ; **48**:[2]bis ; **50E**:2 ; **50F**:[1] ; **51**:3, 10, 11, 12 ; **52**:8, 10 ; **64**:1.7, 8, 9 ; 3.1 ; **68**:1, 2-3

'nw (these) : *'nw*, **64**:3.6

'nwn (they, them) : *'nwn*, **3C**:3, 5 ; **3D**:[2] ; **3F**:9 ; **14**:2.1 ; **16**:2.8 ; **18**: 6, [7] ; **23**:1.11 ; 3.[1] ; **24**:2 ; **25**:1. [3] ; **29B**:20.[31] ; 22.7, 9, 24 ; **32G**: 5.3 ; **62**:13 ; **150**:12

'nwš : see *'nš*

'nḥn' (we) : *'nḥn'*, **23**:1.[11] ; **29B**:19. 12 ; **46**:[2] ; **58**:2

'ns (oppress, overwhelm) : *'nsny*, **18**: [9] ; *'nst*, **29B**:2.13

'ns (force) : *'wns*, **29B**:20.11

'np (nostril, nose ; face) : *'nph'*, **29B**: 20.3 ; *'py*, **5**:10.10 ; *'ph* (its nose), **5**:35.3, 5 ; *'npy* (cst. pl.), **3C**:[1] ; **5**:29.1, 3 ; 31.7 ; 33.3, 4 ; *'npy* (my face), **21**:1.[8] ; **29B**:2.12 ; **49**:1.6 ; *npy*, **39**:3 ; *'npyk*, **29B**:2.17 ; *'npwhy*, **5**:6.8 ; 23.4 ; 25.5 ; **22**:2.[5] ; **23**:1.14 ; *'npyh'*, **29B**:20.2, 4 ; *'npyhwn*, **3C**:1

'nš (man, human being) : *'nš*, **5**:2.8 ; 9.9 ; 12.[9] ; 13.[9] ; 21.[5] ; 24.5 ; 26.3 ; 28.[1] ; 31.4 ; **23**:2.[6] ; **25**:1. [2] ; **59**:2 ; **69**:1 ; **150**:12 ; *'nš* (cst.), **5**:11.3 ; 19.[7] ; 24.4 ; 25.6 ; **20**:8.2 ; **29B**:20.16, 17, 18, 19 ; 21.21 ; *'nš'*, **2**:1.[3], 6 ; **5**:22.6 ; 28.2bis ; **13**:8 ; **28**:1.8 ; **29B**:22.15 ; *'nšy* (my men), **29B**:21.19 ; *'nšy* (Hebraized cst. pl.), **150**:3bis ; *'nwš* (Hebraized form, abs.), **28**:1.[4] ; **29B**:19.15, [23] ; 20. 32 ; 21.13

'nth (woman, wife) : *'nth*, **5**:18.[2] ; 36. 2 ; **29B**:20.27, 34 ; **40**:6 (*'nt*, but read *'nt*<'>) ; **41**:3 ; **42**:[7] ; *'nt'*, **29B**:20. 9 ; 40:18 ; *'ntt*, **29B**:20.25 ; **45**:1.3 ; **98**:1 ; **122**:1 ; *'yntt*, **147**:1 ; *'tt*, **51**:12 ; **84**:1 ; **97A**:1 ; **103**:1 ; **104**:1 ; *'ytt*, **94B**:1 ; *'ntty*, **5**:2.6 ; 18.[3] ; **29B**: 2.[3], 8, 12 ; 19.17, 24 ; 20.14, 15 ; **40**:16 ; *'nty*, **40**:3, 5, 14 ; *'nttk*, **29B**: 20.27bis ; *'ntth* (his wife), **29B**:20. 23bis

'nth (you) : *'nth*, **2**:4.4 ; **20**:7.1 ; **21**:1. 10, [11] ; **23**:1.[12] ; 2.[5] ; **29B**:19.7 ; 20.12, 13bis, 15 ; 21.9 ; *'nt'*, **64**:1.5, 9 ; *'nt* (masc.), **49**:1.9 ; *'nt* (fem.), **42**:[7], 12, [14] ; *'t* (masc. [Hebrew?]), **60**:3 ; *'ty*, **40**:17 ; see also *'t* and *'ty*

'ntwn (you, pl.) : *'ntwn*, **23**:1.11

's' (heal, cure) : *'sy* (peal ptc., cst. pl.), **29B**:20.19 ; *'sy'*, **29B**:20.20 ; *'sywth* (pael inf.), **29B**:20.19, 20

'swr (bond) : *'swrkwn*, **16**:2.14

'sp (threshold) : *'sp*, **8**:1 i 18, [19] ; *'sp'*, **8**:1 i [16], 17, [17], 18 ; *'spy'*, **8**:2.3

'sply' (assurance [= Gk. ἀσφάλεια]) : *'sply'*, **5**:23.[4] ; **53**:2

'sprk (buckler [Pers.]) : *'sprk*, **29B**: 22.31

'sr (bind, tie ; imprison) : *'sr* (impv.), **5**:30.1 ; **34**:2 ; *yysr* (?), **150**:12 ; *'syryn* **5**:27.2 ; **29A**:1 i 4

'' (wood) : *'''*, **2**:1.8 ; *''y*, **150**:5

'p (moreover, also) : *'p*, **5**:20.8 ; 21.1, 9 ; 27.2 ; 29.1 ; 34.3 ; **10**:4 ; **13**:7 ; **17**:2.15 ; **26**:[9] ; **29B**:1.2 ; 20.17, 32, 33, 34 ; 21.6, 13 ; **22**:11

'p (nose) : see *'np*

'pw (then ?) : *'pw*, **5**:1.1 ; 4.3 ; 9.2

'pṭrp' (guardian [= Gk. ἐπίτροπος]) : *'pṭrp'*, **62**:[12]

'ṣb' (finger) : *'ṣb't*, **21**:1.9 ; **29B**:20.5

'rbysr (fourteen) : *'rbysr*, **150**:12

'rb' (four) : *'rb'*, **3B**:[1] ; **8**:1 i [5], [8], [15], 16, 19 ; 1 ii [1], 1, 3, 5, 8bis, 9, [10], [15] ; **14**:13.[1] ; **29B**:12.13 ; 21.27 ; 22.8 ; **64**:3.2, 3 ; *'rb'h*, **4B**:1.5 ; **7**:4.[10] ; 8.[2] ; **9**:3 ; **50E**:1 ; **150**:4, 5, 6 ; *'rb't*, **7**:4.13 ; **9**:4 ; **150**:2, 3

'rb'yn (forty) : *'rb'yn*, **7**:1.4 ; **8**:1 i 2, [14] ; 3.[3]

'rgwn (purple) : *'rgw'n*, **29B**:20.31

'rw (for, that) : *'rw*, **5**:3.6 ; 4.3 ; 5.7 ; 13.4, [4] ; 14.[4], [6] ; 18.[3], [4], 7 ; 19.[2] ; 20.[3] ; 21.1, 3 ; 22.6, 7, [8] ; 24.2 ; 25.8 ; 26.8, [10] ; 27.3 ; 28.1, 4, 8 ; 29.8 ; 32.[10] ; **16**:2.12 ; **18**:10 ; **19**:1.6

'rz (cedar) : *'rz*, **29B**:19.14 ; *'rz'*, **29B**:19.[15], [16], 16

'rḥ (path) : *'rḥ*, **5**:31.3 ; *'rḥ'*, **29B**:21.28 ; 22.4 ; *'rḥy*, **5**:15.2 ; 23.6 ; *'rḥk*, **5**:6.2 ; *'rḥh*, **5**:25.[3] ; **23**:2.[4] ; *'rḥt*, **21**:1.[12] ; *'rḥy* (my paths), **5**:22.[5] ; *'rḥwhy*, **5**:10.[5]

'ry (stall) : *'wryk*, **5**:32.9

'ry (for [conj.]) : *'ry*, **20**:23.1 ; **26**:[9], [10], 12, [12] ; **29B**:2.[17] ; 3.3 ; 19.16, [23] ; 20.20, 22 ; 21.14

'ryk (long) : *'rykn*, **29B**:20.5

'rk (length) : *'rk*, **29B**:2.23 ; **67**:3 ; *'rwk*, **8**:1 ii 7, [10] ; *'wrkh*, **7**:5-6.2 ; **8**:1 i 17 ; 1 ii [1], 3, [4] ; *'rkh'*, **29B**:21.14 ; *'rkyn*, **8**:1 ii 15 ; *'wrkhwn*, **8**:1 i 12 ; 1 ii [10], [13]

'rkh (authorization ?) : *'rkt*, **17**:3.3

'rkwbh (knee) : *'rkwbth*, **28**:1.[6]

'rmlh (widow) : *'rmlh*, **5**:14.8 ; *'rmlth*, **5**:11.6

'rmlw (widowhood) : *'rmlw*, **41**:11 ; **42**:15

'rs (engage) : *'rs* (I engage), **47**:2.4

'rʿ (land) : *'rʿ*, **5**:32.5 ; *'rʿ* (cst.), **5**:31.3 ; 35.[9] ; **29A**:1 ii 6 ; **29B**:16.11 ; 19.11, 13bis, 14 ; 21.11 ; *'rʿ'*, **1**:1 ; **2**:1.[1] ; **5**:13.5 ; 24.7 ; 26.[6] ; 30.2, [10] ; 31.2 ; **10**:[6] ; **11**:[3] ; **12**:6 ; **13**:8 ; **14**:9-14-15.3 ; **16**:2.[9]bis ; **17**:2.16 ; 3.8 ; **20**:26.1 ; **29B**:10.13 ; 12.13 ; 17.9 ; 19.10 ; 20.13, 16 ; 21.4, 10bis, 12, 13, 15, 16 ; 22.16, 21, 25 ; **31**:2.[2] ; **33**:1.[3] ; **35C**:[1] ; *'rʿh* (emph.), **29B**:7.1 ; *'rʿn'*, **29B**:19.12, 13 ; *'rʿhwn*, **3C**:3

'rʿ (happening) : *'rʿy'*, **23**:2.6

'š (foundation) : *'šyh*, **5**:30.4 ; *'šy*, **7**:9.2

'šd (pour), **5**:16.5

'šh (fire), *'šh*, **5**:23:2 ; 36.5

'šp (wizard) : *'špy'*, **29B**:20.19, 20

'štdwr (revolution) : *'štdwr*, **5**:31.[1] ; 33.6

't (you, fem.) : *'t*, **40**:5 ; see also *'ty* and *'nth*

'th (come) : *'th*, **17**:2.21 ; **18**:8 ; **29B**:20.21 ; 21.23 ; 22.1, 13 ; *'tt*, **19**:2.2 ; **150**:12 ; *'tyt*, **29B**:2.[24], 25 ; 21.15, 19 ; *'tw*, **17**:2.5 ; **29B**:19.15 ; *'twn*, **5**:2.[2] ; 38.4 ; **29B**:19.[24], 26 ; **33**:5.3 ; *yth*, **58**:2 ; *t'th*, **5**:30.[9] ; *'th*, **29B**:20.21 ; *ytwn*, **3B**:2 ; **5**:16.1, 2 ; *m'th*, **28**:1.6 ; 2.4 ; *'th* (peal ptc.), **29B**:21.17 ; *hyty*, **5**:38.7 ; *'yt'h*, **150**:11 ; *htyt*, **70**:1

'twn (you, masc. pl.) : *'twn*, **5**:11.[2] ; see also *'ntwn*

'ty (you, fem. sg.) : *'ty*, **41**:[3]

'tr (place) : *'tr*, **10**:[2] ; **29B**:19.[20] ; 21.9 ; *'tr* (cst.), **5**:13.1 ; 25.[2] ; **29B**:21.1 ; *'tr'*, **29B**:21.1 ; **44**:1.[4], [7] ; **45**:1.[5], [8] ; **47**:1.12 ; **52**:3, 5, ‹7›, 9 ; *'try*, **5**:12.[2] ; *'trh*, **5**:1.[8] ; 13.[4] ; 30.[10]

'trg (citron) : *'trgyn*, **60**:3

b- (in, on, by, for [prep.]) : *b-*, **2**:1.2ter, [2], 6bis ; **3A**:9 ; **3B**:3 ; **3C**:3 ; **3F**:[2] ; **4B**:1.3 ; **5**:5.1, 2, 5 ; 8.4, 5, 8 ; 9.[5] ; 10.3, [10] ; 11.[1] ; 13.3, 6, 7bis ; 14.[1], 1bis, [8] ; 15.3, 4, 6, [7] ; 16.2 ; 18.2, 6 ; 19.5, [8] ; 20.[4] ; 22.2, 5, 7, 8, [9], 9, [10] ; 23.4, 7, [8], 10 ; 25.2, 3, [6] ; 26.1, 6 ; 27.2bis, 5, 6bis, [7], 8 ; 29.5 ; 30.2, 4, 6bis, 7, [9], 9, [10] ; 32.5, [9], 9 ; 33.1, 2bis, 3, [9] ; 34.5, 9, [9] ; 35.3bis, 4bis, 5bis, 6bis, 8, 9, [10] ; 36.5, 7 ; 38.2, 3, 4, 6 ; **6**:3.2 ; **7**:1.[1] ; 4.20 ; **8**:1 i [12], 13bis, [14], 14, 17 ; 1 ii 3, 4, [4], [5], 6bis, [9], [15] ; 2.2 ; 3.3 ; **12**:2 ; **14**:9-14-15.3 ; 17.2 ; 21.2 ; 29.1 ; **16**:2.4, 9bis, 13bis ; **17**:2.10, 16bis ; 3.3, 4 ; **18**:3bis, [6], 6 ; **21**:2.11, 16 ; **22**:2.5 ; **23**:1.10, 12, 14, [14] ; 2.4 ; **24**:2bis, [3] ; **26**:11 ; **27**:12 ; **28**:1.4, 7bis ; 2.13 ; **29B**:2.1, 4ter, 5, [6], 6, 7ter, 8, 10, 14bis, 18, 20, 22 ; 3.3 ; 7.[1], 1 ; 12.13bis, 15, 16bis ; 19.[7], 10bis, 14bis, 15, 16,

17, 20bis, 21, 23, 26, 27bis ; 20.10, 11bis, 12bis, 13bis, 14, 15bis, 16, 22, 30, 33bis ; 21.[1], 2, 4, 5, 6, 7, 8, 19ter, 27bis, 28, 29bis, [29], 30bis, 32, 33 ; 22.1, 3, 8bis, 9, 13, 17, 24, 27, 28, 30 ; **32B**:2 ; **32F**:2 ; **33**:4.5, 6 ; **39**:2, 3, 4, 6bis ; **40**:1bis, 3, 5, 6, 10, 12bis, 16, 18, 23 ; **41**:[1], 15, 16 ; **42**:[1], [6], 14bis, 19 ; **43**:1-3, 5 ; **44**:1.1, [1] ; 6.2, 5 ; **45**:1.[6], [8] ; **47**:2.[10] ; **49**:1.6 ; **50E**:1 ; **51**:1bis, 5bis, 7, 10, [11], 13, 14 ; **52**:5, 6, 7, 9 ; **53**:2 ; **55**:4 ; **61**:24, 25bis, 26 ; **62**:12, 13 ; **64**:1.[1], 2bis, 4, 8, 10, 11 ; 2.2 ; 3.[3], 4, 5, 6, [6] ; **68**:4, 6, 7 ; **69**:1, 2 ; **149**:[1] ; **150**:2quater, 3quater, 4bis, 5ter, 6quater, 7bis, 8ter, 9quinquies, 10, 11quater, 12 quattuordeciens ; *by*, **5**:2.3 ; 5.[8] ; **20**:30.3 ; **21**:1.17 ; **64**:1.9 ; *bk*, **5**:26.1 ; *bh*, **5**:13.4 ; 28.[3] ; 31.4 ; 32.[10] ; 35.8 ; **7**:8.5 ; **8**:1 ii 6 ; **10**:[2] ; **13**:6, 8 ; **14**:9-14-15.4 ; **16**:2.11 ; **19**:4.2 ; **20**:53.2 ; **21**:2.[17] ; **29B**:19.[20] ; 20. 15 ; 21.1, 7, 27 ; **44**:1.[3] ; **51**:7 ; **52**:6bis, 10 ; **64**:1.5 ; 3.2 ; *byh*, **150**: 1bis, 2ter, 3ter, 5, 6bis, 8bis, 9ter, 11bis, 12nonies ; *bh'*, **29B**:20.17 ; *bhwn*, **4B**:10 ; **5**:28.8 ; 29.1 ; **7**:4.13 ; **9**:[4] ; **10**:4 ; **20**:25.2 ; **27**:12 ; **29B**: 22.9 ; **150**:1bis, 9 ; see also *b'dyn*, *bdy*, *bdyl*, *bḥd'*, *blḥwdy*

b'dyn (then) : *b'dyn*, **4B**:1.8, 15 ; **5**: 13.8 ; **11**:8 ; **14**:20.3 ; 22.3 ; **17**:2.3, 15, [20] ; **21**:2.11 ; **28**:1.[6] ; **29B**:2.1, 3, 13, 19 ; 20.21 ; 22.2, 18 ; see also *'dyn*, *bdyn*

b'yš (bad, evil) : *b'yš*, **5**:3.[1] ; 8.8 ; **16**:2.14 ; **28**:2.2 ; *b'yš'*, 2:1.2, [2], [6] ; **21**:1.[13] ; *b'yšyn*, **5**:26.[8] ; *b'yšh*, **5**:15.8 ; 16.3 ; *b'yš'* (abs. fem. sg.), **29B**:20.17 ; *b'yšt'*, **29A**:1 ii 8 ; **29B**: 20.28, 29 ; *b'yš* (evil [as noun]) ; *b'yšth*, **5**:13.[10] ; 19.4 ; *b'yšn* **5**:11. [11] ; *b'yšth* (emph. pl.) **5**:38.6 ; *b'yšthwn*, **5**:27.4 ; cf. *b'š*

b'r (well) : *b'r*, **20**:53.2 ; *b'rh*, **14**:19.1

b'š (be evil) : *b'š*, **20**:43.1 ; **29B**:21.7

b'šwšh (stinkweed) : *b'šwšh*, **5**:20.2

b'tr (after) : *b'tr*, **64**:1.2 ; see also *btr*

bb (gate) : *bbn*, **28**:2.14 ; *bby'*, **8**:1 i [10]

bdh (invent) : *ybdh*, **35A**:1.5

bdy (because) : *bdy*, **13**:6, 7bis ; **28**:1. 10 ; **29B**:2.20

b̄dyl (because of, inasmuch as) : *bdyl*, **5**:29.[7] ; **29B**:20.25, 26 ; *bdylyky*, **29B**:19.20 ; *bdylh*, **5**:38.3 ; *bdylh'*, **29B**:20.10

bdyn (now) : *bdyn*, **40**:[7], 8, 20, [21] ; see also *'dyn*, *b'dyn*

bdq (break through) : *bdqw*, **32C**:1

bdr (scatter) : *bdr*, **3C**:5

bhl (hurry ; be frightened) : *bhlh*, **4B**: 1.[3] ; *'tbhlt*, **29B**:2.3

bwzy (Buzite) : *bwzy'*, **5**:20.[6]

bwṣ (fine linen) : *bwṣ*, **29B**:20.31

bzh (booty, spoils) : *bzt'*, **29B**:22.13

bzz (plunder) : *bz*, **29B**:21.33 ; *bzw*, **29B**:22.11 ; *bzyn*, **29B**:21.28 ; 22.4

bḥd' (together) : *bḥd'*, **29B**:12.16

bḥn (test) : *bḥn*, **19**:3

bḥr (choose) : *bḥr*, **29B**:22.6 ; *bḥrt* (I chose), **5**:15.2 ; *bḥrw*, **3C**:1 ; *ybḥr*, **5**:32.7 ; *tbḥr* (you choose), **5**:25.[9] ; *bḥr* (peal ptc.), **23**:1.[12] ; *bḥyr*, **28**: 1.10 ; *bḥyryn*, **20**:25.[3] ; **29B**:22.6

bḥš (hot ash) : *bḥšyn*, **31**:1.2

bṭl (remove) : *bṭylt*, **150**:7, 11 ; *bṭln*, **44**:1.7 ; **45**:1.5

bṭn (womb) : *bṭn*, **5**:31.6

by (house) : *by*, **29B**:21.6 ; *bt* (= *byt*, as abs.), **42**:14, 15 ; *byt* (cst.), **8**:1 ii [2], 11 ; **41**:7, 9, [12] ; **44**:1.4 ; 9-10.1 ; **50B**:1 ; **50C**:1 ; **52**:2 ; **149**:6 ; *byt'*, **8**:1 ii 9 ; **42**:[10] ; *byth* (emph.), **5**:32.5 ; **51**:3, 7, 8, 11, 13 ; *byty*, **5**:2.4 ; 19.8 ; **29B**:20.28 ; 21.19, 21 ; 22.33, [34] ; **42**:11 ; *bty*, **64**:1.10, 11 ; *btk*, **51**:4 ; *byth*, **4B**:[14] ; **5**:5.2 ; 38. 6 ; **29B**:20.15, 16, 17, 18, 20 ; *bythwn*, **42**:15 ; *b'tyn*, **8**:1 ii 6 ; *bty*, **8**:1 ii [10] ; *bty'*, **8**:1 ii [7] ; 2.2 ; *btykwn*, **4A**:1 ii 7 ; *btyhwn*, **5**:4.7

byn (between) : *byn*, **5**:36:4 ; **8**:1 i [2] ; **14**:27.3 ; **20**:50.1 ; **29B**:21.24 ; *byny*,

64:1.13 ; *bynyk*, **64**:1.13 ; 2.2 ; *bynhn*, **5**:36.2(?)

byt (spend the night) : *bt*, **33**:1.2 ; *ybyt*, **5**:19.[9] ; 32.8 ; 36.7

bk' (weep) : *bk'*, **29B**:22.5 ; *bkt*, **29B**: 2.[8] ; 19.21 ; *bkyt*, **29B**:20.10, 16

bkwr (first-born) : *bkwry*, **20**:26.[1]

bky (weeping) : *bky*, **29B**:20.11 ; **35B**: 2.3

blzm (balsam) : *blzmh*, **66**:1 ; *blzm* (prob. Hebr.), **66**:1

blḥwdy (alone) : *blḥwdwhy*, **5**:25.7 ; *blḥwdyk*, **21**:1.11 ; *blḥwdyhh*, **29B**: 19.15

bll (mix) : *bll*, **35A**:1.1

bl' (suffer loss) : *bl'*, **64**:2.5

bn (son [Hebr.]) : *bn* (cst.), **91A**:2 ; **92C**:2 ; **93B**:1 ; **144A**:1 ;

bnh (build) : *bnh*, **149**:6 ; *bnt*, **89**:1 ; *bnyt*, **29B**:19.[7] ; 21.1, 20 ; *bnyth*, **29B**:21.1 ; *mbny*, **150**:12 ; *bn'* (peal ptc.), **85B**:2 ; *bnh*, **85A**:1 ; *bnh* (peil ptc.), **51**:9 ; *'tbny't*, **29B**:19.[9] ; *ytbnwn*, **28**:2.16

bnyh (building, construction) : *bnyh*, **51**:8(?)

bnyn (building) : *bnyn'*, **3A**:[9]

bsr (despise) : *tbsrwn*, **53**:3

b'h (seek, ask) : *b''*, **20**:7.3 ; 11.1 ; 30. 3 ; **29B**:20.9, 21 ; *b'yt*, **29B**:20.12 ; **64**:1.9 ; *b'w*, **17**:2.[21] ; *b'wn*, **29B**: 19.15 ; *tb'y*, **64**:2.[1] ; *'b'y*, **64**:2.1 ; *yb'wn*, **29B**:19.19, [21] ; *b'h* (peal ptc.), **17**:3.[7] ; **64**:2.4 ; *b't* (?), **6**:16.1

b'l (master, husband) : *b'lh*, **29B**:20. 25 ; *b'lh'*, **29B**:20.23 ; *b'ly* (cst. pl.), **18**:5

b'lyn (marriage) : *b'lyn*, **41**:9 ; **42**:12

b'yr (beast, cattle) : *b'yr'*, **5**:1.[6] ; *b'yry*, **5**:26.[6]

bṣ' (settle) : *bṣ'*, **64**:1.5

bṣr (shorten, curtail) : *ytbṣr*, **5**:37.4

bq' (gaze) : *ybq'*, **5**:13.[5] ; *ybqwn*, **5**: 28.3

bq' (valley, plain) : *bq'*, **5**:33.2

bq'h (valley) : *bq't*, **29B**:21.5 ; 22.8, 14 ; *bq'h*, **5**:32.9 ; *bq't'*, **150**:3

bqr (examine) : *bqr* (pael impv.), **29B**: 22.29 ; *bqrh* (inf.), **3A**:9

br (son) : *br* (cst.), **3E**:5 ; **4B**:1.6 ; **5**: 9.[9] ; 20.[6] ; 26.3 ; **21**:2.10 ; **24**: 1bis ; **29B**:19.[23] ; 20.11, 34 ; 21.7, 13, 34 ; 22.3, 5, 11, 34 ; **36**:1 ; **38**:4 ; **39**:2, 3bis, 9, [10], 11, [12] ; **40**:{3}, 3, 14, 26, [27], 28, 29 ; **41**:[2], 18 ; **42**:[17], [21], [22], [24], [25], [26] ; **44**:1.[1] ; 4.1 ; **46**:6 ; **47**:2.6, 9, 12 ; **49**:1.2 ; **50E**:2, 3, 4, 5 ; **51**:2bis, [9], 15, 17, 18, 19, 20 ; **52**:3, 4 ; **53**:1, 3, 4 ; **55**:1, 2 ; **56**:1, 2, 3, 5, 7 ; **58**:1bis, 2, 3 ; **59**:1 ; **60**:1, 2 ; **61**:24, 25bis, 26 ; **62**:11, [11], 13 ; **64**:1.4bis, 7 ; 3.1, [2] ; 4.3 ; **65**:1 ; **68**:1, 2, 6 ; **72**:1 ; **75**:1 ; **76**:1 ; **77**:1 ; **78**:1quinquies ; **79**:1 ; **80**:1 ; **81**:1 ; **82**:1 ; **83**: 1 ; **89**:1 ; **90**:1 ; **91B**:2 ; **92A**:1, 2 ; **92C**:1 ; **93A**:1bis ; **93B**:1 ; **94B**:2 ; **99**: 1 ; **100**:1 ; **101**:1 ; **102**:1 ; **105**:1 ; **106**: 1 ; **109**:2 ; **112**:1 ; **113**:1 ; **121**:1 ; **122**: 1 ; **123**:1bis ; **124**:1 ; **126A**:1 ; **129**:1 ; **130**:1 ; **131**:1 ; **133**:1 ; **135**:1 ; **136**:1 ; **138**:1 ; **140**:1 ; **142**:1bis ; **143**:1 ; **144B**: 1 ; **145C**:1 ; **146**:1 ; **148**:1 ; **149**: 4bis ; see also *brḥryn* ; *bry*, **27**:9 ; **62**:12, [12] ; *brk*, **20**:50.1 ; **29B**:5.[4], 10 ; *brh*, **29B**:5.25 ; **61**:26 ; **110**:3 ; *bryh*, **145C**:2 ; *brh* (her son), **97A**:1 ; **97B**:1 ; *bnyn*, **29B**:22.33 ; *bnn*, **41**:8, [10] ; *bny* (cst. pl.), **2**:1.[4] ; **3C**:1, 4 ; **5**:13.9 ; 28.2 ; **13**:8 ; **14**:20.4 ; **19**: 26.4 ; **22**:1.2 ; **23**:1.12 ; 3.[1] ; **26**: [9], [10]bis, 11, [12], 13 ; **28**:2.1 ; **29B**:2.5, 16 ; 5.[4] ; 12.10 ; 19.13, [15] ; 22.33 ; **35C**:1 ; **41**:2, 17 ; **91A**: 1, 2 ; **91B**:2 ; **150**:2 ; *bry* (cst. pl. !), **91B**:3 ; *bny* (my sons), **29B**:12.13, 16ter ; *bnyk*, **42**:13 ; *bnykh*, **27**:[10] ; *bnwhy*, **24**:2 ; *bnyh* (her children), **5**:31.9 ; *bnyn'*, **42**:[15] ; *bnykwn*, **16**: 2.10 ; *bnyhwn*, **3B**:4 ; **3C**:2 ; **16**:2. [8]bis ; **27**:10 ; *bnyhn*, **5**:32.2, 3

br (outside ; field ; except) : *br* (cst.), **2**:4.1 ; **7**:8.4, 7 ; *br'*, **5**:19.[8] ; **7**:4. [9] ; **9**:2 ; **14**:1.3 ; **18**:8bis ; **29B**:22. 23bis, 31 ; **35A**:1.[6] ; **42**:[14]

br' (create) : *br'*, **5:**29.3

bry (exterior) : *bry'*, **8:**1 i [19] ; 1 ii 2 ; *bryt*, **8:**1 i 1 ; *bryt'*, **8:**1 ii [12]

brh (daughter) : *brt*, **40:**4, ‹14› ; **42:**2, [18], [23] ; **51:**12, 16 ; **62:**11 ; **63:**1 ; **74:**1 ; **88:**1 ; **94A:**1 ; **94B:**2 ; **111:**1 ; **119:**1 ; **134A:**1 ; *brth*, **141:**4 ; *brth* (her daughter), **88:**2 ; *bnt*, **5:**17.[6] ; **29B:**20.34 ; *bntk*, **5:**35.8 ; *bnthwn*, **29B:**12.16

brḥryn (free) : *brḥryn*, **5:**32.4

bryḥ (bolt) : *bryḥyn*, **5:**30.[8]

brk (bless) : *bryk*, **29B:**20.12 ; **22:**16bis ; *brk* (pael), **29B:**22.15 ; *brkt* (you blessed), **21:**2.[6] ; *brkt* (I blessed), **29B:**21.2

brkh (blessing) : *brkt*, **5:**14.7

brm (but) : *brm*, **18:**4

brq (lightning) : *brqy'*, **31:**1.7

bśwrh (tidings) : *bśwrt'*, **150:**12

bśm (fragrance, odor) : *bśm'*, **10:**2, 3, [7]

bśr (flesh) : *bśr*, **18:**4 ; *bśr'*, **28:**2.[5] ; *bśrh*, **5:**36.8 ; *bśrhwn*, **7:**4.1

btwlh (maiden) : *btwln*, **29B:**20.6

btr (after) : *btr*, **3A:**2 ; **5:**24.[3] ; 32.7 ; **28:**1.[3] ; **29B:**12.10 ; 21.5 ; 22.27 ; *btry*, **41:**[11] ; **42:**[12] ; *btryk*, **5:**32.[10] ; *btrhwn*, **29B:**22.7 ; see also *b'tr*, *lbtr*

g'h (haughty) : *g'h*, **5:**34.7

g'wh (pride, haughtiness) : *g'wt*, **5:**26.[7], [9]

gb (ridge ; height) : *gbh*, **35A:**1.[3]

gbh (make high, lift) : *ytgbh*, **5:**33.[8]

gbwrh (power) : *gbwrh*, **5:**29.[7] ; **21:**1.14 ; *gbwrt*, **5:**29.5 ; *gbwrty*, **18:**3

gbr (be strong) : *gbrw*, **29B:**20.18 ; *mtgbr*, **18:**[3]

gbr (man) : *gbr*, **2:**1.[4] ; **5:**15.3 ; 23.[7] ; 24.[1], 3 ; 25.[6], 10 ; 28.[2] ; 30.1 ; 34.3 ; 38.7, 8 ; **7:**4.18bis ; **29B:**6.6 ; **40:**6, 19 ; **53:**3 ; *gbryn*, **4B:**1.5 ; **5:**14.2 ; 19.24 ; 22.6 ; **60:**2 ; *gbry'*, **5:**20.[2] ; **29B:**22.23

gbr (giant) : *gbryn*, **14:**9-14-15.5 ; *gbry'*, **17:**2.13, 15, 20, 21 ; 3.3

gbrw (wondrous thing) : *gbrw'*, **17:**2.16

gw (interior, midst) : *gw* (cst.), **4B:**1.4 ; **29B:**2.10 ; **51:**5, 10 ; *gw'* (cst.), **3B:**2 ; **8:**1 i 17, 18 ; 1 ii 2, 4, [6] ; *gw'* (emph.), **6:**2.2 ; **8:**1 i 13 ; 1 ii 4, [15] ; 2.2 ; **64:**3.5, [7] ; *gh* (?), **51:**4bis; *gwh*, **51:**14 ; **69:**2 ; *gwhwn*, **8:**1 ii 9

gwh (pride) : *gwh*, **5:**34.6

gwḥ (gush) : *hngḥwth*, **5:**30.[6]

gwy (interior [adj.]) : *gwyh*, **8:**1 i 18

gwp (bank) : *g'ph*, **5:**35.2

gzr (diviner) : *gzr*, **2:**1.4

gzr (cut) : *gzyryn*, **5:**5.3

gzrh (decree) : *gzrt'*, **150:**4

gṭ (writ of divorce) : *gṭ*, **40:**8, 21 ; *gṭh*, **68:**7

gl' (uncover) : *ygl'*, **5:**27.3

glgl (wheel) : *glgl'*, **6:**14.[2], 3

glh (go into exile) : *gl'*, **68:**5 ; *glw*, **150:**3

glw (exile) : *glwt*, **24:**4 ; *glwt'*, **2:**1.[4] ; **3C:**4

glyd (ice) : *glyd'*, **5:**31.6

gll (roll, wave) : *gllyk*, **5:**30.[9]

gmyq (dowry [perhaps = Gk. γαμικόν]): *gmyq'*, **40:**[8], [21]

gmyr (complete) : *gmryn*, **51:**6

gmyrh (accomplishment ; decision) : *gmyrt*, **31:**7.2

gmr (coal) : *gmryn*, **5:**36.[6]

gn (garden) : *gn*, **64:**3.7 ; *gnt'*, **64:**1.2, 3, 4

gnb (thief) : *gnby*, **127:**1

gnwn (wedding canopy, bridal chamber) : *gnwn*, **29B:**20.6

gnn (enclosure) : *gnny*, **19:**5.1

gs' (spew forth) : *tgs'*, **5:**36.6

gʿr (shout at, rebuke) : *htgʿr*, **29B:**20.28 ; *'tgʿrt*, **29B:**20.29

gʿrh (cry) : *gʿrh*, **18:**[8]

grm (bone) : *grmy*, **5:**16.7 ; **67:**2 ; *grmwhy*, **5:**5.5

gšm (body) : *gšmhwn*, **4B:**[12]

d- (who, which, what ; of ; that) : *d-* (used as rel. pron.), **15:**3 ; **21:**1.16bis ; **29B:**20.7 ; **46:**4 ; **53:**3 ; **55:**2 ; **64:**1.3 ; 3.2 ; **68:**7 ; **69:**2 ; **150:**12 ;

d- (used as determinative pron.), **21**:2.7 ; **23**:2.[6] ; **29B**:21.29 ; 22.14, 21 ; **37**:1.3 ; **65**:[1] ; **150**:1, 12 ; *d-* (used as a conjunction), **18**:5 ; **23**: 3.2 ; **29B**:2.25 ; 20.10 ; 22.22 ; **55**:2 ; see also *dlm'*

d' (this [fem.]) : *d'*, **5**:3.[5] ; 23.9 ; 29.5 ; **29B**:2.6 ; 19.10, 19 ; 20.28 ; 21.4, 10, 11, 12 ; 22.25 ; **61**:25 ; *dh*, **3D**:2 ; **39**:7 ; **40**:5 ; **69**:1 ; **141**:1

dbḥ (sacrifice) : *dbḥyn*, **3C**:[2]

dbq (cling to ; touch, reach) : *dbq*, **5**: 14.[4] ; **21**:2.17 ; **29B**:16.11 ; 17.8, 9, 10, 16 ; 21.6 ; 22.7 ; *dbqt*, **29B**:19.9, [11] ; 21.1, 16, 17bis, 18bis ; *dbqth*, **29B**:19.8 ; *dbqw*, **29B**:21.29 ; 22.10 ; *ydbqn*, **5**:36.2 ; *dbqyn*, **5**:36.8

dbr (lead) : *dbr*, **29B**:21.27 ; *dbrh'*, **29B**:20.9 ; *dbrt*, **29B**:6.2 ; *dbrw*, **29B**: 20.[30] ; *tdbrwn*, **58**:2 ; *tdbrnh*, **5**: 35.7 ; *dbrh* (impv. with suff.), **29B**: 20.27 ; *mdbr*, **13**:8 ; *dbyrt*, **29B**:20. 11, 14

dbrt (account, sake) : *dbrt*, **5**:34.4 ; *dbrtk*, **5**:1.[7]

dgwg (boat) : *dgwgyn*, **5**:35.[10]

dgl (detachment) : *dglyhwn*, **32A**:2

dd (uncle) : *ddy*, **29B**:20.22 ; **64**:1.7bis, 8 ; 2.3 ; 3.[2]

dh : see *d'*

dhb (gold) : *dhb*, **5**:38.8 ; **29B**:20.[31], 33 ; *dhb'*, **2**:1.7

dwḥ (wash) : *y'dyḥw*, **15**:1

dwq (grind) : *mdqyn*, 10:7 ; see also *dqq*

dwr (dwell) : *dyry*, **5**:2.[3]

dḥ' (repel) : *dḥ'* (impv.), **21**:1.13

dḥl (fear) : *dḥlt*, **29B**:19.[23] ; *dḥlw*, **17**:2.20 ; *tdḥl*, **29B**:22.30 ; *'dḥl*, **29B**: 19.[18] ; *dḥyl*, **23**:1.[13] ; **29B**:2.26

dḥlh (fear [noun]) : *dḥlh*, **5**:33.2, 3

dḥšt (desert [Pers.]) : *dḥšt*, **5**:15.[7] ; 32.5

dy (who, which, what ; of ; that) : *dy* (used as rel. pron.), **2**:1.1, 8 ; **5**:2.8 ; 3.[5] ; 7.1 ; 14.[7] ; 15.3, [4], 8 ; 21.4 ; 25.1 ; 26.5bis, 6 ; 28.1, 4 ; 29.3, 7 ; 31.[1], 4 ; 32.5 ; 34.4 ; 38.4, 6 ; **6**:15.3 ; **7**:3.3 ; 4.11, 13, 14, 16, 17, 19 ; **8**:1 i [3], [4], 4, [5], [13], [18] ; 1 ii 5 ; 2.2 ; 9.2 ; 16.[2] ; **9**:5 ; **10**:2, 4, [5] ; **14**:9-14-15.5 ; 21.2 ; **16**:2.11, 13, [13] ; **17**:2.22 ; 3.11 ; **18**:10 ; **19**:1.5 ; 2.2 ; **20**:1.1 ; 7.2 ; 10.1 ; 25.2 ; 55.2 ; 56.1 ; **23**:1.11 ; **24**:[1], 2, 3 ; **28**:1.4bis ; 2.1, 13 ; **29A**:4.2 ; **29B**:1.2, 3 ; 2.24 ; 5.27 ; 7.1 ; 12.17 ; 16.11 ; 17.9bis, 16 ; 19. 9, 11, 12, 20, [20], 26bis ; 20.6, 25, 30, 32 ; 21.1bis, 3, 8, 9, 10, 12, 13, 15, 17bis, 18ter, 19, 23, 26, 28, 29bis, [29], 30, 32 ; 22.1, 2bis, 10bis, 11, 12, 15, 17, 19ter, 23ter, 25, 29bis, 30, 33, 34 ; **30**:4 ; **31**:7.3 ; **35A**:1.2 ; **35B**:2.2 ; **39**:5, 8 ; **40**:5, 7, 10, 16, 19, [24] ; **41**:11 ; **42**:[5], [10], 13, [13]bis, [15], 17, 18, 19 ; **44**:1.[3]bis, [6]bis, 7 ; 13.2 ; **45**:1.[3], [5], [6]bis, 8 ; **46**:5 ; **47**:1-2 i [2], 2 ; 1-2 ii 10 ; **50D**:[2] ; **51**:4bis, 6, 7, [8] ; **52**:4, 6bis, 7, 9, 10, 11bis ; **53**:4 ; **54**:1 ; **60**:1 ; **61**:24 ; **62**:13, [13] ; **64**:1.5bis, 8, 10, 12 ; 2.1ter, 2 ; 3.2, 3, 5 ; 3.4 ; **68**:4 ; **69**:1 ; **88**:2 ; **89**:1 ; **150**:1quinquies, 2quater, 5, 6, 9bis, 11ter, 12bis ; *dy* (used as a determinative pron.), **2**:1.[1] ; **4B**:1.[1], 6 : **5**:35.10 ; 38.2, 8 ; **7**:4.18 ; **8**:1 i [8], 9bis, [16] ; 1 ii 4, 9 ; **10**:2 ; **14**:1.[1] ; **16**:2.3, 7, [8] ; **18**:8 ; **23**:1.10 ; **28**:1.1 ; **29B**:19. 24 ; 20.31 ; 21.7, 8, 16, 25, 28, [32], [33], 33bis ; 22.1, ‹4›, 17, 18, 22bis, 28 ; **33**:8.2 ; **35C**:1 ; **42**:15, [15] ; **51**: ‹8› ; **62**:[12] ; **141**:3 ; *dy* (used as a conjunction), **2**:1.8 ; **4A**:1 ii 6 ; **4B**: 13 ; **5**:35.2 ; 37.3 ; **16**:2.[6] ; **17**:2.23 ; **27**:12 ; **29B**:2.1, 12, 15, 25 ; 19.10, 19, 20, 23 ; 20.8, 13, 14, 15, 21, 27 ; 21.3bis, 7 ; 22.3bis, 12 ; **36**:1 ; **40**:5, 17 ; **53**:2 ; **56**:4 ; **57**:2 ; **58**:2 ; **59**:3 ; **60**:2 ; **64**:1.‹5›, 7, 8, 9 ; **150**:12 ; see also *bdy*, *bdyl*, *dyl*, *dy lmh* (under *dlm'*), *zy*, *kdy*

dyl- (= possessive pronoun) : *dy l-* (written as two words), **41**:11 ; **42**: [15] ; **47**:1-2 i [2] ; *dyly*, **51**:3, 10 ; *dylh*, **29B**:21.6 ; *dylh'*, **29B**:20.10

dymwsn' (tax-collector, revenue farmer [= Gk. δημωσιώνης]): *dymwsn'y*, **150**:3

dyn (to judge) : *ydyn*, **5**:28.8 ; *d'nyn*, **23**:1.10 ; *mdyn*, **5**:5.4

dyn (a judge) : *dyn*, **64**:2.8

dyn (justice) : *dyn*, **5**:18.6 ; **6**:17.2 ; **21**:2.9 ; **29B**:20.13, 14 ; **41**:3 ; *dyn'*, **5**:24.[7] ; **150**:10 ; *dynh*, **5**:34.4 ; *dyny*, **18**:5 ; *dynn'*, **150**:5

dynr (denar [= Lat. *denarius*]) : *dynryn*, **62**:12

dk (that): *dk*, **42**:14 ; **44**:1.[4], [7]bis ; **45**:1.[4], [5], [8] ; **47**:2.8 ; **50B**:[1] ; **50C**:1 ; **51**:5, 7, 8, 11, 13 ; **52**:3, 5, 7, 9, 12 ; see also *zk*

dk (hall) : *dk'*, **8**:1 ii 10

dky (clean, pure) : *dkyt'*, **7**:4.[8], [14]

dkn (platform) : *dwkny'*, **8**:1 ii [13]

dkr (ram) : *dkryn*, **14**:1.[1]

dkr (remember) : *dkr* (impv.), **5**:28.[1] ; **29B**:2.9, [13]

dkrn (memorial) : *dkrn'*, **9**:[1]

dlm' (lest) : *dlm'*, **29B**:22.22 ; *dy lmh* (written as two words), **5**:21.4

dlq (kindle) : *tdlq*, **5**:36.3 ; **17**:2.10

dm (blood) : *dm*, **29B**:11.17

dm' (be like) : *dmyn'*, **5**:1.6 ; *dm'* (peal ptc.), **2**:4.4 ; **4B**:1.[6] ; **10**:[3], 6

dmyn (price) : *dmyn*, **50A**:2 ; **50E**:3 ; **51**:6 ; **52**:8 ; *dmy*, **64**:1.5

dmk (sleep, rest) : *tdmwk*, **20**:3.[2]

dmʿ (tear ; sap) : *dmʿ'*, **10**:[5] ; *dmʿy*, **29B**:20.12

dn (this) : *dn*, **5**:5.[4], 5 ; **7**:5-6.4, [5] ; **8**:1 i 19 ; 1 ii 2 ; **17**:2.16 ; **19**:2.3 ; **23**:2.2bis ; **28**:1.3bis ; **29B**:2.15bis, [15] ; 16.12 ; 17.10bis ; 19.12, 18bis, [19], 21 ; 20.7, 12, 15, 16, 19, 26 ; 21.5, 16 ; 22.21, 34 ; **46**:[6] ; see also *kdn*

dn' (this) : *dn'*, **29B**:2.2 ; **40**:17 ; *dnh*, **3F**:2, [5] ; **4B**:15 ; **7**:3.[3] ; **39**:6 ; **40**:2, 13 ; **44**:17.[1] ; **45**:1.[2], [7] ; **47**:2.[10] ; **50D**:1 ; **51**:3bis, 11bis, 12, ‹13›, 14 ; **52**:4, 10 ; **64**:1.6, 7, 8, 9ter ; 2.1 ; 3.2 ; **67**:1 ; **150**:12 ; see also *znh*

dnḥ (shine) : *dnḥ*, **5**:19.1 ; *dnḥyn*, **13**:7 ; *hdnḥ*, **5**:10.[4]

dqq (grind) : *mdqq*, **12**:3 ; see also *dwq*

drg (stair, step) : *drg*, **8**:1 ii [2] ; *drg'*, **8**:1 i [13] ; 1 ii 4, 5 ; *drgy'*, **8**:1 i [14] ; **51**:7

drh (courtyard) : *drt'*, **44**:6.2 ; **150**:9 ; *drth*, **51**:5, 9, 10 ; *drty*, **51**:4

drwm (south) : *drwm*, **11**:3 ; *drwm'*, **8**:1 i [4] ; **11**:4 ; **29B**:19.9 ; 21.9, 18 ; **44**:9-10.2 ; **52**:4 ; *drm'*, **51**:9

drk (tread) : *hdrkh*, **5**:12.[4]

drʿ (arm) : *drʿ*, **5**:34.5 ; *drʿy*, **18**:3 ; *drʿyh'*, **29B**:20.4

dš (door) : *dšyn*, **5**:30.6, [8] ; **8**:1 i 9, [11], 19 ; *dšy'*, **8**:1 i [9], [11], [17]

dt' (green grass) : *dt'h*, **5**:31.5

h- (interrogative particle) : *h-*, **5**:1.2(?), [3], 7 ; 3.[5] ; 5.3 ; 6.[4] ; 9.5, 10 ; 24.6, 10 ; 29.[6], [7], [8] ; 30.6, 9 ; 31.5 ; 32.8bis, 9, [10] ; 33.1, 7 ; 34.3 ; 35.4, 5, 6, 7 ; **23**:2.2 ; **29B**:2.6

h' (look! behold!) : *h'*, **5**:11.[2] ; 13.[9] ; 23.7 ; 28.3 ; 34.5 ; **8**:1 i [18] ; **17**:2.16 ; **22**:2.[4] ; **23**:1.10, 14 ; **29A**:1 i 4 ; **29B**:2.1 ; 19.[14] ; 20.27, 30 ; 22.27

h'ḥ (aha!) : *h'ḥ*, **5**:33.5

hbl (emptiness, vanity) : *hbl'*, **5**:26.[8]

hdbr (counselor) : *hdbry*, **4B**:9

hdm (piece) : *hdmyn*, **4B**:14

hds (myrtle) : *hdsyn*, **60**:4

hdr (honor, glory) : *hdr*, **2**:1.[5] ; **5**:34.6

hw (that) : *hw*, **29B**:20.29 ; **64**:1.2, 3, 4, 5ter, 8, 10, 11bis, [11] ; 2.3 ; 3.3, 4, 6

hw' (he) : *hw'*, **2**:1.4 ; **5**:5.4 ; 13.4, [4] ; 18.[3], 4, [4] ; 24.[7] ; 28.3 ; 29.2, 8 ; 37.2 ; **10**:[3], 6 ; **20**:55.2 ; **23**:2.2, 4, 5 ; **28**:1.10 ; **29A**:1 i 1 ; **29B**:2.20 ; 19.7, [11], 20 ; 20.3, 10 ; 21.24 ; 22.14, 15 ; **52**:4

hw' (be) : *hw'*, **2**:1.[1] ; **5**:15.6, 7 ; 20.4 ; 38.4 ; **29B**:19.10, [10] ; 20.17, 20 ; 21.6 ; 22.1, 2, 7, 9, 15 ; *hwh*, **16**:2.9 ; **17**:2.[15] ; **19**:1.4 ; **20**:57.2 ; **49**:1.3, 4, [7] ; **64**:1.9 ; 2.2 ; **150**:12 ; *hww'* (3d sg. masc.), **29B**:22.8 ; *hw't*, **29B**:

20.17, 27 ; 22.25 ; *hwt*, **7**:4.[14] ; **9:** 5 ; *hwyt*, **2**:1.[7] ; **5**:30.2 ; **89**:3 ; *hwyt* (2d sg. fem.), **40**:5, 16 ; *hwyt* (I was), **2**:1.3, 6, [8] ; **5**:14.8 ; 15.2 ; **7**:4.15, 17 ; **14**:3.2 ; **18**:[3], [5] ; **19**:2.2 ; **21**:2.[17] ; **29B**:19.9 ; 20.10, [34] ; 21.17bis ; **49**:1.5, 8 ; 2.2 ; *hww*, **3C**: [2] ; **20**:22.2 ; 55.1 ; *hww'*, **29B**:19. 24, 26, 28 ; 22.9 ; *yhw'*, **20**:11.1 ; 59:3 ; *lhw'*, **3B**:[3] ; **5**:29.4 ; **16**:2.6 ; **41**:6 ; *lhwh*, **3F**:3 ; **28**:1.4 ; *lhwy*, **40**:7 ; *thw'*, **20**:1.[2] ; **28**:1.9 ; *thwh* (you [masc.] are), **29B**:22.22 ; *thw'* (you [fem.] are), **41**:3 ; *thwh*, **42**:[7], [14] ; *'hw'*, **5**:37.8 ; **14**:29.1 ; **29B**:22. 30 ; *yhwn*, **42**:[10] ; *lhywn*, **7**:8.5 ; *lhwwn*, **26**:10bis, [11] ; **28**:1.[7], 11 ; 2.[7] ; **41**:[8] ; *yhwn* (they [fem.] are), **42**:[11]bis ; *lhwyn*, **20**:1.1 ; 9.[2] ; 10. 1 ; *nhwh*, **29B**:19.[20] ; *hw'* (masc. impv.), **55**:5 ; **60**:5 ; *hwh*, **89**:1 ; *hww*, **58**:3 ; *mhw'*, **5**:15.5 ; **21**:1.18

hwk (go) : *thk* (3d sg. fem.), **28**:1.8 ; *thk* (you go), **41**:7, [12] ; *'hk*, **29B**: 22.33 ; **41**:[9] ; **42**:14 ; *yhkwn*, **26**: [13], 14 ; **28**:2.14 ; *yhkn*, **5**:28.5 ; *mhk*, **40**:6, [18]

hwr'h (law) : *hwr'h*, **41**:8

hy' (she ; that) : *hy'*, **3D**:4 ; **24**:3 ; **29B**:2.[1] ; 20.27bis ; 22.13 ; **44**:1. [3] ; **64**:1.2, [3]

hyh (be [Hebraized form]) : *yhy*, **40**: 9, [23] ; *lhy*, **40**:20 ; *mhy*, **40**:6, 18

hyk (how) : *hyk*, **5**:7.6 ; **20**:3.[2]bis ; *hyk'*, **5**:31.2

hykl (temple) : *hykl'*, **7**:4.3, [9] ; **9**:2 ; **150**:11 ; *hklh*, **85A**:1 ; **85B**:2

hk (surely) : *hk*, **5**:22.2

hlk (go, walk) : *hlkt*, **5**:17.4 ; *hlk* (pael impv.), **29B**:21.13 ; for forms in *-hk*, see *hwk*

hll (praise) : *hllt* (I praised), **5**:19.[3] ; **29B**:21.2

hmwn (they, them) : *hmwn*, **2**:1.[8] ; 4.1 ; **5**:25.2 ; 28.[2] ; **34**:[9] ; **50D**:2 ; **51**:6 ; **52**:7

hn (if, whether) : *hn*, **4A**:1 ii 6 ; **5**:8. [1] ; 10.9, 10 ; 11.4, [7] ; 18.5, 8 ; 19.[7] ; 22.1, [4] ; 23.[10] ; 26.[1], 9 ; 27.4, 5, [6] ; 29.3, 4ter ; 30.2, 3 ; **19**:1.6 ; **29B**:2.5 ; 20.19 ; **39**:7 ; **41**: [7], 9 ; **42**:[9], 10, [12], [14] ; see also *lhn*

hn (adverbial) : *hn*, **5**:28.6

hnh (use, profit from) : *mthnh*, **69**:1

hnn (they, them [fem.]) : *hnn*, **42**:[11]

h'kn (snake) : *h'kn*, **23**:1.14 ; but see *ḥ'kyn*!

hpk (turn) : *'thpkw*, **5**:2.[3]

hr (mount, mountain) : *hr*, **150**:9

hrh (be pregnant) : *hrythwn*, **5**:4.9

hrynh (conception) : *hry'nt'*, **29B**:2.1 ; *hrywn'* (Hebraized form), **29B**:2.15

w- (and) : *w-*, **2**:1.3, [3], 4bis, [4], 5bis, [5], [6], 7, [8] ; **3A**:8 ; **3B**:2bis, 3, 4 ; **3C**:[2], 2bis, 3, 5 ; **3D**:2, 3 ; **3F**:3, 4, 10 ; **4A**:5, 7, 8 ; **4B**:3, 4, 7, 9bis, 10, 11bis, 12bis, 13, 14 ; **5**:1.[1]bis, 1, [4], [6] ; 2.[1], 1, 2, [2], 3, 5 ; 3.[3], 4, [8] ; 4.5, 6 ; 5.1, [3], [4] ; 6.7 ; 7.4, 5bis ; 8.[1], 5bis, 7 ; 9.[1], 2, [4], 4, 7, 8, [9], [10] ; 10.2, 3, 8 ; 11.1, 5, 6, [8], 10 ; 12.2 ; 13.[1], 9, 10 ; 14.[2], 2, [3], 3, 5, 9, [10] ; 15.1, 2, 3, [4], 6, [7], [9] ; 16.1, 4bis, 5, [6], 7 ; 17.3 ; 18.4, [6] ; 19.1, 2, [3], 5, 6 ; 20.[1], 8 ; 21.3, [3], 5, 6, 7bis, 8, [9] ; 22.2, 3bis, 5 ; 23.1, 2, 3, [3], [4], 4, 5bis, [9] ; 24.1, 5, 7, 8, [8], 9 ; 25.1, 2, 3, 4, [5]bis, 9, 10 ; 26. 1, 3, 4, 5, [6], 7, [8] ; 27.[1], 2, 3, [3], 4, 5bis, 6, [6], 7, [7], 9 ; 28.[2], 2, 3, 4, 5bis, 7 ; 29.1, 2bis, 4bis, 5, [6] ; 30.[1], 1, 5, 7bis, 8ter, [8], 9 ; 31.1, 2, 3, 4, 5, 6bis, 7 ; 32.1, [1], 2bis, 3ter, 4, 5, 6, 7, [7], 9, 10 ; 33. 2quater, 3bis, 4, 5quater, 6bis, 7, 9bis ; 34.2bis, 3, 4, 6quater, 7ter, 8bis ; 35.5, 7, [8], 8, 9, [10] ; 36.2, 3, 6bis, 7, 9bis ; 37.2, 3, 4bis, 5ter, 6, 7bis, 8bis, 9 ; 38.2bis, 3, 4bis, 5ter, 6, 7, 8 ; **6**:2.2 ; 16.2 ; **7**:1.1, 2, 3, 4 ; 3.2 ; 4.[3], 5, [6], [7], 9, 10, [10], 11, 13, 16, 18 ; 5-6.2, [4], 5, 6 ; 7. [1], 1, 2 ; 8.5, 6, [6], 7, 8 ; **8**:1 i [1],

1bis, [2], 2bis, [3], 3, [4]bis, 4, 5bis, [5], 6quater, 7, [8], 9, [10]bis, 11ter, [12], 12bis, [13]bis, 14, [14], [15]bis, [16]bis, [17], 17bis, 18bis, [18], 19 bis ; 1 ii 1bis, [1], 2, [3], 3bis, 4bis, [4], 5bis, [5], 6bis, [7]ter, 8, [8]bis, 9bis, [10]bis, 11bis, [11], 12bis, [12], [13]bis, 13, 14, [15]ter, 15 ; 2.3 ; 3. [3] ; 6.1 ; 8.1 ; 10.2 ; 11.1 ; **9:**3, 4 ; **10:**1, [2]bis, [3], 3, [4], 4, [5]bis, [6], 6, [8] ; **11:**4 ; **12:**[3], 5ter, [5], 6, 7bis, 8 ; **13:**[6], 6ter, [7], 7, [8], 8, [9]ter, 9 ; **14:**1.[3] ; 3.3 ; 9-14-15.2, 4 ; 17.1, 3 ; **16:**1.2, 3 ; 2.[4], 5bis, 7bis, [8], 8, 9, [9], 10bis, [10]bis, 13ter, 14, 15 ; **17:**2.4bis, 5, 10, 14, 15, [21]bis, 21ter, 22bis, [23]bis, 23 ; 3.4, 5, 6ter, 7, 8 ; **18:**3bis, 4, 6bis, 8, 9 ; **19:**1.2, 3 ; 2.[1], 3 ; 4.2, 4 ; 26.3 ; **20:**3.[1] octies, 2, [2]ter ; 6.1 ; 8.1bis, 2 ; **21:**1.7, [8], 9bis, [10]bis, 13, 14bis, 16, 18 ; 2.12, 14, 16, [16], [17]bis ; **22:**1.1bis ; 2.2bis, 3, 4bis, 5, [6] ; 3.2 ; **23:**1.10bis, 11, [11]bis, 12bis, [12], [13]bis, 13, [14], 14ter, [15] ; 2.2, 3bis, [4], 4bis, 5bis, 6, [6] ; 3. [1]ter, 1, [2]bis ; **24:**2, 3bis, 4bis ; **25:**1.2, [3]bis ; 2.2 ; **26:**[9], [10], 11 bis, 12ter, [13], 13, 14bis ; **27:**9, 10bis, 11bis ; **28:**1.[2], 3, 6, 7quater, [8], 8bis, [9], 9, 10 ; 2.7, 12, 13bis, 16, 17, 18 ; **29A:**1 i 1bis, 3bis, 4 ; 1 ii 8 ; 2.2 ; 3.2 ; **29B:**1.1, 3 ; 2.1bis, 2, 3bis, 6, 7, 8, 9bis, 10bis, 11, 12, 13ter, 15bis, 16ter, 17bis, 19, 20ter, 21bis, 23bis, 24bis, 25 ; 5.9bis, 24, 25, 26 ; 6.2 ; 7.1, 7 ; 12.11, 13ter, 15, 16quinquies ; 17.11, 16 ; 19.7ter, 8, 9ter, 10ter, 11, 12, 13, 14quater, 15quater, 16ter, 17ter, 18quater, 19ter, 20bis, 21bis, 22bis, 23, 24bis, 25quater, 26, 27 ; 20.2bis, 3ter, 4bis, 5ter, 6quater, 7ter, 8bis, 9quinquies, 10ter, 11, 12quater, 13ter, 14, 15ter, 16bis, 17quinquies, 18quater, 19bis, 20ter, 21ter, 22ter, 23quinquies, 24 bis, 25, 26quinquies, 27ter, 28ter, 29quater, 30ter, 31quinquies, 32ter, 33quinquies, 34ter ; 21.1, 2quinquies, 3quater, 5ter, 6quater, 7ter, 8bis, 9quinquies, 10ter, 11quater, 12ter, 13ter, 14ter, 15quater, 16bis, 17bis, 18, 19quinquies, 20quinquies, 21quinquies, 22, 24ter, 25ter, 26ter, 27bis, 28quater, 29ter, 30bis, 31 sexies, 32quater, 33bis, 34 ; 22.1bis, 2, 3quater, 4quinquies, 5ter, 6ter, 7quater, 8bis, 9ter, 10, 11quinquies, 12, 13quater, 14bis, 15quater, 16ter, 17bis, 18, 19, 21, 23, 24bis, 25bis, 26, 27, 28bis, 29ter, 30bis, 31quater, 32ter, 33bis, 34 ; **30:**1bis, [1], 2, 3, 4 ; **31:**1.1, 2, 3, 4, 5, 7 ; 3.[2] ; 5.3, 4bis, [5] ; **32A:**4 ; **32C:**1 ; **32E:**1 ; **32I:**3.1bis ; **33:**1.2, 3 ; 7.1 ; 8:2 ; **35B:**2.3 ; **35D:**1.2 ; **35E:**2, 3 ; **39:**[4], 6, 7bis, 8 ; **40:**2, 6, 7, 8bis, 9, 10bis, 13, 21, 22, [22], 23bis ; **41:**[4], 4, [6], 8, 10bis, 12, 13 ; **42:**6, 10bis, 11bis, [12], 13, [13], 14, 15, [16], 17, 18, 19 ; **44:**1.[3]bis, 3, 5, [6]bis, 6, [7]bis, 7 ; 23.2 ; **45:**[2], 2, [3]bis, 4bis, [4], [5], 5, 6bis, [6]bis ; **46:**[3], 3, 4, 5 ; **47:**1.2 ; 2.4, 6bis, 9, 10, [10] ; **48:**2, 3, 4ter ; **49:**9, 10bis ; **50D:**3 ; **50E:**1 ; **51:**5, 6, 7, 8, 9bis, 10bis, 11bis, <11>, 12bis, 13quater, 14 ; **52:**2bis, [3], 4, 6quater, 7, 8bis, 9bis, 10quater, 11ter, 12bis ; **53:**1bis, 2, 3 ; **54:**1bis, [2] ; **55:**3 ; **56:**3 ; **57:**1, 2 ; **58:**1, 2bis ; **59:**2ter ; **60:**2, 3ter, 4quater ; **61:**25 ; **62:**[12], 12, 13 ; **64:**1.2bis, [3], 4, 5ter, 7ter, 8ter, [8], 9, 10ter, 11ter, [11], 12, 13 ; 2.1ter, 2, 3, 4ter, 5bis, 8ter ; 3.2, 4, 5ter, 6 ; 4.1, 2 ; **67:**4 ; **68:**5bis, 6 ; **70:**4 ; **71:**2 ; **91A:**1 ; **91B:**1bis ; **95B:**1 ; **97A:**1 ; **97B:**4 ; **139:**1 ; **141:**4 ; **149:**3 ; **150:**1ter, 2quater, 3quater, 4bis, 6 bis, 8ter, 9bis, 10, 11ter, 12sexies

wt : see *kwt*, *lwt*

zbd (present a gift) : *zbdtwn*, **32D:**2

zbn (buy [peal]; sell [pael]) : *zbn*, **29B:**21.6 ; *zbnt*, **68:**7 ; *zbynt*, **39:**5 ; *mzbnh* (peal inf., but means " sell ") **52:** 9 ;

zbnh (the buyer), **51:8** ; *zbny'*, **52:9** ; *zbnyh*, **45:1.8** ; *zbnt* (pael), **43:5** ; **51:** 3, 5 ; **52:7** ; *zbnh* (inf.), **52:3** ; *mzbnh* (ptc.), **44:1.6** ; **52:11** ; *mzbnth*, **45:1.** [3] ; *mzbnyn*, **46:2**
zbn (purchase ; sale) : *zbn* (cst.), **51:7**, [11], 13 ; *zbn'*, **44:1.[7]** ; **50D:1** ; *zbnh*, **45:1.[4]** ; **52:12**
zhr (warn) : *tzdhrwn*, **27:12**
zhr (shine) : *mzhr* (inf.), **5:30.4**
zwz (zuz) : *zwzyn*, **39:4** ; **41:5** ; **48:[2]**, 3, 4 ; **51:6** ; **52:7** ; *zzyn*, **36:2** ; *zwzy'*, **5:11.7**
zwy (corner) : *zwyt'*, **8:1** ii [6], [7]
zwn (nourish) : *mtznh*, **41:10** ; **42:15** ; *mtznn*, **42:11**
zw' (tremble) : *yzw'*, **5:33.4** ; *yzy'*, **5:** 10.[2] ; *htzy'nh*, **5:33.1**
zy (who, which, what ; that) : *zy* (used as rel. pron.), **48:3** ; **49:1.6**, 7, 9 ; **89:3** ; *zy* (used as conjunction), **49:** 1.4, 5bis
zyb (ooze) : *yzyb*, **5:35.3**
zyw (splendor) : *zwy*, **5:34.6**
zyn (arms) : *zyn*, **5:33.6**
zyq (chain) : *zyqyn*, **5:27.[2]** ; 36.6 ; *zyqy*, **5:28.5**
zk (that) : *zk*, **48:2**, 3bis ; see also *dk*
zky (be innocent) : *zkyt*, **5:26.[1]** ; *tzk'*, **5:34.4** ; *zky*, **5:9.8** ; 20.[4] ; 22.[3]
zmn (ring) : *zmn*, **5:35.5**
zmn (invite ; join) : *'zdmnw*, **29B:21.25**
zmn (time) : *zmn* (abs.), **5:23.8** ; 31.3 ; **40:[10]**, 23 ; **42:[19]** ; **45:1.[6]** ; **46:5** ; *zmn* (cst.), **150:5** ; *zmn'*, **29B:19.[9]** ; **39:[5]** ; *zmnyn*, **20:3.[1]**ter, 2, [2]bis
znh (this) : *znh*, **49:1.3**, 5bis, 6, [7], [8], [10]
znw (fornication) : *znw*, **20:30.2** ; *znwt'*, **21:1.13** ; *znwtkwn*, **16:2.9**
z'q (call out) : *z'qh* (3 sg. m. pf. peal with suffix), **17:3.6** ; *z'qt*, **5:17.5** ; *yz'qwn*, **5:26.[3]**, 7 ; 30.[5] ; *mz'q* (pael ptc.), **16:2.[10]** ; *mz'qh*, **16:2.[9]**
z'qh (cry) : *z'qt* (cst.), **5:25.[4]** ; 33.6
z'r (young) : *z'ryn*, **5:15.4**
z'yr (small) : *z'yr'*, **150:2** ; *zw'yrn*, **28:1.3**
zqynh (old age) : *zqynh*, **28:1.7**
zqp (erect) : *zqpyn*, **32C:2**
zr (stranger) : *zr*, **29B:2.16**
zrḥ (rise) : *zrḥyn*, **13:7**
zr' (seed, descendants) : *zr'* (abs.), **21:2.7** ; **52:2** ; *zr'* (cst.), **5:20.7** ; **20:** 28.1 ; *zr''*, **29B:2.15** ; *zr'k* (your seed), **29B:21.10**, 12, 13bis, 14 ; **30:1** ; *zr'hwn*, **5:4.[6]**

ḥ'k (laugh) : *ḥ'kw*, **5:15.[4]** ; *yḥ'k*, **5:** 32.6 ; 33.3 ; *tḥ'k*, **5:35.7** ; *'ḥ'k*, **5:15.** 1 ; *yḥ'kwn*, **5:7.5** ; *mḥ'k* (inf.), **32F:1**
ḥbl (harm) : *ḥbltwn*, **16:2.11** ; *ḥbl'* (pael inf.), **5:24.5**
ḥbl (harm) : *ḥbl'*, **5:23.[1]** ; **16:2.11**
ḥbl (tie) : *mḥbl* (pael ptc.), **16:2.[14]**
ḥbl (rope) : *ḥbl*, **5:35.4** ; *ḥbly* (cst. pl.), **5:27.2**
ḥbl (alas) : *ḥbl*, **37:1.2** ; **141:4**
ḥbl (travail) : *ḥbl*, **5:32.[1]**
ḥbl (fetus ?) : *ḥblyhn*, **5:32.3**
ḥbr (dark fog) : *ḥbry'*, **31:1.4**
ḥbr (associate) : *mtḥbr*, **5:24.1**
ḥbr (companion) : *ḥbry*, **61:25** ; *ḥbrwhy*, **16:1.[1]** ; 2.[5] ; **29B:20.8** ; 21.26, 28 ; 22.17
ḥbrh (neighbor) : *ḥbrth*, **5:36.3**
ḥg (feast) : *ḥg'*, **150:1**
ḥgyr (lame) : *ḥgyr*, **5:14.10**
ḥd (one) : *ḥd*, **5:18.[8]** ; 38.4, 8 ; **6:3.2** ; **7:1.[1]** ; 3.1 ; 4.18, [20] ; **8:1** i 5, [9], 11, 12bis, [19] ; 1 ii [10] ; **13:8**bis, [9] ; **21:2.18** ; **22:2.2** ; **23:1.[13]** ; **29B:** 10.12 ; 12.15 ; 19.11, 14 ; 20.8; 22.1 ; 22.33 ; **52:8** ; **150:9** ; *ḥd'*, **5:22.8** ; 36.2 ; **7:4.15** ; **5-6.2** ; **29B:19.15**, [16] ; 22.28 ; **62:12** ; *ḥdh*, **5:37.5** ; 38.7 ; **8:1** i [2], 6, [10], [12], [16] ; 1 ii 3, [6], [7], [11], [15] ; **41:1** ; **43:1**, 3 ; see also *bḥd'*, *kḥd'*, *lḥd'*
ḥdw (joy) : *ḥdwt'*, **26:[13]**
ḥdy (rejoice) : *ḥdyt* (I rejoiced), **29B:** 7.7 ; *yḥd'*, **5:33.2** ; *yḥdh*, **5:33.7**
ḥdy (breast) : *ḥdwhy*, **28:2.18** ; *ḥdyh*, **29B:20.14**
ḥdyd (sharp experience) : *ḥdydy*, **5:22.9**
ḥwb (be guilty) : *ḥybn'*, **5:21.5** ; *tḥybnny*, **5:34.4**

ḥwb (guilt) : *ḥwbth*, **28**:2.17
ḥwd : see *blḥwdy*
ḥwh (inform) : *ḥwyh* (told him), **29B**: 22.3 ; *ḥwyt*, **29B**:2.[19] ; 19.[19] ; *yḥwynk*, **17**:2.[23] ; *tḥwynny*, **29B**: 2.5, 6 ; *nḥwh*, **4A**:5 ; *ḥwy'* (inf.), **17**: 2.13 ; *mḥwh*, **29B**:5.9 ; *mḥwyn*, **29B**: 2.21 ; *hḥwy* (haphel), **2**:1.5 ; *yḥw'*, **5**:27.3 ; *'ḥw'* (I shall make known), **5**:21.[9] ; *'ḥwynk*, **29B**:2.[10] ; *'ḥwy*, **19**:1.[3] ; **24**:2 ; *hḥwyny*, **5**:30.2
ḥwh (beast) : *ḥwh*, **14**:1.3 ; *ḥwt*, **14**:1. [2] ; **35A**:1.6
ḥwṭ (thread) : *ḥwṭ*, **29B**:22.21 ; *ḥwṭ'*, **5**:30.3 ; 35.8
ḥwlq (portion) : *ḥwlq*, **29B**:22.23 ; *ḥwlq'*, **29B**:17.10 ; *ḥwlqy'*, **29B**:17.11 ; *ḥwlqhwn*, **29B**:22.24
ḥwr (white) : *ḥwr*, **7**:8.[3] ; **8**:1 i 6
ḥwry (Hurrian) : *ḥwry'*, **29B**:21.29
ḥzh (see) : *ḥzh* (he saw), **17**:3.[6] ; *ḥzny*, **29B**:20.[22] ; *ḥzh'*, **29B**:20.9 ; *ḥzt* (she saw), **5**:14.[5] ; **29B**:2.12 ; *ḥztk*, **5**:37. 8 ; *ḥzyt* (I saw), **7**:4.11 ; **10**:[3], 4 ; **17**:2.16 ; **21**:2.[16], 16 ; **22**:2.2, 4 ; **23**:1.[12], [14] ; **25**:2.1 ; **29B**:19.14 ; 21.10 ; *ḥzw*, **5**:28.[2] ; *ḥzwny*, **5**:14.2 ; *ḥzytwn*, **5**:11.2 ; *yḥz'*, **5**:23.4 ; *yḥznh*, **29B**:19.23 ; *tḥz'*, **5**:23.7 ; *'ḥzy*, **29B**: 20.14 ; *ḥz'* (impv.), **5**:34.7 ; *ḥzy*, **20**: 3.[2] ; **29B**:21.9bis, 14 ; 22.29 ; *mḥz'* (inf.), **18**:10 ; **29B**:21.15 ; *ḥzh* (ptc.), **4B**:5 ; **23**:2.5 ; *ḥzy*, **7**:4.[14], 17 ; **19**: 2.[1] ; *ḥzyn*, **5**:28.2 ; *'ḥzyny*, **7**:1.[3] ; 8.7 ; *'ḥzy'ny*, **8**:1 i [2], [8], [10], [15] ; 1 ii [2], 6, [10] ; *'ḥzyk*, **19**:1.3 ; *'ḥzyt* (I was shown), **11**:5 ; **12**:[4] ; **21**:2. 15 ; *'ḥzy't*, **10**:[2], [4], 5, 8 ; *yhḥzh*, **20**:54.1 ; *'tḥzy*, **29B**:21.8 ; 22.27 ; *'tḥzy'*, **13**:8
ḥzw (vision) : *ḥzw'*, **29B**:21.8 ; 22.27 ; *ḥzwy* (my vision), **23**:1.10 ; *ḥzwh*, **18**:10 ; **23**:1.10, 13, 14 ; *ḥzwn*, **28**:1. 6 ; *ḥzwt* (cst. pl.), **24**:1 ; *ḥzyw'*, **21**: 2.16
ḥzy (vision) : *ḥzyt*, **21**:2.16
ḥzy (cornerstone ?) : *ḥzyth*, **5**:30.4
ḥzywn (vision) : *ḥzywn*, **21**:2.15
ḥṭ' (sin [verb]) : *yḥṭ'*, **5**:8.7 ; *mḥṭ'*, **5**: 19.[6]
ḥṭ' (sin) : *ḥṭ'*, **5**:18.4 ; 22.3 ; 24.1 ; *ḥṭ'y* (my sins), **2**:1.4 ; *ḥṭyk*, **5**:26.2 ; *ḥṭ'h*, **28**:2.17 ; *ḥṭy'*, **5**:24.1 ; *ḥṭ'hwn*, **5**:38.3
ḥṭ' (wheat) : *ḥṭ'*, **5**:20.1 ; see also *ḥnṭh*
ḥy (living ; animal) : *ḥy*, **5**:10.8 ; *ḥy'*, **40**:11, [25] ; **41**:[14] ; **42**:20 ; **52**:6, 7 ; *ḥyy'*, **28**:1.8, 9 ; *ḥywt* (cst. pl.), **18**:8
ḥyy (live [verb]) : *ḥ‹y›*, **29B**:20.29 ; *yḥh*, **29B**:20.22, 23 ; *'ḥy*, **29B**:19.20 ; *ḥyy* (impv.), **4A**:[4] ; *'ḥyw* (they revived), **26**:14
ḥyn (life) : *ḥyn*, **28**:1.7 ; *ḥyyn*, **5**:23.[9]
ḥyl (force) : *ḥyl* (abs.), **5**:16.8 ; 33.3 ; *ḥyl* (cst.), **18**:3 ; *ḥylh*, **5**:15.3
ḥymr (bitumen) : *ḥymr'*, **29B**:21.[33]
ḥk : see *ḥnk*
ḥkh (hook) : *ḥkh*, **5**:35.3 ; *ḥk'*, **5**:35.4
ḥkym (wise) : *ḥkymy* (cst. pl.), **29B**:20. [19] ; *ḥkymy'*, **29B**:20.20
ḥkm (know) : *ḥkm*, **5**:25.[2] ; *ḥkmnh*, **5**:26.7
ḥkmh (wisdom) : *ḥkmh*, **5**:30.2 ; 37.4 ; **21**:1.[14] ; *ḥkm'*, **29B**:20.7 ; *ḥkmt'*, **29B**:19.25 ; *ḥkmtk*, **5**:33.7 ; *ḥwkmth*, **28**:1.8
ḥlbnh (galbanum) : *ḥlbnh*, **10**:[5]
ḥld (cultivated land) : *ḥld*, **17**:3.5
ḥlh (ossuary) : *ḥlt* (cst.), **88**:1 ; *ḥlth*, **69**:1
ḥlh (valley) : *ḥlt'*, **29B**:22.4
ḥly (mound) : *ḥlyh*, **5**:12.[2]
ḥll (pierce) : *ḥllt*, **5**:10.4 ; *ḥllyn* (wounded), **5**:8.[1]
ḥlm (be strong) : *'tḥlm*, **29B**:22.5
ḥlm (dream [verb]) : *ḥlmt* (I dreamed), **29B**:19.14, 18 ; *ḥlmw*, **17**:2.3 ; *'ḥlmt* (aphel), **2**:4.1
ḥlm (dream [noun]) : *ḥlm*, **29B**:19.14, 17 ; 20.22 ; *ḥlm'*, **17**:2.12, [14], 15, 20 ; **23**:1.10 ; **29B**:19.18bis, 19 ; *ḥlmy* (my dream), **17**:2.16 ; **18**:9 ; **29B**: 19.14 ; *ḥlmk*, **29B**:19.18 ; *ḥlmyn* (abs. pl.), **5**:22.9 ; **17**:2.3 ; *ḥlmy'*, **17**:2.23
ḥlp (pass over, cross) : *ḥlp*, **17**:3.5 ; *ḥlpt* (I crossed), **29B**:19.[12] ; *ḥlpn'*, **29B**:19.13 ; *'ḥlp* (I will exchange),

40:10, [24] ; **42**:[19] ; **46**:5 ; *nḥlp*, **45**:1.7 ; *'ḥlp* (aphel), **2**:4.[2] ; *'ḥlpt*, **12**:[6], 8
ḥlp (instead of) : *ḥlp*, **28**:2.17
ḥlṣ (loins ; vigor) : *ḥlṣ*, **29B**:2.8 *ḥlṣyk*, **5**:30.[1] ; 34.3
ḥlq (set apart) : *ḥlq*, **5**:26.5
ḥmd (attractive) : *ḥmyd*, **29B**:20.[5]
ḥmdh (delight) : *ḥmdt* (cst.), **20**:26.[1]
ḥmh (wrath ; heat) : *ḥmt* (cst.), **5**:5.[1] ; 34.7 ; **29A**:1 i 2
ḥmym (hot) : *ḥmym*, **5**:29.[8]
ḥmysr (fifteen) : *ḥmysr*, **150**:3, 12
ḥmyšy (fifth) : *ḥmyšyt'*, **29B**:12.15
ḥmr (wine) : *ḥmr*, **29B**:12.13 ; *ḥmr'*, **29B**:19.27
ḥmr (ass) : *ḥmryn*, **14**:1.1 ; **60**:1
ḥmš (five) : *ḥmš*, **8**:1 i [13]bis, 14 ; **29B**:19.23 ; **39**:6 ; **149**:3 ; *ḥmš'*, **150**:8 ; *ḥmšh*, **8**:1 i [12]bis, [14]bis ; **36**:2 ; **150**:3, 9 ; *ḥmšt*, **8**:1 ii [6] ; **150**:5
ḥmšyn (fifty) : *ḥmšyn*, **7**:1.1 ; **8**:1 i 1 ; **24**:4 ; **33**:7.2
ḥn (favor) : *ḥnh*, **22**:3.2 ; **23**:3.[1]
ḥnw (shop) : *ḥnwt'*, **64**:1.12 ; 3.5 ; 4.[1]
ḥnṭh (wheat) : *ḥnṭyn*, **52**:2 ; see also *ḥṭ'*
ḥnk (palate) : *ḥnk*, **5**:14.4 ; *ḥky*, **5**:19.7
ḥnkh (dedication) : *ḥnkt*, **150**:2, 6 ; *ḥnkt'*, **150**:9
ḥnn (beg) : *'tḥnnt*, **29B**:20.12 ; *htḥnnh*, **5**:35.6
ḥnp (hypocrisy) : *ḥnpy*, **5**:27.[7]
ḥnq (tether) : *ḥnqy*, **5**:32.4
ḥs (far be it !) : *ḥs*, **5**:24.4
ḥsyn (mighty) : *ḥsynyn*, **3D**:3
ḥsn (force) : *ḥsn*, **18**:3
ḥsp (clay) : *ḥsp'*, **2**:1.8
ḥsr (lack) : *mḥsr*, **52**:[2]
ḥsrn (lack) : *ḥsrnh*, **5**:29.4
ḥ'kyn (serpent) : *ḥ'kyn*, **22**:2.5
ḥ'n (hold tight) : *ḥ'nn*, **5**:36.3
ḥpr (dig ; spy out) : *ḥpr*, **5**:33.2, 10
ḥqq (determine) : *ḥqq*, **64**:1.10
ḥqr (search) : *tḥqrwn*, **5**:21.2
ḥr (free) : *ḥryn*, **5**:32.4
ḥrb (sword) : *ḥrb* (abs.), **5**:11.[5] ; 33.3, 4 ; *ḥrb'*, **5**:27.6 ; **20**:3.[1]
ḥrb (devastate) : *yḥrbwn*, **28**:2.13 ; *yḥrbn*, **28**:2.14 ; *ḥrybyn*, **40**:8, [22] ; *'ḥrb'* (aphel inf.), **3C**:3
ḥrgh (horror) : *ḥrgty*, **5**:22.1
ḥrw (freedom) : *ḥrwt* (cst.), **43**:1, [3] ; **44**:1.1 ; **51**:1
ḥrz (string) : *tḥrz*, **5**:35.4
ḥrk (singe) : *htḥrk*, **4B**:10
ḥrp (edge) : *ḥrp*, **5**:33.5
ḥrr (litigation) : *ḥrr*, **44**:1.[7] ; **45**:1.5 ; **46**:[3]
ḥrt (gimlet, awl) : *ḥrtk*, **5**:35.5
ḥśk (hold back) : *ḥśkt*, **5**:31.[1]
ḥšb (consider ; evaluate) : *ḥšb*, **64**:2.5 ; *ḥšbny*, **5**:2.[1] ; *ḥšbt*, **64**:1.11 ; *ḥšbt* (I considered), **29B**:2.1 ; *tḥšb*, **64**:1.10 ; *nḥšb*, **64**:1.13
ḥšbwn (calculation) : *ḥšbwn*, **28**:1.[13] ; *ḥšbwnwhy*, **28**:1.[10], [11] ; 2.[7] ; *ḥšbwnyhwn*, **11**:2 ; **28**:1.9
ḥšwk (darkness) : *ḥšwk*, **5**:10.1 ; **22**:2.3 ; *ḥšwk'*, **12**:8 ; **23**:1.13 ; 2.4, 5 ; **26**:10, 11, [13]bis ; **31**:3.[2]
ḥšy (be silent) : *ḥšyt*, **29B**:20.16 ; *ḥšw*, **5**:14.3 ; *hḥšyw*, **5**:21.7
ḥšyk (dark) : *ḥšyk*, **22**:2.3 ; **23**:1.13 ; 2.[4] ; *ḥšykh*, **23**:2.[4] ; *ḥšykyn*, **26**:10, [12]
ḥtl (swaddling clothes) : *ḥwtlwhy*, **5**:30.7
ḥtm (seal [verb]) : *ḥtmw*, **51**:14
ḥtp (despoiler) : *ḥtpwhy*, **5**:2.2
ḥtr (break in) : *ḥtr*, **5**:8.[7]

ṭb (good) : *ṭb*, **5**:27.5 ; 29.4 ; **12**:5 ; **21**:1.16 ; **29B**:21.3 ; **41**:5 ; **150**:9, 11 ; *ṭbt'*, **150**:12 ; *ṭby'*, **10**:2
ṭbh (goodness) : *ṭbt'*, **29B**:19.25 ; 21.3 ; *ṭbty*, **5**:16.4 ; *ṭbthwn*, **29B**:22.11
ṭbw (good) : *ṭbwt'*, **29B**:19.19
ṭby' (coinage) : *ṭby'*, **41**:5
ṭwr (mountain) : *ṭwr* (abs.), **10**:5 ; *ṭwr* (cst.), **29B**:17.10 ; 21.16bis ; *ṭwr'*, **3A**:[3] ; **21**:2.[16] ; **29B**:12. 13 ; 19.8 ; 21.7 ; *ṭwryn*, **5**:32.[7] ; **10**:[4], [8] ; **12**:4 ; *ṭwry* (cst.), **29B**: 10.12 ; 21.29 ; *ṭwry'*, **10**:5, [8] ; **12**: [4], 6

ṭhn (grind) : *tṭhn*, **5**:18.3
ṭyn (clay) : *ṭyn'*, **5**:11.7 ; 16.[9]
ṭl (shade) : *ṭl*, **11**:4 ; *ṭl'*, **5**:31.6 ; **31**:5.[4]
ṭlwl (lintel) : *ṭlwl*, **8**:1 i [16]
ṭlwpḥ (lentil) : *ṭlwpḥ'*, **28**:2.2 ; *ṭlwpḥyn*, **28**:1.2
ṭll (provide shade) : *ṭll*, **5**:28.7
ṭll (for the sake of) : *ṭll*, **29B**:19.16 ; *ṭlyky*, **29B**:19.20
ṭm (bone) : *ṭmy* (cst. pl.), **70**:2 ; see also *'ṭm*
ṭm' (defile) : *ṭmy'* (pael inf.), **29B**:20.15
ṭmr (hide) : *ṭmr* (impv.), **5**:34.8 ; *hṭmrw*, **5**:14.4 ; *'ṭmrt*, **5**:18.[2]
ṭ'' (err) : *yṭ'w*, **3F**:8 ; *'ṭ'w* (aphel), **3F**:1
ṭ'w (error) : *ṭ'wt'*, **3C**:2 ; **20**:31.1
ṭ'm (command) : *ṭ'm*, **4B**:13
ṭpy (snuff out) : *hṭpy* (haphel impv.), **5**:34.8
ṭrp (lentil ?) : *ṭrp'*, **38**:3
ṭš' (hide) : *ṭšw*, **5**:14.2

y' (O !) : *y'*, **29B**:2.9bis, 13bis, 24bis
y'' (beautiful) : *y''*, **29B**:20.4, 8 ; *y'y'*, **29B**:19.[15] ; *y'yn*, **29B**:20.3, 5
y'š (set free) : *ty'š*, **5**:31.9
yb' (be willing) : *yb'*, **5**:32.8
ybl (bring) : *'wblt* (I was brought), **11**:3 ; *hwblt*, **12**:5 ; *ywbl'*, **3B**:3
ybl (dog-grass) : *ybl'*, **5**:9.1
yd (hand) : *yd* (cst.), **3B**:3 ; **3C**:3 ; **5**:11.[1] ; **8**:1 i [12], [13], 18, [18] ; 16.2 ; **12**:8 ; **16**:2.4 ; **29B**:21.15, [16], 16, 17bis ; **61**:26 ; *yd'*, **28**:1.1 ; *ydy* (my hand), **5**:19.2 ; **29B**:22.21 ; *ydk*, **5**:26.2 ; **29B**:20.14 ; 22.17 ; *ydh* (his hand), **5**:10.4 ; **8**:1 ii 5, [12] ; **55**:4 ; *'dy* (cst. pl.), **3C**:3 ; *ydy* (my hands), **21**:1.9 ; **29B**:20.22, 29 ; *ydwhy*, **17**:3.4 ; *ydyh'* (her hands), **29B**:20.4, 5bis, 7 ; *ydykwn*, **5**:4.4 ; *ydyhwn*, **14**:17.2
yd' (thank ; declare) : *'wdyt* (aphel), **29B**:21.3 ; *hwdh*, **17**:2.15 ; *'ytwdy*, **39**:2
yd' (know) : *yd'h'* (he knew her), **29B**:20.17 ; *yd't* (you knew), **5**:3.[5] ; 30.2 ; *yd't* (I knew), **5**:5.7 ; 14.[11] ; 37.3 ; *yd'w*, **14**:9-14-15.2 ; *yd'* (he will know), **28**:1.3, 6, 8bis ; *ynd'*, **5**:29.9 ; **28**:1.[5] ; **29B**:2.20 ; *tnd'* (you know), **5**:29.[6], [7], [8] ; 30.3 ; 32.2 ; *'nd'*, **29B**:19.18 ; *ynd'wk*, **29B**:20.15 ; *nnd'*, **5**:28.[4] ; *mnd'* (inf.), **29B**:2.22 ; *yd'* (ptc.), **5**:29.8 ; **18**:10 ; **21**:1.[11]bis ; **28**:1.4 ; **49**:1.4 ; *yd'y* (my acquaintances), **5**:2.3 ; *yd'why*, **5**:38.5 ; *ydy'* (pass. ptc.), **16**:2.6 ; **59**:3 ; *'wd'* (aphel), **29B**:20.[29] ; *hwd't* (you showed), **5**:30.[10] ; *thwd'wnny*, **4A**:[6] ; *mwd'* (ptc.), **26**:9 ; *mhwd'*, **26**:[9]
yhb (give) : *yhb* (he gave), **5**:38.4 ; **27**:[11] ; **29B**:17.16 ; 20.31 ; 21.3 ; 22.2, 17, 25 ; **42**:1-3.[3] ; *yhbw*, **4B**:12 ; **5**:38.7 ; **27**:11 ; *yhbn'*, **20**:3.[2] ; *hb* (impv.), **21**:1.[15] ; **29B**:22.19 ; *yhb* (ptc.), **29B**:21.10 ; **48**:2 ; *yhbn'* (masc. sg. peal ptc. with an elliptical form of *'nh*), **40**:8, 21 ; *yhbyn*, **29B**:19.24 ; 21.27 ; **46**:4 ; *yhyb*, **7**:4.17 ; *yhybt*, **7**:4.15, [16] ; **9**:[6] ; for imperfect forms, see *ntn*
yhwdy (Jew) : *yhwdy*, **2**:1.4 ; **40**:7, 19 ; *yhwd'y*, **150**:12
yhlm (jasper) : *yhlm*, **8**:1 i 7
ywm (day) : *ywm* (abs.), **7**:8.6, [6] ; **9**:1 ; **29A**:1 ii 3 ; **29B**:12.15 ; 22.28 ; **31**:7.1 ; **33**:1.1 ; **64**:1.[8] ; 3.[3] ; **150**:9, 11 ; *ywm* (cst.), **3F**:3 ; **5**:31.1 ; **24**:2 ; **29B**:22.30 ; **150**:9, 12quater ; *ywm'*, **3F**:5 ; **29B**:21.5 ; 22.21 ; **40**:2, 13 ; **44**:17.[1] ; **45**:1.[2] ; **49**:1.7, 8 ; **51**:3, [13] ; **52**:10 ; *ymh*, **51**:3, 11bis ; *ywmyn*, **5**:15.4 ; **150**:9 ; *ymyn*, **42**:15 ; *ywmy*, **5**:16.[6] ; 23.3 ; **29B**:3.3 ; **150**:12 ; *ywmy'*, **29B**:21.23 ; **150**:1 ; *ywmy* (my days), **29B**:6.2 ; *ywmyk*, **5**:30.9 ; *ywmwhy*, **5**:28.3 ; *ymhwn*, **5**:27.5
yḥl (despair) : *'yḥl*, **5**:25.7
ykl (be able) : *ykl*, **29B**:20.17 ; *yklt* (I could), **2**:4.3 ; *yklw*, **29B**:20.20 ; *ykwl* (imperfect), **29B**:20.22 ; *tkwl*, **5**:37.4 ; *ykwlwn*, **29B**:20.19

yld (bear) : *yld*, **5**:31.6 ; *yldh*, **5**:31.[7] ; *yldt*, **19**:1.6 ; *yldn*, **5**:32.2 ; *ylyd*, **68**:4
yld (child, offspring) : *yld*, **64**:1.8
yll (lament) : *yll*, **35E**:2.1
ym (sea) : *ym* (cst.), **29B**:21.18 ; *ym'*, **5**:10.3 ; 30.6 ; **12**:[7] ; **29B**:16.12 ; 21.11, 15, 16, 17, 18bis ; *ymyn*, **9**:2 ; *ymy'*, **13**:[8] ; **16**:2.13 ; **29B**:7.1
ym' (swear) : *ym'*, **29B**:20.30 ; *y'my'*, **29B**:2.14
ymyn (right) : *ymyn*, **7**:4.[9] ; **8**:1 i [13] ; *ymyn'*, **8**:1 i [12], [18]
ysd (base [verb]) : *ysdwn*, **28**:2.17
yswd (foundation) : *yswdh*, **28**:2.17
ysp (increase) : *'wspt* (aphel), **29B**:21. 6 ; *twsp*, **5**:30.9 ; *'wsp*, **5**:25.8 ; 37.6
y'l (mountain goat) : *y'lyn*, **14**:1.[1] ; *y'ly*, **5**:32.1
y'nh (ostrich) : *y'nh*, **5**:17.6
yp' (shine) : *hwp'*, **5**:29.[6]
yṣb' (certainty) : *yṣb'*, **29B**:2.20 ; *yṣbth*, **26**:9
yqd (burn) : *yqdwn*, **5**:16.7 ; *yqd* (ptc.), **5**:36.6
yqyr (precious) : *yqry'*, **30**:3
yqr (bear heavy) : *yqr*, **5**:22.[2]
yqr (honor) : *yqr*, **2**:1.5 ; **5**:27.6 ; 34.6
yrwq (green) : *yrwq*, **5**:32.7
yrḥ (moon ; month) : *yrḥ*, **13**:[8] ; **149**: [1] ; *yrḥ'*, **150**:1 ; *yrḥyn*, **62**:[13] ; *yrḥwhy*, **5**:5.3 ; *yrḥyhwn*, **5**:32.[1]
yrkh (thigh) : *yrkth*, **28**:1.3
yrq (verdure) : *yrq*, **5**:15.7
yrt (heir) : *yrt* (cst.), **64**:1.7, [8] ; *yrtkn*, **45**:1.5 ; **52**:12 ; *yrthn*, **52**:9, 10 ; *yrtyk*, **41**:13 ; **44**:23.[2]
yrt (inherit) : *yrtnny*, **29B**:22.33, 34 ; *yrtnk*, **29B**:22.34 ; *yrtwn*, **42**:[13] ; *yrtwnh*, **29B**:21.12
yš' (save) : *ywš'*, **3D**:2
yšr (send forth) : *twšr*, **5**:32.3
yt (accusative marker) : *yt*, **8**:1 i [16], 17 ; **42**:19 ; **53**:3, 4 ; **54**:1 ; **56**:4 ; **58**:2 ; *yth*, **5**:35.9 ; *ythn*, **53**:2 ; **59**:2 ; **60**:4bis
ytb (dwell) : *ytb*, **29B**:21.5, 7 ; *ytbt* (I dwelt), **21**:2.14 ; **29B**:19.9 ; 21.19 ; *ytbw*, **7**:4.19 ; *ytb* (ptc.), **29B**:21.7, 9 ; 22.1, 3 ; **39**:4 ; **40**:3 ; *ytb'* (fem. ptc.), **40**:4, 15 ; **42**:[14] ; **50G**:1 ; *ytbyn*, **18**:6 ; **28**:2.13 ; *ytbn*, **42**:11 ; *ytby* (cst.), **5**:27.1
ytyr (excessive) : *ytyr*, **52**:[3] ; *ytyr'*, **29B**:19.[23]
ytybh (seating) : *ytybt* (cst.), **150**:10

k- (like, as [prep.]) : *k-*, **3F**:8 ; **5**:9.1 ; 11.[7], 7, 9, 11 ; 14.9 ; 15.[3], 3 ; 16.[4], 4 ; 23.4, 6 ; 24.[1], [5] ; 29. [9] ; 30.1 ; 31.7 ; 34.3, 5 ; 35.3, 8 ; 36.4 ; 39.9bis ; **8**:1 i [18] ; 1 ii 2, 4 ; **17**:3.4bis ; **23**:1.[13] ; **28**:1.4, [4] ; 2. 16 ; **29B**:21.13 ; **41**:3 ; **42**:11 ; **44**:13.2 ; **61**:24 ; **64**:1.4, 5 ; 2.2 ; see also *kdy*, *kdn*, *kdn'*, *kdnh*, *kwt*, *kḥdh*, *km'*, *kmh*, *kmn*, *lkmh*, *klmdnḥ*, *klṣpwn*, *klqbl*
k' (here) : *k'*, **17**:2.12, 20 ; *kh*, **70**:1
k' dy : see *kdy*
k'n (here) : *k'n*, **7**:5-6.3, [4] ; 7.[1]bis
kbr (already) : *kbr*, **29B**:22.23 ; **38**:[5]
kbš (trample down) : *kbšw*, **5**:2.2
kdb (lie) : *kdbt* (I lied), **5**:19.[2]
kdb (lie) : *kdbyn*, **29B**:2.6, 7
kdy (when, as) : *kdy*, **2**:1.[1]bis ; **5**:18.7 ; 19.[1] ; 27.[9] ; **10**:7 ; **20**:6.1 ; **21**:2. [12] ; **29B**:2.12, 21 ; 5.24, 26 ; 20.8, 10, 11, 24 ; 22.33 ; **40**:11, 24 ; **41**: [14] ; **42**:[20] ; **61**:25 ; **64**:1.2 ; 3.2, 6 ; *k' dy*, **64**:1.3
kdn (thus) : *kdn*, **7**:1.3 ; **8**:1 ii 2, 8 ; **18**:9 ; **20**:56.1 ; **23**:1.11 ; **29B**:2.17 ; **40**:9, 22
kdn' (so) : *kdn'*, **29B**:2.17
kdnh (so) : *kdnh*, **4B**:15
kdn (join) : *kdnyn*, **89**:3
kdš (smite) : *mkdš*, **29B**:20.16 ; see also *ktš*
khn (priest) : *khn* (abs.), **7**:4.[15] ; *khn* (cst.), **29B**:22.15 ; *khn'* (emph.), **9**: 14.6 ; *khnh* (emph.), **68**:1 ; **139**:1 ; *khnyn* (abs.), **7**:4.[10], [13] ; **9**:14.3, [4] ; *khny'* (emph.), **7**:4.14, [17] ; **150**:5
khnw (priesthood) : *khnwt'*, **20**:1.2

kwh (window) : *kwt'*, **8:**1 ii 12 ; *kwyn*, **8:**1 ii 11 ; 2.1
kwk (sepulchral chamber) : *kwkh*, **67:** 1 ; see also *qwq*
kwkb (star) : *kwkby* (cst.), **5:**30.5 ; *kwkby'*, **5:**9.8
kwt (like) : *kwtk*, **5:**28.[2] ; *kwth* (like him), **5:**34.5
kḥd' (together) : *kḥd'*, **5:**1.[3] ; 30.5 ; 34.[9] ; **29B:**21.21, 25 ; 22.1 ; *kḥdh*, **5:**5.6 ; 30.5
ky (for) : *ky*, **14:**27.5 ; **30:**3 ; *ky'*, **6:** 14.3
kl (all) : *kl*, **2:**1.[7] ; **5:**2.8 ; 22.[5], 7 ; 25.3 ; 28.[2] ; 29.3 ; 30.5 ; 32.7 ; 34. 7bis ; 37.2 ; 38.5ter, 6 ; **8:**1 i 1, 6, 9, [10], [12], 14, [16], [17] ; 1 ii 8 ; 2.2 ; 5.2 ; **12:**6 ; **13.**6, [8], [9] ; **14:**1.[3]bis ; 3.1 ; 20.4 ; 21.2 ; **17:**2.10, 20 ; 3.8 ; **19:**5.1 ; **20:**8.2 ; 37.2 ; **21:**1.7, [12], 17 ; 2.[9] ; **22:**1.[2] ; 2.[6] ; **23:**2.[4], 4 ; **26:**[9], [10], 11, 12bis, [12], 13 ; **29B:**20.6 ; **30:**1, [1], 2, [4], **4** ; **37:**1.3 ; **40:**22 ; **42:**5, 10, [13], 15 ; **44:**1.[3], [6], [7] ; 13.2 ; **45:**1.[3], 5 ; **46:**3 ; **52:**6, 10, 11 ; **53:**3 ; **55:**2 ; **61:**24 ; **64:**1.4, 12 ; 2.1, 2 ; **69:**1 ; **150:**12 ; *kl'* (emph.), **5:**24.[8] ; 37.3 ; **19:**1.3 ; **20:**3.[2] ; **64:**1.13 ; *klh*, **19:**2.3 ; *kln*, **46:**3 ; *klkwn*, **5:**11.2 ; *klhn*, **8:**1 ii [2] ; **28:**2.[16] ; *kwl*, **4B:**3 ; **5:**38.4 ; **6:**14.1 ; **7:**1.3 ; 4.[11], [17], 18, 20 ; 5-6.[7] ; 7.2 ; 8.6 ; 9.2 ; **9:**[1], 3 ; **10:**6 ; **16:**2.5 ; **18:**[4] ; **23:**1.12, [15] ; 2.5, [5], 6, [6] ; 3.[1] ; **24:**[1] ; **27:**12 ; **28:**1.8bis, [9], 9 ; 2.14 ; **29A:**1 i 8 ; 1 ii 4 ; 3.2 ; **29B:**2.4, 7, 16ter ; 6.2 ; 7.1 ; 10.13 ; 11.17 ; 12.10 ; 16.11 ; 19.19, 20, 23 ; 20.3, 4, 5bis, 6, 7, 9, 12, 13, 15bis, 16, 17, 18, 19ter, 20bis, 24, 28 ; 21.1, 3, 5, 9, 10, 11bis, 12bis, 13, 14, 19, 21, 25, 26, 27, 33 ; 22.1, 3, 10, 11 quater, 12, 13, 15, 17, 22bis, 24bis, 25, 29, 30, 33 ; **31:**1.5 ; 3.2 ; 4.[1] ; 5.3, [5] ; 6.1, [2] ; **33:**4.5, 6 ; **35A:** 1.6 ; **40:**6, 8, 19, [21] ; **41:**13 ; **51:**7 ; **54:**1 ; **59:**2 ; *kwl'* (emph.), **29B:**2.5, [10], 19, 20, 21, 22 ; 19.10 ; 20.13 ; **31:**7.2 ; *kwlh*, **8:**2.3 ; *kwlh'*, **29B:**10. 13 ; 16.11 ; *kwln'*, **29B:**12.16 ; *kwlhwn* **3B:**2 ; **29B:**12.10, 13 ; 20:13, 20 ; 22.9, 20, 26 ; *kwlhn*, **29B:**20.7
kl' (cry out) : *'kly't* (she cried out), **29B:**19.16
kl' (withhold) : *ykl'*, **5:**24.8 ; *yklnh*, **5:**35.3 ; *ytkl'*, **7:**8.6
kl' (bride) : *kl'n*, **29B:**20.6
klb (dog) : *klby* (cst.), **5:**15.5
klyl (crown) : *klyl'y*, **150:**2
klyl (perfect) : *klyln*, **29B:**20.5
klmdnḥ (eastward) : *klmdnḥ*, **29B:**21.20
klṣpwn (northward) : *klṣpwn*, **10:**8 ; **12:**4
klqbl (according) : *klqbl*, **49:**1.6
km' (how) : *km'*, **5:**21.6 ; **29B:**20.2, [3], 3, 4ter, 5, 6bis
kmh (how) : *kmh*, **29B:**20.2
kmn (how much) : *kmn*, **29B:**21.14bis ; 22.29
kn (thus) : *kn*, **2:**1.[5] ; **5:**37.8 ; **29B:** 21.10 ; **39:**7 ; **49:**1.5 ; **53:**2
kns (gather) : *mtknsyn*, **13:**6
knp (wing) : *knpy* (cst.), **5:**30.[10] ; *knpwhy*, **5:**33.[8]
knš (gather) : *ytknšwn*, **3F:**2 ; *'tknšn'* (we gathered), **29B:**12.16
knšh (Sanhedrin) : *knšt'*, **150:**10
ks' (cover, hide) : *ksy*, **5:**28.[8] ; *tksh*, **5:**34.9 ; *'ks'*, **5:**11.[2] ; *mksy'*, **41:**10
ksw (clothing) : *kswt*, **62:**12
ksl (foolishness) : *ksl*, **26:**12 ; *ksl'*, **5:** 27.[7]
ksp (silver, sum) : *ksp* (abs.), **29B:**20. [31], 33 ; **50E:**4 ; **51:**5 ; *ksp* (cst.), **39:**4 ; **41:**5 ; **42:**[10], 13 ; **43:**5 ; **48:** 3, 4 ; **52:**7 ; **62:**[12] ; **64:**3.[2] ; *ksp'* (emph.), **2:**1.7 ; **36:**2 ; **39:**[4] ; **44:**1.5 ; **48:**2bis ; **52:**8
k'n (now) : *k'n*, **5:**15.[4] ; 16.5 ; 24.4, 6 ; 37.7 ; **16:**2.14 ; **20:**3.[2] ; **27:**9 ; **29A:**1 i 4 ; **29B:**5.9 ; 19.8, 12, 13 ; 20.13, 23, 28, 29, 30 ; **30:**3
kp (hand, palm) : *kp*, **5:**14.3 ; *kpy*, **21:** 1.9 ; *kpwhy*, **5:**23.5 ; *kpyh*, **29B:**20.5
kp (rock) : *kp'*, **5:**32.1 ; 33.9

kpl (double) : *kplyn*, **29B**:22.29 ; *kpyl*, **35A**:3
kpn (starve) : *tkpn*, **20**:3.1
kpn (famine) : *kpn*, **5**:15.[7] ; 29.4 ; *kpn'*, **20**:3.1 ; **29B**:19.10, 26
kps (interest) : *kps*, **64**:3.2
kpp (bend) : *htkppw*, **5**:9.[1] ; *'tkppt*, **5**:16.3 ; *htkppt* (inf.), **5**:16.3
kpr (atone) : *kprt* (I atoned), **29B**:10.13 ; *mkpryn*, **7**:8.5
kpt (bind) : *mkptyn*, **4B**:2, 4
krwz (proclamation) : *krwz*, **64**:1.3 ; *krwz'*, **64**:1.3, 4, 5bis ; *krwzyn*, **64**:2.4
krz (proclaim) : *krz*, **64**:1.4 ; *kryzt* (it has been proclaimed), **64**:1.3
krm (vineyard) : *krm*, **29B**:12.13
krsy (throne) : *kwrsyhwn*, **5**:27:[1]
kšṭ (set out) : *kšwṭ*, **51**:14
ktb (write) : *ktb*, **2**:1.5 ; **39**:10 ; **42**:23 ; **51**:16 ; **52**:[15], 18 ; *ktbh* (he wrote it), **56**:7 ; **61**:24, 25 ; *ktbyh* (he wrote it), **62**:13 ; *ktbt* (I wrote), **2**:1.5 ; **54**:1 ; *ktbnn*, **61**:25 ; *ktyb*, **42**:[13], [18] ; **49**:1.[6] ; **61**:25 ; **64**:1.4, [6], 8 ; 3.3 ; *ktybyn*, **64**:1.2 ; *'ktb* (he caused to be written), **64**:1.5
ktb (writing) : *ktb* (abs.), **61**:24 ; *ktb* (cst.), **16**:2.4 ; **24**:1 ; **29B**:19.[25] ; **64**:1.3bis, 4 ; *ktbh* (emph.), **51**:14 ; *ktbyn*, **64**:2.4 ; *ktby* (my writings), **27**:12
ktwbh (contract) : *ktbt* (cst.), **63**:1 ; *ktbtyk*, **42**:[10], 13, [16]
ktl (wall) : *ktwl* (cst.), **7**:3.4 ; *kwtl'*, **6**:7.1 ; **8**:1 i 18 ; 1 ii 12 ; *kwtly'*, **7**:8.3
ktwn (tunic) : *ktwn*, **5**:14.9
ktr (circuit) : *ktrh* (its circuit), **29B**:17.16
ktš (smite) : *ktš*, **29B**:20.20 ; *ktš'*, **29B**:20.17 ; *ktyš*, **2**:1.[1], 3, 6 ; *mktš*, **5**:29.3 ; *mktšh* (to afflict him), **29B**:20.16 ; *mtktš*, **29B**:20.25 ; see also *kdš*

l- (to, for [prep.]) : *l-*, **2**:1.[3], 5bis, [7] ; 4.4 ; **3A**:9 ; **3C**:2ter, 3 ; **3F**:[7] ; **4A**:4 ; **4B**:[4], 4, 6, 12, [15] ; **5**:1.[1], 2, 5, [6] ; 2.4, 5, 6 ; 3.7, 8 ; 4.7 ; 5.2, 3 ; 6.[1], [6] ; 7.2 ; 8.3, 4, 6 ; 9.5 ; 10.9 ; 11.[5] ; 13.5, 6, 9 ; 14.4, 6, 8, 10 ; 15.5 ; 16.[1], 9 ; 17.[6] ; 18.3 ; 19.1, 2, 3, [6], 7 ; 20.3, [3] ; 21.[1], 3, 4 ; 23.3, 8 ; 24.2, 4, {5}, <5> ; 26.3, 5bis ; 27.1bis, 4, 7 ; 28.[2] ; 29.2, 3, 4bis, [8] ; 30.7, [10] ; 31.[1], 1, 3ter, 4, 5bis ; 32.7, [8] ; 33.3, 5, 6, 8 ; 34.2 ; 35.7, 8 ; 36.2, 3 ; 37.4, 7, 8 ; 38.3 ; **6**:1.2 ; 4.2 ; **7**:3.3 ; 4.2, 3, 6, [9]bis, [10], [15], 16, 17, 18 ; 5-6.7 ; **8**:1 i 1bis, [2], [3], [5], 5, 6, [12], [13], 14, [18]bis, 18 ; 1 ii 2, 5, [6], 6, [12] ; 2.5 ; 16.2 ; **9**:2bis, 3, 6 ; **10**:[2], 3, [4], [6], 6 ; **11**:3, 4bis ; **12**:6, [6], 8 ; **13**:[6], 6, [7], 8bis, [8], [9], 9ter ; **14**:9-14-15.4 ; 13.1 ; 17.3 ; **16**:1.3 ; 2.5bis, 14 ; **17**:2.13, [14], 14, 16 ; 3.5, 7bis, 8 ; **18**:5, 10 ; **19**:1.2, [5] ; **20**:1.3 ; 3.[1]bis ; 12.1 ; 30.2 ; **21**:1.8, [15], 18 ; 2.5, [8], 9, 10, 17 ; **24**:2, 4bis ; **25**:1.2 ; **26**:13bis, [13]ter, 14bis ; **27**:[10], 10, 11 ; **28**:1.6, 8, 11 ; 2.1, 8 ; **29A**:1 ii 8 ; **29B**:2.1, 10, 22bis, 23ter, 24, 25, 26 ; 5.10 ; 7.7 ; 10.13 ; 12.13bis, 15bis, 16quater, 17ter ; 16.11 ; 17.8ter, 9bis, 10, 11, 16quater ; 19.8, 9ter, 11ter, 13bis, 14, 15quater, 16, 17, 18, 19bis, 21bis, 22bis, 25, 26 ; 20.6, 7bis, 9ter, 10, 12, 13, 15bis, 16bis, 17bis, 18, 19quater, 20ter, 22, 23bis, 24, 25bis, 27, 31, 32 ; 21.1bis, 2bis, 4, 8, 9quater, 10quater, 12bis, 13, 14, 15quater, 16quinquies, 17quinquies, 18bis, 19, 20bis, 21ter, 25bis, 26bis, 27bis, 28, 29quater, 30, 31 ; 22.2, 4, 5, 6, 7, 10, 11, 13bis, 15ter, 16bis, 18, 20, 21, 24, 25, 27, 31 ; **31**:1.4, 5, 7 ; 3.2 ; 4.[1] ; 5.3, 4bis, 5 ; 6.1 ; 7.1 ; **32D**:3 ; **32J**:15.1 ; **33**:1.2 ; 4.4 ; 5.[2] ; **35A**:1.3 ; **36**:2 ; **37**:2.2, 3 ; **38**:1 ; **39**:1 ; **40**:1, 6ter, 10, 12, 18bis, 19, 23 ; **41**:1, 3, 4, 7, [9], 9 ; **42**:[1], [7], 12bis, 14, 16, 18 ; **43**:1bis, 3bis, 7 ; **44**:1.[1], 1 ; 3.1 ; **45**:1.[2], [4], 4, 6, [7] ; **47**:1.1, 2 ;

48:3, 4, 5 ; **49**:1.1, 4, 7, 10 ; **50A**:3 ; **50E**:1 ; **51**:1bis, 2, 3, 4bis, 6, [8], 9, 11, 12, 13bis ; **52**:[3], 3, 4, 9ter, 10 bis, 12bis ; **53**:1bis, 3 ; **55**:2 ; **56**:2, 3 ; **57**:1bis, 2 ; **58**:1bis ; **59**:1, 2 ; **60**: 1bis, 3, 4 ; **62**:12, [12] ; **64**:1.[1]bis, 13 ; 3.3bis ; **67**:2, 4 ; **68**:5bis ; **70**:1, 4 ; **71**:2, 3 ; **89**:1, 3 ; **95B**:1 ; **150**: 1quinquies, 2quinquies, 3, 5bis, 6bis, 8bis, 9bis, 10, 11quater, 12sexies ; *ly*, **2**:1.4 ; **5**:4.1, 5 ; 15.6 ; 22.3, 4 ; 24.[4] ; **20**:9.3 ; **21**:1.[15] ; 2.18, [18] ; **23**:1.[11], 12 ; 2.2 ; 3.2 ; **27**:11 ; **29B**: 2.13 ; 12.13 ; 19.[8], 18bis, [25]bis ; 20.14, 26ter, 27bis, 30bis, [30], 32 ; 21.3, 8bis, 12, 17, 19 ; 22.19bis, 32bis ; **40**:10, 24 ; **41**:3 ; **42**:7, [19] ; **44**:1.[6] ; **45**:1.[3] ; **46**:5 ; **47**:1.2bis ; 2.8 ; **48**:5 ; **51**:13 ; **52**:11 ; **56**:4 ; **64**: 1.9, 11, 13 ; *lk*, **5**:34.5 ; 35.6 ; **20**:3. [2]bis ; 30.3 ; **29B**:2.9, [13], 14, 24, 25, [25] ; 5.9 ; 20.27 ; 21.8, 10, 14 ; 22.20, 22, 24, 29, 30, 31 ; **39**:8 ; **41**: 11 ; **42**:[10], [15], 16 ; **43**:5 ; **46**:4, 5 ; **47**:2.10 ; **48**:4 ; **51**:3, 5ter, [8], 10, [11] ; **55**:3 ; **60**:1, 4 ; **64**:1.10 ; **89**:1, 3 ; *lk'*, **29B**:5.9 ; *lkh*, **17**:2.22 ; 3.7 ; **27**:9 ; *lky*, **29B**:19.19 ; **40**:3, 7, 9, 10, 14, 20, 24 ; **41**:14 ; *lh* (to him), **2**: 1.4 ; **5**:22.[6] ; 23.5 ; 24.5 ; 25.7 ; 26.[1], 2, 10 ; 29.2, 7 ; 30.8 ; 32.7 ; 34.2 ; 38.4bis, 7 ; **8**:1 i [17], 19 ; **17**:2.[21], 22, 23 ; 3.6 ; **18**:9 ; **19**:1. [6] ; **23**:3.[1] ; **25**:1.3 ; **28**:1.6 ; **29B**: 2.19, 21 ; 19.[9], [19] ; 20.9, 16, 17, 22, 34bis ; 21.5, 6bis ; 22.17, 27, 34 ; **32H**:1.2 ; **55**:3 ; **58**:3 ; **64**:1.8 ; *lh* (to her), **29B**:19.18 ; 20.2, 3ter, 4bis, 6, 31 ; *lhh* (to her), **29B**:19.26 ; *ln'*, **5**:7.3 ; 26.5 ; **17**:2.14 ; **19**:1.[4] ; *lnh*, **45**:1.7 ; **46**:4 ; *lkwn*, **16**:2.6 ; **26**:[9]bis; **31**:8.2 ; **54**:1, 2 ; *lkn*, **45**:1.7 ; **52**:7 ; **59**:3 ; *lhwn*, **5**:8.9 ; 14.7 ; 15.1 ; 16. [2] ; 27.3, [4] ; 38.3 ; **17**:2.13, [21] ; **19**:6.1 ; **20**:54.1 ; **29B**:22.9 ; **150**:12 ; *lhyn*, **29B**:20.3 ; see also *bdyl*, *blḥwdy*, *dyl*, *dlm'*, *klmdnḥ*, *klṣpwn*, *klqbl*, *lbtr*, *lhk'*, *lhl'*, *lwt*, *lḥd'*, *lkm'*, *lm'*, *lqbl*

l' (not) : *l'*, **2**:4.3 ; **4A**:6 ; **4B**:10, 13 ; **5**:2.5 ; 4.3 ; 5.[6] ; 6.[4], 6 ; 7.6 ; 9.6, 8 ; 11.[2], 5, 6, 10 ; 12.4, [4] ; 14.7, [11] ; 15.1, 6 ; 16.1 ; 17.3 ; 19.[7], 9 ; 21.3, 5, 6, 8 ; 22.1, [2], 3, [7] ; 23.5 ; 24.2 ; 25.1, 3, 8, 9 ; 26.4, [7], 8, [9] ; 27.[6], 10 ; 28.[4], 4 ; 30.9 ; 31.4 ; 32.3, 6 ; 33.3, 4 ; 36.[2], 3 ; 37.4, 5bis ; **6**:15.3 ; **7**:8.5 ; **14**: 29.2 ; **16**:2.[6] ; **17**:2.[13] ; **18**:4, 6 ; **19**:1.3, 5 ; 4.4 ; **20**:1.[2] ; 7.3 ; 30.2 ; **28**:1.4 ; **29B**:2.6, 7, 16ter ; 5.[4] ; 11. 17 ; 19.8, 17, [22], 23, 26 ; 20.6, 10, 17bis, 20, 22, 30 ; 21.13bis ; 22.3, 33, 34 ; **30**:2, 3 ; **31**:8.2 ; **39**:5, 7 ; **49**:1.4 ; **51**:5, 9, 10 ; **53**:2, 3 ; **54**:2 ; **59**:2 ; **64**:1.7, 8 ; **67**:4 ; **70**:4 ; **71**:2 ; **95B**:1 ; **150**:1quinquies, 2quater, 5, 6, 9bis, 11bis, 12quater ; see also *lhn*

lb (heart) : *lby* (my heart), **5**:18.2 ; 19.[1] ; **29B**:2.1, 2, 11 ; *lbby*, **5**:3.3 ; *lbbh* (its heart), **5**:36.[9] ; *lbbhwn*, **5**:27.[7]

lbwnh (incense) : *lbwnh*, **10**:3 ; *lbwnt'*, **7**:4.[8], [14] ; **9**:5

lbwš (garment) : *lbwš*, **29B**:20.31 ; *lbwšy*, **5**:16.[8] ; *lbwšk*, **5**:29.7 ; *lbwšh*, **5**:30.[7]

lbn (whiteness) : *lbnh'* (her whiteness), **29B**:20.4

lbš (clothe) : *lbšt* (I was clothed), **5**: 14.9 ; *tlbš* (you will be clothed), **5**: 34.6 ; *hlbštny* (it clothed me), **5**:14. [9] ; *hlbš'* (inf.), **5**:29.7

lbtr (after) : *lbtr*, **29B**:19.23 ; see also *b'tr*, *btr*

lgn (make a furrow) : *ylgn*, **5**:32.[9]

lhk' (hither) : **29B**:2.25

lhl' (further) : *lhl'*, **10**:[1], 3, [5], [8] ; **12**:[3]

lhn (but) : *lhn*, **5**:21.5 ; **29B**:5.4 ; 20.6 ; 22.34 ; **150**:12

lwḥ (tablet) : *lwḥ'*, **15**:1, 3bis ; **16**:2.3 ; **30**:5 ; *lwḥy'*, **30**:3

lwṭ (curse) : *lwṭy*, **5**:19.5

lwš (knead) : *tlwš*, **49**:1.9

lwt (to) : *lwt*, **5**:38.4 ; **42**:8 ; **60**:2bis ;

lwtk, **42**:19 ; **60**:3bis ; **64**:1.5, 9 ; *lwth*, **64**:1.5 ; *lw'ty*, **29B**:21.5, 7
lḥd' (exceedingly) : *lḥd'*, **29B**:20.33 ; 22.32 ; *lḥdh*, **22**:2.6 ; **23**:1.[15]
lḥy (bad) : *lḥyn*, **52**:8
lḥm (bread) : *lḥm*, **5**:6.[7] ; 38.6 ; **32I**:3.1 ; **49**:1.11 ; *lḥm'*, **7**:4.5, [6], [8], 9, [9], [10], [11], 14, 15 ; **9**:[5] ; *lḥmhwn*, **5**:15.[9]
lylh (night) : *lyl'*, **5**:22.9 ; *lylh*, **29B**: 19.14 ; *lyly'*, **5**:8.[5] ; 26.6 ; **17**:2.16 ; **29B**:19.17, 21 ; 20.11, 12, 15, 16 ; 21.8bis, 9
lkwš (spark) : *lkwš*, **5**:36.6
lkm' (similarly) : *lkm'*, **5**:10.[9]
lkn (now) : *lkn*, **5**:3.3
llb (palm branch) : *llbyn*, **60**:3
lm' (why) : *lm'*, **5**:1.[6] ; **29B**:2.[16] ; 22.22, 32 ; *lmh*, **5**:11.2 ; 21.4 ; 22.[6]
lst (jaw) : *lsth* (its jaw), **5**:35.5
lpyd (firebrand) : *lpydyn*, **5**:36.4
lqbl (to, for) : *lqbl*, **8**:1 ii [2], [3] ; *lqwblk*, **51**:13 ; *lqblkn*, **45**:1.[6] ; *lqwbly*, **29B**:21.32 ; *lqwblyk*, **39**:8
lšn (tongue) : *lšn* (cst.), **29B**:21.18 ; *lšnh* (its tongue), **5**:35.4 ; *lšnhwn*, **5**: 14.[4] ; *lšny* (cst.), **5**:36.5

m' (what) : *m'*, **5**:1.1 ; 5.[2] ; 7.[2] ; 9.7 ; 10.5 ; 18.6 ; 26.1bis, 2 ; 29.6 ; 30.4 ; **23**:2.3 ; **29B**:2.[16] ; 20.3, 4, 5, 26 ; *mh*, **16**:1.3 ; **19**:1.5 ; **20**:37.3 ; **23**:3.[1] ; **25**:1.3 ; 2.2 ; **64**:1.10 ; see also *dlm'*, *km'*, *lkm'*
m'h (hundred) : *m'h*, **3B**:1 ; **7**:8.8 ; **8**:1 i [1], [4] ; **24**:3bis ; **48**:3 ; **64**:3.2 ; *m''*, **29B**:22.6 ; *mh*, **149**:2
m'kl (food) : *m'kl*, **29B**:19.27 ; 22.15 ; *mkl'*, **8**:1 ii 10
m'mr (word) : *m'mr*, **23**:2.[6] ; **25**:1.1 ; **28**:2.18 ; *m'mrk*, **5**:33.8 ; *m'mrh*, **5**: 28.9
m'n (vessel) : *m'ny* (cst.), **13**:7
m'tyn (two hundred) : *m'tyn*, **14**:1.1, [1]ter, 2, [2] ; **17**:3.[11] ; **48**:2
mbwl (flood) : *mbwl'*, **3A**:2 ; **29B**:12.10
mb' (exulting) : *mb'*, **5**:3.6
mgdl (tower) : *mgdl*, **150**:3 ; *mgdl'*, **3A**: 6, 8 ; *mgdlyn*, **8**:1 ii [12] ; *mgdly'*, **8**:1 i 13bis, [13]
mgmr (live coals) : *mgmr*, **5**:36.6
mgn (shield) : *mgn*, **29B**:22.31
mgn (for nothing, gratis) : *mgn*, **5**:6.5
mdbḥ (altar) : *mdbḥ*, **29B**:21.20 ; *mdbḥ'*, **7**:4.[6] ; 5-6.[5] ; 7.2 ; **29B**:10.15 ; 19.[7] ; 21.1 ; **150**:8
mdbr (desert) : *mdbr*, **5**:31.4 ; *mdbr'*, **17**:3.5 ; **29B**:21.11, 28, 30 ; *mdbry'*, **16**:2.13
mdh (tribute) : *md'*, **29B**:21.26 ; *mdthwn* **29B**:21.27
mdynh (province, city) : *mdynt* (cst.), **29B**:22.5 ; **150**:12 ; *mdynthwn*, **5**:27.8 ; *mdynn*, **28**:2.12 ; *mdynt* (cst. pl.), **29B**:20.28 ; *mdytwn*, **29B**:22.4
mdnḥ (east) : *mdnḥ*, **13**:[7], *mdnḥ* (cst.), **10**:[6] ; **12**:[6], 6 ; **29B**:21.12, 20 ; *mdnḥ'*, **8**:1 i 3 ; **10**:[2], [4] ; **13**:[7] ; **29B**:21.9, 16, 17 ; **44**:1.4 ; 9-10.[1] ; **51**:8 ; **52**:3 ; *mdnḥhwn*, **10**:[8] ; **12**:4 ; *mdnḥy* (cst.), **13**:6 ; see also *klmdnḥ*
md' (knowledge) : *md''*, **5**:29.[8] ; see also *mnd'*
md'm (anything) : *md'm*, **28**:1.[4]
mdr (dwelling) : *mdrh*, **5**:32.5
mh' (dissolve) : *'tmh'* (I am dissolved), **5**:37.8
mhm (turmoil) : *mhm'*, **5**:32.6
mwḥ (marrow) : *mwḥ*, **5**:5.[5]
mwld (birth) : *mwldh* (his birth), **28**: 1.10 ; *mwldhyn*, **5**:32.2
mwmh (oath) : *mwmh*, **29B**:20.30
mwsr (chastisement) : *mwsr*, **5**:27.4
mw'd (appointed time) : *mw'd'*, **150**:1
mwq (mock) : *tmyq*, **5**:4.2
mwt (die) : *myt*, **64**:1.7 ; *mytw*, **5**:7.1 ; *ymwt*, **5**:5.5 ; 24.9 ; *'mwt*, **29B**:22.33 ; *myt* (ptc.), **64**:1.9 ; *mmtyn* (slayers), **5**:27.8
mwt (death) : *mwt'*, **17**:2.22 ; **26**:[13] ; *mtwtk*, **42**:[16] ; *mwth*, **24**:[2], 3
mzg (matching) : *mzghwn*, **42**:[12]
mzwn (food) : *mzwn*, **62**:[12]
mzrḥ (east) : *mzrḥ*, **13**:7
mḥ' (smite) : *mḥw*, **29B**:21.28, 30 ;

mḥyn (ptc.), **29B**:21.28 ; 22.4 ; *mtmḥyn*, **29A**:2.2
mḥwy (oracle) : *mḥwy*, **17**:3.6, 7
mḥzh (appearance) : *mḥzh*, **29B**:20.5
mḥzy (mirror) : *mḥzyh*, **5**:29.[9]
mḥzrw (return) : *mḥzwryt'*, **33**:5.[1]
mḥnh (camp) : *mḥnyh*, **57**:2 ; **60**:3, 4
mḥrt (next day) : *mḥrt*, **33**:1.2 ; *mḥrty*, **29B**:21.10
mṭ' (reach) : *mṭh*, **16**:2.12 ; *ymṭ'*, **5**:3.[8] ; *ymṭwn*, **60**:4
mṭr (rain) : *mṭr*, **5**:28.5 ; **11**:4 ; *mṭr'*, **5**:31.3, 5 ; **31**:5.4 ; **150**:12bis
myn (waters) : *myn*, **5**:11.11 ; 29.1 ; 31.7 ; **10**:[2] ; **28**:2.14 ; *my* (cst.), **21**:2.[4] ; **29B**:16.12 ; *my'* (emph.), **15**:2, 3 ; **31**:4.1
mkylh (measure) : *mkylh*, **5**:13.7
mkk (abase) : *hmkt* (I have abased), **5**:2.6
mks (covering) : *mksh* (his covering), **22**:2.5 ; **23**:1.[14]
mktš (pestilence) : *mktš'*, **29B**:20.19, 26, 29 ; *mktšy'*, **29B**:20.18, 24
ml' (fill) : *mlyn* (ptc.), **10**:6 ; **12**:[5] ; *ytmlyn*, **5**:23.2
ml'k (angel) : *ml'k*, **21**:2.18 ; *ml'ky* (cst. pl.), **5**:30.5
mlbwš (garment) : *mlbwšh* (his garment), **23**:1.[13]
mlh (word) : *ml'*, **5**:10.5 ; *mlyn*, **5**:1.[5] ; 20.[9] ; 21.6 ; 22.[7] ; 23.[10] ; 25.[10] ; **51**:12 ; *mly* (cst.), **2**:1.1 ; **5**:20.[2] ; **24**:1 ; **29B**:7.7 ; 19.25, 26 ; 20.8bis, 24 ; *mly* (my words), **5**:21.1, 9, [10] ; **29B**:19.21, [24] ; *mlyk*, **5**:22.[2] ; **17**:3.8 ; *mlwhy*, **5**:21.4 ; *mlykwn*, **5**:21.[1]
mlḥ (salt) : *mlḥ'*, **29B**:21.16 ; *mlyḥh*, **5**:32.5
mlk (counsel) : *mlkh*, **28**:1.7
mlk (rule) : *mlk*, **3E**:1 ; *tmlk*, **20**:7.2 ; *mmlk* (inf.), **5**:25.6
mlk (king) : *mlk*, **5**:15.[3] ; 37.2 ; **64**:2.8 ; *mlk* (cst.), **2**:1.1 ; **3C**:3 ; **29B**:2.4, 7, 14 ; 20.14 ; 21.23quater, 24ter, 25ter, 26, 27bis, 31quinquies, 32ter, 33 ; 22.12, 17, 19, 20, 25 ; **64**:1.[1] ; 3.3 ; **70**:3 ; *mlk'* (emph.), **2**:1.1 ; **4A**:4, 5 ; **4B**:[3], [4], [9] ; **29B**:20.8, 10, 22, 23bis, 24, 25, 30bis, 31 ; 22.14bis, 18 ; **64**:1.[1] ; 3.3 ; **150**:11 ; *mlkyn*, **5**:27.1 ; *mlky* (cst. pl.), **3F**:3, 4 ; **29B**:20.13, 15 ; *mlky'* (emph.), **29B**:21.26, [32] ; 22.4
mlkh (queen) : *mlkt'*, **132A**:1 ; *mlkth*, **132B**:1
mlkw (kingdom) : *mlkwt* (cst.), **20**:1.2 ; 3.[1] ; *mlkwt'*, **3D**:[2], 4 ; **20**:1.2 ; *mlkwt* (cst. pl.), **3D**:3
mll (speak) : *mll*, **5**:3.[3] ; **29B**:5.25 ; *mllt* (she spoke), **29B**:2.8 ; *mllt* (I spoke), **5**:37.5 ; *ymll*, **5**:22.8 ; 35.5, 6 ; *tmll* (she speaks), **29B**:2.13 ; *tmll* (you speak), **5**:22.7 ; *'mll*, **5**:23.[9] ; 37.6 ; *ymlln*, **5**:10.[11] ; 21.8 ; *tmllyn* (you speak), **29B**:2.7 ; *nmll*, **5**:1.[6] ; *mll'* (inf.), **5**:14.3 ; *mllh* (inf.), **3E**:7 ; *mmll'* (ptc.), **29B**:2.18 ; *mmllyn*, **29B**:20.8
mlp (teacher) : *mlp*, **32E**:1 ; *mlp'*, **35E**:2.3
mmwn (money) : *mmwnh*, **5**:11.[8]
mn (who, whom ?) : *mn*, **5**:9.[2], 6 ; 10.[6] ; 24.[1] ; 25.5 ; 28.6, 7 ; 30.3, 4 ; 31.2, 5, 6, [7] ; 32.4 ; **19**:1.3 ; **23**:1.12 ; 2.2 ; **29A**:1 i 1 ; **49**:1.4
mn (from, by ; than) : *mn*, **1**:1 ; **2**:1.3, [4], [6], 8 ; **3A**:2, 3 ; **3B**:2 ; **3C**:1 ; **3F**:3 ; **5**:1.8 ; 3.5bis ; 5.[1] ; 8.1 ; 10.2 ; 11.[4] ; 13:[1], [10] ; 14.6 ; 17.7 ; 19.[8] ; 20.[6] ; 22.6 ; 23.1, 2 ; 24.1, 3, 4, 5 ; 25.[3] ; 26.3, 4, 6, [6], [7] ; 27.4, 7 ; 29.1 ; 30.3, 6 ; 31.6 ; 32.4 ; 33.4, 5, 7 ; 34.2 ; 36.4, 5, 7 ; **7**:4.[5], [9], 11, 15 ; 5-6.3, [4], 4, [5] ; 7.1, [1] ; 8.4, 7 ; **8**:1 i 3, 4, [12], 12 ; 1 ii 6, 7, [11] ; **9**:2, 3 ; **10**:3, 5, [8] ; **11**:3 ; **12**:3, 5, 7, 8 ; **13**:7, 8 ; **14**:1.3bis, [3] ; 9-14-15.[5] ; 22.2 ; **15**:2, 3 ; **17**:2.7 ; 3.11 ; **18**:[4] ; **20**:1.1, 2 ; 3.[2] ; 28.1 ; 51.1 ; 56.1 ; **21**:2.10, 13 ; **23**:1.11 ; **28**:1.1, 3 ; 2.14 ; **29A**:2.2 ; **29B**:2.1bis, 16ter ; 5.[4], 4 ; 10.12 ; 12.17 ; 19.11, 16, 17, [18], 24 ; 20.7, 19, 27, [32], 33, 34 ; 21.5bis, 7, 10,

11bis, 15, 16, 18, 28 ; 22.1, 2, 6, 8, 9, 17, 19, 21, 22bis, 23bis, 25, 28bis, 29ter, 30, 33 ; **30**:5 ; **35A**:1.2, 4, 7 ; **39**:2 ; **40**:2, 3, [4], 5, 13, [15], 17 ; **41**:2, 4, 11, 13, 17 ; **42**:5, [11], [12], 17, 18, 23, 24 ; **44**:1.[7] ; 17.[1] ; **45**:1.2, 5, 6, 8 ; **46**:[3], 3, 4 ; **47**:1.1 ; **48**:5 ; **49**:1.6, 10 ; **50E**:3 ; **50F**:1 ; **51**: 2, 3bis, [11], 11, <13>bis ; **52**:4, 9, 10, [17], 19, 20 ; **62**:11 ; **64**:1.2, 3, 10 ; 2.1 ; 3.2 ; **69**:2 ; **91A**:2 ; **136**:2 ; **150**:1bis, 2bis, 6, 7, 8, 9, 11, 12bis ; *m-* (*mn* assimilated and prefixed), **3C**:3 ; **5**:15.5 ; 20.3 ; 26.2 ; 28.3 ; **6**: 1.[2] ; **13**:7 ; **39**:8 ; **41**:[7] ; **42**:12, 13, 14, [15] ; **59**:2bis ; **60**:3 ; **62**:12 ; **150**: 3bis ; see also *m'l* ; *mny* (from me), **5**:2.[2] ; 15.4 ; **18**:7 ; **29B**:5.27 ; 19. 21 ; 20.11, 14, 15, 21 ; **32B**:3 ; **40**:7, 20 ; **42**:[10], [13] ; *mnk*, **5**:37.4 ; **29B**:2.15ter ; 22.31 ; **64**:1.9, 10 ; *mnkh*, **29B**:20.26 ; *mnh*, **2**:4.2 ; **5**: 31.7 ; **12**:7, 8 ; **14**:3.1 ; **29B**:2.20, 22 ; 20.14, 23, 29, [29] ; **64**:3.2 ; *mnh'*, **29B**:20.6 ; *mnn'*, **23**:1.12 ; *mnnh*, **29B**: 20.28 ; *mnkwn*, **5**:21.3 ; *mnkn*, **53**: 2, 3 ; **59**:3 ; *mnhwn*, **3C**:3 ; **5**:21.7 ; **8**:1 i 3, [5] ; **10**:1, [2], [5] ; **12**:6 ; **13**:8bis, [9]bis ; **17**:2.4 ; **22**:2.[2] ; **23**: 1.13 ; **29B**:22.10 ; *mnhm*, **64**:3.5

mnd' (knowledge) : *mnd'*, **21**.1.14 ; *mnd'y*, **5**:4.2 ; *mnd'h*, **5**:10.3 ; *mnd'hwn*, **26**:11 ; see also *md'*

mnh (count ; appoint) : *mnyt*, **64**:1.11 ; *tmnh*, **5**:32.[1] ; *mnyh*, **39**:3 ; *mmnyh* (inf.), **29B**:21.13 ; **38**:5 ; *mnyt* (pael), **5**:30.9, *mny*, **29B**:20.32 ; *mny* (impv.), **29B**:22.29 ; *ytmnh*, **29B**:21.13

mnḥh (meal-offering) : *mnḥ'*, **29B**:21. 20 ; *mnḥh*, **29B**:21.2

mnyn (number) : *mnyn*, **5**:5.[3] ; 28.4 ; **36**:2 ; **38**:1

mn' (withhold) : *'mn'*, **5**:18.[9]

mnpq (exit) : *mnpqhwn*, **64**:3.5 ; see also *mpq*

ms'n (sandal) : *ms'n*, **29B**:22.21

msṭ (turning) : *msṭ'*, **5**:13.10

mskn (needy) : *mskn*, **5**:8.5 ; *mskn'*, **5**: 27.[9] ; *msknyn*, **5**:25.4 ; *mskny'*, **5**: 27.2

msrh (opposition) : *msrt* (cst.), **28**:1.9

m'l (entrance) : *m'l*, **51**:10 ; *m'l'*, **44**: 1.3 ; **52**:6 ; *m'lh*, **8**:1 ii 2 ; *mn'lhm*, **64**:3.5

m'l (above) : *m'l*, **6**:1.[2] ; *m'l'*, **5**:19. [3] ; **42**:13 ; *m'lh*, **44**:13.2

m'rb (west) : *m'rb'*, **8**:1 ii [3] ; **29B**:17.8, 10 ; 21.9 ; **44**:1.[4] ; **51**:9 ; **52**:3 ; *m'rbh*, **7**:4.10 ; **9**:[2]

m'rh (cave) : *m'rth*, **68**:6-7

m'śr (tithe) : *m'śr*, **29B**:22.17

mplh (fall) : *mplth*, **5**:5.1

mpq (exit) : *mpq'*, **44**:1.3 ; **51**:10 ; **52**: 6 ; *mpqhn*, **64**:4.2 ; see also *mnpq*

mṣy' (middle) : *mṣy''*, **8**:1 i [5] ; *mṣy't*, **8**:1 i [5] ; 1 ii [9] ; *mṣy't'*, **8**:1 ii [9]

mṣmḥ (brilliance) : *mṣmḥ*, **5**:36.<4>

mṣr (border) : *mṣrh*, **52**:6

mqdš (sanctuary) : *mqdš'*, **8**:1 i [4]

mqm (place) : *mqm*, **29B**:19.26 ; **61**:25 ; *mqmy*, **61**:25

mr' (lord) : *mr'*, **5**:5.[1] ; 7.[2] ; 11.[2] ; 24.[5], 7 ; 26.[8] ; **7**:3.[3] ; *mry*, **29B**: 20.12 ; *mrh*, **29B**:20.13, 15 ; *mrh* (cst.), **29A**:2.5 ; **29B**:2.4 ; 7.7 ; 12.17 ; 21.2 ; 22.16, 21 ; *mr'* (cst.), **35E**:2 ; *mr'y* (my lord), **23**:2.3 ; *mry* (my lord), **20**:52.1 ; **21**:1.10, 18 ; 2.6 ; **29B**:2.9, 13, 24 ; 20.14, 15, 25 ; 22. 18, 32

mrb' (square) : *mrb'*, **8**:1 ii 5

mrd (rebel) : *mrdw*, **29B**:21.27

mrdp (persecutor) : *mrdp'*, **29B**:20.[28]

mrh (mistress) : *mrt* (cst.), **37**:2.2

mrwm (height) : *mrwmh*, **5**:9.[5]

mrq (brighten) : *ymrq*, **5**:29.1 ; *mrq'* (pael inf.), **45**:1.4 ; **52**:12

mšḥ (measure) : *mšḥ*, **7**:3.2 ; **8**:1 i [4], [16], [17], 17 ; 1 ii [9], [12], [13] ; 10.2 ; 13.[1]

mšḥh (measurement) : *mšḥh*, **6**:2.[3] ; **8**:1 i [6], [12] ; 1 ii 3, 4 ; 4.[3] ; **20**: 37.2 ; *mšḥ'*, **7**:5-6.2 ; *mšḥt* (cst.), **7**: 1.3 ; **8**:1 i [2], [8], [10], [15], [18] ; 1 ii 2, [10] ; *mšḥt'*, **8**:1 i [15] ; *mšḥth*, **5**:30.3

mšk (draw) : *tmškwn*, **19**:4.3
mškb (bed) : *mškbh*, **5**:22.10
mškwn (pledge) : *mškwny*, **64**:3.4
mšmʿ (hearing) : *mšmʿ*, **5**:37.7
mšryh (encampment) : *mšry'ty*, **29B**: 21.1
mšth (drink) : *mšth*, **29B**:19.27 ; 22.15
mt (land) : *mt*, **29B**:2.23
mtnh (gift) : *mtnn*, **4A**:8 ; **29B**:19.25

n' (I pray) : *n'*, **5**:30.1 ; 34.3, 6, 7 ; 37.6 ; **21**:2.[7] ; *nh*, **29B**:20.25
nbzbh (reward) : *nbzbh*, **4A**:[8]
ngd (set out, draw out ; afflict) : *ngdt* (I set out), **21**:2.11 ; **29B**:19.8, 10 ; *ngdw*, **29B**:22.4, 7 ; *ngd* (pael), **5**: 30.3 ; *tgd*, **5**:35.3 ; *mtngd*, **29B**:20.25
ngd (affliction) : *ngdy'*, **29**:20.18, 24
ngšh (driving) : *ngšt* (cst.), **5**:32.6
ndd (flee) : *ndt*, **17**:2.4 ; **18**:[10]
ndn (sheath) : *ndnh'*, **29B**:2.10
nh (I pray) : see *n'*
nhwr (light) : *nhwr* (abs.), **5**:23.7 ; *nhwr* (cst.), **5**:23.[8] ; 29.6 ; *nhwr'* (emph.), **20**:24.1 ; **23**:2.[5], 6 ; 3.[1] ; **26**:[9], [10], [12], 13 ; *nhwrh*, **5**:28. [7]
nhr (illumine) : *nhyryn* (peal pass. ptc.), **26**:10, [12]
nhyrw (brightness) : *nhyrwt'*, **26**:14
nhr (river) : *nhr* (cst.), **29B**:21.11 ; *nhr'*, **14**:13.[2] ; **29B**:16.16 ; 17.16 ; 19.11, 12bis ; 21.15, 17, 19, 28 ; *nhryn*, **29B**:21.24 ; *nhry'*, **13**:[9]
nwd (flee) : *tnwd*, **20**:3.[2]
nwḥ (rest) : *nḥt* (she rested), **29B**:10. 12 ; *tnwḥ*, **20**:3.[2]
nwḥ (repose) : *nwḥ*, **109**:1
nwn (fish) : *nwnyn*, **5**:35:10
nwr (fire) : *nwr'*, **4B**:[1], 4 ; **5**:8.[3] ; 18.[4] ; 36.4 ; **17**:2.10 ; *nwrh* (his fire), **5**:29.2
nzk (spear) : *nzk*, **5**:33.5
nzq (damage) : *nzqyn*, **40**:9, [22]
nzr (Nazirite) : *hnzr* (with Hebr. article), **121**:1 ; *hnzyr* (with Hebr. article), **122**:1
nḥyr (nostril) : *nḥyrwhy*, **5**:36.<5>
nḥl (torrent bed) : *nḥl*, **10**:[2] ; *nḥly'*, **10**:[3]bis
nḥm (console) : *nḥmwhy*, **5**:38.6
nḥš (copper) : *nḥš'*, **2**:1.[7]
nḥšyrw (slaughter) : *nḥšyrwt'*, **20**:3.[1]
nḥt (descend) : *nḥt*, **17**:2.16 ; **150**:12 ; *tnḥt*, **5**:1.[2] ; *ynḥtwn*, **5**:28.5 ; *nḥtn*, **29B**:20.12 ; *'ḥtwny* (make me descend), **5**:16.9 ; *hnḥth*, **5**:31.3
nṭl (lift, take) : *nṭlt* (I lifted), **21**:1.8 ; **22**:2 ; **23**:1.[12] ; *ynṭlw*, **15**:3 ; *yṭlwn*, **7**:4.5 ; *mṭl* (inf.), **5**:35.3 ; *'tnṭyl*, **150**: 11 ; *'tnṭylw*, **150**:2, 3, 9
nṭp (resin) : *nṭp*, **10**:6
nṭr (guard) : *nṭr*, **35G**:1 ; *nṭrt* (I kept), **5**:21.7 ; *tnṭr*, **5**:32.[1] ; *mnṭr*, **5**:26.[5]
nywmh (sleep) : *nywmh*, **5**:22.[10]
nyḥ (equanimity) : *nyḥ*, **5**:35.6
nyr (yoke) : *nyryh*, **5**:32.9
nksyn (flocks ; possessions) : *nksyn*, **5**: 4.6 ; **29B**:20.33, 34 ; 22.32 ; *nksy'*, **29B**:21.3, 33 ; 22.17, 19, 24 ; *nksy* (my goods), **29B**:22.22 ; **39**:8 ; **41**:4 ; **42**:[11], [15] ; **46**:3 ; *nksyk*, **29B**:22. 31 ; *nkswhy*, **29B**:21.5, 6 ; 22.1, 3, 11 ; *nksynh*, **45**:1.[6] ; **51**:<13>
nkry (stranger) : *nkry*, **5**:2.[4]
nms (law [= Gk. νόμος]) : *nms'*, **42**:11
nmr (reap) : *tnmrn*, **57**:2
ns' (carry off) : *ynswn*, **5**:11.4
nsb (take) : *nsb*, **29B**:20.34 ; *nsbh'*, **29B**:20.9 ; *nsbth'* (I took her), **29B**: 20.27 ; *ysbwn*, **7**:4.9 ; *'sb*, **29B**:22.22 ; *sb*, **30**:3
nsy (ruler) : *hnsy* (with Hebr. article), **53**:1
nsk (pour) : *nsyk*, **5**:36.[9] ; *nsykyn*, **5**:36.[8] ; *'tnsk*, **5**:37.8
nʿmty (Naamathite) : *nʿmty'*, **5**:3.[3]
npḥ (blow up) : *mnpḥ* (inf.), **5**:29.[8]
npyl (fallen one) : *npylyn*, **29B**:2.[1] ; *npyly* (cst.), **17**:3.8 ; *npyly'*, **17**:2. [21]
npl (fall) : *npl*, **28**:2.1 ; **29B**:21.33 ; *yplwn*, **5**:27.6 ; *mpl* (inf.), **32J**:1
npq (go forth) : *npq*, **5**:31.6 ; **10**:4 ; **29B**:21.31 ; *npqth*, **29B**:22.28 ; *npqw*, **5**:32.3 ; **17**:2.7 ; 3.[11] ; **29B**:22.30 ;

150:6 ; *ypq*, **5**:31.2 ; 36.5 ; **29B**:22. 34 ; *ypwq*, **35A**:1.4 ; *ynpq*, **5**:33.3 ; *ypqwn*, **5**:36.5 ; *ypqn*, **5**:32.3 ; 36.7 ; *mpq* (inf.), **5**:30.7 ; *mpqk*, **29B**:22.30 ; *npq*, **29B**:21.18 ; *npqyn*, **4B**:8 ; **8**:1 i [3], 4 ; *npqn*, **150**:2 ; *'npq* (aphel), **29B**:5.27 ; 22.14 ; *'npqt*, **64**:1.11 ; *ynpq*, **5**:29.1 ; *ynpqwnny*, **29B**:20. [32] ; *tnpq*, **64**:1.9 ; *hnpqh*, **5**:31.5 ; *hnpq* (was issued ?), **64**:1.3

npš (throat ; breath ; soul ; self) ; *npš* (abs.), **5**:5.[5] ; **109**:1 ; *npš* (cst.), **5**:8.[1] ; *npš'* (emph.), **29B**:22.19 ; *npšy* (my soul), **5**:10.9 ; 16.[6] ; 23. [7] ; **29B**:19.20 ; *npšk*, **35F**:2 ; *npšky*, **40**:6, 18 ; *npšh* (his soul), **5**:23.[8] ; 36.6 ; **39**:9 ; **40**:[26] ; **41**:[18] ; **42**:21 ; **46**:6 ; **47**:11, 12 ; **51**:‹15› ; **52**:[15] ; *npšh* (her soul), **29B**:19.23 ; **42**:23 ; **51**:16 ; *npšn'*, **37**:2.3

nṣ (falcon) : *nṣ'*, **5**:33.7

nṣ (radiance) : *nṣ*, **29B**:20.3

nṣb (plant) : *nṣbt*, **29B**:12.13

nṣbh (plantation) : *nṣbt* (cst.), **29B**:2. 15 ; *nṣbt'*, **29B**:1.1 ; *nṣbtn'*, **5**:26.5

nṣyḥ (splendid) : *nṣyḥ*, **29B**:20.[2]

nṣl (rescue) : *'ṣl* (he rescued), **29B**:22. 10 ; *'ṣlth*, **29B**:22.19 ; *hṣlh*, **4B**:15

nṣph (shrieking) : *nṣpt'*, **20**:3.[1]

nqb (pierce, mark) : *tqwb*, **5**:35.5 ; *nqybyn*, **64**:3.6

nqy (clean) : *nq'*, **5**:22.3

nqp (surround) : *y'qpwny*, **5**:16.6 ; *y'qpwnny*, **5**:16.[9]

nqšh (clash) : *nqšt* (cst.), **5**:33.6

nrd (nard) : *nrd*, **12**:[5]

nšb (blow) : *tšwb*, **5**:31.2

nšyn (women, wives) : *nšyn*, **29B**:20.7 ; *nšy* (cst.), **29B**:12.16 ; *nšy'*, **16**:2.8 ; *nšykwn*, **16**:2.7

nšmh (breath) : *nšmty*, **29B**:2.10 ; *nšmh* (his breath), **5**:24.[8] ; *nšmwhy*, **28**: 1.10 ; 2.[7]

nšq (kiss) : *nšqt*, **5**:19.2

nšr (eagle) : *nšr'*, **5**:33.[8] ; *nšryn*, **17**: 3.[4]

ntk (pour out) : *ttk*, **29A**:1 i 1

ntn (give) : *ytnk*, **44**:1.7 ; *ytnkn*, **45**:1. [5] ; *ttn*, **5**:26.2 ; *'ntn*, **29B**:21.12 ; *'ntnnh*, **29B**:21.14 ; *ytnwn*, **7**:4.[8] ; *ttnwn*, **53**:1 ; *ttnwnny*, **16**:1.3 ; *mntn*, **3C**:2 ; **29B**:22.24

s (cipher for *s'h*, " seah ") : *s*, **38**:1bis, 2, 3

s'h (seah) : *s'yn*, **7**:4.4 ; **52**:2

sb (elder) : *sb'*, **89**:1 ; **110**:2 ; see also *śb*

sb' (sate) : *hsb'h* (inf.), **5**:31.4

sbr (wait) : *sbrt*, **5**:21.1 ; *sbr* (ptc.), **2**:1.[8] ; see also *śbr*

sg' (grow numerous, increase ; amass) : *hsgyw*, **5**:4.6 ; *ysg'*, **5**:11.7

sgy' (much) : *sgy'*, **5**:26.1, 3 ; 28.6 ; 32.10 ; *sgy*, **89**:4 ; *sgy'yn*, **5**:26.4 ; *sgy'y'*, **5**:28.[4] ; see also *śgy'*

sgn (chieftain) : *sgnyn*, **5**:14.4

sgp (afflict) : *ysgpwnny*, **5**:2.[7]

sgr (deliver) : *sgr*, **29B**:22.17

sd (stocks) : *sd'*, **5**:22.5

sdr (row) : *sdryn*, **7**:4.7 ; *sdry* (cst.), **7**:4.8

shr (moon) : *shr'*, **5**:19.[1]

swg (shut) : *tswg*, **5**:30.6

swlt (wheat flour) : *swlt'*, **7**:4.[4] ; *slt'*, **150**:8

swp (reeds) : *swp*, **29B**:21.18

swp (end, finish) : *spw*, **5**:20.[2] ; *yswpw*, **28**:1.9 ; *yswpwn*, **28**:2.14 ; *msp*, **3F**: 7 ; *hsypt*, **5**:18.[9] ; *tsypwn*, **5**:21.2

swp (end) : *swp* (abs.), **5**:1.5 ; 25.1 ; 28.4 ; 34.1 ; *swp* (cst.), **5**:21.2 ; **17**: 2.12, 20 ; **29B**:20.18 ; **150**:1 ; see also *syp*

swrygh (partition-wall): *swrygh*, **150**:8

sḥr (journey) : *sḥrt*, **29B**:21.16, 17, 18 ; *msḥr*, **29B**:21.15bis ; *sḥr* (ptc.), **8**:1 ii 3, [4], 5 ; *swḥr*, **8**:1 i 1; *sḥryn*, **13**:6

sḥwr (around) : *sḥwr*, **7**:1.2bis ; **8**:1 i 1, [1]

sḥr (snorting) : *sḥrwhy*, **5**:33.2

syg (circuit) : *syg*, **5**:31.8

sym (place) : *symw*, **5**:4.4

symw'h (image) : *symw't'*, **150**:9

syp (end) : *sypy* (cst.), **5**:10.[1] ; *sy'py*, **10**:[6] ; **11**:[3]

syp (sword) : *syp*, **5:**33.5 ; *syph*, **53:4**
skl (consider) : *hstklw*, **5:**25.[3]; *ystkl*, **5:**10.6 ; *hstkl* (impv.), **5:**7.7 ; 29.5
skr (close up) : *skr*, **5:**22.5
slm (peace) : see *šlm*
sl' (sela) : *sl'yn*, **43:**[5] ; **50D:**[2] ; **51:**6 ; **52:**8 ; **64:**3.[2]
slq (go up) : *slq*, **29B:**22.13 ; *slqt*, **29B:**20.33 ; 21.10 ; **49:**1.10 ; *slqw*, **29B:**21.28 ; *yslqw*, **15:**2 ; *slq* (impv.), **29B:**21.8 ; *msq*, **150:**8 ; *slq* (ptc.), **8:**1 i [13] ; 1 ii [3], [4], 5, [5] ; **16:**2.10 ; *'sqt*, **29B:**21.20 ; **68:** <5>
slt' (wheat flour) : see *swlt*
smk (lay upon) : *smkt*, **29B:**20.29 ; *'smwk*, **29B:**20.22
sn' (enemy) : *sn'h*, **150:**11 ; see also *śn'*
s'd (support) : *s'd*, **29B:**22.31
s'r (stir) : *yst'r*, **5:**33.7
s'rh (barley) : *s'ryn*, **38:**1 ; see also *ś'rh*
spd (mourn) : *mspd* (inf.), **150:**1ter, 2ter, 5, 6, 9bis, 11bis, 12ter
spyr (sapphire) : *spyr*, **5:**12.3 ; *spyr'*, **7:**3.[2]
spr (book ; writing) : *spr* (cst.), **16:**2.1 ; **40:**7, [20] ; **150:**4 ; *spry'*, **28:**1.5
spr (scribe) : *spr* (cst.), **16:**2.4 ; **17:**2.14, [22] ; *spr'*, **42:**[22] ; *sprh*, **51:**17 ; *spry'*, **52:**{18} ; *spry'*, **150:**12 ; *hswpr* (with Hebr. article), **99:**1
srd (terrify) : *tsrdnk*, **5:**22.[1]
sryq (barren) : *sryqh*, **19:**1.[6]
str (hide) : *ystr*, **5:**25.[5] ; *'sttrt*, **5:**13.[2]
str (hideout) : *stry*, **5:**16.[1]
str (tear down) : *stryn*, **33:**6.1 ; *'sttr*, **150:**8

'bd (servant) : *'bd*, **5:**35.7 ; *'bdy*, **5:**2.5 ; 18.[6] ; *'bdk*, **21:**2.[8], 10 ; *'bdyn*, **3F:**[5] ; *'bdwhy*, **4B:**[12] ; **29B:**22.6
'bd (do ; make) : *'bd*, **5:**24.7 ; **29B:**12.13 ; 21.3 ; *'bdny*, **5:**18.[8] ; *'bdnh*, **5:**26.5 ; *'bdt* (you have done), **5:**28.[1] ; *'bdth*, **29B:**20.26 ; 22.28 ; *'bdt* (I made), **18:**4 ; *'bdw*, **29B:**21.24, [31] ; *y'bd*, **5:**7.[2] ; *t'bd*, **5:**26.[1] ; *t'bdyn*, **29B:**19.[20] ; *''bd*, **5:**18.6 ; **39:**7 ; **53:**3 ; **59:**3 ; *y'bdwn*, **5:**27.[5] ; *t'bdwn*, **53:**2 ; **54:**[2] ; *'bd* (impv.), **29B:**20.14 ; **55:**3 ; *'ybd*, **89:**1 ; *m'bd* (inf.), **2:**1.5 ; **5:**37.4 ; **21:**2.[8] ; **29B:**20.13 ; **52:**10 ; *m'bd'*, **89:**3 ; *m'bdy*, **5:**30.2 ; *m'bdh*, **5:**13.6, [7] ; *'bd* (ptc.), **5:**9.[4] ; *'bdy*, **5:**24.2 ; *'byd* (pass. ptc.), **67:**1 ; *yt'bd*, **4B:**14 ; *tt'bd*, **53:**2 ; *tt'bdwn*, **4A:**7
'bd (deed ; work) : *'bd* (cst.), **5:**11.1 ; 23.4 ; 24.[5] ; *'bdh*, **23.**2.4 ; *'bdhwn*, **5:**25.2 ; *'bdwhy*, **5:**28.1 ; *'bdyhwn*, **5:**27.[3] ; 29.2 ; see also *'wbd*
'bwr (grain) : *'bwr'*, **29B:**19.[10]
'by (depth) : *'wby*, **8:**1 ii 12
'bydh (service) : *'bydt'*, **150:**11
'b' (haste) : *'b'*, **5:**3.7 ; see also *'wb'*
'br (pass) : *'br*, **29B:**17.10 ; *''brt* (I was made to traverse), **12:**7 ; *m'brhwn*, **3B:**3
'gy (pit) : *'gy'yn*, **29B:**21.33
'd (witness) : *'d* (Hebr.), **39:**12 ; **42:**[26] ; **51:**18
'd (unto [prep.]) : *'d*, **3F:**5 ; **5:**10.[1] ; 18.4 ; 30.8 ; **6:**17.3 ; **7:**3.2 ; 4.11, 17, 19 ; **8:**1 ii 5, [6], 7 ; **14:**27.4 ; **16:**2.[10], 12 ; **17:**2.12, 20 ; **19:**2.2 ; **20:**9.3 ; **23:**2.6 ; **28:**1.[4] ; **29B:**16.11, [12] ; 17.9, 16 ; 19.8, 9, 26 ; 21.1, 6, 11ter, 12, 14, 15, 17bis, 18bis ; 22.21 ; **35B:**2.2 ; **39:**5 ; **42:**[11], [15] ; **150:**1bis ; see also *'dy*
'd (until [conj.]) : *'d*, **5:**21.[1], 2 ; **7:**4.15 ; **20:**7.1 ; **21:**2.17 ; **29B:**2.5, 7 ; 17.8, 10 ; 21.29 ; 22.7, 10
'db (lot) : *'dbh*, **29B:**2.21
'dh (come upon ; cease), *'dh*, **4B:**[10] ; *'d'*, **150:**4 ; *t'dy*, **21:**2.[9] ; *y'dwn*, **150:**12 ; *'dy* (depart!), **29B:**20.27 ; *t'd'* (3 sg. aphel impf.), **5:**3.7 ; *t'dh* (2 sg.), **5:**34.4 ; *h'dy*, **5:**34.6, 7 ; *''dywtky*, **29B:**19.[21]
'dw' (seizure) : *'dw'*, **64:**1.2, 3, 10, 11bis ; 3.4, 6
'dy (until) : **62:**12
'dynh (pleasure) : *'dynty*, **29B:**2.9, 14
'dn (time) : *'dn*, **7:**4.19 ; **28:**1.4 ; *'dn* (cst.), **5:**31.1 ; 32:2 ; *'dn'*, **3F:**[2] ; *'dny'*, **33:**4.4

ʿdn (pleasure) : *ʿdnyn*, **5**:27.6
ʿdq (sinew) : *ʿdqy*, **5**:16.[7]
ʿdr (help) : *ʿdrt*, **5**:9.[10]
ʿdr (helper) : *ʿdr*, **5**:14.7
ʿwbd (work ; conduct) : *ʿwbd*, **16**:2.10 ; **29B**:21.5 ; *ʿwbdh*, **28**:2.16 ; *ʿwbdkwn*, **16**:2.7
ʿwbʿ (haste) : *ʿwbʿ*, **29B**:20.9 ; see also *ʿbʿ*
ʿwd (yet) : *ʿwd*, **5**:21.[8] ; **7**:8.6 ; **19**:1.[5] ; **29B**:19.[22] ; **30**:2
ʿwz (black eagle) : *ʿwzʾ*, **5**:33.9
ʿwyh (transgression) : *ʿwytk*, **5**:26.1 ; *ʿwythwn*, **5**:27.[3]
ʿwl (iniquity) : *ʿwl*, **30**:2 ; *ʿwlʾ*, **5**:28.[1] ; *ʿwlyn*, **5**:22.4
ʿwlym (youth) : *ʿwlym*, **5**:23.3 ; *ʿlwmyn* (read *ʿwlmyn*), **5**:14.2 ; *ʿwlymʾ*, **29B**:2.2 ; *ʿwlymy*, **29B**:22.23
ʿwp (bird) : *ʿwp*, **14**:1.[3]
ʿwq (wear out) : *ʿqh*, **5**:29.9
ʿwr (blind) : *ʿwr*, **3F**:8
ʿwr (awake) : *ʾtʿyrt*, **29B**:19.17
ʿwrʿ (toward) : *ʿwrʿh*, **29B**:22.13 ; *ʿwrʿhwn*, **29B**:21.31
ʿwt (distort) : *yʿwt*, **5**:24.[7]
ʿzrh (temple court) : *ʿzrtʾ*, **7**:8.7 ; **150**:8
ʿṭyš (sneeze) : *ʿṭyšth*, **5**:36.3
ʿṭm (bone) : *ʿṭmwhy*, **5**:23.[2] ; see also *ṭmy*
ʿṭr (whisp) : *ʿṭr*, **5**:10.5
ʿyṭ (plot) : *htʿyṭtwn*, **5**:5.8
ʿṭh (advice) : *ʿṭt* (cst.), **5**:7.4
ʿyn (eye) : *ʿyn*, **5**:14.5 ; *ʿyny*, **5**:37.7 ; **18**:10 ; **21**:1.[8] ; **22**:2.2 ; **23**:1.[12] ; *ʿynyk*, **20**:3.[2] ; **21**:2.[5] ; **29B**:21.9 ; *ʿynwhy*, **5**:5.[1] ; 20.[4] ; 35.3 ; 36.4 ; **22**:2.6 ; **23**:1.[15] ; *ʿynyhʾ*, **29B**:20.3 ; *ʿynyhwn*, **5**:4.7 ; **17**:2.4
ʿyr (watcher) : *ʿyrʾ*, **16**:2.[4] ; **23**:2.[2] bis ; *ʿyry*, **25**:2.1 ; *ʿyryn*, **28**:2.16, [18] ; **29B**:2.1, 16
ʿkr (?) : *ʿkyr*, **49**:1.9
ʿl (on, upon) : *ʿl*, **3A**:[8] ; **5**:1.[3], 7 ; 4.4 ; 5.6 ; 9.6 ; 14.[3] ; 19.4 ; 20.[8] ; 22.10 ; 24.[9] ; 25.5, [5] ; 28.[6], 9 ; 29.1, 3bis ; 30.4 ; 31.2, 3, 9 ; 32.6, 8 ; 33.3, 8 ; 34.4 ; 37.2, 8 ; 38.6 ; **7**:4.6, 7, [7] ; **8**:1 i [4], [9], [10], 13, [17] ; 1 ii 2 ; **10**:[3] ; **14**:1.4 ; 19.[2] ; **16**:2.10, [10] ; **17**:2.5, 21 ; **18**:10 ; **21**:2.12, [14] ; **23**:1.12 ; 2.5, [5], 6, [6] ; 3.[1] ; **28**:1.2, 3, 6 ; **29B**:2.2, 3, 9, 19 ; 10.15 ; 17.11 ; 19.21, 24bis ; 20.6, 9, 10, 13, 14, 18, 21, 22, 28bis, 29 ; 21.3, 6, 8 ; 22.2, 5, 10 ; **31**:2.2 ; **33**:5.3 ; **35A**:1.[5] ; **39**:[9] ; **40**:26 ; **41**:[4], [18] ; **42**:[21] ; **44**:[7] ; **45**:1.[5] ; **46**:6 ; **47**:11, 12 ; **49**:1.4, [5] ; **51**:15, 16 ; **52**:15 ; **53**:1 ; **61**:24 ; **64**:1.2 ; 3.1, 2 ; **150**:8, 10, 12bis ; *ʿly*, **5**:2.1 ; 15.4 ; 16:[4], 5 ; **21**:1.18 ; **23**:1.10, 11, [11] ; **29B**:2.2, 11, 12, 25 ; 19.20 ; 20.21, 28 ; 21.7 ; **45**:1.[2] ; **51**:10 ; *ʿlyk*, **5**:16.[10] ; **23**:2.1 ; **29B**:2.17, 26 ; 22.31 ; **42**:[10], [13] ; **64**:2.2 ; *ʿlwhy*, **5**:24.8 ; 25.[4] ; 28.2, [10] ; 33.4 ; 35.[9] ; 36.[8] ; 38.7 ; **7**:8.[5] ; **8**:1 ii 4 ; **28**:1.9 ; 2.17, 19 ; **29B**:20.18, 22, 23 ; 21.2, 20 ; **150**:12 ; *ʿlwy*, **53**:4 ; *ʿlyh*, **5**:29.5 ; 30.3 ; *ʿlyhʾ*, **29B**:7.1 ; *ʿlh*, **44**:1.3 ; **52**:6 ; *ʿlykwn*, **16**:2.[9], 10, 14 ; **34**:3 ; *ʿlyhwn*, **3C**:2 ; **5**:4.[8] ; 5.[7] ; 27.8 ; 29.[6] ; **7**:4.[14] ; **29B**:21.26 ; 22.8 ; **31**:7.3 ; **67**:4 ; *ʿlyhn*, **5**:32.4 ; 37.5 ; **9**:[5] ; see also *mʿl*
ʿlʾ (above) : *ʿlʾ*, **8**:1 ii 11 ; **12**:[7]bis ; **15**:2 ; **29B**:20.7 ; **42**:[18] ; **44**:13.2 ; **45**:1.8 ; **49**:1.6 ; **52**:9 ; **61**:25
ʿlh (burnt offering) : *ʿlʾ*, **29B**:21.20 ; *ʿlwʾn*, **29B**:21.2
ʿly (high ; Most High) : *ʿlyʾ*, **2**:1.[2], [3], [5] ; **23**:2.6 ; **25**:1.[1] ; **29B**:2.4 ; 20.7
ʿlyb (low) : *ʿlybʾ*, **29B**:2.17
ʿlywn (Most High) : *ʿlywn*, **20**:1.[3] ; **29B**:12.17 ; 20.12, 16 ; 21.2, 20 ; 22.15, 16bis, 21
ʿlymw (youth) : *ʿlymw*, **5**:36.8 ; *ʿlymwth*, **5**:23.[3] ; **28**:1.4
ʿll (enter) : *ʿlt* (I came into), **29B**:2.3 ; *ʿlw*, **14**:17.1 ; **32C**:1 ; *ʿlnʾ*, **29B**:19.13 ; *yʿl*, **5**:6.[3] ; *tʿwl*, **5**:36.[2] ; *yʿlwn*, **7**:4.[3] ; *yʿln*, **29B**:20.6 ; *mʿl*, **29B**:19.[11] ; **33**:5.2 ; *mʿly*, **29B**:19.14 ; *ʿll* (ptc.?), **8**:1 ii 1 ; *ʿllh*, **8**:1 i [19] ;

yt''l, **30**:4 ; *''lny* (he brought me inside), **8**:1 i [18] ; 1 ii 6

'lm (world ; age) : *'lm*, **5**:35.7 ; **29B**:19.[8] ; **41**:4 ; 45:1.[2], 6, [7] ; **51**:6, 11, 12, 13 ; **52**:9, 10 ; **71**:[3] ; *'lm'*, **5**:3.5 ; **20**:3.3 ; **26**:[13] ; **29A**:2.5 ; **35D**:1 ; **41**:7, [9] ; **42**:[12] ; **89**:1, 3 ; *'lmyn*, **4A**:4 ; **14**:20.3 ; **21**:2.[9] ; **28**:1.11 ; 2.8 ; *'lmym*, **29B**:2.[4], 7 ; 20.13 ; 21.10, 12 ; *'lmy'*, **29B**:21.2, 14

'l'wl (whirlwind) : *'l'wlyn*, **17**:3.4

'm (people) : *'m*, **4B**:13 ; **5**:25.5 ; 28.6 ; **20**:7.2 ; *'m'*, **26**:14 ; **35G**:1 ; **150**:12 ; *'myn*, **35A**:7 ; *'mmyn*, **5**:28.[8] ; *'mmy'*, **3D**:[3] ; **3F**:3, 4 ; **28**:1.8 ; **35C**:[2] ; **150**:12

'm (with) : *'m*, **5**:9.4 ; 15.5 ; 23.[7] ; 27.2 ; **29B**:1.1 ; 2.[20] ; 5.25 ; 20.7, 19 ; 21.24ter, 25bis ; **42**:10 ; *'my*, **5**:1.2 ; **19**:1.4 ; **29B**:2.7, 8, 13 ; 19.[20], [23] ; 20.11, 32, 34 ; 21.3, 22bis ; 22.23, 24 ; **39**:3 ; **42**:[10], [13] ; **51**:5, 10 ; **64**:1.10 ; *'mk*, **5**:6.3 ; 35.6bis, 7 ; **29B**:2.18 ; 22.19, 30bis ; **42**:12 ; *'mh*, **5**:38.6 ; **7**:4.16 ; **29B**:20.23, [34] ; 21.6, 26, 32 ; 22.7, 15, 25 ; **28**:1.7 ; **55**:4 ; *'mh'*, **29B**:20.7, 17 ; *'mkwn*, **58**:2 ; *'mhwn*, **18**:4, <5> ; **29B**:22.1 ; *'mhn*, **60**:2

'mwd (column) : *'mwd*, **8**:1 ii 4 ; 2.5bis ; *'mwd'*, **6**:1.[1], [2] ; *'mwdyn*, **6**:5.[2] ; *'mwdy*, **5**:10.[2] ; *'mwdy'*, **8**:2.[4]

'ml (toil) : *t'ml*, **20**:3.2

'ml (toil) : *'ml'*, **20**:3.[1]

'mq (valley) : *'mq*, **29B**:22.13, 14 ; *'mq'*, **29B**:21.25, 32

'mr (load) : *y'mrn*, **60**:2

'n (flock) : *'n*, **7**:4.18 ; **14**:1.2 ; *'nh*, **29B**:22.2 ; *'ny*, **5**:15.[5]

'n' (answer) : *'n'*, **5**:1.[4] ; 2.[5] ; 9.3, [9] ; 10.[8] ; 34.2 ; 37.3 ; *'nh*, **23**:3.[2] ; *'nyt* (you answered), **5**:30.[8] ; *'nw*, **22**:1.1 ; **23**:1.[11] ; *y'nh*, **5**:26.7 ; *'n'* (ptc.), **4A**:5 ; *'nh*, **49**:2.[2] ; *'nyn* **4B**:4

'nh (fast ; afflict) : *'t'n'h*, **150**:1bis, 2 ; *m'nyh* (the oppressed), **68**:3

'ny (poor) : *'n'*, **5**:14.6 ; *'nyh*, **145C**:1 ; *'nyn*, **5**:25.4

'nn (cloud) : *'nn*, **5**:16.4 ; 29.2 ; *'nn'*, **5**:34.2 ; *'nnh*, **5**:29.6, 7 ; *'nnyn*, **5**:28.[5] ; 29.[1] ; 30.7 ; 31.3, [10] ; *'nny*, **5**:31.[6] ; *'nny'*, **5**:3.8 ; 28.[7] ; *'nnwhy*, **5**:28.5

'nn (gather clouds) : *y'nn*, **5**:28.[5]

'nt (period) : *'nt'*, **29B**:2.10

'sryn (twenty) : *'sryn*, **39**:[4] ; **51**:[1] ; see also *'śryn*.

'pr (dust) : *'pr*, **5**:1.[3] ; 5.[6] ; 24.[9] ; 34.9 ; 37.8 ; *'pr* (cst.), **29B**:21.13 ; *'pr'*, **5**:11.[7]

'ṣb (sorrow) : *'t'ṣb'*, **29B**:20.12

'qh (trouble) : *'qt'*, **5**:31.[1] ; *'qty*, **30**:4

'qr (uproot) : *m'qr*, **29B**:19.15

'qr (root) : *'qr*, **5**:12.[6] ; 15.[9] ; *'qrhn*, **17**:2.7

'rb (evening) : *'rby* (cst. pl.), **13**:6

'rb (surety) : *'rb*, **47**:2.10 ; **51**:11 ; *'rb'*, **48**:4 ; *'rbh*, **45**:1.4 ; *'rbyn*, **41**:[12] ; **52**:[11]

'rb (take in guarantee): *'rbt*, **64**:1.11

'rbh (willow) : *'rbyn*, **60**:4

'rd (onager) : *'rd'*, **5**:32.5 ; *'rdyn*, **14**:1.[1]

'rṭl (barren) : *'rṭly*, **29B**:22.33

'rymw (subtlety) : *'rymwt'*, **5**:13.1

'rm (be wise) : *y'rm*, **28**:1.6

'rmwmh (prudence) : *'rmwmh*, **28**:1.[7]

'rpl (dark cloud) : *'rpl'*, **5**:29.8 ; *'rplyn*, **5**:30.7

'rq (flee) : *'rq*, **29B**:21.32 ; *'rqw*, **29B**:20.21 ; *'rq* (ptc.), **5**:10.4 ; *'rqyn*, **29B**:22.9

'rq (strap) : *'rq'*, **29B**:22.21

'rś (couch) : *'rśyn*, **8**:1 ii [11]bis

'śr (tithe) : *m'śr*, **20**:4.1

'śr (ten) : *'śr*, **7**:4.13 ; 8.8 ; **8**:1 i [4], 6, 10, [11], [17] ; 1 ii [6], [15] ; 5.3 ; **9**:4 ; **29B**:22.6, 27 ; **150**:2, 3bis, 5, 12quinquies ; *'śrh*, **7**:8.[2] ; **8**:1 i 3, [8], [15], 16, [17] ; 1 ii 1, [1], 3, 8, [8], [9], [10], 11bis, 13bis, [15] ; 2.4 ; **29B**:21.26, 27bis ; **41**:[1] ; **52**:8

'śryn (twenty) : *'śryn*, **7**:8.[4] ; **8**:1 i 1, [4], [10] ; 1 ii [7], [11] ; **42**:[6] ; **50E**:

1 ; **62:**13 ; **64:**1.[1] ; 3.[3] ; **150:**2bis, 3, 5, 6, 8ter, 9bis, 10bis, 11bis, 12bis
'tr (wealth) : *'tr*, **29B:**22.32 ; *'trh*, **29B:** 22.22 ; *'trk*, **29B:**22.31

pg'wn (agreement) : *pg'wn*, **64:**1.10 ; *pg'wn'*, **64:**1.10, 11
pgš (struggle) : *pgš'*, **20:**3.[1]
pwry' (Purim) : *pwry'*, **150:**12
pwr'nw (punishment) : *pr'nwt'*, **53:**2, 3 ; **59:**3
pḥd (fear) : *pḥdw*, **5:**36.[10]
pḥh (governor) : *pḥwt'*, **4B:**9
pṭr (divorce) : *'pṭrnk*, **42:**[9]
pl' (depart) : *'tply*, **29B:**20.29
plg (divide) : *yplg*, **5:**11.8 ; *yplgwn*, **5:** 35.9 ; *plyg*, **29B:**2.21 ; *plygh*, **7:**4.[11] *ytplg*, **7:**4.10
plg (half) : **8:**1 i 11bis, [15]
plwgh (division) : *plwgt*, **7:**4.[11] ; **9:**3
plḥ (cultivate ; serve) ; *mplḥ* (inf.), **29B:**12.3 ; **32D:**3 ; *mplḥk*, **5:**32.8
plṭ (release) : *plṭ*, **29B:**22.2 ; *plṭn'*, **29B:**12.17 ; *plṭw*, **5:**4.[9] ; *ypltn*, **5:** 32.2 ; *tplṭ*, **29B:**19.20
plṭh (remnant) : *plṭt*, **150:**12
plpl (pepper) : *plplyn*, **12:**[5]
pm (mouth) : *pm*, **29B:**20.8 ; *pm* (cst.), **5:**14.[8] ; *pm'*, **5:**4.[4] ; *pmy*, **5:**19. [2] ; *pmh*, **5:**36.4, 7 ; *pmhwn*, **5:**14.[3]
pnbd (apart?) : *pnbd*, **7:**4.16
pnh (turn) : *ypn'*, **5:**27.[8] ; *mpnh*, **29B:**19.22
psḥ (Passover) : *psḥ'*, **150:**2
pṣ' (rescue ; open) : *pṣ'*, **29B:**22.11 ; *ypṣwn*, **5:**11.5 ; *pṣ'* (ptc.), **5:**16.1 ; *pṣhy* (rescue him!), **5:**23.1
pqd (command) : *pqd*, **24:**2 ; *ypqdnwn*, **5:**29.3 ; *mpqd* (ptc.), **27:**[9], 10
pr (dawn) : *pr'*, **5:**36.[4]
pr' (wild ass) : *pr'h*, **5:**32.4
prds (garden) : *prds* (cst.) **12:**8 ; **13:**9 ; *prds'*, **19:**2.3
prḥ (fly) : *prḥ*, **17:**3.4
przh (block) : *przh*, **8:**1 i [2]bis ; *przy'*, **8:**1 i [2], [15] ; *przyt'*, **8:**1 i 1 ; 1 ii 2, 6
przl (iron) : *przl'*, **2:**1.7 ; **5:**36.9
pry (fruit) : *pry'*, **29B:**2.15
prs (spread out) : *prs*, **5:**28.6, 7 ; *yprws*, **5:**33.7
pr' (reimburse) : *'prw'*, **40:**[9] ; *'prw'nk*, **39:**6
pr'w (Pharaoh) : *pr'w*, **29B:**19.22, [24] ; 20.14
prq (rescue) : *prq*, **5:**23.[6] ; *yprq*, **5:** 27.9 ; *'prq*, **64:**1.10
prqn (deliverance) : *prqn*, **150:**12
prš (separate) : *prš*, **29B:**21.5, 7 ; *division*, **5:**26.6 ; *ytpršn*, **5:**36.[3]
prš (distinction) : *prš'*, **16:**2.4 ; **17:**2. 14, [22]
pršgn (copy) : *pršgn*, **16:**2.3 ; **24:**1
pšr (interpret) : *ypšwr*, **17:**2.14, [23]; *'pšr*, **39:**6
pšr (interpretation) : *pšr* (cst.), **16:**2. 13 ; **29B:**19.[19] ; *pšr'*, **4A:**5
pt' (be wide) : *pty'*, **5:**18.[1]
ptgm (word) : *ptgm* (abs.), **5:**9.2 ; 20. [3] ; 29.4 ; 30.1 ; 34.3 ; *ptgm* (cst.), **2:**1.2 ; *ptgmwhy*, **5:**22.[7] ; *ptgmy'*, **29B:**2.[21] ; 5.[4] ; 22.27
ptwr (table) : *ptwr'*, **7:**3.[3] ; 4.[7] ; *ptwry*, **9:**3
ptḥ (open) : *tptḥ*, **5:**31.[8] ; *tptḥnh*, **51:** 4 ; *mptḥ*, **67:**4 ; **70:**4 ; **71:**2-3 ; **95B:** 1 ; *ptyḥ* (pass. ptc.), **8:**1 ii 2 ; **51:**4 ; *ptyḥyn*, **8:**2.[3] ; **11:**[1] ; **21:**2.[16] ; *ptyḥn*, **8:**1 ii 14 ; *'tptḥw*, **21:**2.[17]
pty (width) : *pty*, **8:**1 i [3], 4, [4], 10, 11, [15] ; 1 ii [9]bis, 12 ; 8.1 ; 9.[1] ; **29B:**21.16 ; *pwtyh*, **7:**5-6.[2], 6 ; **8:**1 i 3, 4, 5, [6], 9 ; 1 ii [12], [13], [16], [17], [19]bis ; *pth* (defective), **8:**1 i 2 ; *ptyh'*, **29B:**21.14 ; *pwtyhwn*, **7:** 7.1 ; **8:**1 ii 7, [8], [11], 12, [13], [15] bis ; *pwt'hwn*, **8:**1 ii 7
ptn (serpent) : *ptn*, **23:**1.[13]

ṣbh (wish) : *yṣbwn*, **52:**10 ; *tṣbyn*, **40:** 7, 19
ṣbw (concern) : *ṣbw*, **5:**5.2 ; *ṣbwtkwn*, **16:**2.[13]
ṣbyn (delight) : *ṣbyn*, **5:**15.6
ṣb'n (dyed, colored) : *ṣb'nyn*, **22:**2.3 ; **23:**1.13

ṣd' (really) : *ṣd'*, **5**:24.6
ṣdd (side) : *ṣddy*, **10**:[3]
ṣdyq (righteous) : *ṣdyqy'*, **30**:1
ṣdq (be righteous ; have or be right) : *yṣdq*, **5**:9.7 ; *'ṣdq*, **64**:1.7, [8]
ṣdqh (righteousness) : *ṣdqtk*, **5**:26.3
ṣh' (thirsty) : *ṣh'*, **5**:6.6
ṣwḥ (shout) : *yṣwḥwn*, **5**:26.3
ṣwm (fast) : *ṣmwn*, **150**:12
ṣwr (neck) : *ṣwrh*, **5**:36.7
ṣwt (heed) : *yṣtnh*, **5**:26.9 ; *hṣt* (listen !), **5**:23.9 ; 29.5
ṣl' (pray) : *ṣly*, **2**:1.1 ; *ṣlyt* (I prayed), **2**:1.[3] ; **21**:1.[10] ; **29B**:20.12, 28 ; *yṣlh*, **29B**:20.23 ; *'ṣlh*, **29B**:20.21 ; *ṣly* (impv.), **29B**:20.28 ; *mṣl'* (pael ptc.), **2**:1.7 ; *ṣly'*, **29B**:20.22
ṣlw (prayer) : *ṣlw*, **16**:2.15 ; **150**:12 ; *ṣlwt*, **21**:2.8 ; *ṣlt'*, **2**:1.1 ; *ṣlwt'*, **5**: 14.[8]
ṣlm (expression) : *ṣlm* (cst.), **29B**:2. [16] ; 20.2
ṣmḥ (sprout) : *ṣmḥy*, **5**:31.5
ṣp' (spy) : *yṣp'*, **5**:13.[4]
ṣpwn (north) : *ṣpwn*, **13**:[6] ; *ṣpn*, **51**: 4 ; *ṣpwn* (cst.), **10**:8 ; **12**:4 ; **29B**:21. 20 ; *ṣpwn'*, **8**:1 i [5] ; **13**:[6] ; **29B**: 16.11 ; 17.16 ; 21.6 ; **52**:5 ; *ṣpnh*, **51**:9 ; see also *klṣpwn*
ṣpn (hide) : *ṣpnyn* (ptc.), **13**:6
ṣpr (bird) : *ṣpr'*, **5**:35.[8] ; *ṣpry* (cst. pl.), **5**:13.2 ; *ṣpry'*, **5**:26.6
ṣpr (morning) : *ṣpr*, **5**:30.5 ; *ṣpr'*, **5**:30. [10] ; *ṣpryn*, **5**:14.1
ṣpr (?) : *ṣpr*, **12**:5
ṣry (balsam) : *ṣry*, **10**:[5]
ṣryk (need) : *ṣrykyn*, **58**:3

q (cipher for *qb*, " qab ") : *q*, **38**:1, 3
qb (qab) : *qbyn*, **52**:2
qbwr (tomb), **89**:1
qbl (complain) : *qblt* (I complained), **64**:2.8 ; *qbltk*, **29B**:20.14 ; *tqbl*, **5**:8.2 ; *qbl* (peal ptc.), **16**:2.[10] ; *qblh*, **16**:2. 10 ; *qbylt*, **5**:25.4
qbl (receive) : *qbl*, **48**:3 ; *qblt*, **64**:1.12 ; *yqbl*, **5**:26.2 ; *yqblnh*, **5**:35.2 ; *qbl* (impv.), **5**:7.8 ; *mqbl* (pael ptc.), **44**: 1.[5] ; **48**:[2] ; **50E**:2 ; **52**:8 ; *'tqblyh*, **62**:11
qbl (dusk) : *qbl*, **5**:8.6
qbl : see *lqbl.*
qbr (bury) : *qbr*, **145C**:2 ; *qbrth*, **68**:6
qdd (cut) : *ytqdwn*, **26**:11
qdyš (holy) : *qdyš*, **28**:2.18 ; *qdyš'*, **16**: 2.5 ; **29A**:1 i [7] ; **29B**:2.14 ; 12.17 ; 19.8 ; *qdyšyn*, **3F**:[4] ; **29B**:2.1 ; *qdyšy'*, **3F**:[10] ; **29B**:2.[20] ; *qdšy'*, **18**:6
qdm (before) : *qdm*, **5**:26.4 ; 26.[7] ; 37.3 ; **17**:2.15 ; **37**:2.3 ; **40**:5 ; **44**: 23.2 ; **45**:1.[4] ; **52**:12 ; **56**:5 ; *qwdm*, **6**:22.2 ; **7**:4.[7] ; **8**:1 i 19 ; **9**:1 ; **29A**: 2.5 ; **29B**:21.3 ; **41**:13 ; *qdmy* (before me), **41**:[7] ; **42**:[12] ; *qdmyk*, **21**:1. 15, 16 ; 2.[10] ; **42**:[14] ; *qdmk*, **44**: 23.[2] ; *qdmwhy*, **5**:8.3 ; 11.4 ; 31.2 ; 36.7 ; **7**:3.3 ; **29B**:22.9 ; *qwdmyh'*, **29B**:20.32 ; *qmyh* (sic), **61**:24 ; *qdmkn*, **45**:1.[4] ; **52**:[12] ; *qwdmyhwn*, **29B**: 19.25
qdm (east) : *qdm'*, **5**:31.[1] ; *qdmyn*, **7**: 4.6 ; **28**:2.1 ; **29B**:17.6
qdmy (first) : *qdmyt'*, **3D**:[4] ; **8**:1 ii [12]
qdmt (before) : *qdmt*, **29B**:21.23 ; **40**: 17 ; **52**:4 ; **150**:12
qdr (potter [*or* pot-seller, *or* the Black]): *qdrh*, **86**:1
qdš (ring) : *qdš*, **5**:38.8
qwm (rise) : *qm*, **4B**:3 ; **29B**:20.29 ; 22. 5 ; *qmw*, **5**:21.8 ; **17**:2.[4] ; **150**:12 ; *yqwm*, **5**:18.[7] ; **35B**:1 ; *tqwm*, **5**:9.6 ; *yqwmwn*, **3F**:9 ; *qwm* (impv.), **5**: 29.5 ; **29B**:21.13 ; *mqm* (peal inf.), **29B**:20.20 ; *q'm* (peal ptc.), **7**:4.16 ; **49**:1.8 ; *qym*, **40**:9, [23] ; **41**:6 ; **45**: 1.2 ; **47**:2.10 ; *qym'* (pael inf.), **45**: 1.4 ; **52**:12 ; *hqym*, **5**:30.4 ; *yqym*, **5**:25.1 ; 35.6 ; *'twqm*, **150**:1
qwnm (cinnamon) : *qwnm*, **10**:3
qwṣ (cut down) : *tqwṣw*, **29B**:19.16 ; *mqṣ*, **29B**:19.15 ; *'tqṣ*, **29B**:19.[17]
qwq (sepulchral chamber) : *qwq'*, **141**:1; see also *kwk*

qṭwn (reed-hut [= Gk. κοιτών?]): *qṭwt'*, **5**:11.9
qṭyn (fine) : *qṭynn*, **29B**:20.5
qṭl (kill) : *qṭl*, **5**:10.3 ; *qṭlw*, **14**:9-14-15.4 ; *mqṭlny* (to slay me), **29B**:19. 19, 21 ; 20.9 ; *qṭl*, **29B**:22.8 ; *qṭlyn*, **29B**:22.4 ; *qṭylt* (I was slain), **29B**: 20.10 ; *qṭyl*, **29B**:22.3 ; *qṭlh* (pael inf.), **16**:1.[3] ; *qṭl'*, **20**:1.[3] ; **150**:6
qṭm (ashes) : *qṭm*, **5**:34.[9] ; 37.9
qṭr (tie) : *tqṭr*, **5**:32.9 ; *tqṭrnh*, **5**:35.8
qṭr (offer incense) : *'qṭrt*, **29B**:10.15
qym (alliance) : *qym*, **5**:35.7
qyn' (lament) : *qyn'*, **89**:1, 3, 4
ql (voice ; sound) : *ql*, **5**:14.4 ; 22.[2] ; 33.5 ; 34.5 ; *qlh* (his voice), **5**:38.2 ; **16**:2.[10] ; **17**:2.23 ; **28**:2.17
qlyl (light) : *qlylyn*, **5**:13.8 ; 31.3
qllh (disgrace) : *qllty*, **5**:3.[4]
qlp (bark) : *qlpy* (cst. pl.), **10**:6 ; *qlpy'*, **10**:7 ; *qlpwhy*, **12**:3
qn (nest) : *qnh* (its nest), **5**:33.[9]
qnh (acquire) : *qnh*, **29B**:20.34 ; *'qnh*, **39**:8 ; **41**:[12] ; **44**:1.[6] ; **52**:11 ; *nqnh*, **45**:1.[6] ; **51**:13 ; *mqnh* (inf.), **43**:7 ; **50A**:[3] ; **52**:9
qnh (reed) : *qnh*, **8**:1 i 9, [19] ; 1 ii [10], 11 ; *qnyn*, **8**:1 i [1], 2, 3, 4, 5, [6], 8, 10, [12], [14], 15, 16 ; 1 ii 1bis, 3, [5], [7], [8]bis, 9, [14] ; 3. [3] ; 4.3 ; 15.[1] ; *qny'*, **10**:2
qnn (nest [verb]) : *yqnn*, **5**:33.9
qsr (emperor [= Lat. *Caesar*]) : *qsr*, **39**:1
qpl (scale) : *qply* (cst. pl.), **5**:36.8
qpṣ (shrivel) : *ytqpṣwn*, **5**:9.1
qṣ (time) : *qṣ*, **31**:7.1
qṣw (end) : *qṣwy* (cst. pl.), **5**:13.5
qṣr (be short) : *ttqṣr*, **5**:4.[3] ; *'tqṣrt*, **5**: 18.5
qṣt (part) : *qṣt*, **48**:5 ; **49**:1.[11] ; *nṣt* (read *qṣt*), **64**:3.4 ; *qṣthwn*, **150**:1
qr' (call) : *qr'*, **16**:2.[4] ; **29B**:20.19, 26 ; *qryt*, **5**:2.5 ; **29B**:12.16 ; 19.[7], 25 ; 21.2, 21 ; *qryw*, **17**:2.[21] ; *qryn* (peal m. pl. ptc.), **13**:[6], [7] ; **18**:8 ; *qry'y*, **3F**:2 ; *'tqry*, **64**:1.[11] ; *mtqr'*, **10**:[5]
qrb (draw near ; offer) : *qrb*, **29B**:22. 18 ; **64**:1.[5] ; *tqrb*, **14**:4.2 ; *mqrb*, **29B**:20.17 ; *qrbny* (pael impv.), **21**: 1.18 ; *'qrbt*, **29B**:21.2 ; *'qrb* (I offer), **64**:1.10
qrb (war) : *qrb*, **5**:31.1 ; **18**:4 ; **29B**:21. 24, 25 ; 22.6 ; *qrbh*, **5**:33.6; *qrb'*, **20**: 3.[1] ; 51.1 ; **29B**:21.31
qrbn (offering) : *qrbn*, **69**:2 ; **107**:1 ; *qwrbn*, **7**:4.2
qrdmn (cardamom) : *qrdmn*, **12**:5
qry (city) : *qry'*, **5**:14.1 ; 32.6 ; *qryhwn*, **5**:8.1
qryh (city) : *qryh*, **3A**:4 ; *qryt'*, **8**:1 i 5, [6]
qrm (freeze) : *htqrmw*, **5**:31.7
qrn (horn) : *qrn* (cst.), **7**:5-6.[5] ; *qrn'*, **5**:33.5
qrq' (terrain) : *qrq''*, **51**:8
qšṭ (set aright) : *qšṭ*, **5**:24.8
qšṭ (truth) : *qšṭ* (abs.), **21**:1.12 ; 2.9 ; *qšwṭ*, **26**:12 ; *qwšṭ*, **29B**:2.7, 10, 18 ; *qšṭ'*, **12**:[8] ; **21**:2.[7] ; *qwšṭ'*, **13**:9 ; **29B**:2.5, [6], 22 ; 6.2 ; 19.25
qšyṭ (true) : *qšyṭh*, **5**:11.8
qšš (grow up) : *yqšn*, **5**:32.3

r'm (wild ox) : *r'm'*, **5**:32.[8], [9]
r'š (head ; chief) : *r'š*, **5**:15.[2] ; *r'š* (cst.), **5**:15.3 ; **64**:3.2 ; *r'yš*, **29B**:17.9, 11 ; *ryš*, **150**:1 ; *r'š'*, **20**:45.1 ; *r'šh*, **5**:3.[8] ; *r'yšh*, **29B**:20.[29] ; *r'yšh* (her head), **29B**:20.3 ; *r'šy* (cst.), **29B**:19.12bis
rb (great) : *rb*, **5**:22.6 ; 28.3 ; **10**:[2] ; **23**:1.11 ; *rb'*, **2**:1.[1] ; **7**:4.[15] ; **9**:[6] ; **17**:3.5 ; **20**:1.2 ; **29A**:1 i 7 ; **29B**:2.14, 17 ; 16.12 ; 21.11, 12, 16 ; **44**:15.1 ; *rbh*, **68**:2 ; *rbh* (fem. sg. absol.), **14**:9-14-15.3 ; **19**:3.1 ; *rbt'* (fem. sg. emph.), **3D**:2 ; **29B**:20.14 ; 22.4 ; *rbnw* (our leader), **58**:3 ; *rbrbyn* (nobles), **5**:14.3 ; 25.[1] ; 28.1 ; **17**: 2.7 ; **20**:22.[1] ; *rbrby* (cst.), **29B**:19.24; *rbrby'*, **8**:1 i 3 ; 3.[2] ; *rbbrn* (for fem. pl. abs. *rbrbn*), **5**:22.7
rbh (be great) : *rbw*, **35E**:2 ; *rbynk*, **20**.3.[2]
rbw (greatness) : *rbw*, **5**:9.4 ; *rbwt* (cst.),

2:1.[5] ; **20**:3.[3] ; *rbwt'*, **29B**:2.4 ; *rbwty*, **5**:16.4
rby (interest) : *rbyn*, **64**:3.2
rb'yn (fourfold) : *rb'yn*, **40**:10, 23 ; *rby'y'*, **4B**:6
rgg (desire) : *rgg* (peal pass. ptc.), **29B**: 20.3 ; *rgyg*, **29B**.2.[20]
rgz (be angry) : *rgz*, **3C**:2 ; **5**:20.6 ; *trgz*, **29B**:2.25
rgz (anger) : *rgz*, **5**:18.3 ; 27.7 ; *rgzy* (my anger), **5**:19.5 ; *rgzk*, **5**:34.7 ; **29A**:1 i 1, 2 ; *rgzh*, **5**:2.1
rgl (foot) : *rgl*, **5**:12.1 ; *rglyn*, **5**:14.10 ; *rgly*, **5**:22.5 ; *rglyh'*, **29B**:20.5
rdp (pursue) : *rdp*, **29B**:22.7, 9 ; *yrdp*, **5**:32.8 ; *mrdph* (the persecuted), **68**: 3-4
rhwmy (Roman) : *rhwmyh*, **58**:2 ; *rwm'y*, **150**:6
rwḥ (wind ; spirit) : *rwḥ* (abs.), **5**:3.4 ; 16.4 ; 31.[1] ; 34.6, 8 ; 36.2 ; **7**:1.[2] ; 5-6.[8] ; **8**:1 i [1], 14 ; 1 ii [6] ; **29B**: 20.16bis ; **31**:1.1 ; **35D**:3 ; *rwḥ* (cst.), **5**:2.6 ; **11**:4 ; **28**:1.10 ; 2.7 ; **29B**:20. 26 ; *rwḥ'*, **5**:13.6 ; **29B**:20.20, 28, [29]; *rwḥy*, **5**:4.[3] ; *rwḥk*, **29B**:2.17 ; *rwḥh'*, **29B**:2.13 ; *rwḥyn*, **5**:33.8 ; *rwḥy* (cst. pl.), **20**:31.[1] ; *rwḥyhwn*, **29B**:22.8
rwṭ (run) : *rṭ*, **29B**:2.[22] ; *rṭt* (I ran), **29B**:2.19 ; *yrwṭ*, **5**:33.2 ; *trwṭ* (it runs), **5**:36.8 ; *yrṭwn*, **5**:36.5
rwm (be exalted) : *yrwn*, **5**:27.1 ; *yrym* (aphel), **5**:33.9 ; *mrym* (ptc.), **29B**: 22.20 ; *htrwmmw*, **5**:27.3
rwm (height) : *rwm*, **8**:1 i 13 ; 1 ii 5, [10], [12] ; *rwmh* (its height), **3A**: [6] ; **8**:1 i [19] ; 1 ii 1, 12, [15] ; *rwmhwn*, **8**:1 ii [8], [14]
rz (secret) : *rz*, **29B**:1.2 ; *rz'*, **29B**:1.3 ; *rzy* (cst. pl.), **14**:9-14-15.[2] ; **28**:1. 8bis
rḥyq (afar) : *rḥyq*, **5**:28.3 ; 33.6 ; **10**:[2] ; **12**:6, [8]
rḥm (love) ; *rḥmh* (he desired her), **29B**:20.8 ; *rḥm* (peal ptc.), **20**:57.2 ; *rḥym* (the beloved), **29B**:2.20
rḥm (friend) : *rḥmy'*, **89**:3 ; *rḥmy* (my friends), **29B**:21.21 ; *rḥmwhy*, **5**:20. [8] ; 27.[1] ; 38.5
rḥm (womb) : *rḥm* (cst.), **5**:30.6 ; *rḥmy*, **2**:4.3
rḥmyn (mercy) : *rḥmyn*, **5**:38.3 ; *rḥmyk*, **21**:1.15
rḥ' (wash) : *'trḥ't*, **21**:1.[7]
rḥṣ (be confident) : *ytrḥṣ*, **5**:35.2 ; *ttrḥṣ*, **5**:32.10
rḥṣn (confidence) : *rḥṣn*, **5**:9.5 ; 27.1
rḥq (be far) : *hrḥqw*, **5**:2.3 ; *'rḥqt* (I was removed), **10**:1, [4] ; **12**:7 ; *'rḥq* (be far !), **21**:1.12
rḥš (creeping thing) : *rḥš*, **5**:37.2
ryḥ (sniff) : *yryḥ*, **5**:33.6
ryḥ (smell) : *ryḥ*, **10**:7 ; *ryḥwhy*, **32F**:2
ryq (invalid) : *ryq*, **44**:1.7
ryqn (empty) : *ryqnh*, **5**:6.[9]
rm (high) : *rm*, **5**:34.6 ; **21**:2.17 ; *rmy'*, **5**:5.4
rm' (cast oneself) : *rmh*, **29B**:22.8 ; *yrm'*, **5**:25.2
rmh (height) : *rmt* (cst.), **5**:34.8 ; *rmt'*, **29B**:21.11
r'h (herd [verb]) : *r'h*, **29B**:21.6
r'h (herdsman) : *r'h*, **29B**:22.1 ; *r'wtn'* (our herdsmen), **29B**:21.5
r'w (pleasure ; will) : *r'w'*, **7**:4.2 ; *r'wty* (my will), **50F**:1 ; **51**:3 ; *r'ty*, **40**:2, 13 ; *r'wth*, **20**:53.[2] ; *r'wth*, **29B**:2.23
r'yn (attraction) : *r'yn*, **5**:15.[7]
r'm (thunder) : *tr'm*, **5**:34.5
rṣṣ (smash) : *'rṣ'* (aphel inf.), **5**:29.4
rṣp (pave) : *rṣypyn*, **8**:1 i [6]
rqyq (soft) : *rqyq*, **29B**:20.3
rš' (be permitted, authorized) : *ršy*, **51**: 6 ; *ršy'* (peal ptc. fem. sg.), **40**:6, 17 ; *ršyn*, **45**:1.8 ; *rš'yn*, **52**:9
ršwt (authority, power) : *ršwt*, **48**:[5]
ršh (authorization) : *ršh*, **51**:5, 9
ršy' (evil) : *ršy'yn*, **5**:2.7 ; 3.[6] ; 7.[4] ; 11.3 ; 34.[8] ; *ršy'y'*, **5**:25.6
ršmh (inscription) : *ršmt'*, **7**:4.12
rš' (wickedness) : *rš'*, **5**:24.[2] ; **26**:[12] ; *rš''*, **3F**:[1], [7], 11 ; **29B**:1.2
rtḥ (seethe) : *rtḥw*, **5**:17.[3]
rtm (broom tree) : *rtmyn*, **5**:15.[9]
rtt (tremble) : *mrtt* (pael ptc.), **19**:1.3

śb (old) : *śby'*, **7**:4.13
śb' (be sated) : *śb't*, **9**:3 ; *yśb'wn*, **5**:11.5
śbr (hope) : *śbrt*, **88**:2 ; see also *sbr*
śgy (be great ; multiply) : *śgy*, **29B**:22.32 ; *śgyw*, **29B**:22.29 ; *'śgh*, **29B**:21.13 ; *yśgwn*, **29B**:22.32
śgy' (much [noun ?]) : *śgy'*, **14**:9-14-15:[4] ; **28**:1.9 ; **64**:2.1, 2
śgy' (much [adj.]) : *śgy*, **29B**:19.27, [27] ; 20.31 ; *śgy'*, **20**:18.1 ; **29B**:20.[31] ; *śgy'* (= *śgy'h*), **29B**:20.7 ; *śgy'yn*, **29B**:20.33, 34 ; *śgy'n*, **20**:9.[1] ; **29B**:19.[25] ; see also *sgy'*
śgy' (greatly [adv.]) : *śgy'*, **12**:7 ; **29B**:19.[15] ; *śgy*, **29B**:2.11 ; 20.8 ; 21.6
śhd (witness) : *śhd*, **39**:10, 11 ; **40**:27, 28, 29 ; **42**:27 ; **51**:19, 20 ; **52**:[17], 20
śhdw (testimony) : *śhdw*, **27**:12 ; *śhdt* (cst.), **61**:[24] ; *śhdt'*, **61**:25
śṭn (adversary) : *śṭn*, **21**:1.17
śyḥ (tell) : *yśyḥ*, **5**:28:[10]
śym (place) : *śm*, **5**:30.3 ; **29B**:20.[31] *śymw*, **4B**:13 ; *śym'*, **29B**:22.10 ; see also *sym*
śkwl (discretion) : *śwkl'*, **28**:1.[6]
śm'l (left) : *śm'l*, **8**:1 i [4] ; 1 ii 2 ; **29B**:21.8 ; 22.10 ; *śm'l'*, **8**:1 i [12]
śmḥh (happiness) : *śmḥt* (cst.), **26**:[13]
śmwq (red) : *śmwq'*, **12**:7 ; **29B**:21.17, 18bis
śn' (enemy) : *śn'yk*, **29B**:22.17
ś'r (hair) : *ś'r* (cst.), **29B**:20.3
ś'rh (barley) : *ś'rh*, **28**:1.2 ; *ś'rt'*, **5**:20.[1] ; see also *s'rh*
śph (lip) : *śpty*, **5**:10.[10]
śrbl (mantle) : *śrblyhwn*, **4B**:[10]

š'wl (Sheol) : *š'wl*, **5**:1.2
š'l (ask) : *š'lt* (I asked), **23**:1.11 ; *š'lth*, **23**:3.1 ; **25**:1.3 ; *š'lw*, **29B**:19.[25] ; *'š'lnk*, **5**:30.[1] ; 34.3 ; 37.6 ; *mš'l*, **5**:19.[7]
š'r (remain) : *yšt'rwn*, **30**:1
š'r (remainder) : *š'r'*, **48**:4
šb' (take captive) : *šbw*, **29B**:21.34 ; *šbw'*, **29B**:22.10, 12 ; *šbyn*, **29B**:22.4 ; *šby*, **29B**:22.3
šbh (Sabbath) : *šbh*, **56**:6
šbḥ (praise) : *šbḥtny*, **5**:14.5 ; *šbḥh* (pael inf.), **21**:1.15
šby (captive) : *šby'* (abs. fem. sg.), **29B**:22.19, 25 ; *šbyt'*, **29B**:22.12bis, 25
šbyh (captivity) : *šby'*, **29B**:22.2
šbyl (way) : *šbylwhy*, **5**:8.4 ; 25.3
šby'y (seventh) : *šby'y*, **9**:1
šbyqh (abandoned vine) : *šbyqh*, **5**:31.4
šb' (seven) : *šb'*, **2**:1.3, 7 ; **8**:1 i 1, 5, [9] ; 1 ii 1, [10], 19 ; **13**:[9] ; **29B**:22.28 ; **62**:13 ; *šb'h*, **8**:1 ii [7] ; **41**:1, 15 ; **150**:2bis, 8, 9 ; *šb't*, **7**:4.[11] ; **29B**:19.12 ; *šwb't*, **150**:12
šbsr (seventeen) : *šybsr*, **150**:6
šb'yn (seventy) : *šb'yn*, **3D**:[1] ; **8**:1 i [3] ; **52**:7
šbq (peristyle) : *šbq*, **7**:1.2 ; **8**:1 i 1
šbq (leave, forgive, divorce) : *šbq*, **2**:1.4 ; **5**:38.2 ; **28**:1.[1] ; **29B**:22.25 ; **64**:1.7 ; *šbqt* (you left), **64**:1.13 ; *mšbq*, **29B**:19.19 ; *mšbwq*, **29B**:19.15 ; *šbq* (ptc.), **40**:2, 13 ; *šbyq*, **29B**:19.16 ; *šbyqt* (I was saved), **29B**:20.10 ; *šbyqyn*, **29B**:22.20 ; *tštbqy*, **41**:[6]
šbqyn (divorce) : *šbqyn*, **40**:8, [21]
šdr (send ; make an effort) : *tšdrwn*, **59**:2 ; *htšdr* (impv.), **55**:3
šh' (keep) : *hšhyh*, **5**:9.[5]
šhwh (wasteland) : *šhwyn*, **17**:3.5
šw' (vanity) : *šw'*, **5**:26.8
šw' (place ; be equal) : *šw'*, **5**:22.5 ; *šwy'*, **5**:29.6 ; 31.2 ; *šwyt* (I made), **5**:32.5 ; *šwyw*, **29B**:21.26 ; *tšw'*, **5**:1.5 ; 35.4 ; *tšwh*, **5**:30.7 ; *yšwwn*, **7**:4.[6] ; *yšwn*, **5**:14.3 ; *šw'* (peal ptc.), **89**:3 ; *šwyn*, **62**:[13] ; *šwy*, **2**:1.3, [6] ; *hšwhy*, **49**:1.11
šwh (immediately) : *šwh*, **56**:5
šwḥ'y (Shuhite) : *šwḥ'y'*, **5**:1.[4] ; 9.[3]
šwyh (donning) : *šwyt* (cst.), **5**:30.7
šwmh (mark) : *šwmh*, **28**:1.1 ; *šwmn*, **28**:1.3
šwq (market) : *šwq* (abs.), **8**:1 i 1, [2], 5 ; *šwq* (cst.), **64**:3.5 ; *šwq'*, **5**:14.[1] ; **8**:1 i [3] ; *šwqy'*, **8**:1 i [3], [4], [6] ; *šqy'*, **64**:1.2

šwr (wall) : *šwr* (cst.), **150:**2, 6, 8 ; *šwr'*, **7:**8.2 ; **150:**12
šḥwh (perdition) : *šḥwh*, **28:**2.1
šḥlny (purulence) : *šḥlny'*, **29B:**20.26
šḥn (inflammation) : *šḥn'*, **2:**1.2bis, 6
šḥnw (purulence) : *šḥnw*, **5:**16.2
šḥr (dawn) : *šḥr'*, **5:**30.[10]
šḥt (destroy) : *šḥt* **29B:**2.17 ; *šḥyt*, **14:**3.3
šṭr (document) : *šṭr* (cst.), **64:**1.2, 3, 9, 10, 11 ; 3.4, 6 ; *šṭr'*, **41:**14 ; **42:**[19] ; **45:**1.[7] ; **46:**[6] ; **47:**2.10 ; **51:** 2 ; **64:**1.8 ; 3.3 ; *šṭrh*, **40:**11, 24 ; *šṭryn*, **64:**2.4 ; *šṭry'*, **150:**7
šyd (demon) : *šydy* (cst. pl.), **3C:**2
šyzb (deliver [Akkadianism]) : *šzb*, **4B:** 12 ; *šyzbt*, **5:**14.6
šyṣy (complete [Akkadianism: cause to go forth]) : *šyṣy*, **14:**29.2 ; **19:**1. [5] ; **32H:**1
šyqw' (covering) : *šyqw'*, **5:**31.[6]
šyt (thornbush) : *šyt'*, **5:**31.4
škb (lie down) : *škbt* (I lay down), **21:**2.14 ; *yškb*, **5:**11.[10] ; *yškbw*, **5:** 5.[6] ; *yškbwn*, **5:**24.9 ; *nškb*, **5:**1.3
škḥ (find ; be able) ; *'škḥ*, **29B:**22.7 ; *hškḥ*, **5:**22.4 ; *'škḥh* (he found him), **29B:**2.23; *'škḥt* (I found), **29B:**21. 19 ; *hškḥw*, **17:**2.13 ; *yškḥ*, **29B:**21. 13 ; *mhškḥ*, **18:**5 ; *yštkḥ*, **30:**2
škn (dwell) : *yškwn*, **5:**33.9
šlwh (repose) : *šlwty*, **2:**4.[2]
šlḥ (send) : *šlḥ* (he sent), **5:**32.4 ; **29B:** 20.8, 16, 18 ; 22.26 ; *šlḥt* (I sent), **29B:**21.21; **54:**1 ; **60:**1 ; *šlḥwhw* (they sent him), **17:**2.21 ; *yšlḥ*, **29B:**20.23 ; *tšlḥ*, **60:**1 ; *yšlḥn*, **60:**3 ; *tšlḥwn*, **56:**4 ; *tšlḥn*, **57:**2 ; *šlḥ* (impv.), **60:**3, 4
šlṭ (lance) : *šlṭ*, **5:**33.4
šlṭ (rule) : *yšlṭ*, **29B:**20.15 ; *tšlṭ*, **21:** 1.17 ; **29B:**7.[1] ; *mšlṭ* (pael ptc.), **23:**2.5, [5] ; *mšlṭyn*, **23:**1.[11] ; *'šlṭt*, **23:**3.1 ; **25:**1.[3] ; *mhšlṭ*, 23:2.[1] ; *mhšlṭyn*, **23:**1.[12]
šlṭn (dominion, ruler) : *šlṭn*, **5:**9.[4] ; **17:**2.16
šlyṭ (powerful) : *šlyṭ*, **5:**32.6 ; **22:**3.1 ; **23:**2.6, [6] ; **25:**1.2 ; **29B:**20.13bis; *šlyṭyn*, **23:**1.12 ; **29B:**22.24
šlm (be complete ; requite, pay) : *šlm'*, **29B:**20.6 ; 22.8 ; *šlmyn*, **5:**32.2 ; *šlm* (pael), **31:**8.2 ; *yšlm*, **5:**23.[5] ; 24.5 ; *yšlmwn*, **5:**27.[5] ; *tšlmn*, **36:**[2] ; *mšlm*, **39:**[4] ; **40:**10, [23] ; *'šlmh* (3 sg. masc. aphel pf. with 3 sg. fem. suffix), **29B:**20.[32] ; *hštlmt*, **5:** 23.[6]
šlm (at peace) : *šlm*, **29B:**21.19 ; **55:**5 ; **58:**3 ; **60:**5 ; **89:**1
šlm (peace) : *šlm* (abs.), **5:**9.[4] ; **20:** 8.1 ; **26:**[12] ; **29B:**21.4, 19 ; **36:**1 ; **55:**1 ; **57:**[2] ; **89:**3, 4 ; *slm*, **53:**1 ; *šlm* (cst.), **2:**4.[2] ; **20:**3.3 ; *šlmh*, **22:**3.[2] ; **23:**3.[1]
šm (name) : *šm* (cst.), **2:**1.5 ; **29B:**19. [7] ; 21.2bis ; **64:**1.4 ; *šmy* (my name), **64:**2.2 ; *šmhn* (their name[s]), **64:** 3.6 ; *šmhty* (my names), **23:**3.[2] ; *šmhtk* (your names), **23:**3.[1]
šmd (do evil) : *mšmdy'*, **150:**6
šmṭh (release) : *šmṭh*, **39:**7
šmyn (heavens) : *šmyn*, **17:**3.11 ; **29B:** 2.5, [16] ; 5.4 ; *šmy'*, **5:**10.[2] ; 13.2 ; 31.[6] ; **13:**6bis, 7 ; **16:**2.[10] ; **17:**2. 16 ; **18:**[6] ; **20:**32.1 ; 37.3 ; **21:**1.8 ; 2.[16], [17], 18 ; **29B:**2.[14] ; 7.7 ; 12.17 ; 22.16, 21 ; **33:**1.3
šmʿ (hear) : *šmʿ*, **5:**38.2 ; **29B:**2.21 ; 5. 24 ; 20.8, 24 ; 22.12 ; *šmʿth* (you heard), **17:**2.23 ; *šmʿt* (I heard), **19:** 1.6 ; **29B:**19.10 ; *šmʿtk*, **5:**37.7 ; *šmʿn'* (we heard), **5:**13.3 ; *yšmʿ*, **5:**19.5 ; 25.4 ; 26.[8] ; 32.7 ; *yšmʿnh* (he will hear him), **5:**23.3 ; *yšmʿwn*, **5:**27.5, [6] ; 29.2 ; *tšmʿ*, **5:**14.[5] ; *'šmʿ*, **5:**3.4 ; *nšmʿ*, **5:**10.[5] ; *šmʿ* (impv.), **5:**37.6 ; **21:**2.[7] ; *šmʿw*, **5:**24.[4] ; *šmʿ* (ptc.), **49:**1.5
šmʿh (hearing) : *šmʿh*, **5:**13.[3]
šmš (sun) : *šmš*, **13:**8
šn' (change) : *šn'*, **29B:**2.17 ; *yšn'*, **5:** 24.3 ; *šnyw* (pael), **4B:**12 ; *'štny*, **29B:**2.11, 12 ; *mštny*, **29B:**2.2
šnh (sleep) : *šnt* (cst.), **17:**2.4 ; **18:**[10] ; **20:**3.[2] ; *šnty*, **29B:**19.17
šnh (year) : *šnh*, **43:**1, 3 ; *šnt*, **24:**2, 3 ; **29B:**21.27bis ; **39:**1, 7 ; **40:**1, 12 ;

41:1 ; **42**:1 ; **44**:1.1 ; **51**:1 ; **62**:13 ; **64**:1.1 ; 3.[3] ; **149**:2 ; *šnt'*, **24**:3 ; *št'*, **29B**:12.15 ; *šnyn*, **2**:1.3, 7 ; **3B**:1 ; **3D**:1 ; **3E**:1, [4], 6 ; **28**:1.3 ; **29B**: 12.10, 13 ; 19.[10] ; 20.18bis ; 21. 26 ; 22.27 ; *šny'*, **29B**:19.23 ; *šnwhy*, **5**:28.4 ; *šnyhwn*, **5**:27.5

šnn (sharpened) : *šnn*, **5**:33.5

šnq (snuff) : *yšnqnh*, **5**:23.2

š'' (tell) : *'št'y*, **29B**:19.18 ; *'št'y'* (inf.), **29B**:19.18 ; *'št'yh* (inf.), **19**:1.5

špyr (beautiful) : *špyr*, **21**:1.16 ; **29B**: 20.2, 4 ; *špyrn*, **29B**:20.4, 6

špl (be low) : *hšplh* (bring him low!), **5**:34.7

špr (be fair) : *šprh*, **29B**:20.7 ; *yšprn*, **29B**:20.6

špr (beauty) : *šwpr*, **29B**:20.7 ; *špr'*, **29B**:20.7 ; *šprh'*, **29B**:20.7, 9

špš (postern gate) : *špšy'*, **8**:1 i [8], 8

šq (leg) : *šqyh'*, **29B**:20.6

šql (lift up) : *šqwl* (impv.), **29B**:21.9

šqr (deceive) : *yšqr*, **5**:24.7

šqr (deceit) : *šqr*, **5**:24.2, 4, 10 ; **30**:2

šr' (loose, encamp ; begin) : *šr'*, **5**:32. 5 ; **29B**:22.13 ; *šrw*, **14**:17.3 ; **20**:54. 2 ; *šr'w* (impv.), **16**:2.14 ; *šr'* (ptc.), **29B**:20.[34] ; *šryn*, **4B**:[5] ; **18**:6 ; **29B**:22.8 ; *šryt* (pael, I began), **29B**: 12.13, 15 ; 19.18 ; 21.15 ; *šryw*, **150**: 12

šrb (family) : *šrb'*, **29B**:19.16

šry (beam) : *šryt'*, **51**:[7]

šrr (make firm) : *'štrrh*, **18**:5

šrš (shoot) : *šršyn*, **17**:2.7 ; *šršwhy*, **19**: 2.1

šš (marble) : *šš*, **8**:1 i 7

št (six) : *št*, **8**:1 i 4 ; 1 ii [4]bis ; **24**:3 ; **40**:1, 12 ; *šth*, **8**:1 i [2] ; 3.3, [3] ; *štt*, **150**:3, 12 ; *štyh*, **62**:12

št' (drink) : *'štyt* (I drank), **29B**:21.20 ; *'štyw*, **29B**:21.22 ; *mštyh* (inf.), **29B**: 12.15

štyn (sixty) : *štyn*, **8**:1 i 5

t'n (fig) : *t'ny'*, **52**:6

tbw (ark) : *tbwt'*, **29B**:10.12

tbl (world, earth) : *tbl*, **5**:24.[8] ; 29.3

tbr (crush) : *tbr*, **29B**:22.9 ; *ttbr*, **5**:34.8 ; *'tbr* ('ithpeel), **29B**:21.32

tgr (debate ; claim) : *tgr*, **23**:1.11 ; **44**: 1.[7] ; **45**:1.5 ; **46**:[3]

tdmry (Palmyrene) : *tdmryh*, **53**:3

thwm (deep) : *thwm'*, **5**:30.6 ; 31.[7]

twb (return) : *tb*, **5**:23.3 ; 38:3 ; **14**:19.2 ; *tbt* (she returned), **150**:8 ; *tbt* (you returned), **29B**:22.29 ; *tbt* (I returned), **29B**:21.19 ; *tbw*, **29B**:21.30 ; **150**: 6 ; *tbn'*, **150**:5 ; *ytwb*, **5**:33.4 ; *tbw'* (3 pl. fem. pf. peal), **5**:32.3 ; *ytwbwn*, **3F**:10 ; **5**:27.4 ; *'tyb* (aphel), **29B**:22. 12bis, 24 ; *htyb* **5**:3.[3] ; *'tybny*, **29B**: 21.3 ; *ytyb*, **5**:22.[8] ; *ytybny*, **5**:3.[3] ; *ytybnny*, **5**:9.2 ; *ytybnh*, **5**:21.6 ; 25. 5 ; *'tyb*, **5**:37.5 ; *'tbnk*, **42**:[10] ; *ytybw*, **29B**:20.25 ; *htybny* (answer me), **5**: 30.1 ; 34.3 ; 37.7 ; *htbh* (haphel inf.), **5**:20.[3] ; *'tbh*, **5**:23.[8] ; *mtyb*, **5**:21. [3] ; *'twtb*, **150**:1

twh (be astonished) : *twh*, **4B**:3

twk (depart) : *ytwk*, **29B**:20.26

twl'h (worm) : *twl'th*, **5**:1.[1] ; *twl't'*, **5**:9.[9]

twn (chamber) : *tny* (cst. pl.), **64**:4.1 ; *twny'*, **8**:1 ii 8, [9] ; **64**:3.5

twr (ox) : *twr'*, **29B**:17.10 ; 21.16bis

tḥwm (boundary) : *tḥwm'*, **29B**:16.12 ; *tḥm'*, **51**:8 ; *tḥwmh* (its boundary), **52**:5 ; *tḥwmyn*, **5**:30.8 ; **64**:3.6 ; *tḥwmy*, **8**:1 ii [13] ; **44**:1.[4] ; **52**:3 ; *tḥwmyh*, **64**:1.2

tḥwt (beneath ; in place of) : *tḥwt*, **5**: 16.[3] ; 20.1, [1] ; *tḥwty*, **21**:2.17 ; *tḥwtyhwn*, **5**:34.[8]

tyš (he-goat) : *tyšyn*, **14**:1.2

tlh (hang, brandish) : *ytlh*, **5**:33.4

tlyty (third) : *tlyty*, **32G**:2 ; *tlyty'*, **8**:1 i 3 ; *tlytyn*, **20**:1.1

tlt (three) : *tlt*, **6**:15.2 ; **8**:1 i [1] ; 1 ii [15], [17] ; **29B**:21.27 ; 22.6 ; **44**:1.1 ; **51**:1 ; **52**:2 ; **149**:2 ; **150**:12 ; *tlth*, **5**: 20.[2], [8] ; 23.8 ; **8**:1 i [1], 10 ; 1 ii [7] ; **11**:[5] ; **23**:3.2 ; **52**:2 ; **62**:13 ; *tlt'*, **150**:2, 7, 8, 9 ; *tltt*, **8**:1 i [6] ; **19**:2.1 ; **28**:1.5 ; **29B**:17.11 ; 19.24 ; 21.21 ; 22.23 ; *tlthwn*, **29B**:20.8

tltyn (thirty) : *tltyn*, **8:**1 i [13] ; **24:**3 ; **62:**13
tmh (there) : *tmh*, **5:**26.7 ; see also *tmn*
tmh (be amazed) : *ytmhwn*, **5:**10.2 ; *'tmh* (aphel), **29B:**20.9
tmh (amazement) : *tmh'*, **5:**4.5 ; *tmhyn*, **19:**1.6
tmyd (daily sacrifice) : *tmyd'*, **150:**1
tmymw (entirety) : *tmymwt'*, **39:**[6]
tmk (hold) : *tmkyn*, **14:**21.2
tmn (there) : *tmn*, **11:**3 ; **12:**5 ; **13:**7 ; **29B:**2.23; 19.[7]bis, [10] ; 21.1, 2, 3, 20bis ; **49:**1.10 ; **51:**3
tmn' (eight) : *tmn'*, **7:**4.4 ; *tmny'*, **51:**[6] ; **150:**1, 9, 10, 12 ; *tmnyh*, **8:**1 ii [6] ; **52:**7 ; **150:**1, 11, 12 ; *tmnyt*, **8:**1 i 4 ; *tmny't*, **29B:**22.6
tmnyn (eighty) : *tmnyn*, **7:**4.[10] ; **8:**1 i [8] ; **9:**3
tmrh (palm tree) : *tmr'*, **29B:**19.14 ; *tmrt'*, **29B:**19.15, 16bis
tmryrw (bitterness) : *tmryrwt'*, **32B:**2
tn' (recount) : *mtn'*, **49:**1.3
tn' (here) : *tn'*, **5:**30.8 ; **17:**3.7 ; *tnh*, **29B:**22.28
tnyn (dragon) : *tnyn*, **5:**10.4 ; 12.5 ; 35.4
tnyn (second) : *tnynh*, **7:**4.16 ; **16:**2.[3] ; *tny'ny*, **29B:**21.1
tnynw (a second time) : *tnynwt*, **17:**3.7
tnn (smoke) : *tnn*, **5:**36.5
tqw'y (Teqoan) : *tqw'y*, **53:**3
tqyp (strong) : *tqyp*, **29B:**2.8 ; 20.11 ; 22.31 ; *tqypyn*, **18:**7
tql (shekel) : *tql*, **52:**8
tql (stumble) : *htqlw*, **5:**25.6
tqn (prepare) : *tqn* (pael impv.), **60:**4
tqp (prevail) : *tqp*, **5:**2.[1] ; **29B:**21.25 ; *tqpw*, **29B:**20.18
tqp (force) : *tqp*, **5:**16.2 ; 32.6 ; 33.1 ; 37.4 ; **29B:**22.31 ; *twqp* (cst.), **29B:**20.14 ; *tqwp*, **18:**3 ; *tqph*, **5:**36.7
trw'h (trumpet) : *trw't* (cst.), **150:**12
tryn (two) : *tryn*, **5:**23.8 ; 38.4 ; **6:**5.[2] ; **7:**4.[6] ; **8:**1 i [3], [5], 8, 9, [11], 15, 16, 19 ; 1 ii 1bis, 3, [3], [5], 8, [8], [9], 14 ; 15.[1] ; **23:**1.10 ; **29B:**20.8 ; **33:**6.2 ; **48:**4 ; **150:**6, 11bis, 12bis ; *try* (cst.), **7:**4.8 ; **8:**1 i 10, [12] ; **60:**1, ‹2› ; *tryn'*, **29B:**19.16 ; *tryhwn*, **17:**2.3 ; *trtyn*, **5:**37.5 ; **7:**1.4 ; **8:**1 i 2, [6] ; 1 ii [11], 12 ; 3.[5] ; 7.2 ; **24:**4 ; **28:**1.1, [3] ; **29B:**12.10 ; 19.[10] ; 20.18bis ; 22.28 ; **39:**[1] ; **51:**6 ; **67:**3 ; *trty*, (cst.), **7:**4.14, 15 ; **8:**1 ii [11], [13] ; 2.4 ; 6.1 ; 11.1 ; **9:**[5] ; **29B:**21.26 ; **64:**1.12 ; 3.5 ; 4.1
trk (repudiate): *mtrk* (pael ptc.), **40:** 2, 13
trkyn (repudiation) : *trkyn*, **40:**7, 20
tr' (gate) : *tr'*, **8:**1 i 9, [11], [12] ; 1 ii [1], [2], 6, [6] ; 5.2 ; 12.[2] ; *tr'* (cst.), **7:**3.2 ; **8:**1 i 9, [11] ; *tr''*, **6:**4.[2] ; **7:**11.[1] ; **8:**1 i 13, [14], 18, [18], [19] ; 1 ii 2, 7 ; 2.[3] ; *tr'hwn*, **8:**1 ii [8] ; *tr'yn*, **8:**1 ii [3], 4 ; **11:**1, 5 ; *tr'y* (cst.), **5:**14.1 ; **8:**1 i [15] ; **16:**2.[10] ; **21.**2.18 ; *tr'y'*, **8:**3.[2] ; 9.[2] ; *tr'yhwn*, **8:**1 i 10
tšwyt (base) : *tšwyt*, **6:**1.1
tšbr (disgrace) : *tšbr'*, **5:**16.6
tšlwmh (indemnity) : *tšlwmt'*, **39:**[7] ; **45:**1.6 ; **51:**[13]
tš' (nine) : *tš'*, **6:**16.2 ; **8:**1 ii 10, 13 ; **52:**8 ; *tš'h*, **8:**1 i [5] ; **150:**12
tš'yn (ninety) : *tš'yn*, **8:**1 i [6] ; **48:**[4]

Names of Months, Persons, and Places

'b (Ab), **150:**5
'bh (Abba), **68:**1, 3
'byšlwm (Abishalom), **115:**1
'bl myn (Abel-main), **21:**2.13
'brm (Abram), **29B:**19.14 ; 20.10, 11, 22, 25bis, 33 ; 21.15 ; 22.1, 2ter, 5bis, 12, 13, 15, 16bis, 18bis, 20, 23, 24, 27, 32
'bšlwm (Absalom), **39:**2
'grh ('Agrah), **80:**1 ; **81:**1
'dmh (Admah), **29B:**21.24, 31
'dr (Adar), **41:**1 ; **150:**12
'hrn (Aaron), **68:**2
'whyh ('Ohyah), **17:**2.15 ; **18:**9 ; **19:**1.2, 6
'ḥy ('Aḥai), **38:**[2]
'ywb (Job), **5:**9.[10] ; 10.[8] ; 20.[2], [3], 4 ; 21.[3] ; 23.[9] ; 24.[1] ; 29.5 ; 34.2 ; 37.3 ; 38.2, 3, 5
'yyr (Iyyar), **150:**2
'ylwt' ('Ilutha), **61:**25
'lwl (Elul), **62:**13 ; **64:**1.[1] ; **150:**6
'lyhw (Elihu), **5:**20.[6]
'ly'zr (Eliezer), **29B:**22.34 ; **40:**27 ; **130:**1
'lyšb' (Elisheba' or Elizabeth), **104:**1
'lyšyb (Eliashib), **41:**2, 17
'lyš' (Elisha), **55:**2
'lks ('Alex), **61:**26
'lnh (Elnah), **52:**3
'l'zr (Eleazar), **40:**29 ; **51:**2bis, 7, 8, 17, 19 ; **56:**4 ; **64:**1.7, 8, 9 ; 2.1, [2] ; 3.1 ; **68:**1-2 ; **77:**1 ; **98:**1 ; **99:**1 ; **101:**1 ; **138:**1 ; **146:**1
'yl prn (El-Paran), **29B:**21.29-30
'lqṣdryn (Alexandrin[us]), **140:**1
'mrpl (Amraphel), **29B:**21.23
'nṭywkws (Antiochus), **150:**11
'nyn ('Anin), **145C:**1
'ptḥ ('Aphtaḥ), **64:**1.[4]
'ptlmys (Ptolemaios), **52:**5
'rywk (Arioch), **29B:**21.23
'rm (Aram), **29B:**17.9
'rpkšd (Arpachshad), **29B:**12.10 ; 17.11
'rrṭ (Ararat), **29B:**10.12
'šwny (name ?), **123:**1bis
'šwr (Asshur), **29B:**17.8
'škwl (Eshcol), **29B:**21.21 ; 22.7

bbl (Babel, Babylon), **2:**1.[1] ; **3C:**[3] ; **29B:**21.23 ; **68:**5
bbly (Babelis), **62:**13
bbth (Babatha), **61:**24bis ; **63:**1 ; *bbtyh*, **62:**11
bṭnyh (Beṭenyah), **58:**3
byt 'l (Bethel), **29B:**21.1, 7, 9
byt zbdy (Beth-Zabdai), **150:**12
byt krm' (Beth-haccherem), **29B:**22.14
byt š'n (Beth-shean), **150:**3
bldd (Bildad), **5:**1.4 ; 9.[3]
blkrws (Balakros), **3E:**2
bl' (Bela), **29B:**21.25, 31
bny (Bannai), **64:**1.3, 7bis, 8 ; 2.3 ; 3.2, 4
b'yh (Ba'yah), **55:**2
b'yn (Ba'yan), **56:**2 ; **58:**1 ; **60:**2
brk'l (Barachel), **5:**20.[6]
brsb' (Barsabba *or* son of Sabba), **118:**1
br' (Bera), **29B:**21.24
brq'l (Baraqi'el), **19:**1.4
bršb' (Barsabba), **44:**1.4 ; 9-10.[1]
brš' (Birsha), **29B:**21.24
bt'nwš (Bitenosh) **29B:**2.3, 8, 12

gbl (Gebal), **29B:**21.11, 29
gbnys (Gabinius), **47:**1-2 ii 6
gwym (Goiim), **29B:**21.23
gḥwn (Gihon), **29B:**21.18 ; *gyḥwn* **29B:**21.15
gml' (Gamla'), **94A:**1 ; **94B:**2
gmr (Gomer), **29B:**17.16
gny (Gannai), **146:**1
grzym (Gerizim), **150:**9
gryd' (Gerida'), **125:**1

dwsts (Dosithos), **95A:**1 ; **95B:**1
dn (Dan), **21:**2.14 ; **29B:**22.7, 8
dny'l (Daniel), **2:**4.4
drmšq (Damascus), **29B:**22.5, 10

hgr (Hagar), **29B:**20.32
hwš' (Hosea), **133:1**
hnblṭ' (Hanabalaṭa), **40:4**, [15]
hqrywt (Hakerioth), **29B:**21.29

zwmzmy' (Zumzammin), **29B:**21.29
zkryh (Zechariah), **39:3**, [9] ; **83:1**

ḥbb (name ?), **141:2**
ḥbrwn (Hebron), **29B:**19.9bis ; 21.19, 20 ; 22.3 ; **52:20**
ḥgy (Haggai), **148:1**
ḥdql (Tigris), **29B:**17.8
ḥwbbš (Ḥobabesh), **16:**1.2
ḥwny (Ḥoni), **52:4**
ḥwrn (Hauran), **29B:**21.11, 12
ḥṭh (name ?), **56:5**
ḥysh (name ?), **126B:1**
ḥlbwn (Helbon), **29B:**22.10
ḥm (Ham), **29B:**19.13 ; **35C:1**
ḥmlt (Ḥamilat), **149:4**
ḥnwk (Enoch), **16:**2.4 ; **17:**2.[14], 21; 3.6 ; **29B:**2.[19], 22, [23], 24 ; 5.3 ; 19.25 ; **33:**7.1
ḥnwn (Ḥannun), **131:1**
ḥny (Ḥoni), **89:4**
ḥnyn (Ḥannin), 39.2 ; **50E:2**, 4
ḥnyn' (Ḥannina), **44:**1.[1], 6
ḥnynh (Ḥannina), **44:**4.[1], 6
ḥnnh (Ḥanana), **40:29**
ḥnny (Ḥanani), **136:1**
ḥnnyh (Ḥananiah), **78:1**quinquies ; **82:**1bis ; **102:1** ; **121:1** ; **122:1**
ḥsdy (Ḥasdai), **42:25**
ḥṣṣn tmr (Hazezon-Tamar), **29B:**21.30
ḥqwh (name ?), **79:1**
ḥqr' (Acra), **150:2**
ḥrdwn (Ḥarodon), **41:16**
ḥrn (Haran), **29B:**22.28, 30
ḥrqnwš (Hirqanos), **29B:**20.8, 21, 24
ḥrqq (Harquq), **38:4**

ṭbt (Tebet), **64:**3.3 ; **150:10**
ṭwbyh (Tobiah), **81:1**
ṭwr twr' (Taurus Mountain), **29B:**17. 10 ; 21.16bis
ṭwrynws (Trajan), **150:12**
ṭynh (Tina), **29B:**16.16 ; 17.16
ṭpz'y (Ṭiphzai), **129:1**
ṭrwsyh (name ?), **141:3**
ṭrpwn (Tarphon *or* Tryphon), **104:1**

yhwd (Judah), **68:6**
yhwdh (Judah), **41:18** ; **48:3** ; **51:2**, 15, 20bis ; **56:7** ; **60:1**; **61:**24bis ; **64:**4. 3 ; **70:3** ; **99:1** ; **102:1** ; **124:1** ; **142:1** ; **144:**1bis ; **150:3**
yhwdn (Judan), **39:**[12]
yhwḥn' (John), **39:11**
yhwḥnn (Yehoḥanan), **39:3**, [9] ; **42:**[26] ; **44:**1.[1] ; 4.[1] ; **49.**1.[1], 3, [5], 5, 6, [10] ; 2.[1] ; **61:26** ; **105:1** ; **116:1** ; **124:1** ; **126A:1**, **134A:1** ; **135:**1 ; **142:1** ; **143:1**
yhwntn (Jonathan), **39:11** ; **40:4**, 15 ; **48:3** ; **51:9** ; **52:**[4] ; **53:1** ; **55:2** ; **56:**2 ; **58:1** ; **59:1** ; **60:2** ; **76:1** ; **86:2** ; **121:1**
yhwsp (Joseph), **39:10**, 12 ; **40:2**, 3, 14, 26, 28 ; **42:**[22] ; **47:**3.[1] ; **51:18** ; **61:26** ; **62:12** ; **75:**[1] ; **80:1** ; **90:1** ; **106:1** ; **110:3** ; **113:1** ; **127:1** ; **135:1** ; **143:1** ; **145C:1** **148:1**
yhw'zr (Yeho'azar), **91B:1** ; **92A:1** ; **92C:1** ; **93A:1** ; **93B:1** ; **94B:2**
yw'mṣ (Yo'amaṣ [if correctly read]), **112:1**
ywḥnh (Yoḥanah), **61:25** ; **62:**[11]
ywnh (Jonah), **134C:1**
ywsp (Joseph), **47:**1-2 ii 6 ; **50B:**[1] ; **50C:1**
yw'zr (Yo'azar *or* Yo'ezer), **91A:1** ; **92B:1**
yḥwny (Yeḥoni), **131:1**
yḥzq (Yeḥzaq), **91A:1** ; **91B:2**
yḥzqyh (Yeḥezqiah *or* Hezekiah), **103:1**
ymlyk (Yamlik), **64:**1.4, 5, 9 ; 3.[1]
ym swp (Sea of Reeds), **29B:**21.18
ym' śmwq' (Red Sea), **12:7** ; **29B:**21.17, 18bis
yntn (Jonathan), **57:1**
yswn (Jason), **89:1**
ysp (Joseph), **64:**4.3
y'qb (Jacob), **20:**4.[1] ; 19.[1] ; 29.[1] ; **21:**2.12
y'qybyh (Ya'aqibyah), **139:1**

yṣḥq (Isaac), **20**:5.1
yqym (Yaqim), **149**:3
yrd (Jared), **29B**:3.3
yrdn' (Jordan), **3B**:3 ; **5**:35.2 ; **29B**: 21.5
yrwšlm (Jerusalem), **29B**:22.13 ; **43**:[1], [3] ; **44**:1.1 ; **52**:19 ; **68**:4 ; **150**:2ter, 3, 6bis, 11, 12
yśr'l (Israel), **3C**:1 ; **20**:58.[1] ; **24**:[4] ; **32C**:[3] ; **51**:1 ; **53**:1
yšb'b (Yeshab'ab), **91A**:2 ; **91B**:3
yšw' (Jesus), **38**:2, 4 ; **51**:[9] ; **53**:3 ; **62**:12bis ; **100**:1 ; **106**:1
ytr' (Yitra), **142**:1

kdrl'wmr (Chedorlaomer), **29B**:21.23, [32]
kwsbh (Kosiba), **53**:1 ; **55**:1 ; **58**:1
kwśbh (Kosiba), **59**:1 ; *kśbh*, **56**:1
kym' (Pleiades), **5**:31.8
klqys (Calchis), **150**:12
kn'n (Canaan), **29B**:12.11
kslw (Kisleu), **150**:9
kslwn (Cheaslon), **39**:4
kprbbyw (Kephar-Bebayu), **51**:1, 2
kptwk (Cappadocia), **29B**:21.23
krmwn (Carmon), **29B**:19.11
kśbh, see *kwśbh*
ktwśywn (Chthusion), **61**:24

lbnn (Lebanon), **29B**:21.11
lwbr (Lubar), **3A**:3 ; **19**:1 ; **29B**:12.13
lwṭ (Lot), **20**:12.1 ; **29B**:20.11, 22, 24, [33], 34 ; 21.5, 7, 34 ; 22.2, 3, 5, 11
lwy (Levi), 21.2.8 ; **24**:1 ; **27**:11
lmk (Lamech), **29B**:2.3, 19 ; 5.4, 10, 25, 26
l'wtwn (Le'uthon), **42**:[2], [3], [17], [18], [23]

mgwg (Magog), **29B**:17.16
mhwy (Mahaway), **14**:27.2 ; **17**:2.21 ; **19**:1.2, 5
mwšh (Moses), **41**:3
mḥwz 'gltyn (Maḥoz 'Eglatain), **64**:1.2 ; 3.5
mysh (Misa), **58**:3
mlkh (Malka), **40**:27, 28
mlkyṣdk (Melchizedek), **29B**:22.14
mlkyrš' (Malkî-reša'), **23**:2.3
mmrh (Mamre), **29B**:21.19, 21 ; 22.7
mnḥm (Menaḥem), **36**:[1] ; **42**:17, [21] ; **62**:13 ; **78**:1quinquies ; **109**:2
mnkw (Maliku), **64**:1.1 ; 3.3
mnšh (Manasseh), **41**:2 ; **52**:18 ; **60**:1
msblh (Masabbala), **53**:1 ; **57**:1 ; **58**:1 ; **60**:2
m'zy (Ma'azi), **36**:1
mṣd' (Masada), **40**:1, 3, 5, 12, 16 ; **49**:1.10
mṣryn (Egypt), **3B**:3 ; **24**:4 ; **29B**:19.10, 11, 13, 14, [24] ; 20.14, 19bis, 28, [32], [33], [34] ; 21:11, 28, 29
mrḥšwn (Marḥeshwan), **40**:1, [12] ; **44**: 1.[1] ; 3.[1] ; **150**:8
mrym (Miriam), **40**:4 ; **91A**:1 ; **91B**:1 ; **103**:1 ; **119**:1
mrt' (Martha), **87**:3
mśblh (Masabbala), **56**:3 ; **59**:2
mtwšlḥ (Methuselah), **29B**:2.19, [21] ; 5.24
mšk (Meshach), **4B**:[7], 11
mty (Mattai), **120**:1
mtyh (Matthiah), **79**:1 ; **97A**:1 ; **97B**:1
mtt' (Mattathah), **51**:17
mtty (Mattatai), **68**:5-6

nbwm' (Neboma), **64**:1.[7] ; 3.2
nbṭw (Nabatea), **64**:1.[1] ; 3.3
nbkdnṣr (Nebukadnezzar), **3C**:3
nbny (Nabonidus), **2**:1.1
nwḥ (Noah), **3A**:[3] ; **29B**:6.6
nykrqs (Nikarchos), **64**:3.4
nysn (Nisan), **150**:1
nyqnwr (Nicanor), **150**:12
nyqrks (Nikarchos), **64**:1.6, 7, 8
npyl' (Orion), **5**:31.8
nṣrmlk (Neṣarmilk), **149**:5
nqnr (Nicanor), **108**:1
nqsn (Naqsan), **40**:3, 14, 26
nrwn (Nero), **39**:1
nty (Nattai), **101**:1

sbwr' (Sibbura), **128**:1
sdy' (Siddim), **29B**:21.25, [32]
swdm (Sodom), **29B**:21.6bis, 24, 26,

31, 32, 33 ; 22.1, 12, 18, 20, 25 ; *sdwm*, **33**:2
sw'm (So'am), **109**:1
sywn (Siwan), **150**:3
smwn (Simon), **85A**:1 ; **85B**:1
srw (Saru), **130**:1
sry (Saray), **126B**:1

'bdy ('Abdai), **64**:1.4, 12 ; 3.1
'bdngw (Abednego), **4B**:[11], [14]
'bd'bdt ('Abdo'abdat), **61**:25bis
'gl' ('Egla), **61**:25
'wy ('Awwai), **74**:1
'wzyh (Uzziah), **70**:2
'wmrm (Gomorrah), **29B**:21.24, [31], 32, [34]
'zryh (Azariah), **83**:1
'ylm (Elam), **29B**:21.23, 26, 27bis, [32], 33 ; 22.17, 19
'my ('Ammi), **53**:4
'mn (Ammon), **29B**:21.29
'mrm ('Amram), **24**:1 ; **27**:9
'rnm (Arnem), **29B**:21.21 ; 22.6
'štr' (Ashteroth), **29B**:21.28

pdwy (Paddui), **49**:1.2
pwṭ (Put), **29B**:12.11
pwrt (Euphrates), **29B**:21.12, 17bis, 28
pnḥs (Phinehas), **47**:1-2 ii 9 ; **139**:1
prwyn (Parvaim), **29B**:2.23

ṣbwym (Zeboiim), **29B**:21.25, 31
ṣby' (Sibya'), **126A**:1
ṣwyh (Ṣiwaya), **39**:2bis
ṣwpr (Zophar), **5**:3.3
ṣwq (Ṣûq) **38**:5
ṣwr ([Beth-]Zur), **150**:3
ṣ'n (Zoan), **29B**:19.[22], 22, [24] ; 20.14
ṣrh (Ṣarah), **132B**:1
ṣrn (Ṣaran), **132A**:1

qdš (Kadesh), **29B**:21.11
qht (Qahat), **24**:1
qymw (Qaymu), **141**:2
qlwn (Kallon), **91A**:2 ; **91B**:2 ; **92A**:3 ; **92C**:2 ; **93A**:1 ; **93B**:1 ; **94B**:2
qlwpw (Klopas), **50E**:5
qryt 'rbyh (Qiryat 'Arabaya), **60**:1
qrnym (Karnaim), **29B**:21.29
qrs' (Qarsa), **137**:1
qtrs (Qathros), **65**:1

rwb' (Roba), **52**:[4]
rwm'h (Rumah), **5**:20.[7]
rmn (Rimmon), **47**:1-2 i 1
rmt hṣwr (Ramath-Hazor), **29B**:21.8, 10
rp'y' (Rephaim), **29B**:21.28
rp'l (Raphael), **16**:2.12

śnyr (Senir), **29B**:21.11, 12
śry (Sarai), **29B**:19.17, 21, 22 ; 20.9, 11, 23, 25bis, [26], [31]
š'wl (Saul), **88**:1
šbt (Shebat), **43**:1, 3 ; **49**:1.7 ; **150**:11
šdrk (Shadrach), **4B**:[7], [8]
šwh (Shaveh), **29B**:21.29 ; 22.14
šlwm (Salome), **84**:1 ; **88**:1, 2 ; **89**:1 ; **122**:1 ; **134A**:1 ; **134B**:1
šlm (Salome), **51**:12, [13], 16 ; **74**:1; **97B**:1
šlm (Salem), **20**:8.2 ; **29B**:22.13, 14
šlmṣywn (Shelamṣion), **94A**:1 ; **94B**:1 ; **96A**:1 ; **96B**:1 ; **111**:1
šm (Shem), **29B**:12.10
šmw'l (Samuel), **53**:4
šmy'bd (Shemiabad), **29B**:21.25
šmyḥzh (Shemiḥazah), **16**:2.5 ; **17**:2.5
šm'h (Shim'ah), **136**:2
šm'n (Simeon), **47**:1-2 ii 9 ; **50A**:[4] ; **50C**:[2] ; **50E**:2, 4 ; **51**:12, 16, 18 ; **53**:1 ; **55**:1 ; **56**:1, 3, 7 ; **57**:1 ; **58**:1 ; **59**:1, **60**:1 ; **62**:11bis ; **63**:1 ; **72**:1 ; **82**:1 ; **90**:1 ; **91A**:1 ; **91B**:1 ; **92A**:2 ; **92C**:2 ; **93A**:1 ; **93B**:1 ; **100**:1 ; **110**:2 ; **111**:2 ; **112**:1 ; **113**:1 ; **118**:1 ; **119**:1 ; **123**:1 ; **129**:1 ; **133**:1 ; **136**:1 ; **138**:1 ; **147**:1
šmrwn (Samaria), **150**:8
šn'b (Shinab), **29B**:21.24
špyr (Shappir), **84**:1
špyr' (Sapphira), **73**:1 ; **147**:1
špr' (Sapphira) **117**:1

td'l (Tidal), **29B**:21.23
twdws (Theudos), **144A**:1 ; **144B**:1

tym'lhy (Taim'ilahi), **64:1.4**
tymn (Teman), **2:1.2, 6**
tynynws (Tininos), **58:2**
tyrsys (Tirsis), **58:2**
tl 'rzyn (Tell Arza), **59:2**
tmwz (Tammuz), **62:12 ; 150:4**
tqw' (Teqoa), **59:2**
tšry (Tishri), **150:7**

GLOSSARY TO THE APPENDIX

GLOSSARY TO THE APPENDIX

The references in brackets indicate that some part of the word has been emended. But the degree of certainty or probability for the restoration varies considerably, and one should always consult the passage itself before discounting the bracketed references.

'dn (pedestal, column ?) : *h'dn* (with Hebr. article), **A25:2**
'w (or) : *'w*, **A5:2**
'wmn (craftsman) : *'wmnh*, **A9:1 ; A14:1**
'wrḥtw (caravan hospitality) : *'wrḥtwh*, **A48:1**
'ḥ (brother) : *'ḥwy*, **A42:3**
'mn (amen) : *'mn*, **A1:[5] ; A3:2 ; A5:8 ; A7:[4] ; A8:[3] ; A9:[1] ; A13:3 ; A22:8 ; A26:10bis ; A27:3bis, 4bis ; A28:2bis, 4bis ; A29:[5] ; A30:3ter ; A33:2bis ; A34:[6] ; A35:1 ; A36:5 ; A39:4bis**
'mr (say, speak) : *ymrwn*, **A22:8** ; *'mr* (peal act. ptc.), **A22:2**
'nh (I) : *'nh*, **A9:1 ; A23:1**
'nwn (they) : *'nwn*, **A22:10** (see also *hnwn*)
'nš (man) : *'nšy* (Hebr. cst. pl.), **A34:4**
'p (face) : *'pwh*, **A22:6**
'rbyly (Arbelite) : *'rbylyy*, **A27:4**
'rb' (four) : *'rb'*, **A52:6** ; see also *rb'*
'rd (builder ?) : *'rdh*, **A27:3**
'r' (land) : *'r'h*, **A22:5**
't' (come) : *'ytwn*, **A5:[6]**
'th (woman, wife) : *'th*, **A28:2** ; *'tth*, **A2:6**
'tr (place) : *'tr*, **A26:7** ; *'trh*, **A3:2 ; A5:3, 7 ; A7:3, 4 ; A8:[3] ; A13:2 ; A30:2 ; A35:1**

b- (in, on, by, for [prep.]) : *b-*, **A3:2 ; A5:3, 7 ; A7:[3], 4 ; A8:3 ; A11:1 ; A13:2, 3, 4 ; A22:5, 6, 7 ; A26:7, 10 ; A27:3, 4 ; A28:2, 3 ; A30:1 ; A34:5 ; A45:3, 4 ; A46:1, 3, 5 ; A50:3 ; A51:4 ; A52:3bis, 4bis**
b (cipher for 2) : *b*, **A52:[4]**
byš (evil) : *byš*, **A22:3 ; A45:4 ; A46:6**
byt (house) : *byt* (cst.), **A20:1** (?) ; **A48:1 ; A50:8 ; A51:8 ; A52:8** ; *btyhwn*, **A34:5**
bn (son [Hebr.]) : *bn* (cst.), **A22:9bis**
bn (= *byn*, between, either ... or) : *bn*, **A5:4bis, 5 ; A22:2**
bnh (build) : *bnhw* (built it), **A49:[1]** ; *bnyn* (peal act. ptc.), **A48:1**
br (son) : *br* (cst.), **A2:1 ; A4:3 ; A8:2 ; A9:1 ; A12:[3], 4 ; A15:1bis ; A16:1 ; A17:1 ; A18:[1] ; A24:1 ; A25:1 ; A27:[1], 2 ; A29:1, [2], [3] ; A31:2, 3 ; A33:3, 4, 5 ; A36:1, 2 ; A38:1bis ; A41:[3], 3 ; A43:[1] ; A46:2 ; A48:1 ; A49:1 ; A50:2 ; A53:1** ; *brh* (his son), **A7:3 ; A26:4, 6** ; *bryh*, **A44:3** ; *bny* (cst. pl.), **A11:4, [7] ; A13:1** ; *bnwh*, **A22:1** ; *bnwy*, **A36:2 ; A48:1 ; A56:2** ; *bnyhwn*, **A26:6 ; A34:4**
brh (daughter) : *brt* (cst.), **A3:1** ; *brth* (his daughter), **A51:2 ; A52:2**
brwk (blessed [Hebr. pass. ptc.]) : *brwkh*, **A32:1**
brby (BeRabbi) : *brby*, **A32:1**
brkh (blessing) : *brkth* (emph. st.), **A13:3 ; A15:3 ; A17:[2] ; A19:[2] ; A20:3 ; A25:4 ; A29:5 ; A30:3 ; A32:[2] ; A36:4 ; A37:3 ; A41:[6]** ; *brkth* (suf-

fixal or emph. st.), **A26:9** ; **A27:3**, 4 ; **A28:2**, 3

g (cipher for 3) : *g*, **A51:5**
gbr (man) : *gbr* (abs. st.), **A22:2** ; *gbrh* (emph. st.), **A22:6**
gw (interior) : *gw* (cst. st.), **A29:4** ; *gwh* (suffixal), **A45:3**
glh (reveal) : *gly* (peal act. ptc.), **A22:4**
gnb (steal) : *gnyb* (peal act. ptc.), **A22:3**
grm (gram [?]) : *grmyn*, **A27:2**

d- (who, which, what) : *d-* (used as rel. pron.), **A1:3** ; **A2:1**, 3 ; **A3:2** ; **A5:**[2], [3], [6] ; **A7:3** ; **A9:1** ; **A12:5** ; **A13:2** ; **A14:1** ; **A16:2** ; **A17:1** ; **A22:**2, 4, 5 ; **A26:7**, 8 ; **A27:1**, 2bis, 3, 4 ; **A28:1**, 3, 4 ; **A29:2**, ‹3› ; **A30:1**, 2 ; **A32:**[2], 3 ; **A34:2**, 4 ; **A36:3** ; **A39:1**, 3 ; **A40:4** ; **A41:**[4] ; **A43:2** ; **A45:1**, 3 ; **A46:1**, 4 ; **A47:1** ; **A48:1** ; **A50:3** ; **A51:3** ; **A52:2**, 5 ; **A54:3** ; **A56:2** ; *d-* (used as determinative pron.), **A11:2** ; **A12:6** ; **A13:2** ; **A22:1**, 4bis, 10 ; **A27:1**, 2 ; **A28:1**, 3 ; **A32:1** ; **A34:3**, 4bis ; **A35:1** ; **A42:4** ; **A48:1**, 2 ; **A50:2**, 5 ; **A51:2**, 3, 5 ; **A52:1**, 5 ; *d-* (that), **A46:3**
dh (this [fem. dem. pron.]) : *dh*, **A48:1**
dhb (gold) : *dhb* (abs. st.), **A5:4** ; **A26:9**
dy (who) : *dy*, **A40:**[2] (correctly restored ?)
dyn (judge) : *dyn* (abs. st.), **A22:5**
dynr (denar) : *dynr* (abs. st.), **A28:3** ; **A29:**[4] ; *dynryn*, **A26:8** ; **A40:4**
dkr (remember) : *dkyr* (peal pass. ptc.), **A1:1** ; **A2:1** ; **A4:**[1] ; **A6:1** ; **A7:**[1], ‹2› ; **A8:1** ; **A12:1** ; **A14:1** ; **A16:1** ; **A22:9** ; **A26:1** ; **A27:**[1], 1, 3, [4] ; **A28:**‹1› ; **A29:**[1] ; **A31:1** ; **A32:**[2], 3bis ; **A36:1** ; **A38:1** ; **A41:**[1] ; **A43:**1 ; **A54:1** ; **A56:1** ; *dkyrh*, **A2:4** ; **A3:1** ; **A28:2** ; *dkyryn*, **A5:**[1] ; **A11:**[6] ; **A13:1** ; **A22:1** ; **A28:4** ; **A35:1** ; **A40:**[1] ; **A48:1** ; *dkyrn*, **A34:1** ; **A55:**[1]
dkrwn (remembrance [Hebraized form ?]) : *dkrwnhwn*, **A34:1**
dmk (sleep, die) : *dmyk*, **A48:2**
dn (this [masc. dem. pron.]) : *dn*, **A35:1** (correctly read ?)
drg (step) : *drgy* (cst. pl.), **A22:10** ; *drgwh*, **A16:3**

h- (Hebr. article) : *h-*, **A9:1** ; **A22:7** ; **A25:2** ; **A27:1**
hdh (this [fem. dem. pron.]) : *hdh*, **A14:1** ; **A36:3** ; **A37:2** ; **A39:1** ; **A41:**4 ; **A45:2** ; **A51:1** (see also *dh*)
hdyn (this [masc. dem. pron.]) : *hdyn*, **A1:**[4] ; **A3:2** ; **A9:**[1] ; **A11:**[1] ; **A12:**5 ; **A46:1** (see also *hdn, dn*)
hdn (this [masc. dem. pron.]) : *hdn*, **A5:3**, 7 ; **A7:**[3], 4 ; **A8:**[3] ; **A15:2** ; **A16:2** ; **A29:4** ; **A30:1** ; **A40:2** ; **A42:**4 ; **A43:**[2]
hw (that) : *hhw* (with Hebr. art.), **A22:7**
hw' (he) : *hw'*, **A22:6**
hwh (be) : *yhwy*, **A34:1** ; *thwy*, **A13:3** ; **A29:4**
hy (either ... or [prob. = Gk. εἰ]) : *hy*, **A22:2**, 3, 4
hy' (she) : *hy'*, **A5:6** ; **A52:5**
hyh (be [Hebraized form ?]) : *yhy* **A16:3** ; **A30:1** ; **A46:4** ; *thy*, **A15:**[3] ; **A17:**[2] ; **A20:2** ; **A30:3** ; **A32:2** ; **A36:**4 ; **A37:**[2] ; **A41:**[6] ; *t'h* (form ?), **A25:3**
hkh (here) : *hkh*, **A26:8**
hnwn (they) : *hnwn*, **A7:3** ; **A13:2** ; *hnnwn*, **A26:6** (see also *'nwn*)

w- (and) : *w-*, **A1:**[3] ; **A2:3** ; **A5:2**, [6] ; **A7:2** ; **A13:3** ; **A16:3** ; **A17:2** ; **A22:**1bis, 6, 7bis, 8bis ; **A26:1**, 2, 3, 4, 5bis, 6 ; **A27:1**bis, 2bis, 3, 4 ; **A28:**1bis, 2, 4 ; **A29:**[1], 2, 3 ; **A30:2**, 3 ; **A32:1**, 2 ; **A33:5** ; **A34:2**, 3bis, 4bis ; **A36:2** ; **A39:3** ; **A40:3**ter ; **A42:2** ; **A46:3** ; **A48:1** ; **A50:6**, 7 ; **A51:6** ; **A52:6**, 7 ; **A55:1** ; **A56:2**
wrth (?), **A32:1**

zbn (purchase) : *zbn*, **A12:5**
z'wr (youth): *z'wryh* (emph. st. pl.), **A34:2**

zr' (seed) : *zr'yh* (suffixal form), **A22:7**

ḥbr (fellow, associate) : *ḥbryh* (his fellow), **A22:2**, 3, 4 ; *ḥbryn*, **A34:6**
ḥbwrh (community) : *ḥbwrth*, **A13:1**
ḥd (one) : *ḥd*, **A27:1** ; **A28:3**, 4 ; **A29:** 2, 3 ; **A56:2** ; *ḥdh*, **A28:2**
ḥd'śr (eleven) : *hd'śr* (but read *ḥd'śr*), **A52:3**
ḥwlq (lot, portion) : *ḥwlq*, **A16:4** ; *ḥwlqhwn*, **A5:**<6> ; **A8:3** ; **A48:2**
ḥzn (sexton) : *ḥz'nh* (emph. st.), **A23:** [1] ; *ḥznh* (emph. st.), **A42:1**
ḥzq (be strong ; *refl.* : gather one's resources) : *'tḥzq*, **A1:3** ; *'tḥzqt*, **A3:** [2] ; *'tḥzqwn*, **A34:3** ; *mtḥzq*, **A5:2** ; *mtḥzqyn*, **A7:3** ; **A13:2** ;
ḥṭh (wheat) : *ḥṭyyh* (emph. st. pl.), **A11:3**
ḥy (living) : *ḥyyh* (emph. st. pl.), **A34:5**
ḥmh (see) : *ḥmy* (peal act. ptc.), **A22:6**
ḥmš (five) : *ḥmš*, **A52:7** ; *ḥmyšh*, **A26:8**
ḥsd (piety) : *ḥsd*, **A13:4**
ḥrbn (destruction) : *ḥrbn*, **A50:7** ; **A51:** 7 ; **A52:7**
ḥtn (son-in-law) : *ḥtnh* (his son-in-law), **A26:4**, 5

ṭb (good) : *ṭb*, **A1:1** ; **A2:1**, 5 ; **A3:1** ; **A4:1** ; **A5:1** ; **A6:[1]** ; **A7:2** ; **A8:1** ; **A11:6** ; **A12:2** ; **A13:1** ; **A14:1** ; **A16:** 1 ; **A22:1**, 9 ; **A26:1** ; **A27:[1]**, 1, 3, [4] ; **A28:1**, 2, 4 ; **A29:1** ; **A31:1** ; **A32:[2]**, 3bis ; **A34:1bis** ; **A35:1** ; **A36:1** ; **A38:1** ; **A40:1** ; **A41:[2]** ; **A43:1** ; **A48:1** ; **A55:1** ; **A56:1**
ṭblh (panel [?] ; prob. = Lat. *tabula*) : *ṭblh*, **A36:3** ; **A37:[2]** ; **A41:[4]**
ṭbryh (Tiberias) : *ṭbryh*, **A10:1**
ṭymy (value ; = Gk. τιμή) : *ṭymy*, **A2:2**
ṭrymysyn (*trimēsion* ; = Gk. τριμήσιον, Lat. *tremis(sis)*, a coin = ⅓ of *aureus*) : *ṭrymysyn*, **A27:1** ; **A28:**<4> ; **A29:2** ; **A56:[2]**

yd (hand) : *ydh* (his hand, i.e., his own resources), **A2:3**
yd' (know) : *yd'* (pf. or ptc.?), **A34:4**

yhb (give) : *yhb*, **A2:1** ; **A5:[3]** ; **A27:3** ; **A29:2** ; **A32:2**, [3] ; **A44:1** ; **A54:3** ; **A56:2** ; *yhb* (peal act. ptc.), **A5:2** ; *hb* (= *yhb*, with prefix *d-*), **A27:1** ; *yhbh* (seems to be 3d sg. fem. pf. peal ; but could it be peal act. ptc. fem.?), **A28:[3]** ; *yhbwn*, **A27:2**, 4 ; **A29:**<3> ; *yhbw*, **A40:4** ; *hbwn* (with prefixed *d-*), **A26:8** ; **A28:[1]**, 4 ; *yhwb* (?), **A22:2**
ywm (day) : *ywm*, **A52:3** ; *ywmyn*, **A52:4**
yqr (honor) : *yqrh*, **A12:6** ; **A28:[1]**, 3
yrḥ (month) : *yrḥ*, **A50:3** ; **A51:4** ; **A52:4**
yt (sign of accusative) : *ytyh*, **A22:7** ; *ythwn*, **A34:3**, 5

khn (priest) : *khn'*, **A56:[1]** ; *khnh*, **A2:1**
kl (all) : *kl* (cst. st.), **A5:1**, 5 ; **A11:4**, 6 ; **A13:1** ; **A22:2**, 5, 8 ; **A26:7** ; **A30:1** ; **A32:[2]** ; **A33:1** ; **A34:1**, 6 ; **A40:1** ; **A45:1** ; **A46:3** ; **A47:1**
klyl (circle) : *klylh*, **A35:1**
kn (thus) : *kn*, **A40:3**
knyšh (congregation) : *knyšt'*, **A12:6** ; *knyšth*, **A28:1**, 3
ksp (silver) : *ksp* (abs. st.), **A5:[5]**
kph (arch) : *kpth*, **A17:2**
kpr (village) : *kpr* (used in proper names of places), **A27:**<2>, 2 ; **A35:1**
ktb (write) : *yktwb*, **A34:5**

l- (to, for [prep.]) : *l-*, **A1:1** ; **A2:1**, 5 ; **A3:1** ; **A4:1** ; **A5:1** ; **A6:1** ; **A7:2** ; **A8:1** ; **A11:[2]**, [6] ; **A12:2**, 6 ; **A13:** 1 ; **A14:1** ; **A16:1**; **A22:1**, 2, 3, 5, 9, 10 ; **A26:1** ; **A27:[1]**, 1, 3, [4] ; **A28:1**, [1], 2, 3, 4 ; **A29:[1]**, 4 ; **A31:1** ; **A32:[2]**, 3bis ; **A34:1bis**, 6 ; **A35:1bis** ; **A36:1** ; **A38:1** ; **A40:1** ; **A41:[2]** ; **A43:1** ; **A48:1** ; **A50:7** ; **A51:** 7 **A52:7** ; **A55:1** ; **A56:1** ; *ly*, **A30:3** ; *lh*, **A16:4**; **A17:[2]** ; **A20:2** ; **A25:3** ; **A30:3** ; **A41:6** ; *l'* (read *lh*), **A15:3** ; *lhwn*, **A13:3** ; **A29:4** ; **A32:[2]** ; **A36:** 4 ; **A37:[2]**

lwy (levite) : *hlwy* (with Hebr. article), **A9:1** ; **A27:1**
lšn (tongue) : *lšn*, **A22:3**

m'h (hundred) : *m'h*, **A52:6** ; *m'*, **A50:6** ; **A51:6** ; *m't*, **A11:3**
mḥy (woven goods) : *mḥythwn*, **A27:**‹4›
myt (die) : *myt*, **A50:3** ; *mytt*, **A51:3** ; **A52:2** ; *ymwt*, **A45:4** ; *m'yt* (peal act. ptc.), **A46:5**
mlk (king) : *mlk* (cst. st.), **A10:2** ; **A26:9** ; **A27:2**, 4 ; **A28:2**, 3 ; *mlkh* (emph. st.), **A11:[2]** ; *mlkyh*, **A34:3**
mlkw (kingdom) : *mlkwth* (suffixal or emph. st. ?), **A11:[2]**
mn (who ? whoever) : *mn*, **A5:1** ; **A22:** 2, 4 ; **A30:1** ; **A32:[2]** ; **A45:1**, 3 ; **A47:1**
mn (from) : *mn*, **A2:3** ; **A16:3** ; **A17:1** ; **A22:7** ; **A27:2**, 3 ; **A39:2**, 3 ; **A50:** 4 ; **A51:7** ; **A56:3**
mnḥm (counsellor) : *mnḥmh*, **A55:1bis**
mṣwh (commandment ; donation) : *mṣwth*, **A30:1**, 2 ; *myṣwtwn*, **A26:7**
mqdš (sanctuary, temple) : *mqdšh*, **A50:** 8 ; **A51:8** ; **A52:8**
mqm (property ?) : *mqmh*, **A5:5**
mry (lord) : *mry*, **A42:4**
mrwšt (basin ?) : *mrwšt*, **A2:3**

ndb (volunteer) : *'tndbwn*, **A11:4**
nwḥ (to rest) : *ttnyḥ*, **A50:1** ; **A52:1**
nyḥ (repose) : *nyḥ*, **A12:3**
npš (soul, self ; tomb) : *npš*, **A12:[3]** ; *npšh* (suffixal or emph. st. ?), **A50:1** ; **A51:1** ; **A52:1** ; *npšyh*, **A44:2**
ntn (give) : *ytn*, **A22:6** ; **A26:9** ; **A27:** [3], 4 ; **A28:2**, 3

sgy (great [Hebraized meaning ?]) : *sgy*, **A22:10**
sdrh (meaning uncertain) : *sdrh*, **A1:2**
swp (end) : **A45:4** ; **A46:5**
sṭwh (colonnade [= Gk. στοά]) : *sṭwh*, **A16:2**
sy' (aid, help) : *syy'*, **A34:2**
skwph, see *šqwph*
slh (selah) : *slh*, **A9:1** ; **A22:8** ; **A26:10** ; **A27:3**, 4 ; **A28:2**, [4] ; **A29:[5]** ; **A30:** 3 ; **A33:3** ; **A34:[6]** ; **A35:1** ; **A39:4**
spr (book) : *spr* (cst. st.), **A34:5**
str (hide, secret) : *styrth* (peal pass. ptc. fem. pl.), **A22:6**

'bd (do, make) : *'bd*, **A1:[3]** ; **A9:1** ; **A14:1** ; **A15:2** ; **A16:2** ; **A17:1** ; **A21:** 1 ; **A25:2** ; **A30:1** ; **A41:[4]** ; *'bdw*, **A20:1** ; **A22:10** ; **A40:2** ; **A42:3** ; *'bdwn*, **A34:3** ; *m'bd*, **A30:2** ; *'byd* (peal act. ptc.), **A43:2** ; *'bdyn*, **A36:3**
'bydh (work) : *'bydth* (read *'bydth*), **A14:1**
'yn (eye) : *'ynwh*, **A22:5**
'yr (watcher, guardian) : *'yry'*, **A28:4**
'l (on, upon, against, above) : *'l*, **A17:** 1 ; **A22:3** ; **A30:1** ; **A33:1** ; **A44:2** ; **A45:3** ; **A52:9** ; *'lyw* (should it be *'lwy* ?), **A46:4**
'll (enter) : *'lt*, **A51:10**
'lm (universe) : *'lmh*, **A10:2** ; **A26:9** ; **A27:[3]**, ‹4› ; **A28:2**, 3 ; **A34:3**
'm (people) : *'mh*, **A22:8** ; *'mmyh* (Gentiles), **A22:3**, 5
'm (with) : *'m*, **A16:4** ; **A34:[5]** ; **A48:[2]**
'mwd (column) : *'mwd'*, **A12:5** ; *'mwdh*, **A15:2** ; **A43:[2]** ; *'mwdyh*, **A17:1**
'ml (toil, undertaking) : *'mly*, **A39:3** ; *'mlh* (suffixal), **A28:2**, 3 ; *'mlhwn*, **A26:10** ; **A27:[3]**, 4
'mr (citizen) : *'mrym*, **A53:**‹1›
'qr (uproot) : *y'qwr*, **A22:7**
'tyd (prepared, ready [used to express future]) : *'tyd*, **A30:2**

plgw (division, discord ; half) : *plgw*, **A22:2** ; *plgwt*, **A29:3**
psyps (mosaic [= Gk. ψῆφος]) : *psypsh*, **A2:2** ; **A11:[1]** ; **A29:[4]** ; **A34:4** ; *pspsh*, **A40:**‹2›
psq (pledge) : *psq*, **A32:[2]**
psqh (pledged donation) : *psqth*, **A32:2**
p'l (skill, work) : *p'lh* (suffixal), **A16:3** ; **A56:[3]**
pṣym (beam) : *pṣymyh* (emph. st. pl.), **A17:[2]**

prns (administrator) : *prnsh*, **A4:**[2]
ptḥ (open) : *yptḥ*, **A45:**1 ; **A46:**4 ; **A47:** 1

ṣbw (goods) : *ṣbwtyh*, **A22:**4
ṣdyq (righteous) : *ṣdyqyh*, **A16:**4 ; **A34:** 6 ; **A48:**[2]
ṣpwry (Sepphorite) : *ṣpwryh*, **A27:**1

qbwrh (grave) : *qbwrth*, **A45:**2
qb' (fix, compose) : *'tqb'*, **A11:**1
qbr (bury) : *qbyr*, **A46:**1
qdyš (holy) : *qdyšh* (emph. st. masc.), **A3:**[2] ; **A5:**4, 7 ; **A7:**4 ; **A8:**[3] ; **A13:**[3] ; **A30:**2 ; **A34:**[2] ; **A35:**1 ; *qdyšth*, **A13:**1
qdm (before) : *qdm*, **A48:**2
qdmy (first) : *qdmyth*, **A50:**5
qhl (assembly) : *qhlh*, **A34:**2 ; **A40:**1
qwms (Comes, a title [= Lat. *comes*]) : *qwms*, **A26:**4
qyrh (Lady, a title [= Gk. κυρία]) : *qyrh*, **A26:**2 ; **A28:**1
qyrys (Lord, a title [= Gk. κύριος]) : *qyrys*, **A26:**5 ; **A28:**1 ; *qyrs*, **A26:**2, 3, 5 ; **A27:**[2]
qrth (city, town) : *qrth*, **A11:**[5] ; **A22:**4

r'š (head, leader) : *r'š*, **A1:**1 ; *rš*, **A53:** 1 ; *ryš*, **A50:**3
rb (Rab, a title) : *rb*, **A27:**1
rb (elder; great) : *rbh*, **A17:**[1] ; *rbyh* (emph. st. pl.), **A34:**2
rby (Rabbi, a title) : *rby*, **A3:**1 ; **A11:**5 ; **A22:**9 ; **A41:**[2] ; **A48:**1 ; *r'*, **A43:**1
rb' (four) : *rb'*, **A50:**7 ; see also *'rb'*
rwb (abundance, much) : *rwb*, **A13:**4
rz (secret) : *rzh* (emph. st.), **A22:**4

rḥmn (merciful one) : *rḥmnh* (emph. st.), **A22:**10 ; *rḥmnh*, **A39:**3

śhd (witness) : *śhdh* (emph. st.), **A55:**1

šbw'h (oath) : *šbw'h*, **A46:**3
šmy' (heaven) : *šwmyh*, **A22:**7 ; **A42:**5
šṭṭ (roam, range) : *mšwṭṭn*, **A22:**5
šlwm (peace [Hebr.]) : *šlwm*, **A1:**5 ; **A12:**7 ; **A13:**4bis ; **A22:**10 ; **A27:**3 ; **A28:**2, 4 ; **A29:**5 ; **A33:**1 ; **A34:**[6] ; **A35:**1 ; **A51:**9bis ; **A52:**8, 9
šlm (peace) : *šlm*, **A50:**8 ; *šlmh* (suffixal or emph. st. ?), **A30:**1
šlm (completion) : *šlmh* (suffixal), **A 13:**3
šm (name) : *šmh* (suffixal), **A22:**10 ; *šmhtwn*, **A34:**4
šmṭh (release) : *šmṭth*, **A50:**5 ; **A51:**[5] ; **A52:**5
šnh (year) : *šnt* (cst.), **A50:**6 ; **A51:**5, 6 ; **A52:**4,5 ; *šth*, **A11:**1 ; **A50:**4 ; *šnyn*, **A50:**7 ; **A51:**7 ; **A52:**7
šqwph (lintel) : *šqwph*, **A10:**2 ; *skwpth*, **A39:**2
šrh (loose ; begin) : *šrn*, **A39:**1
štyn (sixty) : *štyn*, **A50:**6

tg (sum ? = Gk. ταγή) : *tg*, **A40:**4
tdyr (constant) : *tdyrn*, **A26:**7
tḥwt (beneath) : *tḥwt*, **A22:**7
tlt (three) : *tlt*, **A27:**2, 3 ; **A50:**6 ; **A51:** 6, [6] ; *tlth*, **A52:**3 ; *tltyhwn*, **A27:**2
tltyn (thirty) : *tltyn*, **A52:**6
tqwn (repair) : *tqwnh* (emph. st.), **A13:**2
tryn (two) : *try*, **A40:**4
tr' (gate) : *tr'h*, **A1:**4 ; **A21:**1 ; **A48:**2 ; *tr'*, **A42:**4

Names of Months, Persons, and Places

'dh ('Adah), **A29:1**
'wksnṭys (Auxentios), **A12:4**
'lwl (Elul), **A52:4**
'ly'zr (Eli'ezer), **A17:[1]** ; **A48:1**
'l'zr (Eleazar), **A17:1** ; **A49:1**
'nṭwlyh (Anatolia), **A28:3**
'str (Esther), **A51:2**

bwṭh (Butah), **A36:2** ; **A41:[4]**
bynymyn (Benjamin), **A4:2**
brwk (Baruch), **A33:4**
brkh (Berakah), **A1:2**

d'yśn (Daisan), **A40:3**
dwsty (Dositheos), **A27:2**
dyṭws (Dioṭos), **A53:1**

hwplys (Hoples), **A26:2**
hym'ym (place name ?), **A27:3**

zbyd' (Zebida), **A15:1**

ḥzyqyw (Ḥezeqyo), **A22:1**
ḥzqyh (Ḥezekiah), **A33:5**
ḥzqyw (Ḥizqio), **A22:9**
ḥynnh (Ḥaynanah), **A19:[1]**
ḥlpw (Ḥalphu), **A15:1** ; **A38:[1]** ; **A52:1** (fem.)
ḥlpy (Ḥalphay), **A22:1**, 9bis
ḥlyph (Ḥalipah), **A27:[1]**
ḥlypw (Ḥalipu), **A3:1**
ḥnynh (Ḥaninah), **A26:6**
ḥnn (Ḥanan), **A38:[1]**
ḥnnyh (Ḥananiah), **A24:1** ; see also *kpr ḥnnyh*

ṭd'wr (Ṭedeor), **A48:1**

yhwdh (Judah), **A23:1** ; **A40:3**
yhwntn (Jonathan), **A49:[1]**
yhwšw' (Joshua), **A44:1**
ywdh (Judah), **A18:1**
ywdn (Judan), **A16:1** ; **A27:3** ; **A33:[5]** ; **A41:2** ; **A54:2**
ywḥnn (John), **A15:1** ; **A46:2**
ywntn (Jonathan), **A31:[2]**
ywsh (Jose), **A4:3** ; **A9:1** ; **A22:1**, 9 ; **A25:1** ; **A27:2** ; **A29:2** ; **A33:4** ; **A36:1** ; **A38:1**
ywsṭh (Justus), **A2:1**
ywsṭynws (Justinus), **A11:2**
yw'zr (Yo'ezer), **A42:1**
ywšw' (Joshua), **A54:2**
ywšyh (Josiah), **A32:3**
y'y[y]r (name ?), **A7:[2]**
y'qb (Jacob), **A24:1**
yśr'l (Israel), **A33:2** ; **A34:6** ; **A52:9**
yšw' (Yeshua', Jesus), **A55:1**
yšm''l (Ishmael), **A16:**‹1›

kpr ḥnnyh (Kefar Ḥananiah), **A35:1**
kpr nḥwm (Capernaum), **A27:2**
kpr 'qbyh (Kefar 'Aqabyah), **A27:**‹2›
krysph (Crispos), **A8:[2]**

lwy (Levi), **A9:1**
ly'nṭys (Leontios), **A28:1**
l'zr (La'zar, Lazarus), **A56:1**

mwnyqh (Monika), **A27:1** ; **A29:[2]**, 3
mrwth (Marutah), **A7:[2]** ; **A8:[1]**
mrḥšwn (Marḥeshwan), **A50:4**
mtyh (Mattiah), **A43:1**

nḥwm (Nahum), **A25:1** ; see also *kpr nḥwm*

sbrs (Severus), **A31:2**
swsyph (place name ?), **A27:**‹1›
slwsṭys (Sallustius), **A26:3**
sprh (Saprah), **A3:1**

'dyw ('Idyo), **A51:3**
'yrwn ('Iron), **A22:1**
'qbyh (Aqabyah), **A27:**‹2›; see *kpr 'qbyh*

pwṭys (Photius), **A26:5**

pṭryq (Patrikos), **A27:2**
pynḥs (Phinehas), **A2:1**, 7 ; **A33:3**
prwṭwn (Proton), **A26:3**
prwrws (Phroros), **A26:4**

qlnyq (Kalonike), **A28:1**
qwrys (Kyrios), **A12:2**
qṭynh (Qetinah), **A7:[2]**
qnrws (Kynoros), **A53:1**
qrwṣh (Qaroṣah), **A29:3**

rbqh (Rebecca), **A2:5**

š'wl (Saul), **A50:2**
šbṭ (Shebat), **A51:4**
šmw'l (Samuel), **A6:2** ; **A33:5**
šm'wn (Simeon), **A42:2** ; **A46:2**
š'yy (She'ay), **A12:[3]**

tmh (Thomas), **A40:3**
tnḥwm (Tanḥum), **A27:1** ; **A29:1** ; **A36:2** ; **A41:[3]** ; **A44:3**

INDEXES

I. INDEX OF SUBJECTS

(Listed here are persons and topics mentioned in the sections called "Text Description." For names of persons and places in the texts themselves, consult the two glossaries. The numbers here refer to pages.)

'Abellin, 280
Abraham, 204, 206, 288
Abu Gosh, 241
Acre, 300
Acts of the Apostles, 225, 238, 246
Adam, 288
Aḥmedieh, Wadi, 241, 242
'Ain Duk, 281, 282, 283, 301
Alexander Balas, 193
Alexander Janneus, 231
Alexandra, Queen, 231
'Alma, 283
Altar of holocausts, 198
'Amram, 204, 205
Antiochus IV Epiphanes, 232
Arabia, Province of, 211
'Araq el-Emir, 227
Ark of the Law, 293
Aromatic trees, 199
Arza, Tell, 216
Azariah, 288

Babel, Tower of, 193
Babylonia, 191
Balakros, 193
Bar Cochba, Simon, 212, 215, 216
Baraqi'el, 202
Beit Jibrin, 284
Beit Saḥur, 246
Belvoir Crusader Castle, 297
Bersabee, 299
Beth Alpha, 284
Beth Gubrin, 284, 293
Beth She'an, 285
Beth She'arim, 299, 300

Bîr-'Ayyub, 222
Bread of presence, 198
Bread offering, 198

Calligraphic script, 213, 226, 227
Cana, 295
Canaan, 206
Capernaum, 285
Chorazin, 286
Chronicles, Books of, 223, 230, 243, 245, 288
Cursive script, 210, 212, 213, 225

Dabbura, 287, 288
Daniel, Book of, 191, 192, 193, 194, 195, 198, 288
Deir es-Senneh, 237
Diocaesarea, 298
Dominus Flevit, 224, 225, 226, 227

Egypt, 193, 206
'Eilabun, 298
Eleutheropolis, 284
Eleazar ben Judah, R., 281
Eliezer bar Teodor, R., 300
Eliezer ha-Qappar, R., 287
'En Gedi, 288
'En Rogel, 236
Enoch, 199, 200, 201, 205, 208
Eshtemoa', 303
Exodus, 193
Exodus, Book of, 204
Ezekiel, Book of, 198

Fiq, 289
French Hill, 247

Gadara, 291
Galilee, 295, 298
Galilee, Lake of, 289, 291, 296
Gallus, 298
Garden of truth, 199, 200
Gaza, 290
Genesis, Book of, 208
Genesis Apocryphon, 195, 205, 206, 207, 208
Gezer, 242, 247
Ghor eṣ-Ṣâfieh, 300, 301, 302
Giants, 200, 201, 202
Gischala, 290
Giv'at ha-Mivtar, 221, 227, 228, 303

Hadrian, Emp., 248
Haifa, 280
Ham, 208
Hammath-Gadara, 291, 292, 295
Hammath-Tiberias, 292
Hananiah, 288
Hasmonean script, 209
Hebron, 293, 302
Helen of Adiabene, Queen, 243, 247
Herod the Great, 228, 235
Herodian script, 194, 198, 200, 205, 206, 208
Ḥever, Naḥal, 213, 214, 215, 216, 217
Ḥizmeh, 244
Hula, Lake, 298
Hyrcania, 209

Isaac, 288
'Isfiya, 293, 294
Israel, 193
Issachar, 297
Issawiya, 244

Jacob, 288
Jaffa, 244, 246
Japhet, 288
Jason, 229
Jebel Ḫallet eṭ-Ṭûri, 222
Jerash, 294
Jeremiah, Book of, 191
Jericho, 294
Jerusalem, 198, 212, 218, 221, 222, 223, 224, 228, 229, 230, 231, 232, 233, 234, 237, 238, 241, 243, 244, 245, 246, 247, 248
Job, Book of, 194, 195, 196, 197
John the Baptist, Church of, 290
Jose ben Perida', R., 281
Josephus, 205, 223, 230, 243, 246
Jubilees, Book of, 200, 205, 208
Judah I, R., 299
Judea, 248
Judean Desert, 209, 214
Justin I, Emp., 284
Justin II, Emp. 284

Kafr Bir'im, 283, 300
Kafr Ḥananiah, 295
Kafr Kenna, 295, 296, 298
Kallon family, 229, 230
Kanef, Khirbet, 296
Karm el-Wiz, 247
Kefar-Bebayu, 214
Kidron Valley, 221, 222, 224, 236, 241, 242, 245, 246
Kings, Books of, 223
Kokhav ha-Yarden, 296

Levi, 202, 203, 205
Luke, Gospel of, 204

Maccabees, Books of, 232
Magen-Nirim, 297
Mahawai, 201, 202
Mal, el, 247
Malki-reša', 204
Manichean literature, 200, 201
Mal, el, 247
Ma'on, 297
Mark, Gospel of, 222, 241
Masada, 209, 245
Masḥara, 247
Matthew, Gospel of, 204, 222
Mĕgillat Ta'ănît, 248, 249, 250
Melchizedek, 204
Menorah, 290
Mird, Khirbet el, 209
Mishael, 288

Mishnah, 230
Moses, 204
Murabba'at, 209, 210, 211, 212, 213

Nabonidus, 191, 192, 193
Nâr, Wadi en, 222
Nazareth, 235
Nebuchadnezzar, 191
Nehemiah, Book of, 280
Nero, Emp., 210
Nethopha Valley, 298
Nicanor, Gate of, 234, 235
Nir-Yiṣḥaq, 297
Noah, 205, 206

Offense, Mt. of, 232
'Ohyah, 202
Olives, Mt. of, 223, 224, 232, 246
Origen, 204
Ossuaries, 219-41

Patriarchs, 200, 206
Persian campaign of A.D. 614, 289
Proclamation, Writ of, 218
Promised land, 206
Psalms, Book of, 226

Qahat, 205
Qasr el-Tuba, 301
Qaṭ'a, 245
Quneitra, 247

Ram, er, 246
Rama, er, 300
Ramat Raḥel, 245

Safed, 283, 290, 300
Šaf'at, 246
Samak, Wadi, 296
Samuel, Books of, 243
Scopus, Mt., 237, 239, 240
Seleucid Aramaic script, 247
Seleucids, 193
Semicursive script, 209
Sepphoris, 298
Shemiḥazah, 201
Siloam, 236, 237
Silwan, 237
Sulṭan, Tell es, 294
Susiya, Khirbet, 302, 303
Synagogues, 279-303

Talmud, Babylonian, 223, 230, 285
Talpioth, 238, 239
Teima, 191
Temple of Jerusalem, 198, 228, 231, 234, 239
Teqoa, 215, 216
Testaments of the Twelve Patriarchs, 200, 202, 203
Theodosius, Code of, 291
Trajan, Emp., 248

Umm el-'Amed, 298
Uzziah, 223

Yarmuk River, 289, 291
Yasul, Wadi, 244, 246
Yesud ha-Ma'ala, 298

Zif, Khirbet, 302
Zif, Tell, 302
Zion, Mt., 234, 247
Zoar, 301

II. INDEX OF MODERN SCHOLARS

(Numbers refer to pages)

Abel, F.-M., 234, 245, 246
Abramson, S., 214
Agnello, S. L., 238
Aharoni, Y., 215, 245
Akavya, A. A., 301
Albright, W. F., 223, 224, 236, 243, 244
Alexander, P. S., 197
Amiran, R. B. K., 283, 300
Amusin, I. D., 192, 206, 209, 214
Andersen, F. I., 196
Archer, G. L., Jr., 207
Arendzen, J., 202
Arensburg, B., 247
Ascoli, G. I., 219
Attema, D. S., 193
Attwater, D., 220
Avigad, N., 206, 218, 219, 220, 221, 223, 224, 229, 231, 235, 239, 240, 241, 242, 243, 244, 245, 298, 299
Aviram, J., 297
Avi-Yonah, M., 221, 225, 245, 279, 280, 281, 284, 291, 293, 294, 296, 297, 298
Avneri, Z., 250

Bacher, W., 195
Bagatti, B., 220, 221, 224, 225, 238, 280, 296
Bahat, D., 285
Baillet, M., 198, 200, 201, 202, 208
Barag, D., 240, 285, 289, 293
Baramki, D. C., 294
Bardtke, H., 191, 192, 193, 195, 196, 207, 215
Barkay, G., 248
Barrois, A., 284, 294
Barthélemy, D., 194
Becker, J., 203
Ben-Dov, M., 296, 297
Benoit, P., 195, 229, 282
Ben-Zvi, I., 283, 300
Berger, K., 204
Bickerman, E., 249
Bie, H. J. de, 195
Biran, A., 285, 287, 290, 293
Birnbaum, S. A., 211, 214
Black, M., 195, 199
Bligh, J., 223
Boer, P. A. H. de, 301
Bogaert, P.-M., 195
Borger, R., 197
Bornkamm, G., 192
Boyarin, D., 196
Brann, M., 249
Braslavsky, J., 279
Braslawski, J., 280
Brown, R. E., 206
Brownlee, W. H., 195, 197
Büchler, A., 289
Burchard, C., 203
Burrows, M., 192, 203
Bushell, G., 220

Cantera, J., 195
Caquot, A., 196
Carmignac, J., 192, 205
Carrière, B., 281, 282, 283
Cassuto, M. D., 301
Cassuto Salzmann, M., 215, 222
Charles, R. H., 202, 203
Christ, F., 221
Christ, H., 221
Chwolson, D., xv, 219
Clarke, E. G., 196
Clermont-Ganneau, C., 219, 232, 233,

234, 235, 237, 241, 243, 244, 246, 279, 281, 289, 290, 295, 296, 298
Clifford, R. J., 207
Colella, P., 211
Conder, C. R., 291
Cook, S. A., 242, 281, 290
Coppens, J., 195
Cortes, E., 195
Cowley, A. E., 202, 301
Cowling, G., 207
Coxon, P. W., 197, 207
Cross, F. M., 191, 201
Crowfoot, J. W., 294

Dahood, M., 195, 196, 197
Daiches, S., 301
Dalman, G., 219, 235, 249, 283, 286, 290, 291, 296
Daniélou, J., 220
Dehandschutter, B., 207
Delcor, M., 193, 195, 196, 207, 210
Denis, A.-M., 199
Derenbourg, J., 248
Detweiler, A. H., 294
Diakonoff, I. M., 192
Dickson, G., 235
Díez-Macho, A., 196
Dinkler, E., 220, 221, 238
Dion, P.-E., 222
Dommershausen, W., 193
Dotan, A., 289
Dothan, M., 292, 293
Driver, G. R., 195, 301
Dunayevsky, I., 240
Dupont-Sommer, A., 192, 195, 202, 203, 205, 206
Dussaud, R., 219, 235, 243, 279, 300

Edel, E., 287
Edersheim, A., 249
Emerton, J. A., 192, 207
Epstein, J. N., 224, 287
Euting, J., 246

Falk, Z. W., 223
Feliks, J., 289
Finegan, J., 220
Fishwick, D., 239
Fitzgerald, G. M., 293
Fitzmyer, J. A., xi, xiv, 194, 196, 199, 202, 205, 207, 209, 210, 216, 217, 223
Foerster, G., 280, 286
Fohrer, G., 192, 195
Fraenkel, A. H., 302
Freedman, D. N., 192, 195
Frey, J.-B., xv, 220, 279, 281, 295, 298
Fritsch, C. T., 195
Frizzell, L., 197

Galling, K., 224, 279, 287
Garbini, G., 208
Geraty, L. T., 247
Germer-Durand, J., 232, 234
Geus, C. H. J. de, 221
Gevaryahu, H. M. I., 192
Ginsberg, H. L., 209, 214, 221, 280
Gispen, W. H., 193
Glatzer, N. N., 250
Goodenough, E. R., xvi, 220, 238, 279, 298
Graetz, H., 249
Gray, J., 197
Greenfield, J. C., 195, 196, 206, 223
Grelot, P., 192, 195, 196, 199, 203, 204, 206, 207
Grimme, H., 219, 229, 230
Guérin, M., 283
Günczler, P., 249
Gustafsson, B., 239
Gutman, S., 302, 303
Gutmann, J., 280

Habermann, A., 192
Haenchen, E., 192
Halévy, J., 296
Hamilton, R. W., 294
Hamp, V., 192, 193, 207
Hänsler, H., 230
Harding, G. L., 195, 211
Hartman, L. F., 192
Haspecker, J., 193
Heitmann, P., xiv
Hempel, J., 209
Herr, M. D., 249

Hestrin, R., xv, 283, 285
Hillers, D. R., 210
Hiram, A., 280
Hoade, E., 221
Hornstein, C. A., 237, 241
Hospers, J. H., xvi
Howard, G., 197, 217
Hruby, K., 280
Hüttermeister, F., 280

Jacobson, H., 204
Janzen, J. G., 191
Jastrow, M., 294
Jensen, J., xiv
Jeremias, G., 200, 201
Jonge, M. de, 202, 203
Jongeling, B., xv, 194, 196, 197, 198, 199
Juster, J., 279

Kahane, P., 220
Kane, J. P., 239
Kapera, Z. J., 195
Kaufman, S. A., 196
Kautzsch, E., 241
Kirchschläger, W., 193, 207
Kitchener, H. H., 291
Klein, S., xvi, 220, 231, 242, 279, 280, 285, 287, 298, 300
Kloner, A., 228
Koffmahn, E., xv, 210, 211, 212, 213, 218
Kohl, H., xv, 279
Komlosh, Y., 196
Koole, J. L., 193
Koopmans, J. J., xv
Kraeling, C. H., 238, 294
Krauss, S., 220, 279, 281, 284, 285, 287, 290, 294
Kuhn, K. G., 200, 201
Kutscher, E. Y., 206, 207, 209, 215, 216, 220, 243, 280, 291, 297, 302

Labuschange, C. J., xv
Lagrange, M.-J., 234
Laperrousaz, E. M., 210
Larsson, E., 203
Lauterbach, J. Z., 249
Lebram, J. C. H., 194
Le Déaut, R., 195, 197
Lehmann, M. R., 210, 215
Lerner, B. M., 289
Lévi, I., 202
Lichtenstein, H., 248, 249
Lidzbarski, M., xv, 219, 236, 237, 238, 241, 246
Liebermann, S., 289
Lietzmann, H., 281
Lifshitz, B., xv, 217, 229, 293
Littmann, E., 227
Loeb, I., 290
Loffreda, S., 286
Ludin Janzen, H., 238
Lugscheider, B., 241
Luncz, A. M., 225, 279, 301
Lurie, B., 249
Lys, D., 195, 207

Macalister, R. A. S., 235, 237, 238, 242, 247
Macfarlane, J., 279
Mader, A., 279
Maisler (Mazar), B., 299
Mancini, I., 220, 225, 239
Mantel, H. D., 249
Marmorstein, A., 281, 287, 300, 301
Martini, C., xiv
Mayer, L. A., 236, 237
Mazar, B., 223, 224, 288, 289
McCown, C. C., 293
McKenzie, J. L., 192, 209, 216
McNamara, M., 193, 207
Medala, S., 195
Ménard, J.-E., 196
Mertens, A., 193, 194
Meyer, M. A., 290
Meyer, R., 192, 197, 207
Meyers, E. M., 221
Michelini Tocci, F., 206
Michon, E., 290
Mielgo, C., 207
Milik, J. T., xiv, 191, 193, 194, 198, 199, 200, 201, 202, 203, 204, 205, 206, 208, 209, 210, 211, 212, 213, 214, 222, 224, 225, 226, 227
Millar, F., 250

Moe, O., 238
Moore, G. F., 249
Moraldi, L., 193, 198, 206
Morgenstern, J., 249
Morrow, F. J., Jr., 196
Mueller, J., 249
Mulder, M. J., 197
Müller, D. H., 296
Munck, J., 238
Muraoka, T., xiii, 197, 207
Murray, R., 207

Naveh, J., 209, 222, 227, 228, 244, 247, 280, 285, 286, 287, 295, 297
Neeman, D., 286, 292
Negev, A., 221
Netzer, E., 289, 302, 303
Neubauer, A., 249
Novotný, G., 207

Obed, B., 293
Oliphant, L., 296
Orfali, G., 285, 286
Ory, J., 286
Ovadiah, A., 290

Padberg, J. W., xiv
Pardee, D., 197
Pass, H. L., 202
Paul, A., 207
Payne, J. B., 207
Pelletier, A., 250
Pestman, P. W., 196
Peterson, F. P., 225
Philby, H. St. J. B., 300
Philonenko, M., 200, 203
Ploeg, J. P. M. van der, 194, 195, 196, 221, 224
Polotsky, H. J., 217
Pope, M., 196
Porat, Y., 289
Power, E., 234
Poznański, S., 235
Prado, J., 204
Press, I., 225, 279, 301
Puech, E., 214

Rabinowitz, J. J., 209, 214, 217, 218
Rahmani, L., 221, 229, 302
Rak, Y., 247
Rapp, E. L., 287
Reeg, G., 280
Rehm, M., 193
Reicke, B., 238
Reifenberg, A., 234
Reinach, T., 301
Renan, E., 291, 300
Renov, I., 293
Ringgren, H., 207
Robert, J., 197
Robert, L., xvi
Roberts, B. J., 195
Rosenthal, E. S., 221, 289
Rosenthal, F., xv, 280
Rost, L., 207
Roussel, P., 235
Rundgren, F., 196

Safrai, S., 280
Saller, S. J., 280
Sanders, J. A., 195
Sapir, B., 286, 292
Sarfatti, G. B., 207, 289
Saul, D. J., 290
Saulcy, F. de, 219, 243
Savignac, M.-R., 220, 236
Schiffman, L. H., 197
Schilling, O., 193
Schultze, V., 219, 244
Schumacher, G., 289
Schürer, E., 250
Schütz, D., 231, 235, 243
Schwab, M., 249
Schwabe, M., 284, 293
Schwarz, A., 249
Segert, S., 191, 193, 195, 201, 207, 210
Sellin, E., 296
Shaked, S., 196
Shazar, Z., 228, 239
Shelton, J. C., 217
Simonsen, D., 249
Skehan, P. W., 195
Slousch, N., 281, 293
Smith, G. A., 229
Smith, M., 207
Smith, P., 222

Smith, R. H., 219, 221, 225, 232, 234, 235, 239
Sokoloff, M., 197, 280
Sperber, D., 196
Spoer, H. H., 224, 233
Starcky, J., 198, 201, 205, 206, 217
Stauffer, E., 238
Stegemann, H., 203
Stewart, A., 232, 243, 279
Stone, M. E., 203
Storme, A., 286
Strack, H. L., 248
Strange, J. F., 247
Sukenik, E. L., xv, 192, 217, 220, 221, 223, 224, 225, 230, 231, 233, 235, 236, 237, 238, 239, 240, 241, 242, 244, 245, 246, 247, 279, 282, 284, 285, 286, 287, 291, 292, 294, 296, 299, 301, 302
Szörényi, A., 193

Taylor, W. R., 290
Testa, E., 220, 221, 223
Testuz, M., 208
Themele, I. T. P., 243
Thompson, T. L., 207
Thomsen, P., xvi
Tod, M. N., xvi
Togan, Z. V., 206
Torrey, C. C., 281
Trever, J. C., 194
Tromp, N. J., 221
Tsori, N., 285
Tuinstra, E. W., 196
Tyloch, W., 207
Tzaferis, V., 222, 227, 228

Unnik, W. C. van, 199, 207
Urbach, E. E., 289
Urman, D., 248, 287, 288

Vattioni, F., 207
Vaux, R. de, xiv, 192
Veenhof, K. R., 196
Vermes, G., 192, 250, 303
Viaud, P., 298
Vincent, L.-H., 220, 227, 234, 235, 240, 241, 242, 243, 246, 281, 282, 283, 292, 293, 296, 299, 301
Vogt, E., 192
Vriezen, T. C., xvi

Wacholder, B. Z., 195, 210, 301, 302
Watzinger, C., xv, 279, 284, 287, 291
Weiss, I. H., 249
Weiss, R., 197
Wellhausen, J., 248
Willoughby, H. R., 238
Winter, P., 195
Woude, A. S. van der, xv, 194, 195
Wright, W., 202

Yadin, Y., 206, 209, 211, 214, 215, 216, 217, 218, 228, 298, 302
Yaron, R., 209, 211
Yeivin, D., 209
Yeivin, S., 228, 229, 297
Yeivin, Z., 287, 302, 303
Yellin, A., 231
Yellin, D., 235
York, A. D., 197

Zeitlin, S., 223, 249
Ziebarth, E., xvi
Zunz, L., 248

COMPARATIVE TABLE

COMPARATIVE TABLE OF TEXTS IN THIS COLLECTION WITH OTHER COLLECTIONS

	AC	*AH*	*ASG*	*ASH*	*ASP*	*ATQ*	*CIH*	*CII*	*CIS*	*DadWJ*	*Ephem*	*Epigr*
1												
2	62					121-31						
3												
4												
5						1-73						
6												
7	61											
8-19												
20	60											
21	60											
22-27												
28												
29	66	I/1. 51-52				75-119						
30-37												
38												
39										80-89		
40										148-55		
41	63									114-19		
42										120-25		
43										163		
44										164-65		
45										166-68		
46												
47										169		
48-50												
51	64											
52	65									170-75		
53-55												
56		I/1. 53										
57-59												
60		I/1. 53										
61												
62												
63												
64												
65												
66												
67		I/1. 52						1300				
68												
69		I/1. 53										
70		I/1. 52										
71		I/1. 52						1334				
72-84												
85												
86-87												
88												
89												
90								1350				
91								1352				
92								1351				
93								1354				
94								1353				
95								1359				
96								1363				
97								1362				
98								1356				
99								1308				
100								1318				

	IR	*JPCI*	*JS*	*PI*	*PS*	*SEG*	*SHY*	*SWDS*(pl.)	*Thomsen*	*Yediot 2*
1										
2										
3										
4										
5										
6										
7										
8-19										
20										
21								8		
22-27										
28								11		
29										
30-37										
38	193									
39										
40	189									
41										
42										
43										
44										
45										
46										
47										
48-50										
51	192									
52										
53-55										
56										
59-59										
60										
61	191									
62										
63	190									
64										
65	233									
66	248									
67				38-40						
68	263									
69										
70	255			39-40						
71										
72-84										
85	170									
86-87										
88	261									
89										
90		1							206	
91		2								
92		3								
93		4								
94		5								
95										
96										
97										
98										
99		10, 35								
100		67								

	AC	*AH*	*ASG*	*ASH*	*ASP*	*ATQ*	*CIH*	*CII*	*CIS*	*DadWJ*	*Ephem*	*Epigr*
101								1304				
102												
103								1341			3.50-51	
104								1338			3.51	
105								1335			3.51	
106												
107								1407				
108								1256			2.197-98	
109								988				
110								1299				
111								1297				
112-13												
114								1298				
115											3.52	
116												
117-25												
126								1248-49			1.186-87	
127								1190			2.72	
128-29												
130								1181				
131								1177				
132							72	1388	2.156			117
133												
134								1245				
135							11	1379				
136-38												
139								1221				
140								1217				
141								1222				
142								1301				
143								1348				
144								1255				
145								1373				
146								1176				
147								1384				
148-50												

	IR	*JPCI*	*JS*	*PI*	*PS*	*SEG*	*SHY*	*SWDS*(pl.)	*Thomsen*	*Yediot* 2
101		19								
102										
103		7				8.202				
104		18								
105										
106										
107		101								
108		9				8.200			200	
109		166								
110										
111	256									
112-13										
114	257									
115		14								
116		14								
117-25										
126		69-73								
127	164									
128-29										
130		160								
131		161								
132		57								
133										
134										
135		42								
136-38										
139		73								
140		81								
141		82								
142										
143		39								
144		36								
145		12							204	
146										
147										
148-50										

	AC	*AH*	*ASG*	*ASH*	*ASP*	*ATQ*	*CIH*	*CII*	*CIS*	*DadWJ*	*Ephem*	*Epigr*
A1												
A2		I/1.70			28-31, 72-76			1197-98				
A3								1199				
A4								1202				
A5								1203				
A6												
A7								1204				
A8								1205				
A9-10												
A11					31-35			1165				
A12					72			1195				
A13-14												
A15		I/1.70	4-40		7-21, 71-72			982				
A16	71	I/1.70	41-58		60			981				
A17-21												
A22												
A23		I/1.70						855				
A24								967			2.72	
A25		I/1.70	107-11				94-96	976				
A26								856-60				
A27-29				47-57								
A30-31												
A32					85-86			885				
A33					77			866				
A34		I/1.69										
A35												
A36		I/1.70						987			1.313-15	
A37												
A38								854				
A39-40												
A41								989				
A42		I/1.70	71-79									
A43								971				
A44								1196				
A45		I/1.70										
A46-47												
A48				77-78				979				
A49			89-100		24-26, 70-71		87-94	974-75				
A50								1208				
A51-55												

	IR	JPCI	JS	PI	PS	SEG	SHY	SWDS(pl.)	Thomsen	Yediot 2
A1							1			
A2			1.253-57		1/2.34-35		109-10			17-25
A3										
A4										
A5										
A6										
A7										
A8										
A9-10										
A11			1.241-53				12			
A12			1.212, 215				13			
A13-14	184									
A15			1.181-92 ; 3.451		1/4.49-50		94			16
A16			1.193-99		1/4.57-59		98			
A17-21										
A22	185									
A23		13	1.221				7			11
A24		2	1.223			8.276	113-14			4
A25		7	1.205		1/2.35		29			12
A26			1.239-41				46			
A27-29										
A30-31										
A32										
A33			1.180 ; 2.259-60				34			
A34			1.260-62				88			
A35										
A36		4	1.264		1/2.34		93			13-14
A37										
A38		12	1.212-13		1/2.36 ; 1/3.48					10
A39-40										
A41		5					141			
A42			1.199-200							
A43					1/4.59-60					
A44							11			
A45			1.208-11 ; 3.535							
A46-47										
A48			1.213				153			
A49		9	1.201-3				91			5, 9
A50							126			
A51-55										